INTELLECTUAL SUPPRESSION

INTELLECTUAL SUPPRESSION

AUSTRALIAN CASE HISTORIES, ANALYSIS AND RESPONSES

EDITED BY
BRIAN MARTIN,
C. M. ANN BAKER, CLYDE MANWELL
AND CEDRIC PUGH.

ANGUS
& ROBERTSON
PUBLISHERS

ANGUS & ROBERTSON PUBLISHERS

Unit 4, Eden Park, 31 Waterloo Road,
North Ryde, NSW, Australia 2113, and
16 Golden Square, London W1R 4BN,
United Kingdom

First published in Australia
by Angus & Robertson Publishers in 1986

Copyright © this selection and presentation,
Brian Martin, 1986
Copyright in the articles is retained by their authors

National Library of Australia
Cataloguing-in-publication data.

Intellectual suppression.

  Includes index

  ISBN 0 207 15132 6.

  1. Academic freedom — Australia. I. Martin, Brian, 1947-

323.44 '0994

Typeset in 10pt Bembo
by Setrite Typesetters
Printed in Shenzhen, China

CONTENTS

PART THREE: RESPONSES

NOTES ON CONTRIBUTORS

C. M. Ann Baker has the degrees of B.Sc. and M.Sc. in agriculture from the University of Durham. Her employment has included periods with the Hill Farming Research Organisation, Welsh Plant Breeding Station, and the Ministry of Agriculture, Fisheries and Food in the United Kingdom. She went to the United States on a Fulbright travel grant where she did research on the molecular basis of hybrid vigour and on biochemical markers in egg white and other tissues, in collaboration with her future husband (Clyde Manwell). At present she is a Visiting Research Fellow at the University of Adelaide. Her research interests cover the genetics and evolution of animals in environments altered by humans. She also works on the politics of agriculture and is active in organisations devoted to the defence of academic freedom. Together with her husband she has participated in the analysis of the social structure of science and of universities. She has written a number of research papers, including four major reviews, on egg quality, egg proteins, genetics of protein polymorphisms in the chicken, and molecular variability in domesticated mammals. She is co-author with her husband of *Molecular Biology and the Origin of Species*.

Jean Buckley-Moran has worked as a journalist and film director. She currently teaches part-time in Technology and Society at the University of New South Wales, and is writing a thesis on industrialisation and innovation in post-World War II Australia.

Richard Davis was born in India in 1935 and educated mainly in Ireland, graduating in history at the University of Dublin. Before coming to Australia he was on the staff of the Queen's University, Belfast, and the University of Otago, Dunedin. He is now Reader in History at the University of Tasmania and has published seven books and fifty articles. Richard Davis is married with two children.

Cheryl Hannah is a committed feminist who has been active in student and worker politics since the mid-1960s. She has an honours degree in political science from the Australian National University and ten years' experience working first with federal politicians and then international relations theorists. She has taught Australian foreign policy to undergraduates and women's studies to high school students. For her *the personal is political*. She is also fond of her two cats.

Evan Jones is a lecturer in economics at the University of Sydney. His special interests are in the methodology and sociology of the economics profession, and in the structural constraints on capitalist development. He has spent the last ten years trying to escape the clutches of a rigorous education.

Clyde Manwell has the degrees of B.S. and Ph.D. from Stanford University. His employment has included teaching at the University of Utah and the University of Illinois, as well as research fellowships at the Scripps Institution of Oceanography, and at the Marine Biological Laboratory and the National Lending Library of Science and Technology in the United Kingdom. His research interests include comparative biochemistry, population genetics (especially of marine organisms and of domesticated animals), and molecular aspects of pollution. His publications include *Molecular Biology and the Origin of Species* (with C. M. Ann Baker) and reviews on respiratory transport proteins, on molecular variation in animal populations, on oil and detergent pollution, and on the social structure of science. He is at present Professor of Zoology at the University of Adelaide — a position he was nearly forced to vacate as a consequence of the criticisms he and his wife made of fruit fly spraying in South Australia. As a consequence of first-hand experience, he became active in attempting to protect the right to dissent in academic and scientific institutions.

Brian Martin was born in 1947, received a B.A. from Rice University (Houston, Texas) and a Ph.D. in theoretical physics from Sydney University. He has worked as a research assistant and research associate doing applied mathematics at the Australian National University since 1976. His many technical scientific papers are mainly in the areas of stratospheric modelling, numerical methods, wind power and astrophysics. He also has written widely on the critique of science and technology, nuclear power, war and peace issues, and social action, including the books *The Bias of Science* and *Uprooting War*. He has been active for many years in environmental and peace movements in Canberra, and has played an important role in publicising the issues and organising support in a number of cases of suppression of intellectual dissent.

Val Plumwood has been a social activist, working on a range of environmental issues, especially forestry and nuclear power, since the early 1970s. Her academic background is in philosophy, where she has published numerous papers and books in virtually all areas. She currently teaches social philosophy at Macquarie University. Her political consciousness was considerably raised by the Australian National University suppression attempts (documented in this book) and the years of activism. Both her academic work and activism now have a strongly political, anarchist and feminist orientation.

Cedric Pugh was born in 1938. He read Politics and Economics for his B.A.(Hons.) at the University of Wales, and his masterate and doctorate degrees were in Australian and international housing policy. Dr Pugh has taught in universities and polytechnics in four countries in three continents, living in both democratic and non-democratic societies. He has written a wide range of journal articles, monographs and international textbooks on urban economics, housing policy and public finance. Dr Pugh has been active in environmental and social reformist causes, sometimes acting as media spokesperson. He became interested in human rights issues in his undergraduate work at the University College of Swansea, where he was encouraged by the eminent scholars and authors, the late Frank Stacey and John C. Rees. Frank Stacey wrote extensively on ombudspersons and bills of rights, and John C. Rees had a continual research programme in the ideas of John Stuart Mill. Dr Pugh's candidature for promotion was campaigned in Australia and overseas in response to the South Australian Institute of Technology's policy that its internal critics be prevented from achieving senior status.

Stuart Rees is Professor of Social Work at the University of Sydney. He has worked for several years as a probation officer in London and Vancouver and has taught at universities in Scotland, Canada and the United States. His publications have included *Social Work Face to Face* and *Verdicts on Social Work* (published by Edward Arnold) and most recently a research report on family care of disabled children, *Disabled Children: Disabling Practices*, published by the University of New South Wales Social Welfare Research Centre.

Richard Routley, senior fellow in philosophy at the Australian National University, engages in research in logic and metaphysics as well as environmental philosophy. His work on environmental theory has always been coupled with more practical applications, in the early 1970s to forestry and the comparatively natural environment, more recently to nuclear power and then nuclear war, and now to the transformed environment and especially to agriculture.

Peter W. Sheehan, Professor of Psychology at the University of Queensland, is Chairman of the Australian Research Grants Scheme.

Deborah Smith is a journalist with the *National Times*, specialising on issues in science and medicine. She has written a number of important stories on academic freedom cases.

Peter Springell has been active in the environmental movement since the early 1970s on a range of issues. He worked in the CSIRO, beginning in 1953, and rose to the position of Principal Research Scientist. Beginning in 1974 he undertook research work and published on environmental topics. The resulting conflict with CSIRO management led to his resignation in 1976.

Frank Stilwell is an associate professor of economics at the University of Sydney. His special interests are in urban and regional studies and in progressive economic policies. His most recent book is *Economic Crisis, Cities and Regions* (1980).

ACKNOWLEDGEMENTS

The following authors and publishers kindly have granted permission to reprint material from their publications:

Liz Burdon, "Sexual harassment on campus", *On Dit*, vol. 51, no. 5, 11 April 1983, p. 11. Reprinted by permission of *On Dit*, the newspaper of the Students' Association of the University of Adelaide.

Deborah Smith, "A victory for academic freedom", *National Times*, 18–24 October 1981, p. 47. Reprinted by permission of the author and John Fairfax and Sons, Limited.

Peter Springell, "For the freedom to comment by scientists", *Arena*, no. 44, 45, 1976, pp. 28–33. Reprinted by permission of the author and the editors of *Arena*.

Clyde Manwell, "How to get rid of environmentally oriented teaching", *On Dit*, vol. 50, no. 9, Fifty Year Memorial Issue, 7 June 1982, p. 16. Reprinted by permission of *On Dit*, the newspaper of the Students' Association of the University of Adelaide.

INTRODUCTION

Dr John Coulter worked for twenty years as a medical researcher at the Institute of Medical and Veterinary Science (IMVS) in Adelaide, South Australia. During this time he was, in his private capacity, a leading environmentalist. He spoke out on many occasions on issues such as uranium mining and the hazards of environmental chemicals. In addition, Dr Coulter in the late 1970s headed within the IMVS a small mutagens testing unit. By testing substances for their capacity to cause mutations, a good indication of their potential for inducing cancer can be obtained.

Dr Coulter's activities posed a threat to various vested interests, in particular certain chemical companies and their supporters within the IMVS. For example, in 1979 Dr Coulter gave a lecture, in his private capacity, in which he mentioned the way the Velsicol company in the United States had handled information on the cancer-causing properties of two of their products, chlordane and heptachlor. After the lecture, Velsicol Australia complained about it to the Director of the IMVS — not directly to Dr Coulter.

Dr Coulter's work in the environmental mutagens testing unit also was unwelcome in some places. Dr Coulter on occasion tested substances such as polycyclic hydrocarbons to which workers or the public were being exposed. Furthermore, sometimes he gave reports of his testing to workers or trade unions as well as to the appropriate IMVS committees.

Dr Coulter was dismissed from his job at the IMVS on 30 June 1980. Several reasons were offered for the dismissal by the then Director of the IMVS. But in later court hearings, initiated by Dr Coulter to gain reinstatement, none of these reasons were substantiated. Therefore it seems a reasonable inference that Dr Coulter was dismissed not because of any deficiencies in his job performance, but because his environmental activities were found objectionable by certain people in positions of power.

The Coulter case has much more detail and further ramifications, some of which are described in later chapters. But this basic outline illustrates most of the key features of what we call *suppression of intellectual dissent* or, more briefly, intellectual suppression.

First, a person or group, by their public statements, research, teaching or other activities, threatens the vested interests of elites in corporations, government, professions or some other area. Typically this is by threatening profits, bureaucratic power, prestige or public image, for example by providing support to alternative views or by exposing the less attractive sides of the powerful group.

By speaking out on environmental issues, Dr Coulter provided support for community groups opposing policies of uranium mining companies, government departments and other powerful interests. By providing information about the hazards of environmental chemicals directly to workers, he provided support for workers and also undercut the power of employers to the extent to which it was based on a monopoly of information about health hazards on the job. In short, the first main feature of suppression cases is a threat to vested interests.

The second feature of suppression cases is an attempt by a powerful individual or group to stop or to penalise the person or activity found objectionable. This may involve denying funds or work opportunities, blocking appointments, blocking tenure, blocking promotion, blocking courses, blocking publication, preventing free speech, dismissal, harassment, blacklisting, and smearing of reputations. These are examples of what we call *direct suppression*. *Indirect suppression* occurs when people are inhibited from making public statements, doing research and the like because of the implied or overt threat of sanctions or because of a general climate of fear or pressures for conformity.

Dr Coulter was directly suppressed by being dismissed. At the same time, the activity of testing for environmental mutagens was directly suppressed by the closure of the testing unit which he had headed. Indirect suppression is harder to pinpoint. But it is probably responsible for the rarity with which professional scientists speak up on social issues, and in the scarcity of scientific research, such as environmental mutagens testing, which is both directly useful to workers and community groups and which is made available to them.

There are several other typical features of suppression cases. For example, when complaints are made about a person's activities, they are usually made not to the person concerned, but to her or his boss. This occurred when companies complained to the IMVS about Dr Coulter's public statements. The companies' responses were to the source of power over Dr Coulter, namely the IMVS, rather than to the source of the information in question, namely Dr Coulter himself.

Another typical feature of suppression cases is a lack of any substantive reasons given for the action taken. In societies in which freedom of speech and inquiry are formally subscribed to, suppression is seldom justified by saying outright that public criticism or critical teaching is being penalised. "Acceptable" reasons usually are given: that a person has not been doing a satisfactory job, that a proposal is not a high enough priority to warrant funding, and so forth. In many cases such reasons are entirely correct; they are not the suppression cases we are concerned with here. We are concerned with the cases in which the suppression is entirely or in part a response to the expression of intellectual dissent, and in which other explanations for the suppression do not stand up to scrutiny.

Often it is difficult to "prove" conclusively that suppression of intellectual dissent has actually occurred. Only occasionally do suppressors openly admit their motivations and actions. Therefore the number of cases of suspected suppression is much larger than the number of cases in which suppression can definitely be said to be involved. Suppression can be strongly suspected whenever the formal reasons offered for penalising a person or activity are demonstrably inadequate. If the performance of a dissident — a person whose activities provide some challenge to prevailing views or interests — is not significantly worse than that of other individuals who are not dissidents and who are not punished, this is strong evidence of suppression.

For example, other scientists in the IMVS whose scientific performances were less impressive than Dr Coulter's were not dismissed. This suggests that explanations for his dismissal based on poor scientific productivity are suspect.

Suppression of intellectual dissent is only one kind of suppression. Also possible, and common, is suppression instigated because of a person's political affiliation or activity, ethnic origin, sex, sexual preference, age, religion, occupation, personality or superior competence. All these forms of suppression are vitally important. But to limit the treatment in this book we have focused mainly on intellectual suppression. For example, blocking of a person's appointment to a job because of her sex would not count as suppression of intellectual dissent, but blocking of a person's appointment because of her outspoken feminist views would fall into this category.

We have chosen to distinguish suppression from *repression*[1], reserving for the latter term instances involving physical violence, such as beatings, imprisonment, torture and murder. Direct suppression thus essentially covers nonviolent restraint or inhibition of people or their activities: withdrawal of funds, jobs or publication outlets, damaging reputations, or harassment or social ostracism. *Oppression*, another term, refers to institutionalised lack of justice or freedom, such as apartheid, or poverty maintained by exploitative social arrangements. Oppression is often enforced by both suppression and repression.

Suppression is a general term, and both censorship and discrimination can be considered as types of suppression. In this book the unqualified use of the term suppression will refer to suppression of intellectual dissent.

Although suppression in any individual case is often difficult to demonstrate conclusively, we think the available evidence suggests that suppression is a widespread occurrence. How common is it? In some circumstances, suppression is the rule rather than the exception. For example, in authoritarian societies such as military dictatorships and communist regimes, suppression of dissident views is standard policy. In many countries in which routine repression occurs — torture, imprisonment and murder — such violent means of smashing dissent are essentially a supplement to routine suppression, such as firing dissidents from government employment and censoring the media.[2]

Although suppression is sometimes the initial, nonviolent aspect of attempts to deter and penalise dissent, with violent repression reserved for the more recalcitrant cases, the distinction is usually more complex. Suppression is essentially an expression of political power in circumstances in which knowledge and information rather than brute force is paramount. The very concept of "intellectual dissent" assumes the existence of a group of people who produce and distribute information, and of a standard set of ideas from which dissent can be made. Although suppression of intellectual dissent has occurred for thousands of years, it is especially characteristic of modern industrial societies with a high degree of literacy, in which communications and mass media are well developed, and in which the standard organisational form is bureaucracy.

Modern industrial societies are held together less by force than by common acceptance of the status quo. Of course, "common acceptance" may not be representative of the best interests of everyone: opinions can be shaped or manipulated through schooling and advertising, and perceptions of what is socially possible are shaped by the current distribution of social power and the existing social institutions. Those who are in the best position to shape perceptions of reality are those in powerful positions: elites in government, in government bureaucracies, in corporations. Intellectual dissent usually means dissent from the established policies or practices of elite groups. The most effective way for these groups to maintain their privileged and powerful positions is by shaping people's perceptions, by making the existing distribution and use of power in society seem reasonable, beneficial and inevitable. If everyone saw things in these ways, there would be no need for direct suppression. It is usually only when individuals or groups criticise this state of affairs that elites resort to suppression.

Does suppression really matter all that much? Would not society carry on much the same with or without an extra amount of open dissent? We believe that suppression has important consequences for society. In some spectacular cases the stakes are enormous. A. Ernest Fitzgerald was sacked because he exposed cost overruns in United States military contracting. The overruns, which were being obscured by misleading accounting practices, which Fitzgerald revealed, amounted in the case of the C5-A transport aircraft to US$2000 million.[3] John Bradley lost his job because he tried to expose shortcomings in the computer system used in the US missile tracking early warning system. At stake was the conventionally assessed security of the US people against nuclear attack.[4]

The success of either dissent or suppression also may decide whether millions of people are exposed to harmful drugs or environmental chemicals, whether dangerous defects in everyday consumer products are corrected, whether funds are diverted from the poor and the ill, whether corrupt politicians or business executives remain in positions of power, and whether wars are fought under false pretences. But perhaps more fundamentally, suppression may make the difference between a society in which dissent helps sustain continual efforts to address social problems and a society in which intellectual conformity helps sustain domination by particular groups and exploitation of others.

It is important to make one point clear. We and most of the other contributors in this book do not wish to draw any conclusions about the motivations of those people who carry out suppression. Almost everyone has the best of intentions. Many of those who carry out suppression genuinely believe they are acting on proper grounds, such as ensuring top quality scholarship or preventing harmful public statements. Others carrying out suppression may justify it by appealing to what are for them higher goals, such as maintaining professional decorum or organisational efficiency. Rather than focusing on psychological motivations for suppression, we prefer to emphasise the social dynamics of the process, including mechanisms, contexts, power relationships and opposition to it.

Where is suppression most frequent? Indirect or institutionalised suppression — in which a climate of fear or threat of penalties inhibits dissent — is most common in authoritarian societies and organisations. For example, in communist countries significant open dissent from the line of the Communist Party is sure to cause repercussions, and will, among other things, severely limit potential career advancement. More generally, bureaucracy is an authoritarian form of social organisation: internal dissent is discouraged, and dissent to a public audience is usually severely penalised. The prevalence of bureaucracy has been increasing steadily in the last several hundred years, and as bureaucracy spreads so the market for dissenting ideas gradually shrinks.

It is no coincidence that the form of social organisation in which bureaucracy is most dominant and pervasive, namely communist regimes, is also where suppression of intellectual dissent is most rigorously enforced. But the importance of bureaucracy, and of suppression, has greatly increased in Western societies too. Government bureaucracies and large corporations (also organised in the form of bureaucracy) are the most important, but other parts of society are also bureaucratised, including churches, trade unions and academia. This means that intellectual activity is more and more done by professionals working for large bureaucratised organisations. Independent intellectuals are ever rarer, as are the channels by which they can express their opinions to more than a minority.

In these circumstances, intellectual dissent from within the ranks of intellectual workers plays an ever-increasing role. Dissidents may be found at any level in the flow of information. Journalists, writers, artists, librarians, secretaries, lawyers, engineers and computer programmers all play vital roles in the flow of information in modern industrial societies. Companies and governments can muster enough of their own experts to promote their own interests. On issues such as uranium mining, it rests to a considerable extent on professional intellectuals, such as John Coulter, to help present contrary views on a technical level. And if activities such as mutagen testing are to be done in the public interest, it often depends on individuals such as Dr Coulter to carry them out within a bureaucratic work setting and to make them available to a wider audience.

Although suppression is an important phenomenon in modern industrialised society, its significance has been generally overlooked in the West. The finger is often pointed at communist and other repressive governments, but the same problems at home are not seen in a coherent framework. Most often suppression is seen — if suppression is acknowledged at all — as an occasional abuse rather than a systematic occurrence. And periods such as the late 1940s and early 1950s, in which suppression became rampant — called in the United States the McCarthy era — are seen as a sort of aberration rather than a temporary accentuation of an ever-present problem. It is because the systematic discussion of suppression has been avoided in the West that we focus on suppression in the so-called "Free World". The problem is as bad and usually worse in communist countries and military dictatorships, but at least the problem is well recognised. Suppression in the West also needs to be studied, exposed and resisted — not only to maintain freedom, but also to learn how to overcome suppression in countries where dissent is even less welcome.

Most of our case histories involve academic or scientific institutions. We chose this focus for several reasons.

First, academic institutions play a central role in the flow of information in modern industrial society. Not only are they primary centres for the creation and integration of knowledge, but they pass on that knowledge through teaching. They also play a major role in the training and certification of other information professions.

Second, although suppression is generally more frequent in government bureaucracies and corporations, well-documented cases of suppression in these areas are less frequent than in academic organisations. This is partly because there are fewer mechanisms in corporations and state bureaucracies by which to openly oppose suppression, and less access to information to expose it.

Third, science and academia are often said to be havens for dissent, under the protection of scientific freedom and academic freedom. By illustrating suppression in these areas, we hope to show by implication the pervasiveness of suppression in other areas in which intellectuals are employed. Finally, our own experiences are mainly in science and academia, and this experience gives us greater feeling for the operation of suppression in these areas.

Our emphasis on academic organisations should not be taken as any suggestion that suppression problems are less important in other parts of society. Indeed, we do not see a clear separation between bureaucracies and academia, but on the contrary perceive close similarities. Universities are often bureaucratic in many aspects of their operation. In addition, universities provide ''tangible services'', namely the production of students with degrees, and of publications. This process is more easily quantified and evaluated than the ''production process'' of many governmental institutions. Another point here is the exchange of personnel between academia and other state bureaucracies, and the convergence of styles of work and work management in their arenas. For these reasons we see the chapter by Stuart Rees on authoritarianism in state bureaucracies as closely linked to experiences in science and academia.

Documented cases of suppression are in several ways an unrepresentative sample of all cases of suppression. As mentioned before, expectations of scientific and academic freedom mean that a disproportionate fraction of challenged and publicised suppression cases are from these areas. In addition, only some types of cases are readily documented: dismissals usually require justification, whereas blockings of appointments are difficult to verify. Documented cases of suppression overemphasise the major and dramatic events, such as dismissals and cutting off of funding, and underemphasise problems such as blocking of publication and subtle harassment by collegial disapproval. Documented cases also overemphasise instances in which channels for formal redress are available.

The nature of science and academia, and the unrepresentativeness of documented cases of suppression, lead to other biases. For example, there are relatively few documented cases of suppression of women dissidents in science and academia, since due to discrimination few women are found in science and academia in the first place, and those who are there are mostly in lower-level positions with less security and protection and therefore less opportunity for resisting or publicising suppression when it occurs. We have tried to overcome some of these biases, without being tokenistic. Nevertheless, our sample of cases is far from ideal. We only hope that the treatments here encourage the further study of other types and instances of suppression — and, even more importantly, resistance to suppression.

The documented cases here may suggest that suppression is a spectacular and therefore fairly rare occurrence. But in practice suppression is a routine phenomenon. When discrimination is institutionalised, as against women or against followers of a particular way of organising knowledge, then suppression can occur so effortlessly that it is difficult to recognise. Once debate in an area of intellectual discourse is considered to be outside the realm of acceptability — for example the issue of fluoridation — then instances of overt suppression may be few. It is simply considered ridiculous to allow publication of the unorthodox opinion or to hire supporters of the unorthodox position. But in such cases suppression may be at work via interest groups and the squashing of challenges to received opinion. This has been the process behind most of the suppression of feminist critique, the subject of Cheryl Hannah's chapter: the power of men within tertiary institutions has been used in a routine way to silence challenges to patriarchal ideas, rather than normal academic processes being used to do this.

Routine, institutionalised suppression is often more important than the notable examples of overt suppression. But it is partly by studying the more dramatic instances of suppression, for which more information is available, that the dynamics of routine suppression can be elucidated.

Part One presents a set of case studies of suppression. These studies should give a feeling for what suppression is like at the nitty gritty level of dissident actions, harassment, patterns of action and responses. For several of the chapters we have invited comment from the institution implicated in the alleged suppression. If comment was received, we have invited the author of the chapter in question to respond. We have restricted the cases to those from Australia. To give an idea of the variety of other cases which have not been presented in such detail, a series of thumbnail sketches of other instances of suppression is presented.

Part Two begins with a chapter on the common origins of suppression cases in the vested interests embodied in the power structures in government, business and academia. The second chapter analyses the institutionalised suppression of feminist critique in universities. Next the role of authoritarian behaviour patterns in state bureaucracies is examined. The final chapter addresses academic suppression in the context of human rights.

Part Three addresses the question of how to oppose individual cases of suppression and more generally to oppose the institutional structures which give rise to suppression in the course of serving vested interests. Special attention is given to challenging suppression by obtaining publicity, and through social action. The final chapter looks in detail at how performance is evaluated in scientific and academic organisations, and thereby provides information for challenging suppression of dissidents whose job performance is adequate.

One final comment: not everything can be told about most suppression cases. Australian defamation laws are among the most severe in the world, and are often used to suppress free expression.[5] Significantly, most defamation cases are brought by powerful organisations or leading public figures, the same groups who are more often responsible for suppression than victims of it. In most of the suppression cases documented here, there is information which cannot be revealed because of the possibility of attracting defamation suits. Suffice it to say that the extent and viciousness of suppression is certainly greater than can be spelled out here.

References

1. For definitions of political repression (including what is here called suppression) see Alan Wolfe, *The Seamy Side of Democracy: Repression in America* (New York: David McKay, 1973) and Robert Justin Goldstein, *Political Repression in Modern America from 1870 to the Present* (Cambridge, Mass.: Schenkman, 1978), p. xvi.

2. On repression see the publications of Amnesty International. On both suppression and repression see the excellent journal *Index on Censorship*. A recent bibliography and analysis of repression can be found in Thomas Plate and Andrea Darvi, *Secret Police: The Inside Story of a Network of Terror* (London: Abacus, Sphere, 1983).

3. A. Ernest Fitzgerald, *The High Priests of Waste* (New York: Norton, 1972). A similar story, including dismissal of those who provide examples of waste, occurs in various branches of local and national government in the UK. See Leslie Chapman, *Waste Away*

(London: Chatto and Windus, 1982), as well as his earlier *Your Disobedient Servant* (London: Chatto and Windus, 1978).

4. Rhonda Brown and Paul Matteucci, "The high cost of whistle-blowing", *Inquiry Magazine*, vol. 4, no. 15, 1 September 1981, pp. 14–19; Peter Pringle and William Arkin, *SIOP* (London: Sphere, 1983), pp. 109–12.

5. Robert Pullan, *Guilty Secrets: Free Speech in Australia* (Sydney: Methuen Australia, 1984).

Part One:
CASES

AUSTRALIAN SCIENTISTS AND THE COLD WAR

Jean Buckley-Moran

INTRODUCTION

In the late 1940s and through the 1950s, Western countries underwent a period of anti-communist hysteria. As the military necessity for Western alliance with the Soviet Union against Nazi Germany collapsed, earlier anticommunism resurfaced and the Soviet Union was fostered as a feared enemy. The hysteria manifested itself in an elite-sponsored paranoia about communist agents who somehow threatened to topple Western institutions by working from the inside and providing information and comfort to the Soviet state. In practice, anticommunism served to mobilise national chauvinism and to oppose emerging support for internationalism in politics and economics. The cold-war crusade in addition ably served the careers of many politicians who joined the cause, helping them to discredit political opponents.

The anticommunist hysteria was also used to eliminate left-wing and other critical people from a wide range of institutions, including trade unions, schools, universities, artistic endeavours, and science. This process was most intense in the United States, and there is a wealth of documentation on the events there.[1] But other countries were not untouched.

This chapter[2] examines the nature of the cold-war suppression of Australian scientists, its motivation and impact. As such it focuses on political suppression by the state. With the advent of the "atomic age" the acerbic and sustained assault on scientists was not an isolated attempt to quell dissent among a now strategically placed professional group. The attacks provided a political key for confirming the premises of the cold war in Australia. They also provided a springboard for generalising the attack to other intellectual vanguard groups.

A little-known organisation, the Australian Association of Scientific Workers (AASW) became an unwitting focus of the attempt to gain more concerted control over the future direction of science and the determination of policies for its institutional development. In contrast with the conservative, isolationist mould in which Australian science had grown, the AASW offered a different set of ideals for science — that science be centrally related to social ends and be more vitally connected with industry. AASW's premature demise cannot be considered separately from a whole range of social alternatives that were dislodged in the early cold-war years.

To state the obvious, the price of suppression is always greater than the sum total of individuals damaged in the process. It visibly affects the process by which countervailing orthodoxies may be regenerated and reproduced institutionally. It limits the horizons of what is perceived as possible, feasible or even desirable. The following account attempts to demonstrate skeletally and sharply how state apparatuses can be mobilised to suppress dissent — in this instance, with the belated but ready support of a professional elite.

11

THE AUSTRALIAN ASSOCIATION
OF SCIENTIFIC WORKERS

Formed in July 1939, AASW represented a distinct break in the elitist, "advancement of science" orientation of existing scientific societies. Its membership was open to all scientists irrespective of professional standing and in its heyday it could claim to represent one-third of the total scientific population. Its uniquely broad-based support was facilitated by the outbreak of war, which united scientists of very different political persuasions. Science was projected as a vital national resource, critical for "winning the war, as well as winning the peace" — with scientists at the helm in their role as social engineers.

By 1943 AASW had gained much credibility in government circles and its track record was indeed impressive. It was instrumental in having Australia's first scientific manpower registers compiled and in establishing a Scientific Liaison Bureau. The Bureau's brief was to act as an information and referral service for industry, to relieve "technical" bottlenecks and to overcome duplication of research effort. It set up joint production committees in strategic industries to advise on manufacturing processes, and was represented on numerous wartime committees. It investigated ways of overcoming critical shortfalls of raw materials previously imported from Germany. It lobbied for urgent funding to develop indigenous manufacturing processes for essential supplies such as acetone, butyl alcohol, aluminium sheet and potash salts.

Individual subcommittees made outstanding contributions. For instance the AASW Drugs Committee, a small team of research chemists who worked around the clock to develop pilot-scale synthesis of essential drugs, was a pioneering effort given that Australia had never before undertaken commercial synthesis of drugs. Their breakthrough in developing an anti-malarial drug became as important as ammunition when the incidence of malaria threatened to reach epidemic proportions among troops fighting in New Guinea.

As the gruelling exigencies of war slowly subsided, AASW was able to concentrate on community-based projects, and conducted a series of sweeping investigations into health, industrial relations, safety and work conditions, education, housing, nutrition and family budgets, social security provisions and rationing anomalies. Underlying these efforts was the promotion of science as a means for reducing social inequality.

AASW's twin constitutional goals of promoting science for society as well as the interests of scientists ultimately proved irreconcilable and deeply polarised its membership. Essentially the progressive-liberals argued for piecemeal reform based on incontrovertible "facts", while a small but disproportionately influential radical nucleus[3] asserted that socially productive science could not be achieved without radical social change.

This polarisation first became evident in moves to unionise the AASW and later over the question of whether "planned" science was the appropriate strategy for making science publicly accessible and connecting science more vitally with industry and social produc-tivity. In both instances, the progressive-liberals won out over the emerging anti-capitalist critique of its radical core. In the event AASW failed to become a scientists' union and a separate organisation, the Federation of Scientific and Technical Workers, was created for this purpose. The planning controversy, identified in its timing with Labor government moves towards a planned economy and "socialisation" of industry, ultimately alienated a sizeable proportion of AASW's senior "respectable" membership. Even so, AASW's demise at this stage was by no means self-evident.

The AASW was affiliated with the World Federation of Scientific Workers (WFSW) which was established in July 1946. The WFSW was to provide a forum to promote the political responsibility of scientists, the international collaboration of associations of scientific workers, and to lobby for disarmament and the abolition of nuclear weapons.

Most of the overseas scientists' protest movements (such as the many bodies affiliated with the WFSW) were expressly politically motivated. AASW's constitutional apoliticism was critically at odds with these developments. To the extent that it followed the thrust of the WFSW, the AASW could not avoid the dilemma of responding politically to the atomic energy and defence debates in Australia and later in countering parliamentary insinuations of espionage.

The AASW scientists' early public visibility and pronouncements about atomic energy were to play directly into the hands of their critics. Eager endorsement of the internationalist ethos of science and appeals for the unfettered exchange of scientific knowledge were later interpreted as either evidence of scientists' ostrich-like naivety or as a subterfuge for sinister acts of disloyalty, even treason.

In its early public statements, the AASW urged the Australian government to initiate research on atomic energy and provide forms of "adequate control and development of Australian resources of uranium and thorium and . . . other sources of atomic energy". "Full international co-operation" was seen as a precondition both for acquiring the technical information and expertise necessary to initiate such a programme in Australia, and for ensuring that this project would in fact be turned to peaceful ends.

In conferences and other statements in the mid-1940s, members of the AASW emphasised the "special duty" of scientists as one in which their "special knowledge lays on them a special responsibility above that of other citizens". The possibility that the interests of governments might conflict with those of scientists and deny them their social engineering role was not an issue directly confronted or tackled. Rather, emphasis was put on the themes of international cooperation, opposition to secrecy, and devising a system of international control of nuclear power and weapons through the United Nations as essential for the future survival of humankind. At the time, it was perhaps impossible to predict how elusive such self-evident objectives were destined to be. Nevertheless, AASW's response to the dilemma the "atomic age" and internationalism posed for the social relations of science could not, and did not, take into account the impending cold war which effectively placed the option on social responsibility beyond its reach.

While for scientists the outcome of secrecy measures and the international control of atomic energy were inextricably linked, the presentation of atomic energy as a *public* issue depended very much on the public's appreciation of a distinction between the spirit of science and the practice of power politics. The timing of espionage charges against scientists in Canada, and potentially in Australia, both complicated and coloured public response to the issue.

THE CANADIAN CONNECTION

According to a statement released by the Canadian Association of Scientific Workers (CASW) in May 1946, thirteen scientists were "virtually kidnapped" during the night of 15 February. They were held incommunicado without access to legal counsel, friends and in some instances without charges being laid, for periods of two to six weeks. Canadian press accounts also commented on the extraordinary nature of the arrests: "the search and seizure powers conferred on police resulted in fantastic excesses of zeal; one policeman, for example, considered that share certificates, Hansard, and a copy of the Basic Writings of Freud were evidence 'that secret information had been communicated' to foreign agents".

The detainees were then subjected to the gruelling cross-examination of a Royal Commission. The Commission had been appointed within hours of revelations being made to the Canadian Ministry of Justice by Igor Gouzenko, a cipher clerk at the Soviet Embassy in Ottawa. Its mandate was to investigate the nature and extent of espionage activities perpetrated by a conspiracy whose immediate objective was to convey "the secret of the atomic bomb to Russia".[4] Effectively acting as both judge and jury, the Commission proclaimed some of the detained guilty before criminal proceedings had started. It also charged others who "did not so far as the evidence discloses take any part in the subversive activities but would have done so if required".[5] Specific allegations contained in reports of the Commission's hearing before criminal trials were held made the verdict of trial proceedings a "foregone conclusion".

The CASW in its statement alleged that the Royal Commission's sole justification was that "some of the accused had stated that they had a higher loyalty than that which they owed their country". As CASW dryly observed, "it would be difficult to find many scientists who have been engaged on war work, who though perfectly innocent, could not be convicted under this Act". Beyond deploring the use of legal procedure to repress scientific exchange, CASW found its hands tied. The arrest of Dr Raymond Boyer, then Assistant Professor at McGill University and National Chairman of CASW, made the CASW an easy target for a hostile press.

On 1 May 1946, Dr Alan Nunn May was charged with "communicating information prejudicial to the safety and interest of the State". Formerly Reader in Physics at London University, May had in 1943 joined the British research team to work on atomic energy in the United States, later moving to Canada to continue his research. In his daze May claimed that the information he passed on to the Soviet Union was "mostly of a character which has since been published or is about to be published". May pleaded guilty and was subsequently sentenced to 10 years' imprisonment.

J. B. S. Haldane, for the British Association of Scientific Workers, claimed in May's defence that May's actions occurred at a time when the Soviet Union was still officially an ally, and that he was motivated by the "great tradition of internationalism in science". AASW followed the British Association's lead in protesting against the severity of May's sentence. AASW saw the conviction of May as part of an attempt to stifle protest by scientists. AASW members were also concerned that secrecy restrictions on the technical aspects of atomic energy were being applied in blanket fashion to *all* information with any relevance to atomic processes. With the arrest of prominent Canadian scientists on charges of espionage, the threat of military control of science was seen in some quarters as a "threat of the military control of labour, for it is the beginning of Fascism".

As CASW itself anticipated, there was a strong possibility that the spy scare would be used to discredit the scientific profession and that it would be used to stampede the United States public and legislature into supporting legislation such as the May Johnson Bill. Under the terms of the original May Johnson Bill, the future development of atomic energy would be geared to armament and defence. CASW, along with some of the protest groups of US atomic scientists (which by April 1946 combined to form the Federation of American Scientists) correctly saw the introduction of the May Johnson Bill as compromising freedom of scientific exchange and the chances of developing atomic energy for peaceful purposes.

ATTACKS ON *AASW*

While some AASW scientists absorbed the shock that the internationalist ethos of science guaranteed no immunity from what they interpreted as a clear-cut case of political chicanery, the Australian press and a few vocal politicians seized on AASW's defence of Canadian scientists implicated in the Gouzenko affair as unequivocal evidence of communist infiltration and treason by AASW.

The Australian Labor Party had formed the national government since 1941. The government's outlook favoured a trend towards centralisation and internationalism. Cabinet documents reveal that the government's views on the uses of atomic energy for industrial power production were entirely consistent with AASW's own position at this time. The parties which formed the parliamentary Opposition — the Liberal and Country Parties — were able to use attacks on the autonomous AASW and on the major government scientific research organisation, the Council for Scientific and Industrial Research (CSIR) as a convenient lever for discrediting the Labor government.

One of those leading the attack on AASW was W. C. Wentworth, an aspiring politician, later elected to the House of Representatives in 1949. His antagonism towards AASW had been earlier aroused at AASW's 1944 Planning Conference. There the provocative interjections of Wentworth and his supporters effectively stymied conference approval of a series of specific resolutions of direct political and social significance. This time, however, the stakes were rather higher. After the Canadian Royal Commission, Wentworth lost little time in denouncing AASW. Prominently featured in the pages of the Sydney *Daily Telegraph*, Wentworth claimed that Russia was using "her influence on AASW to get the technique to make atom bombs as soon as possible" and that

> When [Russia] can make [atom bombs], she proposes to distribute them to Communist agents all over the world, so as to hold the world ransom and blow up our vital centres.

He charged that AASW was "a fifth column for Russia" whose "policy" was "that even if ¾ of the people in the world died, that would not matter as long as the remaining ¼ were Communists". Wentworth also alleged that

> (1) "Russia operates largely through a physics lecturer at Sydney University [Dr R. Makinson], the Australian Association of Scientific Workers, the Australian Federation of Scientific Workers"; (2) "that these last two bodies have infiltrated the Council for Scientific and Industrial Research"; and (3) "[the] man who organised this treasonable conspiracy still remains a Lecturer in Physics at Sydney University".

AASW's fear that Wentworth's attack amounted to an attempt to "frame the left" was confirmed when, six months later in March 1947, Country Party parliamentarian Joe Abbott launched a vitriolic attack against AASW. The timing of Abbott's charges coincided with parliamentary discussion of the Anglo-Australian rocket range proposals, acceptance of which federal Cabinet had approved in principle on 19 November 1946. Meanwhile a protest movement hotly contested the establishment of an experimental testing range for guided projectiles in South Australia, mainly on the grounds that it could endanger the lifestyle of tribal Aborigines. By January 1947 the protest movement gathered momentum and had the support of some 36 organisations, including AASW.

On 6 March 1947, the day before Abbott's first attack on AASW, the government's Committee on Guided Projectiles had released its official report on the rocket range. Through a series of conflational acrobatics, Abbott used a recapitulation of the Nunn May case and the Canadian espionage trials to insinuate a concrete espionage connection between the Canadian and Australian Associations of Scientific Workers. He strongly urged that the government hold a Royal Commission to investigate "the whole of the communist activities of Australia", evidence of "spy rings" and communist associations among AASW and CSIR personnel. Abbott then named six AASW members and a member of the executive committee of CSIR as security risks. Abbott's insinuations were seen as both an attempt to silence AASW's ("expert") opposition to the rocket range proposals and to discredit the Labor government's present security arrangements.

Apart from insisting on a Royal Commission as a means to outlaw the Communist Party of Australia for the second time within five years, Abbott was also engineering a case for instituting security screenings on all CSIR research personnel and, effectively, for the control of science in Australia. In claiming that AASW's executive used "secret study groups" to turn its members into "traitors", Abbott's charges of communist infiltration of CSIR through AASW implied a sinister symbiotic connection between the two organisations. Abbott's attack was consolidated by contributions from several other members of the federal Opposition.

Stung by the allegations made under parliamentary privilege, AASW's scope for redress was by now severely circumscribed. Faced with an "orgy of redbaiting" by the press, AASW's Federal Council was reduced to sending letters of protest to the Prime Minister and sympathetic members of the House of Representatives.

After the parliamentary attacks were made on AASW, it became clear to those who still remained sympathetic to AASW's overall platform that they could no longer remain members of AASW without considerable risk to their careers and livelihoods. Initially, many of those who remained with AASW until March 1947 refused to believe that AASW harboured "fellow travellers". After several of its members were named in Parliament in

March 1947, to be a member of AASW *implied* Communist Party membership.

By 12 June 1947 legislation for *The Approved Defence Projects Protection Act* was passed, and on 20 June the Woomera rocket range was declared an approved project. From the point of view of stifling protest and compelling the Labor government to accept the premises of the cold war, the Opposition's campaign had been resoundingly successful.

That the wider base for support for the protest movement's future activities had all but evaporated may be judged by two facts. First, only one Member of Parliament raised any objection to the proposed Approved Defence Projects Protection legislation. Second, earlier trade union moves to organise a black ban on all rocket bomb manufacture and experimentation were successfully countered by the Industrial Groups and other conservative elements in the trade union movement which denounced the proposal as communist inspired.

The *Act* included penalties of up to 12 months' imprisonment and/or £5000 fine for anyone who "by speech or writing advocates or encourages the prevention, hindrance or obstruction or carrying out of any approved defence project". These security measures had obvious implications for the CSIR Division of Aeronautics since the Anglo–Australian Project involved the Division's continued wartime research services on military aircraft for the RAAF and development of a gas turbine engine.

CSIR ATTACKED AND REORGANISED

Early in 1947 the Chief Executive Officer of CSIR, Sir David Rivett, gave an address on "Science and Responsibility" to the Canberra University College. The speech contained a fairly standard defence of autonomy in science:

> If national sovereignty demanded the right to prepare secretly for the destruction of other sovereignties, let those who took the responsibility for such a decision keep their projects clear of national scientific institutions in which traditional freedom of science must be maintained.

On 25 March 1947, Abbott quoted from Rivett's address, urging the Prime Minister to ensure that "only those officers of the council be employed on research into guided weapons who dissociate themselves from his views".

To clinch his case of guilt by association, Abbott then asked John Dedman, the Minister responsible for CSIR, to justify Arthur Rudkin's present employment with CSIR, given Rudkin's previous conviction in Perth under the National Security Regulations on 10 June 1940. At that time Rudkin had allegedly used his honorary position as air raids precaution warden at Victoria in Western Australia to convey privileged information[6] to the Australian and British Communist Parties. Rudkin's "information" was in fact fairly common knowledge in Britain at that time. Rudkin was subsequently sentenced to four months' imprisonment. Soon after his release, Rudkin was given contract work with CSIR's Melbourne Forest Products Laboratory. There he worked on developing plywood products. On 23 April 1947 Abbott produced samples of recent articles written by Rudkin to demonstrate that Rudkin's sympathies had not significantly changed since his conviction in 1940. An example of Rudkin's present "treacherous" activities included his opposition to Nunn May's sentence as an instance of the attempt "to terrorise scientists".

In the following year, any reserves the government might have had to defend the abstract principle of freedom in science were depleted by its struggle to survive a formidable campaign against its bank nationalisation moves. Responding to earlier insinuations against CSIR officers, on 25 August 1948 Chifley instigated a report on CSIR's organisation to be carried out by W. J. Dunk and H. C. Coombs, two high-ranking public servants. Two weeks later, the Opposition lost little time in using the Estimates Debate in Parliament to launch the next battery of indictments against CSIR and Rivett. The Acting Leader of the Opposition, E. J. Harrison, set the pace by asserting that the United States Government would withhold defence information from the United Kingdom and Australia because of the Australian Government's deficient security arrangements for its own science organisation. A similar unsubstantiated claim had been made in the Sydney press some months earlier. This time, however, Artie Fadden, leader of the Country Party and an inveterate anti-communist, produced a "secret document" listing a series of disturbing allegations. This was the Opposition's trump card against Rivett and the CSIR.

Fadden's "secret document" claimed to be a "minute" of two confidential meetings: the first between Prime Minister Ben Chifley and the Executive Committee of CSIR on 6 July 1947; the second between Chifley and the British Cabinet on 8 July 1947. Specifically, the document alleged that the US Government was reluctant to convey "certain specially secret information" to Australian authorities because of its belief that the Australian CSIR "might not be fully under the control of the Australian Government". Fadden repeatedly refused to table this document in Parliament on the grounds that "the Government cannot and must not be trusted".

The Opposition's case soon degenerated into unrestrained invective against Rivett, Makinson and Rudkin. Using Abbott's well-tried technique of precarious innuendo, Harrison connected Rivett's advocacy of "free trade in scientific knowledge" with that of renowned communists, such as Makinson. Abbott then met Dedman's denial of the Opposition's charges with the rejoinder that Dedman was simply protecting his own appointments in the CSIR and was not sufficiently concerned about communist infiltration.

Again Abbott produced Rivett's Canberra speech as evidence of Rivett's desire to "protect certain shibboleths and faiths, to the detriment of the interests of Australia". Abbott then accused Rivett of preaching "wickedly and wrongly, the most dangerous doctrines to our young scientists". Characterising Rivett's approach as "as near to treachery as one can get", Opposition member Archie Cameron recommended that "the proper thing to do with Sir David Rivett would be to relieve him of his duties". The gravity of the Opposition's assertions and its flair for adding inaccuracies to insults were made at a time when CSIR had only two officers working in the area of nuclear energy research.

Press coverage of the debate largely endorsed the Opposition's attack on CSIR, against men with no right of reply or redress. The Sydney *Daily Telegraph* went so far as to suggest that "Mr Fadden holds a whip which he should use without mercy".[7] In turn press reportage had the effect of revitalising the Opposition's unremitting and scurrilous campaign when the debate resumed on 1 October 1948. With few exceptions, little press attention was given to the statements of Sir Henry Tizard, then Chairman of the British Government's Research Policy Committee, which emphatically denied that Australian security presented any problems for negotiations between the UK and the US governments.

Most of the government's defence was sidetracked into attacking Fadden's secret document as a forgery or itself a breach of security. The press interpreted this evasion as a convenient smokescreen which thoroughly vindicated Fadden's claims. Certainly there is circumstantial evidence to suggest that Fadden's allegations had some basis in fact. The government's denials put it at a severe tactical disadvantage. It gave credence to more serious charges later.

But by this time the attacks had led to a number of major concessions by the government. In December 1948, Public Service Bill (No. 2) was ratified in Parliament, enabling the government to transfer work performed by CSIR to other Commonwealth departments. The Division of Aeronautics was duly transferred to the Department of Supply and Development in February 1949. On 19 May 1949, with the passing of amendments to the *Science and Industry Act of 1926*, CSIR was reconstituted and renamed the Commonwealth Scientific and Industrial Research Organisation (CSIRO). A new executive, without Sir David Rivett, took office.

With these amendments, the government assumed full responsibility for CSIRO through the chairman of its executive council, now to consist of five members, three of whom were scientists. The executive council was to be appointed by the Governor-General on the advice of the responsible Minister, and would be in charge of initiating research and investigations and for making funding recommendations to government. All scientific officers were to be employed by the Minister, not the Public Service Board. CSIRO employees were now required to take an oath of allegiance. As Dedman put it, "the present staff would have to pass a 'character test'. There would not be any political test".

Despite AASW's earlier dire warnings, it was not until after the parliamentary attack on Rivett and the CSIR that other scientific bodies reacted sharply to the inevitability of secrecy provisions and the threat that "political exercise of control" in science represented. By this time, such protests awkwardly conceded the necessity for security restrictions in military science, while offering varying rationalisations as to why similar conditions in the conduct of fundamental research would irrevocably compromise its future progress. Not surprisingly, these arguments met a cool response in military circles. The scientists' protests were largely ineffectual.

The *Melbourne Herald*'s tribute to Rivett on his retirement as a "genius for getting things done" and someone who collected honours and exhibitions "as easily as a housewife gathers flowers" must have been small comfort for someone who had made such outstanding contributions to Australian science and to two world wars.

AASW's Demise

Between the passage of the Public Service Bill of 1948 and the 1949 amendments to the *Science and Industry Act*, Jack Lang, a right-wing Labor parliamentarian, renewed the attack on AASW, joining in what had been a campaign conducted by the Opposition. On 5 November 1948, following the parliamentary debate on communism, Lang made several allegations against two former executive members of the AASW, Spencer Smith-White, a geneticist, and Paul Klemens, a postgraduate student in theoretical physics. Both had been signatories to outspoken statements against Abbott's earlier offensives.

In pointing out Smith-White's connections with the "communist-controlled" AASW and his Communist Party membership, Lang called on Chifley to establish whether Smith-White had "gone abroad on a government mission and, if so, will the Prime Minister obtain a report of his communist activities, and forward it to the British authorities?" Given Smith-White's then occupation as lecturer in botany at Sydney University, Lang's insinuations about Smith-White's capacity for espionage were rather far-fetched. In his defence Smith-White denied Communist Party membership, asserting that his loyalties "are neither Russian nor American but British, and that as a geneticist the 'Genetics Controversy' in Russia has caused me considerable concern".[8]

Lang's attack on Paul Klemens was hardly more legitimate, and was clearly designed to curtail any future academic career Klemens might have had in Australia. Criticising the government for rewarding Klemens with a postgraduate scholarship to Cambridge, Lang asked what precautions the government had taken

> to make certain that such scholarship holders are not affiliated with Communist organizations, prior to their being given credentials for overseas study, especially studies that involve contact with the work of nuclear physics? Is Klemens to return as a lecturer in physics at the Australian National University in Canberra?

Klemens, then based at Oxford, not Cambridge, was quickly defended by Ian Clunies Ross, CSIRO's new Executive Chairman. A university medallist awarded a postgraduate scholarship on the recommendation of Mark Oliphant, Klemens had evidently accepted the position of Acting Secretary of AASW in an attempt to counterbalance "increasing influence of extreme left-wing activists".[9] A letter from H. C. Coombs to the Prime Minister's Department reveals that the "Registrar of the National University has been good enough to let me have some information *re* Klemens".[10] (Klemens subsequently had a successful academic career in the US and now holds a professorship at the University of Connecticut.)

While Lang's attack on Smith-White, Klemens and the AASW was mild in comparison with his earlier anti-communist attacks on the Chifley Government, it was motivated by a deep-seated xenophobia with a strong anti-intellectual thrust. Lang made other attacks on Australian intellectuals, particularly those employed by government instrumentalities and writers and artists in receipt of Commonwealth grants.

With Lang's attack on Smith-White and Klemens, AASW's decision to dissolve was sealed. AASW formally wound up its affairs on 31 July 1949. In other circumstances, the organisation might have provided a fertile breeding ground for a coherent rather than an ad hoc scientists' protest movement. The expedient attack effectively put an end to the public articulation of social responsibility in science for a generation of scientists in Australia. The changed ideological climate of the cold war had the effect of turning the quest for autonomy into a utilitarian pursuit for greater funding for fundamental research. Apart from the obvious repercussions this had for the future articulation of science policy, it also cemented the prospect that science in Australia would continue to be marginalised. In an important sense then, AASW's premature demise marked a watershed in the attempt to negotiate a central relevance for science in society and to break down the isolationist mould of scientific production in Australia.[11]

COLD-WAR CASUALTIES

Not surprisingly, most of those attacked in the internal cold-war offensive were physicists or research scientists whose public outspokenness and sympathy for the Soviet mode of science made them ready victims. While some AASW members named in Parliament recovered forfeited promotions ten years later, the scars were to remain permanent. A number of other scientists chose to remain in voluntary exile overseas following the institution of mandatory security checks in several Australian universities. A few were unfortunate enough not to regain professional admission in their chosen area of specialised research.

Following the intemperate parliamentary attacks on Dr R. E. B. Makinson, an officer of the Commonwealth Investigation Branch (CIB) sent a report to Professor V. A. Bailey in an attempt to block Makinson's application for the Chair of Nuclear Physics at Sydney University. With the delicacy of a sledgehammer, this communication states:

> As Chairmanship of Nuclear Physics will carry with it research into atomic energy, you may feel with me [CIB] that the matter of an appointment is of very great national significance and the fact that Dr. Makinson is a professed Communist should be taken into account.

The concern expressed by the CIB evidently carried some weight since this Chair of Physics was to remain vacant for the next seven years.

Following his election to the House of Representatives in 1949, W. C. Wentworth's continuing vendetta against Makinson did little to alleviate Makinson's plight. As late as 1952 Wentworth was still able to gain political mileage by dubbing Makinson a "traitor" on the basis of his "influence" in the now defunct AASW. Makinson was to share the distinction, with fellow founding AASW veteran Jack Legge, of being one of the very few of his academic contemporaries never to be promoted to a professorship.

A different sort of consequence in the wake of attacks on CSIR was a reversion to strictly professional obligations and loyalties by the scientific community. In this context, the neutrality of science was offered as both a defence for, and rationalisation of, the need to protect autonomy in science. Few perhaps understood this dynamic as keenly as Ian Clunies Ross in his handling of the "Kaiser affair".

This incident occurred in late 1949, soon after legislative changes to the *Science and Industry Act*, and renewed the newly formed Executive's anxiety that the government would exercise greater political control over CSIRO. One of its officers, Tom Kaiser, on overseas leave to complete a Ph.D., was involved in a public demonstration outside Australia House in London. Kaiser had distributed leaflets protesting against the gaoling of eight trade union leaders during a recent coal strike in Australia. Kaiser was himself the son of a factory worker and a number of his relatives were working in mines at the time. He had previously been engaged on radiophysics research with CSIR, and had made a "valuable contribution to the Australian war effort in helping to develop means of countering Japanese radar". In 1947 he went to the Clarendon Physics Laboratory, Oxford University, to begin basic research work in nuclear physics. Having completed his Ph.D., Kaiser at the time of his participation in the demonstration was set to return to the Radiophysics Division of CSIRO.

The Australian Government instructed the High Commissioner in London to conduct an enquiry into Dr Kaiser's actions. Press reports seized on the Kaiser incident as an episode in "national humiliation" with serious repercussions for Australian diplomacy. Kaiser's actions, it was claimed, "will undo much work done in recent months to allay British and American suspicions that Australia cannot be trusted with secret information about modern weapons". Rumour also had it that only two months before the Kaiser incident Australian officers were excluded from a British military demonstration of "certain secret types of American weapons". This exclusion was evidently based on American "awareness that some Australians sent abroad on technical missions are Communists". The press was also quick to point out that "when a student is assigned to research on nuclear physics, with the backing of his Government, he is placed in work where no sure line can be drawn between harmless and potentially dangerous knowledge". In the circumstances, an expected "government purge of scientists" seemed more realistic than Dedman's "ridiculous assurance that Kaiser had no access to secret information".[12]

On 19 August 1949, the CSIRO Executive ordered Kaiser's immediate return to Australia, but stated that it "cannot agree to your return to radio physics or to nuclear physics". The Executive insisted that failure to comply would mean immediate termination of Kaiser's employment with CSIRO. Kaiser rejected these directives on the grounds that "just as during the war I regarded it as my first duty to contribute to the defeat of tyranny in other countries, so . . . I will in the future apply my energies to fighting for the retention of free science as the only one that can flourish and raise the prestige of Australian science in the way that C.S.I.R.O. has done since its foundation". What followed for Kaiser was a period of considerable personal and financial hardship, during which time he found it necessary to undertake study of a separate branch of physics — theoretical physics — to gain future employment in England. The flowering of Australian radiophysics during the post-war years is indicative of the professional price Kaiser was to pay for his decision to change research areas. Kaiser later took up a position at Sheffield University where he is now Reader in Physics.

The handling of the Kaiser affair was perhaps the logical consequence of Clunies Ross's concern to appease any doubts the government may have had about CSIRO's ability to deal with its own affairs. To do less would have been to jettison any further appeals to autonomy which was to become the fulcrum in CSIRO's future funding and policy formation.

Following Kaiser's dismissal, Clunies Ross issued a memo to all CSIRO officers forbidding employees from participation in "controversial political issues", including the following justification:

> There may be a few amongst us who confuse scientific freedom with political licence, even to the extent of claiming the right to bring public discredit on the Organization or the Government of which they are the servants . . . Even were there no other consequences arising from the involvement of C.S.I.R.O., however indirectly, in political controversy, scientific discredit may still be brought upon us, since, in such controversy, objective truth and scientific analysis are almost inevitably confused by hearsay, prejudice and emotion . . . [I]n fairness to those who may be tempted to disregard these responsibilities it is only right to let them know the serious view the Executive must take of any such disregard in the future.

As one CSIRO officer later commented, the effect of this memo[13] was to place a binding, "voluntary" censorship on any discussion of political issues on CSIRO premises for a considerable period of time. At the time of Kaiser's likely dismissal, Dr Ralph Traill, Chairman of the Victorian Division until AASW's demise, commented that

> It is not political freedom merely to be allowed to hold what views you like; but to be able to express them in political action ... Kaiser has apparently considerably embarrassed the [CSIRO] Executive; and this clearly shows its dependence on the Government, the opposition, and the powers that stand behind them both.

Eric Burhop was another keenly active and outspoken founding member of AASW's Victorian Division. Early in the war years, Burhop was seconded to CSIR's Radiophysics Laboratory to carry out pioneering work on the production of centimetre valves. In a collaborative effort with Dr D. F. Martyn, he produced Australia's first laboratory model of a magnetron in May 1942. A few months later Burhop was transferred back to Melbourne and, in his capacity as officer-in-charge of the Maribyrnong Munitions Supply Laboratory, was responsible for the pilot production and testing of resonant cavity magnetrons in Australia. However, Burhop's later international reputation evolved from his connection with the Manhattan Project. In 1944 he joined the British party which had been working with the United States team at Berkeley, California, on the electromagnetic separation of uranium isotopes.

Burhop found it impossible to regain employment in his capacity as radiophysicist in Australia after the war. His application for the Chair of Physics at the University of Adelaide was rejected. Shortly afterwards, Burhop was offered lectureships in applied mathematics and later physics at the University College of London, obtaining the Chair of Physics there in 1960. In view of Burhop's superlative contribution to Australian science during the war years, the rejection of his application for academic appointment in Australia was most likely not decided on academic grounds alone, especially considering that at the time most Australian universities required security clearances.

Like his Australian contemporary Mark Oliphant, Burhop was to devote much of the rest of his life working towards disarmament. In 1957 he acted as one of the intermediaries between Joliot-Curie and Bertrand Russell in calling a conference following the Einstein – Russell statement against the hydrogen bomb. These negotiations resulted in the first of the Pugwash conferences in July 1957. In 1969 Burhop became President of the WFSW and was awarded the Joliot-Curie Medal of the World Peace Council. He was belatedly elected a fellow of the Royal Society of London in 1963.

While Burhop's career was not irrevocably impaired by his exclusion from Australian academia for security reasons, his later achievements testify to qualities of personal and political resilience and breadth of vision — qualities which were actively denied expression in Australia's cold-war years.

Less fortunate was the more gradual, although no less invidious outcome in the 1950s for other members of the now defunct AASW who redirected their energy into the peace movement. John Callaghan, a founding member of the Queensland Division of AASW, was sacked from his position as biochemist at the Institute of Medical Research for taking three months' leave of absence to act as the Queensland Peace Council's delegate to Peking in 1952. According to interview sources, the Institute refused to confirm approval or refusal of his request for leave of absence until after the date he had officially requested that the leave begin. He subsequently faced six years' unemployment with a family of seven to support. Dr Steve Macindoe forfeited his career promotion prospects for ten years over his involvement with the Australia–China Friendship League. Dr Len Hibbard's position in CSIRO was placed in jeopardy over the Petrov Affair (which claimed many victims outside science).[14] Most of the AASW members named in Abbott's original parliamentary attack were to experience setbacks in subsequent career options. Particularly poignant was the blacklisting of Arthur Rudkin. Rudkin's appointment with CSIR(O) was terminated in late 1948.

Formerly described as "a brilliant chemist", Rudkin later found work in a boot factory. Rudkin eventually found employment with the Sydney Metropolitan Water Sewerage and Drainage Board as an assistant chemist in the Research Branch. Some fifteen years later, he opted for the precarious vagaries of freelance work as a part-time tutor/demonstrator in physics and chemistry at Sydney University and the University of New South Wales, and translation of scientific papers.

"Victimisation", however, cannot be indexed according to the career loss alone. Arguably, far more damaging was the pervasive environment of political and social repression which stunted the burgeoning of intellectual and cultural life so evident in the early to mid-1940s. The arrival of the *Lucky Country* with the post-war boom was a bitter palliative for those whose earlier endeavours became recessed within the walls of material expansion that Australia enjoyed in the 1950s and 1960s.

Acknowledgements

I thank Ann Baker, Clyde Manwell and especially Brian Martin for helpful comments and editorial support.

References

1. See especially Cedric Belfrage, *The American Inquisition 1945–1960* (Indianapolis: Bobbs-Merrill, 1973) and David Caute, *The Great Fear: The Anti-Communist Purge under Truman and Eisenhower* (London: Secker and Warburg, 1978). See also for example Robert Justin Goldstein, *Political Repression in Modern America from 1870 to the Present* (Cambridge: Schenkman, 1978); Chandler Davis, " . . . From an exile", in Robert O. Bowen (ed.), . . . *The New Professors* (New York: Holt, Rinehart and Winston, 1960), pp. 182–201. For specific accounts of Australia's period of "McCarthyism", see N. R. Whitlam and J. Stubbs, *Nest of Traitors* (Queensland: Jacaranda Press, 1974); H. Radi and P. Spearitt, *Jack Lang* (Sydney: Hale & Iremonger, 1977); the *South Australian White Report* (1978); and J. B. Paul, "Labor's Petrov legend", in R. Manne (ed.), *The New Conservatism in Australia* (London: Oxford University Press, 1982), pp. 114–40, 283–5.

2. Most of the material in this chapter is directly taken from or based on Jean Moran, "Scientists in the Political and Public Arena: A Social-intellectual History of the Australian Association of Scientific Workers, 1939–49" (M.Phil. thesis, School of Science, Griffith University, 1983). Sources for all quotes and other material not explicitly documented in this chapter are given in this work.

3. At this early stage the progressive-liberals numerically outnumbered the more radical members and the progressives had a decided influence on AASW's official line at a policy level. Even so, the influence of the radicals can be said to be "disproportionate" to their numbers in that they were far more active in subcommittee and lobbying activities which to a large extent sustained the momentum of many AASW platforms. The radicals' input was most visible in the Victorian and New South Wales Divisions where, after the resignation of AASW's more senior and "respectable" membership in the mid-1940s, their influence registered even more sharply.

4. R. Bothwell and J. L. Granatstein (eds), *The Gouzenko Transcripts* (1982), p. 4.

5. Paul Dufour, " 'Eggheads' and espionage: the Gouzenko affair in Canada", *Journal of Canadian Studies*, vol. 16, nos 3–4, Fall–Winter 1981, p. 190.

6. Rudkin had forwarded a brief account of existing ARP provisions in Australia to Professor J. B. S. Haldane (then adviser to Churchill on ARP and scientific matters) and sought his advice as to how these could be improved. This request and Rudkin's appraisal of the inadequacy of Australian ARP were later interpreted by security

personnel as an attempt to "sabotage" (rather than improve) existing ARP arrangements. (Personal communication from A. Rudkin, 10 December 1983.)

7. Sydney *Daily Telegraph*, 18 October 1948.

8. Australian Archives, CRS A461 Item 327/1/4, 6 November 1948.

9. ibid.

10. ibid., 12 November 1948.

11. AASW's fate was paralleled by that of several other radical and reformist groups of the period, such as the Studio of Realist Art whose history has been documented by Richard Haese, *Rebels and Precursors: The Revolutionary Years of Australian Art* (London: Allen Lane, 1981).

12. The newspaper quotes are from, respectively: *Melbourne Herald*, 1 August 1949; *Sydney Morning Herald*, 29 July 1949; *Melbourne Herald*, 2 August 1949; *Melbourne Herald*, 1 August 1949; Sydney *Sun-Herald*, 31 July 1949; *Melbourne Herald*, 1 August 1949.

13. Clunies Ross was also alleged to have announced that any officer objecting to the dismissal of subordinates would himself be dismissed.

14. See Bruce McFarlane, "Asio: the past", in Pat Flanagan (ed.), *Big Brother or Democracy?* (Adelaide: Department of Continuing Education, University of Adelaide, c. 1980), pp. 8–23; Don Watson, *Brian Fitzpatrick: A Radical Life* (Sydney: Hale & Iremonger, 1979). On the effect of ASIO and security checks in the cold-war period, see K. P. Barley, letter, *Australian Journal of Science*, vol. 19, April 1957, pp. 203–4; R. M. Hartwell, letter, *Vestes*, vol. 3, no. 4, December 1960, p. 51.

POLITICAL ECONOMY AT THE UNIVERSITY OF SYDNEY

Evan Jones and Frank Stilwell

One of the most substantial and enduring academic conflicts within Australia in the last twenty years has been that within the Economics Department at the University of Sydney. It has generated extreme bitterness of feeling and has been tragically wasteful of energies that might otherwise have been productively engaged. The conflict is a product of a unique set of circumstances but it has wider implications. It raises issues which are fundamental to the role of any educational organisation. It also has implications that are significant for understanding the economic system and for the appropriate direction of economic policy. No more relevant occasion exists than the present: a Federal Labor government in office, committed to economic and social reform in a time of economic crisis, but constrained in its economic policies by a dominant economic orthodoxy.

In general, the "political economy dispute" is a classic manifestation of academic conflict. It has involved substantial differences of opinion on a range of key issues: the appropriate subject content in the syllabus and in research, appropriate methods of inquiry, ideological preferences, the administrative power structure, and attitudes towards teaching and students. Much of this will be considered in some detail below.

It should be stressed that what follows is a one-sided interpretation of the events and their significance by two members of the dissident political economy group. From our perspective, the core of the discipline is intellectually bankrupt, and this structure has been maintained and reproduced by substantially illiberal institutional practices. In an era of relative quiescence in student opinions, the persistence and intensity of widespread student dissent in the Department of Economics at the University of Sydney has been a striking indication of the depth of these problems.

The ongoing dispute is of remarkable duration. Its origins can be traced to the appointment of two new professors of economics in the late 1960s, Professors Warren Hogan and Colin Simkin. They set about restructuring the program of courses offered by the Department, comprising a particular theoretical framework (and its statistical applications) in a structure that had acquired increasing prestige overseas. The proponents of the new approach saw it as leading to a modernisation of the Department and as a foundation for a more "rigorous" training in the subject. However, the nature of the changes and the heavy-handed manner of their introduction succeeded in antagonising most of the teaching staff. A number of staff left the Department at this time, concluding that other avenues provided greater possibilities for a career with some measure of dignity intact. Moreover, the new courses were generally seen by the students as overly theoretical, hopelessly unrealistic, poorly taught, and oriented towards one particular conservative set of economic doctrines.

An unofficial survey of student opinion was conducted in 1970, revealing a high degree of dissatisfaction with the courses, but the survey was impounded by one of the professors, and two tutors who had been associated with the survey were not re-employed at the end of the year. Protest meetings were held, but to no avail. Discontent simmered for the next couple of years and two more dissident tutors had their employment terminated. Tenured staff called for a Senate inquiry into the Department. The students staged a "day of protest" in 1973 and a "day of outrage" in 1974. Students and dissident staff prepared proposals for alternative curricula, which were rejected by the professors. Eventually an official enquiry was held by the Faculty of Economics in 1973, which recommended that the Department be partitioned by the creation of a separate Department of Political Economy, which would put on courses exposing students to more diverse currents of economic thought.

The then Vice-Chancellor, Bruce Williams (himself a conservative economist), refused to act as recommended but the University's Professorial Board did agree to the introduction of new courses in political economy, Economics I(P) and Economics II(P). Sympathetic staff formed themselves into a "political economy group" and mounted the new courses, starting in 1975. Continuing departmental impediments to the establishment of the new courses and discrimination against staff generated further student dissent which in turn led to the establishment of a *second* committee of inquiry in late 1975. The major recommendation of administrative autonomy for political economy staff was again shelved, which resulted in student protest on a massive scale. Reprisals against student leaders were instigated, which further inflamed the protests. The Vice-Chancellor's office was occupied, there was a partial strike of staff, and over 4000 students boycotted classes.

Dissent simmered for another five years, during which time the established bureaucratic procedures proved themselves generally effective in swallowing articulated grievances. In 1981, the rejection of a substantial student/staff proposal for course reform in third and fourth year engendered so much dissatisfaction that a *third* committee of inquiry into the Department was established. The 1982 report blamed the political economy staff for their isolationist mentality, but it legitimised studies in political economy, and recommended a pragmatic institutional change by which the political economy staff could administer their courses with some independence (in effect a *de facto* professor to operate in a bureaucratic structure centred on professorial power). The report was shelved by the Vice-Chancellor and its proposals decried as being impossible to implement. Shortly after the renewed legitimation of political economy courses, the orthodox economists sought to have these courses disbanded and return to the status quo of a decade before. Enrolments in the political economy courses had always been high (over 500 students studying the two courses each year) and were gradually increasing to the point of threatening to absorb over 50 per cent of students entering the Department. The moves against the courses once again generated student protest, escalating into the occupation of buildings and disciplinary proceedings against student leaders.

Finally, in mid-1983, the Academic Board intervened, imposing a compromise on the Economics Department involving more courses in political economy at the third and fourth-year level and the abolition of separate first-year courses to be replaced by a single course in which the political economy staff would be granted one term out of three. These changes were instituted in 1984 but the existence in Economics I of an identifiable term for the teaching of a dissenting economics was wholly unacceptable to the professors and their supporters. Other means of emasculation having now failed, procedures were established to remove the political economy staff and their courses (and other "soft" subjects such as government) to other faculties and to reconstitute a purified Faculty of Economics centred on the "professional" subjects of (orthodox) economics, accounting and econometrics. An Academic Board committee of inquiry was established by the University in 1984 to consider this and other proposals for the restructuring of faculties, and the resolution of the continuing "political economy dispute" was widely seen as the main objective of the exercise.

In what follows we examine (1) the principal *dimensions* of the conflict, (2) its *manifestations* in the form of discrimination against political economy staff and students, and opposition to political economy course developments and (3) the general *significance* of the issues.

1. DIMENSIONS OF THE DISPUTE

Three key dimensions of the dispute deserve elaboration: the nature of economics as a discipline, the teaching of economics and the administrative and decision-making structure.

(a) Economics as a Discipline

The fundamental element in the conflict is to be found in the nature of the economic discipline. The period since the Second World War has witnessed the development of a discipline increasingly monolithic in its attachment to a particular orthodoxy which can be labelled, at the risk of simplification, "neoclassical economics".[1] This approach had its origins around the 1870s, when Marx and other critical thinkers had to be deflected, and when economics developed into a specialised academic discipline separate from the issues of politics, history and social structure which had been the interrelated concerns of the classical political economists.

The core of the neoclassical "paradigm" consists of a body of generally accepted axioms and a set of propositions which follow, in principle, as logical deductions from those axioms. Key axioms are:

a postulate of the primacy of the individual as the basic unit of analysis;

a psychological motivation postulate that the individual is a rational calculating machine in pursuit of maximum material gain;

a postulate delimiting the decision-making environment, namely an economic sphere comprising an all-pervasive competitive market mechanism (which eradicates individual discretion); and a political sphere containing a government structure whose role is to support the appropriate economic environment (but this sphere is shadowy and strictly *off stage*);

a postulate that there exists sufficient information to make (individual) rational calculation possible, namely *full* information or probabilistic uncertainty;

a systems postulate that various mechanisms exist which impart a stabilising tendency to the system following any alteration to the underlying parameters.

The vision appears to have been borrowed from classical mechanics. Social behaviour is constructed in such a way as to parallel this structure from the natural world. At the individual level, (economic) behaviour becomes a mechanical process — a matter of logic; at the aggregate level, social behaviour is structurally constrained by a market-dictated and static environment, and is systems-stabilising following disturbances. At the aggregate level, then, there exists a fundamental emphasis on a concept of "social order". Represented under the label "general equilibrium", it takes an essentially mechanical form because relevant behaviour is dictated by an omnipresent and ruthlessly efficient resource allocation mechanism embodied in the competitive price system. As such, a developed "theory" can take the form of analysis using mathematical techniques borrowed from other disciplines (in particular, the calculus and linear algebra).

A consequence is that conventional economic analysis has been developed, at its best, into an extraordinarily elegant edifice. This edifice serves two functions, in which form and content are brilliantly fused: an analytical one in which an elegance of form is pursued for its own sake; and an ideological one in which all the contradictions of liberalist social philosophy are resolved in the *deus ex machina* of an atomistic self-regulating market economy. Of course, much work of an empirical nature takes place within the economics discipline, but it is ultimately tied to the conceptual "home base" of the neoclassical axioms.[2] Moreover, the status hierarchy of the discipline is directly related to the proximity of an academic's research work to the neoclassical core.[3]

During the twentieth century there has been a persistent confrontation within the discipline between the rigidity of the neoclassical analytical structure and the analytical requirements of studying complex historical processes and institutional behaviour. This confrontation has produced not a modification of the neoclassical analysis, but a stronger commitment to an increasingly refined version. The only conceptual "breakaway" to have been institutionally successful (accepted in the compulsory syllabus and as a basis for respectable research) is Keynesian macroeconomics — an alternative vision of the economy at the aggregate level, and not integrally dependent upon individualist analysis. Keynesian macroeconomics has as its major intellectual (and ideological) contribution the view that "market mechanism" capitalism has an innate flaw: no automatic stabilisation mechanism exists which can guarantee the full employment of resources.

Keynesianism was introduced into the conventional syllabus, but only at substantial cost to its conceptual autonomy. Its role has been reduced to a subsidiary one of generating recommendations for appropriate government economy *policy* while the supposed theoretical integrity of the neoclassical system has remained intact. Even the remnants of Keynesianism (and its progressive ideological implications) have come under sustained attack in the last decade, with the ascendancy of a purist version of macroeconomics ("monetarism"). Monetarism places most of the blame for the problems that beset the economy (economic cycles, inflation) on the excessive variations in the money supply. In turn, monetarism removes the root cause of these problems from the private sector and the profit motive and places the blame on "external" factors such as government incompetence and irresponsibility.

The post-war running debate between Keynesians (liberals) and monetarists (libertarian conservatives) has created the impression of disciplinary diversity and tolerance, but in fact it has defined the limits of acceptable debate. While the exchange has been significant, both its ideological underpinnings and its relationship to the unquestioned core of the discipline has been rendered opaque. Early developments in dissident political economy were especially linked to attempts to discredit the preposterous notion that economic inquiry was essentially "value-free".

More fundamentally, the core of the economics discipline is substantially inadequate as an explanatory device. The commitment to a highly restrictive method (one of logical determinism, as outlined above) and a particular vision (a pervasive and all-powerful market mechanism) produces an analysis ill-suited to explaining the actual economic system, characterised by institutions with varying degrees of power interacting in a complex and discretionary manner, and subject to perennial crises, structural change and institutional reconstruction.

Thus the conventional paradigm serves to support the status quo of the contemporary politico-economic structure, yet it does so not by defending it explicitly but by obfuscation. The defence of the status quo involves an incoherent mixture of a reification of the ideal market economy with a pragmatic acknowledgement of certain contemporary institutional realities, overlaid with an unarticulated class prejudice.

Thus union power is an impediment to a mythical free labour market; whereas corporate market power is a fact of life (though the relation of corporate behaviour to the ideal is obscured as the key concept of "competition" varies enormously to suit the occasion). Government involvement that has always been integral to the capitalist economy is labelled as "intervention" and its impact as "distorting": thus governments, it is said, should get out of, say, the regulation of interest rates, yet the structural inequalities of the relationship between financial institutions and mortgagees is somehow deemed natural and not worthy of detailed scrutiny. At the macroeconomic level there is visceral support of wage reduction through political means in the interests of healthy profit levels and viable "economic growth" but this is disconnected from the respectable theory of national income distribution in which wage and profit shares are dictated by the *objective* contributions of labour and "capital" to aggregate production. The examples could be mutiplied. In general, the *effect* of a convoluted combination of idealist vision plus pragmatism plus prejudice is to support the interests of capital against labour and consumers, and the interests of more powerful sections of business against smaller business, but the support is neither intellectually coherent nor morally explicit.

By contrast, the political economists have sought to examine and develop alternative explanations of contemporary capitalism, and to illuminate (especially as teachers) the character of socio-economic change and the forces generating such change. Their focus has been on the historical development and contemporary behaviour of key institutions and their structure: the business sector, the state apparatus, organised labour, the family, and so on. Their analysis has centred on how these institutions develop and use economic power and on the consequent conflicts and the manner of their resolution. This also involves the study of the way in which production and consumption are influenced by social and cultural norms. There is here also a concept of "social order", but it is one structurally constrained by a historically specific, complex set of institutionalised social relationships, culture and productive technique; it is also an order subject to transformation through a dynamic generated by unstable "contradictions", and moulded by conscious social action in a context of political struggle.

Within this vision, the method of the political economists has been historically based, drawing on the conceptual frameworks of Marxism, institutional economics, post-Keynesian economics, and feminist studies. However, the appropriate method remains an open question. This ambivalence is linked to an aversion to theoretical dogmatism (some Marxist scholarship, for example, is unacceptably dogmatic); but it is also linked to the recognition that substantial insight has been gained from works with quite different methodological commitments.[4] Inevitably this involves a linkage with the concerns of scholars in other social sciences who have become dissatisfied with traditional preoccupations and who are working towards a research program which transcends traditional disciplinary boundaries.

This relative methodological openness has provided the basis for the most persistent and dominant form of criticism by orthodox economists. The political economists, it is said, lack *rigour* in their approach. Apart from the devotion to the *content* of the neoclassical paradigm, rigorous analysis is seen implicitly as being synonymous with the logico-deductive method, preferably in mathematical form.

Criticism of the political economy group along these lines has also come from individuals who would label themselves as "political economists". This is the source of one of the more complex dimensions to the conflict. There has been an attempted appropriation of the term "political economy" by individuals of a generally orthodox persuasion.[5] More importantly, criticism has come from individuals with some formal attachment to the school called "post-Keynesian" economics.[6] A major critical contribution of one branch of this school has been a fundamental critique of the orthodox theory of income distribution between wages and profits. The positive contribution has centred on the attempt to provide an integrated theory of economic growth and income distribution, linked to the dissimilar savings propensities out of profits and wages. The contribution, however, has involved a marked disparity between promise and performance. The promise has involved an adequate theory of the macro-economy, which is social and non-mechanical, to be based on an irreversible historical process and integrally determined by the impact of (non-probabilistic) uncertainty on economic decision-making.[7] In practice, post-Keynesians have shown a predilection for models of economic growth which are logico-deductive, and consequently deterministic and ahistorical.[8] Although the problems posed are significant, there has been a tendency to return to an analytical form which is *integrally* linked to the orthodox tradition; and because this mode of analysis becomes an end in itself rather than a heuristic device in a broader analysis, it is *structurally* unsuited to the differentiated tasks which the post-Keynesians have set themselves.

Some insight into the recent post-Keynesian tradition must come from its social placing in the discipline. Post-Keynesians interpret their approach not so much as dissent but as the recovery of a respectable past. In a selective reading of the classic texts, post-Keynesians claim a royal lineage with all the greats in English economics (David Ricardo, Alfred Marshall, Keynes), and that the neoclassical school has usurped this tradition. There is a manifest need for academic respectability which incorporates the paraphernalia of a weary scholasticism: reflected, at its worst, in turgid footnoting displays of intellectual artefacts gleaned from cultivated heroes both alive and dead. As one tangible product of being influenced by this tradition, the school has remained fairly elitist and generally inaccessible to the bulk of undergraduates. The dominant orthodoxy has shown its qualified deference by accepting token sessions on post-Keynesian economics at professional conferences but has shown its complacency by generally remaining impervious to the post-Keynesian contribution. In turn, the post-Keynesian school has shown itself inextricably placid in the face of the profession's blatant refusal to acknowledge a crucial flaw in its intellectual foundations and to change its vision accordingly. At the University of Sydney the presentation of this school as representing the "real" political economy has played a useful political role: opposition to the dissident political economy tradition can thus be defended as merely a stand against mediocrity and not a clear manifestation of intellectual bigotry. The post-Keynesian school thus has the seemingly paradoxical status of being anti-orthodox (because of its formal concerns and a major critical victory) yet marginally respectable (because of its reversion to a respectable method and because *institutionally* it has proved little threat to the status quo). Post-Keynesian economics, perhaps unwittingly, has become the ideal venue for those who want to be daringly different but in a manner which is not detrimental to one's career.

Consideration of these complex aspects of economics as a discipline are crucial in understanding the general character of the "political economy dispute". Of course, it is not unusual for academic disciplines to be characterised by sharp disagreement among their practitioners. However, the problematic character of the *economics* discipline is fuelled by additional factors. First, an appropriate interpretation of economic behaviour is central to the dominant ideologies of contemporary capitalism. Economic ideas matter in a very obvious way, in that the dominant vision of the discipline has a profound influence on community perceptions and on institutional behaviour (including government economic policy) and ultimately has a direct impact on material well being. Progressive economic ideas play a major role in providing a critical perspective on the existing social and political order. Second, contemporary capitalism has been in a state of crisis, with widespread and persistent unemployment and inflation, which conventional economic theory finds difficulty in explaining and resolving. Indeed, the principal prescriptions of conventional economic theory have proved to be not even satisfactory in serving the specific interests of business. The crisis in the discipline links directly with the crisis in the object of the study. It is pertinent to ask not why there has been a "problem" in the Economics Department at the University of Sydney, but why the problem has not been endemic.

(b) Teaching

Disagreement among the economists at the University of Sydney has not been limited to differing perceptions of the appropriate directions for development of the discipline. Equally important are differences in attitudes to teaching. In part this has been predictably manifest in conflicts over curriculum design. From the early 1970s onwards, the political economy group took the view that students should have the opportunity to explore the major competing paradigms in the discipline at the first-year level and specialise in political economy or orthodox economics thereafter, while other staff (some of whom claimed an interest in political economy) held that a conventional syllabus structure dominated by orthodox economics was appropriate for undergraduate students.

The different attitudes to teaching have involved more than matters of curriculum. Essentially, the political economy group reacted against what they interpreted as authoritarian attitudes and practices — the refusal to institutionalise student course questionnaires and learn from student feedback; a callous attitude towards failure rates; the over-reliance on conventional examinations in aggregate assessment; a reluctance to permit undergraduates to undertake independent self-generated projects and theses, and so on.

Of course, conflict on these issues is fairly standard fare in universities. What appears to be rather distinctive (albeit not unique) about economics is that, given the lack of an obvious association between the orthodox curriculum content and the observable character of the real world, *an authoritarian teaching practice becomes inevitable*. The continued dominance of orthodox economic theory in the compulsory syllabus generates persistent student dissatisfaction, which in turn leads to a situation where alternative or self-directed forms of study must be denied, where the right to define the discipline must be monopolised by the "authorities", and where official student feedback must be either minimised or deflected. This tendency has been well developed at the University of Sydney. Indeed it was the standard of teaching of the compulsory courses in the late 1960s and early 1970s by those of professorial rank and the "denial" of student opinion which fuelled the widespread rebellion by students, overwhelmingly the products of "respectable" homes and of normally reticent dispositions.[9]

On the other hand, the Department of Economics possessed an atypically large number of staff members who rejected substantial parts of their formal education, who rebelled against an illiberal hierarchy and who have found more open methods of teaching to be more effective in developing student interest and a more enlightened education. Of course, teaching competence transcends affiliation to any faction. Yet the political economy group set out to make a systematic *collective* effort at a sympathetic teaching practice, and consistently favourable student feedback has validated such efforts. Although political economy courses have had their quota of weaker students, there has been an unusual amount of intellectual excitement and exchange, manifest partly in an assertiveness and intellectual independence both in and out of the classroom. By contrast, the conventional syllabus has consistently produced, apart from a handful of capable honours students, an ethos of intellectual lethargy and apathy. The perennial product of this conventional tradition has been a minuscule honours school drawn from the hundreds enrolled at the first-year level.

(c) The Administrative and Decision-making Structure

The University administrative structure is strongly hierarchical. Dominant power is vested in the Vice-Chancellor and academics of professorial rank. The by-laws grant those of professorial rank monopoly rights in the definition of the nature of the discipline and in the direction of teaching. In effect, the by-laws are an academic Masters and Servants Act. Heads of departments are chosen by the Vice-Chancellor rather than, as in many other tertiary educational institutions, being elected. Non-professorial staff have had no formal rights at the department level, with the exception of one sub-section of the by-laws which compels a department head to convey to Faculty any proposal supported by a majority of staff who are also members of Faculty. (This singular recognition of the lecturing staff's intellectual capacity has made little difference in practice in the Department of Economics, as the majority of the orthodox staff have never seen fit to support any course proposal against the professorial will. One can only speculate about the reasons for this relative docility, but the evidence indicates that support for the professors' general intellectual position, personal antipathy to the political economists, respect for authority *per se*, fear and careerism have all played a role.)

A strong hierarchy in constitutional terms has been reinforced in the Economics Department by the views of the particular professors. Some departments at the University of Sydney work reasonably well because the professoriate does not attempt to appropriate all administrative and intellectual independence from the non-professorial staff. By contrast, the professors of economics have interpreted their powers in the strictest sense, ensuring that the by-laws are a living and active document. Student representation at the Department level has been persistently denied.

The one significant "imperfection" in this system of professorial power involves the role of Faculties. These sit in the hierarchy between departments and the Academic Board (broadened in membership from its predecessor, the Professorial Board, in 1974, but still dominated by the professoriate). Faculties are relatively democratic institutions, with elected deans, and a membership which includes all full-time lecturing staff and a small number of student representatives. Moreover, the Economics Faculty has represented a broader spectrum of opinion than is typical in Commerce Faculties, with the Department of Government being included, as well as the Departments of Economic History and Industrial Relations. Although access to Faculty procedure is predominantly through the professoriate, Faculty decisions have, in the past, leavened the conservatism of the Economics Department and the University establishment. It was through the intervention of the Faculty of Economics in the early 1970s that the political economy courses were established, and it was through the partial erosion of support at this level that the process of dismantling the political economy courses was pursued in the early 1980s.

During the years of the dispute there has been significant conflict between different elements within the university's decision-making structure. The most obvious illustration of this has been the failure of the University to act on the recommendation of its own committees of investigation into the dispute. In 1974 a committee of the Faculty of Economics recommended the creation of a separate Department of Political Economy: this became the official policy of the Faculty but Vice-Chancellor Williams refused to implement it. In 1976 a committee of the Academic Board recommended the creation of a Unit of Political Economy with a more limited and temporary degree of autonomy, but this was also vetoed by the Vice-Chancellor. In 1982 a further committee of the Academic Board noted that the political economy programme had "met a definite need, had been appreciated by students and has proved generally successful", but its balanced report was shelved by the new Vice-Chancellor, Professor John Ward (who had himself chaired the 1976 inquiry). In effect, the University authorities have shown a disregard not only for the interests of political economy staff and students, but also for the recommendations of its own properly constituted committees.

2. MANIFESTATIONS OF THE CONFLICT

The "political economy dispute" has involved a number of practices by those in authority which have not only impeded the teaching and study of political economy but which are incompatible with the tradition that a contemporary university provide a basis for free intellectual exchange and a liberal education.

(a) Opposition to Course Development

The political economists were successful in the 1970s in establishing first- and second-year courses. This success was attributable to the strong pressures for reform in the early 1970s. Conservative forces subsequently unified in opposition to further course developments which would have provided the basis for any integrated undergraduate program and the possibility of extensions into honours and postgraduate work.

Proposals for third-year political economy courses were systematically frustrated throughout the 1970s and early 1980s. One option proposed by Frank Stilwell was accepted as part of the package imposed on the Department between 1975 and 1977, but this reflected the fact that the subject (Regional and Urban Economics) represented no great threat to the key third-year courses containing the theoretical core of the orthodox discipline. In all other cases the political economy staff were prevented from teaching whole-year options which would provide for students proceeding from the second-year political economy course, right up to 1984.

The most persistent antagonism regarding course developments was towards a proposal titled Capital, Labour and the State. This course was designed to develop in greater depth the emphases of the second-year course, in particular the character of economic power. Despite frequent revision by its proponent, the proposal was rejected by a majority vote of the Economics Department staff, in an almost annual ritual over a six-year period. Not once in six years was there any suggestion as to the character of possible intellectual limitations of the course proposal, or as to ways in which the proposal might be improved for future presentation. Finally, in 1984, a variant of the course was introduced, following further intervention by the Academic Board.

The fate of another course proposal highlights the fundamentally political character of syllabus developments. In 1979, Associate Professor E. L. Wheelwright proposed another Economics III option on Transnational Corporations and the World Economy, supported by a 24-page outline and list of readings. In a rare display of equanimity, Wheelwright's proposal gained the support of some of the orthodox economists on the staff, tipping the balance in favour of a bare departmental majority. The Department Head subsequently gained the Registrar's support for a reinterpretation of the meaning of "majority", the base being redefined to include *all* Department members, whether present or not. By this definition, all staff absent or on leave were deemed to be automatically against any proposal before Department meetings. The upshot was that Wheelwright's proposal did not get the necessary "majority". By way of compensation for this sleight-of-hand, Wheelwright was offered a half of an existing option in a *different* subject (an advance on the original offer of a third) which had become vacant with its contemporary teacher absent on study leave. The result was better than nothing, but the process was classically obstructive and the end result a cynical muddling of the syllabus. Again, the intervention of the Academic Board in 1983 facilitated the introduction of a new option, Australian and World Capitalism, in which Wheelwright's material could be properly accommodated. The two third-year options were introduced, however, at the expense of the termination of Economics I(P).

The development of political economy courses for honours students has been another major problem. During the nine years since the introduction of political economy courses in 1975, the fourth-year honours program had not been revised. Various proposals for a course in Advanced Political Economy were advanced in the 1970s and early 1980s, but it became clear that no honours studies in political economy would be acceptable to the professoriate as a matter of principle. Some of the staff in the political economy group taught in the honours program in the early 1970s, but since the introduction of the new course in first and second year, only the most marginal involvement in honours courses was tolerated, including the supervision and examination of honours theses. The inequity of this situation led the Academic Board in 1983 to single out the development of honours courses in political economy, involving teaching and supervision by the "P" teachers, as one of the matters needing to be remedied (in 1985).

In summary, the professors of economics have consistently opposed the introduction of all proposals for new courses put forward by the political economy group. New courses have only been implemented as the result of intervention by higher bodies such as the Faculty of Economics and the Academic Board. In turn, adequate institutional bases for these courses have been consistently denied by Vice-Chancellors unsympathetic to the institutionalisation of studies in political economy.

(b) Discrimination Against Staff

Discrimination against dissident staff has been persistent and systematic. Reference has already been made to some blatant examples regarding the re-employment of tutorial staff. But, in general, evidence for the claim of discrimination must necessarily be indirect since the information available to promotion and tenure committees is confidential. The inference of persistent discrimination is clearly supported by a letter to the Vice-Chancellor in September 1981, written by Geelum Simpson-Lee, Dean of the Faculty of Economics, and Associate-Professor Wheelwright, drawing on their experience as long-time members of tenure and promotion committees. They state clearly:

> We have served on most of the tenure and promotions committees over the last ten years, and we are deeply concerned and much troubled by the way tenure/promotions procedures have been exploited by the Professors of Economics to block the progress of political economy staff, and the way tenure/promotions committees have allowed themselves to be used. The result has been unconscionable persecution of young academics at a time when they are highly vulnerable personally, in terms of their careers as academics, and their self-esteem as teachers and scholars.

Of the dissident lecturing staff, all except one were tenured by the time the "political economy dispute" erupted. The one without tenure achieved it after six years teaching (a record for the University) and four successive annual applications, while an orthodox economist appointed at the same time and possessing no obvious superior qualities obtained tenure in the normal three-year probationary period. Regarding promotions, the speed of promotion of lecturers within the Department has shown no obvious parallel with their achievements in terms of the formal criteria of research, teaching and administration. Regarding research, much is made of "quality", but quality appears to have been defined in terms of orthodox economics' method and vision. In other words, the work of the political economists as assessed from the orthodox viewpoint must, *in principle*, be of poor quality. Regarding teaching, there appears, if anything, to have been an inverse relation between the speed of promotion and teaching ability. One member of the political economy group, a hardworking and effective teacher, has been denied promotion to senior lecturer over a period of thirteen years while more recently appointed orthodox economists with less commitment to teaching have been promoted above him.

Hiring procedures have also left much to be desired. The Department has refused to allocate to the political economy group any of a substantial number of vacancies for lecturers to adequately staff their courses. The retirement of a member of this group in 1981 elicited no support from the rest of the Department for his replacement. Judgements of the orthodox economics lecturers ranged from the vapid "we want the best person for the job irrespective of field of interest", to the more honest "there is already an excess supply of political economists". At precisely the time that the University was in turmoil with protests by political economy students over the denial of their interests, a selection committee recommended the appointment of an orthodox mathematical economist to replace the retired member of the political economy group. The predictable result was a rise in student-staff ratios in the "P" courses, to the extent that in 1983 the student load per member of "P" staff had increased to twice the level prevailing in the rest of the Department.

The process of appointment of individuals to Chairs has been another area of concern. In 1975 Associate Professor E. L. Wheelwright was passed over in consideration for a Chair (as he had been on previous occasions). The treatment of Wheelwright is perhaps the most observable and telling indication of unequal treatment. The Selection Committee was made up of conservatives (except for the Dean of the Faculty, an elected position) known for their antagonism to the character of Wheelwright's intellectual contribution. The successful applicant's record could not be compared with the record of Wheelwright, who was author (and co-author) of half a dozen books and a plethora of edited collections and essays, and who had had broad overseas experience. Wheelwright also had strong references from six economists of international stature, including Joan Robinson and J. K. Galbraith. The outcome appeared sufficiently inequitable for the University Staff Association to call for an investigation, as did a number of petitions, including one from 49 Members of Parliament.[10] A long and emotional exchange in the press, including overseas coverage[11], was generated by this affair[12], but it was transformed into a debate on the freedom of universities from "outside interference". The University authorities successfully deflected the public outcry, but the decision had a long-term adverse impact on the workings of the Economics Department.

While the 1975 professorial appointment was decided in camera by the professoriate, the next Chair involved a more open process. The retirement of Professor Colin Simkin in 1980 came at a time when non-professorial staff as a whole had managed to secure more participation in departmental procedures. With the support of the Dean of the Faculty, Economics Department staff played a significant role in the consideration of major applicants, by examining curriculum vitae, conducting interviews, and so on. The procedure was careful and involved substantial compromise, given predictable intellectual differences. The official University selection committee, on first meeting, expressed support for hiring the candidate recommended by the non-professorial staff. But, the committee was later recalled by the Vice-Chancellor (after the one political economist on the committee had gone on study leave) and the decision was reversed, offering the post to an internal candidate who had gained no significant support from his colleagues. The administration did not see fit to enquire into the basis for the staff's considered judgement, but rather chose to rebuke the representatives of the staff for their "irresponsible" behaviour.

Thus, the professorial appointment process has been compromised by at least two undesirable practices: first, the flouting of appropriate conventions for appointment (research, teaching, public service, referees' reports) in the interests of denying a dissident the rank of full professor; and second, the making of an appointment in direct opposition to the staff's considered collective opinion. The professorial hierarchy, which is constitutionally unaccountable, has thereby reproduced itself by an objectionable procedure. A broader political economy vision and liberalised teaching practices have both been casualties of this process.

(c) Unfair Treatment of Students

The existence of first- and second-year courses in political economy at the University of Sydney has, to a large measure, sheltered the more questioning and assertive students from the problems of unfair assessment said to be experienced in economics departments elsewhere. Thus, in a general sense, it may well be that the problem of discrimination has been less prevalent than elsewhere. The main discrimination at the University of Sydney has been institutional rather than personal, namely the denial to political economy students of third-year and honours courses comparable to those available to students interested in taking orthodox economics courses at these levels.

This structural inequality has made for particular problems for political economy students intent on doing honours, despite the lack of a suitable programme of studies. One brilliant student, who had been a prominent leader of the student protest movement in the early 1970s, was awarded a class of honours degree below that which he might reasonably have expected on the basis of his previous grades. His marks fell short of first-class standard in two subjects, and it was later revealed that these papers had both been assessed by a conservative professor in the Department, despite the fact that the professor in question had not been involved in teaching one of the courses. In 1978, two students emanating from the political economy courses chose to write honours theses. Political economy staff were denied access to these theses. After the assessment was determined one of the political economy staff obtained copies of the theses and concluded that there was evidence of discrimination in the marking, by contrast with the mark gained for a third thesis by a student from orthodox economics. One student was treated very shabbily and given third-class honours. No redress was available to the dissatisfied student; and requests for a procedure to process a staff member's complaint of a prima facie case of discrimination were refused. The appropriate Faculty body also declined to intervene, either on the specific case of alleged discrimination, or on the general principle of discriminatory exclusion of staff from examination procedures. The predictable outcome of such experiences has been that students from the political economy courses have typically chosen not to do honours in the Department of Economics but have done so in cognate departments such as Economic History, Industrial Relations and Government.

The denial of unfavourable student feedback has also been a persistent element in the political economy dispute. That a discipline of questionable intellectual merits should integrally require an authoritarian teaching practice has already been argued. The resulting student expressions of dissent have been widespread, strong in intensity, persistent, and the product of much disciplined labour; and the rejection of such feedback has been both aggressive and ultimately counterproductive. In 1981, for example, students devoted extraordinary energy to producing a large document comprising desired course developments in Economics III. The proposals were discussed at Department level, summarily rejected, and no acknowledgement made of the disciplined interest of students in their own education. The Vice-Chancellor eventually diverted rising dissent by establishing the third committee of inquiry into the "political economy dispute".

Two years later student opinion was again explicitly rejected in respect of a proposal to abolish the first-year political economy and orthodox economics courses in favour of a common compulsory course for first and second year centred on orthodox economic "principles". A student referendum, organised by the Students' Representative Council, was undertaken in 1983: approximately 40 per cent (an unusually large percentage for student ballots) of a possible 1900 students voted in the referendum, and of these, 80 per cent voted for the maintenance of separate streams. The response of the orthodox economists was to question the legitimacy of the procedure, and to speed up the process for the achievement of a common compulsory syllabus. Widespread student incredulity at the cynicism of this procedure provided part of the basis for the escalation of student dissent into the widely reported forms of demonstrations and occupations in June and July 1983.

3. THE GENERAL SIGNIFICANCE OF THE ISSUES

Which groups then have played a major role in inhibiting the development of studies in political economy? By contrast with other documented examples of academic suppression, corporate elites have played no major observable role (subject to a qualification to be considered shortly). It is possible that an undergraduate economics education is seen to be of less tangible significance to business than is research in the natural sciences, which directly impinges on corporate sector prestige and profitability. Certainly, political economy courses are potentially threatening at the ideological level. However, what evidence exists indicates that students from the political economy courses have been acceptable to employers in both the private and public sectors. It is possible that the manifest narrowness and distorted vision of much of the conventional economics syllabus offers little basis for private employers to mount a campaign of active hostility.

This reticence of business is not universal. United States business has been prepared to intervene in disputes regarding the teaching of economics, the most celebrated example being the shameful harassment of the Marxist development economist, Paul Baran, at Stanford University in the 1950s and 1960s.[13] This country-specific difference may be linked to cultural and institutional differences in education in the United States. In the cultural sphere, US business has placed much higher priority on the ideological component of education in social disciplines.[14] Institutionally, the highest governing body in US universities (the Board of Trustees) is typically dominated by businessmen, who have exhibited a capacity for an intervention role in syllabus development and staffing appointments.[15] These tendencies are not so pronounced in Australian universities.

At Sydney University, the major antagonistic group has been the academic elite, with support from the administrative hierarchy. For some of this group the opposition has been explicitly ideological. Professor Simkin was a founding member of the Sydney-based Centre for Independent Studies, a right-wing think tank. Professor Hogan has been a long-time adviser to the Liberal Party and consultant to the corporate sector. Ted Wheelwright's research programme on transnational corporations has been a focus of hostility for some academics dependent on corporate funding of research (such as in geology, pharmacology and engineering) and those who are uncritically sympathetic to such corporations' values. More generally, the antagonism has derived both from the desire to maintain a rigid institutional hierarchy and from the desire to maintain a monolithic conceptual approach within the academic profession, indeed to define the discipline as being *synonymous* with a particular analytical vision.

The desire of individuals to acquire power and to abuse power once in high office is a perennial curse on the efficient and humane operation of social organisations. This important element in the "political economy dispute" is little different in its significance from numerous other examples of the same ilk. The particular and perhaps most significant element is intellectual suppression. The behaviour of the academic elite can best be likened to a jealous priesthood attempting the dogmatic imposition of a (secular) theology on succeeding generations of novices, and engaging in a persistent inquisition of heretics whenever such dissidence gains sufficient prominence as to cause any trouble to entrenched holy writ.[16] The size of the dissident group at Sydney University is linked to the fact that they were all hired on the basis of orthodox credentials. The processes of appointment and the granting of tenure are means for discrimination, but the key means to disciplinary purity in Australia, one suspects, is the allegiance required at the student level. Most critical students very early decide that a more adequate explanation of economic systems is to be gained from the other social sciences. Without the existence of sympathetic staff, persistent student attempts to have the syllabus modified (such as at Melbourne University and the A.N.U.) have usually failed.

The compulsory imposition of a predominantly orthodox syllabus on all economics students is defended by its academic proponents on various grounds, the essence of which is captured by the standard comments: "this is the body of analysis that we studied"; "this is what economics is"; "students have to study it regardless of the lack of interest it engenders and regardless of its relevance"; "students have to be able to talk the language of the profession". In this context, the best that one can hope for is a critical evaluation of orthodoxy, but *on its own terms*. Methodologically, this is a poor basis for the development of any critical perspective. Pedagogically, it is extremely unsatisfactory, because students complete their formal education with the knowledge that much of what they know is not very useful, and with exposure to only fragments of an alternative perspective.

The most fundamental incongruity is the absence of a clearly articulated philosophical basis for this monolithic vision of the discipline. Exclusionary activities have rarely been attended by any epistemological and methodological defence. Indeed, the indifference and ignorance of methodological issues amongst many academic economists firmly committed to intellectual orthodoxy have been extraordinary. Much use has been made of terms such as "rigorous analysis", but no more detailed explication of the meaning of "rigour" is usually attempted. Those methodological criteria that have had the greatest currency are either philosophically questionable, or are not followed in academic practice.[17] In the case of the Department of Economics at the University of Sydney, the professoriate has typically relied on the prerogative of authority *per se*. Thus intellectual defence is rendered unnecessary.

The most plausible explanation for the overwhelming dominance of the "neoclassical synthesis" in the economics profession at large is a sociological one. New generations of adherents to intellectual orthodoxy are reproduced by a socialisation process and enforced by lines of authority.[18] The apparent cohesion of economics departments elsewhere is not a product of open compromise between a variety of intellectual perspectives but the product of an exclusionary and introverted narrowness. In the words of a dissident contemporary philosopher of science, " . . . the semblance of Absolute Truth is nothing but the result of an absolute conformism".[19] The consequence of this process is that individuals who have mastered the discipline's own apprenticeship are not readily permitted to follow a line of reasoning wherever it leads. By analogy, those in authority stand firmly on the side of the Church and against Galileo. The implications of this are profound. Those with formal authority in the Department of Economics at the University of Sydney, and elsewhere in the discipline, have been engaged in an educational process which is fundamentally anti-intellectual. It is a classic example of academic suppression.

References

1. A good summary of the methodological basis of conventional economics and its limitations can be found in K. W. Rothschild (ed.), *Power in Economics* (Harmondsworth: Penguin, 1971), Introduction.

2. Much work in applied (orthodox) economics is incoherent because of the attempted grafting of detailed empirical work onto an idealist conceptual structure. For example, see F. Scherer, *Industrial Market Structure and Economic Performance* (Chicago: Rand McNally, 1970), probably the best work in the applied field known as "industry economics".

3. The 1983 Nobel prize for economics was awarded to Gerard Debreu, the Berkeley theorist, whose work encapsulates the core of the neoclassical conceptual focus.

4. Compare, for example, Michel Aglietta, *A Theory of Capitalist Regulation* (London: New Left Books, 1979), and E. P. Thompson, *The Making of the English Working Class* (Harmondsworth: Penguin, 1968). Both are masterly works on the "transformation of the conditions of existence of the working class", both claim a Marxist lineage, but the methodological premises underlying each work are substantially different.

5. Conservatives have labelled as "political economy" the application of the neoclassical method to the sphere of politics. There is certainly a "conservative" political economy, but this development is an example of intellectual imperialism, and constitutes false advertising at its best.

6. The most persistent criticism has come from Peter Groenewegen, elevated to a Chair in the Department in 1980. Groenewegen's attachment to post-Keynesian economics is to be distinguished from the varied character of his own published work, mainly in the history of economic thought and public finance. For Groenewegen's views on political economy and political economists, see "Radical Economics in Australia: A Survey of

the 1970s'', in F. H. Gruen (ed.), *Surveys of Australian Economics*, vol. 2 (Sydney: Allen & Unwin, 1979).

7.   See, for example, Paul Davidson, ''Post Keynesian Economics'', in Daniel Bell and Irving Kristol (eds), *The Crisis in Economic Theory* (New York: Basic Books, 1981).

8.   See, for example, Luigi L. Pasinetti, *Growth and Income Distribution* (Cambridge: the University Press, 1974).

9.   Sydney University Economics Society Student Survey, 1973, archival collection of Frank Stilwell; also reported in *Honi Soit*, 18 October 1973.

10.   Graham Williams, ''40 MPs demand inquiry into 'bias' against professor'', the *Australian*, 5 May 1975.

11.   Alan Ashbolt, ''Australian Political Chairs'', *New Statesman*, 9 May 1975.

12.   The official position was stated by the Vice-Chancellor, Bruce Williams, in a letter to the *Australian Financial Review*, 6 May 1975.

13.   Lawrence S. Lifshultz, ''Could Karl Marx Teach Economics in America?'', *Ramparts*, vol. 12, April 1974, pp. 27–30, 52–9.

14.   See, for example, Alex Carey, ''Social Science, Propaganda and Democracy'', in Paul Boreham and Geoff Dow (eds), *Work and Inequality*, vol. 2 (South Melbourne: Macmillan, 1980).

15.   David N. Smith, *Who Rules the Universities?* (New York: Monthly Review Press, 1974).

16.   Such ''disciplinary dogmatism'' has a long history. See, for example, Bernard Barber, ''Resistance by Scientists to Scientific Discovery'', *Science*, vol. 134, Sept. 1961, pp. 596–602.

17.   Evan Jones, ''Positive Economics or What?'', *Economic Record*, vol. 53, no. 143, Sept. 1977, pp. 350–63.

18.   Evan Jones, ''The Socialisation of the Economics Profession'', mimeo, Department of Economics, University of Sydney, 1981.

19.   P. Feyeraband, *Against Method* (London: New Left Books, 1975).

Postscript by Brian Martin

On 2 June 1984 I sent a copy of an earlier version of this chapter to the Vice-Chancellor of the University of Sydney inviting a response from someone representing the University, or anyone else appropriate, to be included in this book. On 8 June the Vice-Chancellor replied with a brief comment which was not for publication.

"NOT MERELY MALICE": THE UNIVERSITY OF TASMANIA VERSUS PROFESSOR ORR

Clyde Manwell and C. M. Ann Baker

In a society which condones corruption all become more or less corrupt, and the traditional ideals of a calling become proportionately corrupted. As a result, what is socially permissible, or even respected, in that society depends upon expediency, not ethics...

In democratic societies two callings accept full personal responsibility to society for knowledge and opinion and integrity of human relations. The Judiciary is one, the University is the other.

The members of the Judiciary may be dismissed only upon the motion in public of both houses of Parliament; the academic can be dismissed upon the motion in camera of what may be a virulent corporation...

The power of corporations over servants exercising personal responsibility for knowledge and opinion constitutes the greatest danger to the Universities as the intellectual sources of adaptation of societies to new problems...

A governing body of an institution ostensibly devoted to truth and justice is obviously corrupt if it obstructs, by every possible means, inquiry into its stewardship, when this is demanded by significant sections of the community it is supposed to serve...

Such a state of affairs is the antithesis of democratic processes and places the society in imminent danger.

> R. D. Wright,
> then Professor of Physiology at the University of Melbourne
> and member of the Council
> of the Australian National University

I must confess to a feeling approaching panic, a kind of fear such as I had never known even in war-time, during the blitzes, the fear of being without the protection of the law; and for the first time in my life I realized something of what it must be like to fall foul of the authorities in a totalitarian regime.

> Professor Sydney Sparks Orr,
> written during one of the Star Chamber trials
> at the University of Tasmania,
> quoted by W. H. C. Eddy.[1]

The sacking of Professor Orr from the University of Tasmania in 1956 has had more effect on Australian universities than any other attempted or effected removal of a staff member. The sacking of Orr forced Australian academics to confront their powerlessness against arbitrary dismissal — though as the recent cases of Dr Spautz[2] and of Professor Burns[3] reveal, some of the basic issues are still not settled. The judgement of the High Court case arising from the dismissal of Orr emphasised that academics were basically servants, servants who could be dismissed at the whim of their master, the governing body of the University.

What improvements there have been, in the creation of specific dismissal statutes and in the implementation of tenure, we owe to Professor Orr's courage to fight against overwhelming odds in the face of indifferent or outright antagonistic academic opinion (until support finally became mobilised two or three years after the sacking).

The Orr case is a reference point in a number of places in our discussion of academic problems. This is largely due to W. H. C. Eddy's searching book, *Orr*. Eddy sifted through the accumulation of some ten thousand pages of courtroom testimony and documents. He interviewed a number of the staff at the University of Tasmania, and he has provided the most comprehensive analysis of academic conflict. Eddy documents the dark side — the obsessive vindictiveness directed against a scapegoat. He reveals the indifference to fair procedures and to the quality of the "evidence", an indifference which many would consider difficult to believe — unless they too had been the object of an academic witch-hunt.

THE ACT OF DISSIDENCE: CALL FOR A ROYAL COMMISSION

Orr's act of dissidence was to write an open letter to the Premier of Tasmania and to the Minister for Education, which was also published in a local newspaper at the end of October 1954. The letter alleged that the administration of the University of Tasmania was guilty of "apathy, neglect and maladministration over recent years".[4] Orr complained of the "Council's intervention in wholly academic matters".[5] He pointed out how the Council had over-reacted to the Staff Association's request for an independent assessment of salary claims. He argued that administrative policies were retarding the growth of the University and that this threatened the economy of the state, which was becoming increasingly dependent on technology.

In particular, Orr called for an investigation of the University of Tasmania. Initially, Orr was by no means alone in agitating for some basic reform. There were a large number of dissatisfied academics, including the local staff association. The unofficial leaders of this dissenting movement were Professor Orr and Associate Professor John Bela Polya, a distinguished chemist. As a consequence of their activities, the Governor of Tasmania appointed a Royal Commission in 1955. Its report was highly critical of a number of aspects of the University. Some of its proposed reforms were implemented but others were not.

ATTACK ON DISSIDENTS

The new *University Act*, incorporating some of the reforms suggested by the Royal Commission, was proclaimed on 15 December 1955. *Next day* the Vice-Chancellor made allegations against Professor Orr before the University Council. Professor Polya was also under attack in the Council. Although he too was victimised in a variety of ways over the years, the attack concentrated on Orr. First, it was his carefully argued letter published in the newspaper which alerted the community about the problems at the University, and which ultimately led to the Royal Commission. Second, Orr's personal life made him vulnerable. He had, earlier in Melbourne, been part of a *ménage à trois*; while this may seem trivial by today's standards, it provided a rich source of scurrilous gossip.

The allegations against Orr were ultimately grouped into five sets by a Supreme Court judge, who named four of the sets after different accusing academics. While the four sets of allegations from academics were accepted by the University of Tasmania's administration, *all* of them were rejected as unproven by the Supreme Court judge and they are, therefore, not discussed here. These four sets of charges show how easily some staff members will join in a campaign once they perceive that there is powerful support from higher authority.

It is the fifth charge that is the problem. In February of 1956, a Hobart businessman alleged that his daughter, Miss Suzanne Kemp, had had sexual intercourse with Professor Orr. This charge was upheld by the Supreme Court judge.

ACADEMIC SEDUCTION
OR A PLATONIC PHILOSOPHICAL RELATIONSHIP?

For approximately three hundred pages of quotations and comments in his book, Eddy focuses on the "evidence" which the judge of the Supreme Court of Tasmania claimed supported the University's allegations about the relationship between Professor Orr and Miss Suzanne Kemp. While the allegation assumed a variety of protean shapes, it was often stated to involve "seduction", even in official documents. There are *no* allegations of any kind of force, including *no* claims of threats to manipulate the marks a student might receive were she to "cooperate".

The "evidence" rested basically on Miss Kemp's testimony and her diary. Eddy reveals a maze of contradictions in her testimony, diary and letters. Even if the allegations were true, there was no indication that Miss Kemp, who was over the age of consent, had not enjoyed herself in an affair which, if it took place, occurred over eight or nine months. The best "evidence" the University administration could produce, independent of Miss Kemp's diary and testimony, was Orr's gift of two philosophy books to Miss Kemp. Each book bore a short inscription from Professor Orr, such as many staff members might write to a promising student. This independent documentary "evidence" is all unromantic.

The picture that emerges from reading Eddy's detailed description is quite ordinary, indeed commonplace. Miss Kemp was a bright student, enthusiastic for Professor Orr's subject. In her own writings (one of which is quoted later), she revealed that she had become attracted to Orr. In so much as it is always pleasant to encounter a student interested in one's subject, Orr encouraged her personally in much the same way as he encouraged his other top students, female and male. For a long period of time Miss Kemp enthusiastically supported Orr in his fight for university reform.

At the time of his dismissal (and ever afterwards) Orr denied that he had had sexual intercourse with Miss Kemp.

Reading Eddy's presentation of the case, in particular his quotations from Miss Kemp's testimony and writings, one notices many flights of fancy. Evidence was produced that Miss Kemp was not a wholly reliable witness. There is also a certain type of power-seeking that becomes apparent in some of the quotations from her diary, which Eddy suggests may well have been written some time after the event:

> [the] power one has over men [is] rather terrifying. I am abusing it. But will it stop? I bet I won't. Why? Because [I'm] afraid I wouldn't have power? It is horrible but very interesting...[6]

Her correspondence with Orr shows similar themes — and also evidence that she resented the fact that Orr was not as responsive to her charms as she would have wished, for example the Orford letter. That letter shows transference, Miss Kemp's hostile relations with her father playing some part, together with a passage, quoted below, indicating role confusion:

> Ah my dear, I am young and foolish. Forgive me for I know not what I do. Don't expect too much of me. I can feel how much you depend on and are sustained by love and it rather frightens me. It gives me so much power...

Do you believe me. Do you think it is my childish streak coming through to hurt? It is what I feel, have always felt, whatever it is.

I am rather hungry...[In the context of the remainder of a long paragraph this hunger is simply for food.]

I don't know when I will be coming to town again. I foresee nothing as yet. I feel no desperate need to be with you, except when I think of Christ. No doubt this has very interesting psychological implications (I hope not too awful) which I am afraid I can't work out. Perhaps you and He have unconsciously swapped places in my mind. No doubt if you took a sample of my handwriting to a specialist he could give you some interesting psychological data too.

I had better stop as I become rather dramatic and peculiar as the night wears on...[7]

Such writings are reminiscent of the "crush" or the "groupie" phenomenon. This is not to ignore the real problem of sexual harassment on campus. The "groupie" phenomenon is the other side of the problem. Impressionable individuals (female or male, often though not always, teenagers) feel compelled to imagine, or in some cases to act out, fantasies of physical involvement with authority figures. This is so common now of the cults promulgated about pop-stars and movie idols that it is big business to media entrepreneurs (and it is passively accepted in Western societies in spite of the harm that is often done to youngsters who are introduced, not only to irresponsible sexual behaviour, but also to drug abuse and to the general nihilistic values of this self-indulgent set). The "groupie" phenomenon also manifests itself occasionally with other authority figures, notably teachers, athletes, fringe religious leaders, and even the occasional politician, caught with more than his charisma down.

The charge against Orr, of "seduction", carried weight among certain of Orr's academic colleagues and with the Supreme Court judge, but it did not evoke the sympathy from the community that the University administration had hoped.

On the whole, the students of the University of Tasmania supported Orr strongly, even defying the academic staff by inviting Orr to University functions. The former editor of the student newspaper (and later Student Representative to the Council) combined with a teacher to write:

Student observations show that Miss Kemp was an emotionally immature student who had developed a "crush" on the Professor. She made no attempt to disguise her efforts to place herself in his company. There is substantiation for the contention that Orr made definite attempts to avoid her.[8]

As guardians of the community's morals, it is of some importance that nearly all the religious leaders supported Orr. The Head of the Scots Kirk and the Roman Catholic Archbishop of Hobart were among those who proclaimed that Orr was innocent. The Anglican Bishop of Tasmania combined with Baptist and Presbyterian Ministers to make the following statement:

One of our number, the Bishop of Tasmania, whose name was closely associated with the origins of this infamous business, has publicly charged that six months before the dismissal University officers made scurrilous and malicious accusations against Professor Orr which he later found untrue and baseless, that he was misinformed and misused as a Bishop by the University lawyers, and that in his absence his name and position were used to give credence to much highly coloured evidence against Orr and an untrue statement relating to himself was made by the then Vice-Chancellor in the Court.[9]

We are grateful to Professor Polya for pointing out other evidence, not adequately emphasised by Eddy, which suggests Orr's innocence:

Even in...circumstances that counselled extreme caution, Orr had been indiscreet with all his associates, female students in particular. He avidly sought human company; he had a philosophically absurd desire to be understood and liked; he had the teachers' and prophets' virtue or vice of burning with a desire to communicate. From my long acquaintance with him I feel that given a choice between a night with a beauty queen and the opportunity tõ talk to her for a week, he would have chosen the second alternative without hesitation.

He was physically weak and had a bad heart — hardly the type for the sexual acrobatics under the bizarre circumstances suggested during the evolution of the Kemp "diaries".[10]

However, in fairness to Miss Kemp, Polya also points out that she was *not* a willing witness against Orr, an erroneous inference one might make from earlier descriptions of her. It is not generally known that Miss Kemp was locked in her room and subjected to physical violence until she agreed to join the frame-up.

REACTION OVER THE SACKING

Initially the University of Tasmania's Staff Association did nothing to help Professor Orr, despite the fact that he had been instrumental in obtaining the Royal Commission and the reforms which the Staff Association had also wanted. At the time of Orr's dismissal the Chairman of the Staff Association was, as Eddy[11] details, also a member of two of the administrative committees which found Orr guilty. After this conflict-of-interest situation was resolved with new Staff Association officials, Orr then got belated support. Eddy writes: "No Australian University Staff Association gave Orr any support for his Supreme Court action, but small sums were contributed a few weeks before the High Court Appeal."[12]

Just before the formal dismissal action, Orr had become almost totally isolated (by methods summarised so well by Eddy and by Professor R. Douglas Wright in the next section of this chapter) that he even swallowed the Vice-Chancellor's bait: Orr was willing to resign in return for six months' salary. However, the University Council used that device to "prove" Orr's guilt and summarily sacked him.[13]

Some overseas academics quickly came to Orr's assistance, notably a number of staff from Orr's former university (Queen's University, Belfast) and also some eminent philosophers, such as Stephen Toulmin (then at Leeds University). In Australia, the most eminent academic to come to Orr's defence was Professor Roy Douglas Wright. It is the compelling words of Professor Wright, from his prologue to Eddy's book, that we use as the beginning of this chapter and to which we will return shortly. Orr also received support from the Australasian Association of Philosophy, who successfully organised a boycott of his vacant post until a settlement was reached in 1963.

Once mobilised, Australian Staff Associations made an important effort on behalf of Orr and finally persuaded the administration of the University of Tasmania to compensate for the damage. In October 1958, Professor R. H. Thorp and K. D. Buckley, as officials of the Federal Council of University Staff Associations of Australia (essentially the forerunner of FAUSA), issued the first report, condemning the University of Tasmania for convicting Orr on evidence that "would not hang a dog".[14]

After another committee's investigation, R. H. Thorp, D. W. Smith and E. L. Wheelwright (President, Vice-President and Acting Secretary, respectively, of the Federal Council of Staff Associations) announced in an official letter on 7 December 1960 the censure against the Administration of the University of Tasmania. That letter summarised the injustices done to Professor Orr as follows:

1. The University Inquiries were defective procedurally, in that they failed to accord "natural justice" to Orr.

2. The findings of the University Inquiries were not supported by adequate evidence.

3. In subsequent litigation, the University of Tasmania conducted its case against the dismissed professor in a manner which warrants explicit condemnation, as conduct totally unworthy of a university.[15]

Other organisations condemned the procedures used by the University of Tasmania. The Scots Kirk Session's summary of the University's inquiry into the allegations by Miss Kemp concluded:

> This committee conducted an enquiry which denied every right of natural justice to Professor Orr, as did Professor Hytten's committee on the other allegations.
>
> 1. Professor Orr was refused a statement of the charges against him in sufficient detail to allow him to prepare a defence.
>
> 2. He was forbidden to attend at the University or interview any students and was thus greatly handicapped in the preparation of his defence.
>
> 3. He was refused time and opportunity in which to collect evidence for his defence.
>
> 4. His accusers were heard in his absence.
>
> 5. Witnesses whose evidence was mutually confirmatory were present together, prompting each other.
>
> 6. Even though no date was fixed for any act of misconduct alleged by Miss Kemp, Professor Orr was expected to prove immediately that these acts had not taken place.
>
> 7. He was refused a transcript of the proceedings.
>
> 8. He was refused the right to assistance by his legal advisers.
>
> 9. In the absence of his legal adviser, legally qualified members of the enquiry insisted on legal interpretations affecting his standing in the matter.[16]

There are no excuses for such violations of natural justice in procedures. If charges are grave, if the evidence for those charges is good, there is no need for a university administration to follow any procedures but those of scrupulous fairness. Ignorance is no excuse. University administrations have largely unlimited access to the taxpayer's purse. Administrations can, and do, buy the best legal advice. University administrations often have some of the most prestigious local legal figures sitting on their governing boards or in their law schools. Is the price of those connections, profitable to the legal elite in terms of self esteem if not financial rewards for themselves or their friends, that a blind eye is turned towards the blatant violations of natural justice in procedures that characterise other cases besides that of Professor Orr? This question has immediate implications, especially in the perspective of certain recent cases, for example that of Dr Spautz.[17] When dismissal cases are brought into court, there is sometimes the plea of absolute privilege, that what is said is exempt from any challenge for defamation. The argument is that universities have their own quasi-judicial system and, like the courts and Parliament, for it to work it must have absolute privilege. That plea of absolute privilege should be challenged on the grounds of the absence of natural justice, or normal legal procedural safeguards to ensure a fair trial.

How to Organise an Academic Witch-hunt

In the book on Orr one of the most valuable contributions is that both W. H. C. Eddy and R. Douglas Wright independently focus on what is the most disturbing aspect of the dismissal of Orr from the University of Tasmania, and which also characterises other Australian cases: the susceptibility of supposedly rational academics to participate in a campaign against a dissident, a campaign that epitomised irrationality. That campaign is summarised by Professor Wright, then Professor of Physiology in the University of Melbourne and a Member of the Council of the Australian National University:

> a. Defamation of the victim related to professional competence, mental balance, truthfulness, drinking habits and corruption of the young, i.e., juniors, by blasphemy, swearing, seduction, etc. This tends to isolate the victim and encourages defamation by his contacts who, then finding that they are at legal and financial risk, serve the corporation as "witnesses".

b. Reward of collaborators from the victim's group, which may vary from slight social advancement to extraordinary promotion, usually with definite pecuniary advantage, which costs the governing group nothing personally.

c. The welding together of the pack of prosecutors, preferably led by a judge and/or clergyman — this misleads the community as to the integrity of the prosecution.

d. The proclamation at all stages of the authority of the corporation.

e. The careful leaking of the defamation through personal links and loyalties to other corporations of similar community standing, e.g., Clubs, Churches, Chambers, Chapters, Associations, State Departments and especially the Press owners, so that the attack is broadly based and protected. In this way the subordinates of these organizations may be enlisted to become defamers.

f. The victim is not told anything, but becomes disturbed by what people do not say, and more especially by the way people move individually or collectively in his presence. This communication of disturbance without conversation is the real basis of a feeling of isolation, and in its crudest form is "sending to Coventry".

g. As a culmination of this stage most accused people leave the group, i.e., resign, and this is accepted as proof of guilt, whereas it is usually an indication of a feeling of loneliness, confusion, fear and unprotected helplessness. If they do not resign, then dismissal as a *fait accompli* is often effective.[18]

Wright is not the only person to suggest that University administrations reward supporters with "extraordinary promotion". Eddy provides examples (including the names, which we delete.) For example, "Mr A ... gave the Vice-Chancellor a statement against Professor Orr ... for the University Council, which received it and forthwith appointed him a Demonstrator in ... *retrospective* ... "[19] Or, if you prefer, "Mr T ..., one of Professor Orr's accusers, was made Professor T ... just before Orr's dismissal, in a manner which called forth the most vigorous protest even from the Tasmanian Professorial Board".[20]

Those who did not support the campaign had a tougher time. The Law School had been a centre of some support for Orr — and by three years after the sacking "every full-time member of the Law Faculty had resigned".[21] One staff member who decided to stay in Tasmania, Associate Professor Polya, found himself blocked for further promotion, given a heavy administrative load, and reduced funds for teaching and research in his specialty.[22]

Eddy perceptively notes how the accusers choose charges which project their own guilt on to the victim:

One method of confusing the issues was to accuse Orr of doing what was done to him, or at least of trying or of threatening to do it. This also confused attitudes.

Orr was accused of trying to dismiss Milanov — Milanov was promoted; Orr was dismissed. Orr was accused of threatening to wreck Townsley's career — Townsley was promoted; Orr's career was wrecked. Orr was accused of "at least technical violence", of threatening violence, or giving rise to a suspicion of a feeling of a little fear of violence. None of the accusers suffered violence; it was Orr who was assaulted, stoned and shot. Orr was accused of violating academic freedom — his dismissal was a gross violation of academic freedom; nobody's freedom was curtailed by Orr.[23]

Allegations are made which may not only reflect the accuser's own weaknesses but the weaknesses of others in order to recruit supporters to the campaign:

The successful framers study men's vulnerabilities and exploit above all weakness which normally would be taken as irrelevant, personal prejudices, irritabilities, vanities, envies and the like. Those who wrong the victim, not those whom he wrongs, are those most hostile to him. Wrongs about which they will feel guilty are most effective. They will then have the vested interest in believing in the victim's guilt — it protects them from their own. This is one of the most common patterns in the attack on Orr. Someone, they must believe, is guilty. Themselves or him?[24]

Allegations involving sexual behaviour are especially useful in recruiting supporters to a campaign because they strike a deep resonance of repression (in the psychological sense of the word) in the minds of the frustrated and the salacious:

> The emotions aroused by sexual charges were exploited to induce people to invent their own Kemp stories. For those who could not accept that he seduced her, there was the bait of the "Diary" to induce belief that she seduced him; for those who thought neither was proved there was the belief that he must have been indiscreet. Sexual charges to discredit leading champions of freedom are regular, deliberate parts of the pattern, which also exhibits a choice of words of a kind which encourages each hearer or reader to fill in the details for himself and make up his own story.[25]

Once the critical mass of supporters has come together, the aggressive drive finds new targets, for example the dissident's students or prospective students[26], or the dissident's wife. As Eddy says:

> Where men are not directly malleable under the pressures used... their wives become special targets...
>
> It is not only in totalitarian countries that family and other close ties are exploited. It is done in "open" societies wherever the techniques of totalitarianism are used. Such methods are especially potent in isolating a victim. Those who wish to manifest solidarity with him are not merely going into a tiny minority group... they are also inflicting on their wives and families isolation and unpleasantness.[27]

"A VIRTUOSITY IN EVIL-DOING FOR WHICH IT WOULD BE DIFFICULT ... TO FIND A PARALLEL"?

Both Professor R. Douglas Wright, in the prologue, and W. H. C. Eddy, towards the end of the book, suggest that what happened at the University of Tasmania is unique. Eddy, in the paragraph which provides the title to our case history, argues:

> They condoned and encouraged violence, covering it by lying; they protected one set of false charges by another, evading clarification of old issues by ever new slanders. No exposure, no harm suffered by individuals or the institution for which they claimed responsibility, deflected them. Publicly condemned by a Royal Commission, after a thorough probing of the facts, they perpetuated their power and ruthlessly struck down the man whose voice had led to that enquiry, and by every device of propaganda, at public expense, sought to destroy him. They then systematically re-wrote history, falsely belittling the role of the man to whom they had falsely attributed all the trouble. They displayed not merely malice, but a virtuosity in evil-doing for which it would be difficult, within their spheres of operation, to find a parallel.[28]

But, is it "difficult... to find a parallel"? While a case will always have some unique elements, might not one see many parallels when different case histories are compared? That exercise is left for the reader.[29]

The administration of the University of Tasmania resisted the censure until December 1963, when it finally settled with the Federal Council of University Staff Associations of Australia. The terms of the settlement included the payment of £16,000 to Professor Orr (at that time this would have been fairly close to the remainder of his salary after tax), plus a separate payment of all Orr's court costs. In addition, the settlement also required: that the Australian Association of Philosophy lift the ban on filling the vacant Chair of Philosophy at the University of Tasmania, that the censure from the Federal Council of Staff Associations be removed, and that "the University undertakes to refrain from legal or other action directly or indirectly against Professor Orr *or his supporters*".[30]

At the end of the document announcing the terms of the settlement, the Federal Council of University Staff Associations of Australia also stated: "that the academic rehabilitation of Professor Orr is essential and the Federal Council assured him of its continued support and assistance to that end".[31] Unfortunately, it was too late for Orr's "rehabilitation". The strain of the original injustice and the initial lack of support had taken their toll. He was an ill man by the time the settlement was reached and he died shortly afterwards.

Orr is dead but the issues live. The problem is not just the abuse of administrative power. That abuse requires compliance. It is not merely the malice of power-seeking personalities. It is the ability of certain intellectuals to rationalise any injustice so long as their own pursuit of glory or comfort is not disturbed. For the ability to rationalise, we let one of the academics quoted by W. H. C. Eddy have the last word:

> If he had had sexual relations with the girl, then there would have been an issue of academic freedom worth fighting for. But Orr will not support that view, so he was unworthy of support.[32]

References

1. W. H. C. Eddy, *Orr* (Brisbane: Jacaranda Press, 1961), pp. xiii–xv, 261.

2. The dismissal of Dr Spautz from Newcastle University is given a short summary in the chapter "Archives of Suppression".

3. The removal by "early retirement" of Professor Arthur Burns from the Australian National University is given a short summary in the chapter "Archives of Suppression". What is important here is that an earlier court decision, which basically upheld the concept of tenure and, in particular, the right of an individual to be given the reasons for his removal, was overturned by a sitting of the Full Bench of the Federal Court: Fia Cumming, "Worrying impact of court rule", the *Australian (Higher Education Supplement)*, 22 December 1982, p. 17. A further complication is that Professor Burns' health has improved and he believes that he is fit to return to work; it is of interest that he had originally been given a pension of half professorial level and was offered more if he would go quietly, but he refused it: Fia Cumming, "Staff association threatens legal action if professor isn't reinstated", the *Australian (Higher Education Supplement)*, 17 August 1983, p. 18.

4. Eddy, op. cit., p. 10.

5. ibid., p. 11.

6. ibid., p. 133.

7. ibid., pp. 482–4.

8. ibid., p. 607.

9. G. Cranswick, M. Holly and A. Christie-Johnson, "Statement issued by the Bishop of Tasmania on 18 April, 1963", *Vestes*, vol. 6, issue 2 (June 1963), pp. 153–6.

10. J. B. Polya, in a ten page document dated 31 January 1984, with minor changes in punctuation and paragraphing, comments upon an earlier draft version of this manuscript. Professor Polya tries to be as even-handed as possible, pointing out that Orr was not without serious faults, though not justifying the treatment he received.

11. Eddy, op. cit.

12. Eddy, op. cit., p. xix.

13. We have reason to believe that this strategy has been attempted in other Australian cases, judging from comments made to us by individuals subjected to administrative harassment and judging from our own experiences.

14. R. H. Thorp and K. D. Buckley, quoted in Eddy, op. cit., p. xix.

15. R. H. Thorp, D. W. Smith and E. L. Wheelwright, "Letter", *Vestes*, vol. 4, issue 1 (March 1961), pp. 69–87.

16. Scots Kirk Sessions summary, quoted in Eddy, op. cit., p. 265.

17. See note 2 above.

18. R. Douglas Wright, "Prologue", in Eddy, op. cit., pp. xiv–xv.

19. Eddy, op. cit., legend on photograph facing p. 157.

20. Eddy, op. cit., p. 680.

21. Eddy, op. cit., p. 668.

22. Richard Davis has written to the authors: "The Polya case, incidentally, seems almost as bad as the Orr case in some ways". (Letter dated 3 February 1984.) Richard Davis is working on a more extensive historical study of the University of Tasmania. See, for example, "Free Academics or Council Servants? Tasmanian University Staff Before the Murray Report", Australian and New Zealand History of Education Society, 13th Annual Conference Proceeding, vol. 1 (1984), pp. 49–61.

23. Eddy, op. cit., pp. 596–7.

24. Eddy, op. cit., p. 587.

25. Eddy, op. cit., p. 594.

26. See note 13 above.

27. Eddy, op. cit., p. 589. The second author encountered much the same experience at the University of Adelaide. At one time or another, at least three different staff members expressed surprise that she stood by her husband. Such openly expressed attitudes suggest that there is a serious lack of moral fibre among some Australian academics.

28. Eddy, op. cit., p. 582.

29. On several occasions we encountered from Staff Association officials or other academics a fascinating phenomenon. On the one hand, they were scathing in their criticism of the University of Tasmania over the Orr case (although sometimes not very knowledgeable about the details). On the other hand, they were very defensive about local cases which had many of the same elements, unfair procedures, witch-hunting, and a general reluctance to admit that the charges were insubstantial or inaccurate. Orr did directly challenge the authority of the administration at the University of Tasmania in a way that other dissidents at other Australian universities did not even remotely approach. Thus, in a way, the heavy-handed responses in some other cases were even less justified. True, not all of the other dissidents were sacked — thanks basically to post-Orr statutes. But the treatment otherwise received differs little from what happened to Orr.

30. *Vestes*, vol. 7, issue 1 (March 1964), p. 78. (Italics have been added by us.)

31. ibid., p. 79.

32. Eddy, op. cit., p. 684.

Acknowledgements

We thank Dr Richard Davis, Department of History, and Associate Professor J. B. Polya for their useful comments and corrections on our manuscript. Among the comments made by Professor Polya is one that is especially pertinent to other cases as well:

"Manwell and Baker should bring out that academic persecution affects not only those who criticise the scum risen to the top of the pseudoacademic soup but that innocents suffer from old vendettas carried on by new administrators". One of the most frightening observations in several cases is how new staff and new administrators, not involved in the original witch-hunt, join to defend the old errors and injustices. The only explanation for such behaviour is that the pressures on certain academics, or perhaps their basic psychodynamics, demand a release of tensions on to a convenient scapegoat; it may also be that, by showing a willingness to victimise a scapegoat, they ingratiate themselves with local power elites.

It may well be that this lack of character and compassion is so common that it has contributed to another curious phenomenon of Australian academic life. Since 1975, Australian academics have sustained severe budget cuts, some caustic (and partly unfair) criticism in the mass media (e.g., Peter Samuel, "The Scandal of our universities", *The Bulletin* (Sydney), 12 March 1977, pp. 14–18), and several examples of unwarranted political interference (e.g., curbs on overseas study leave, attacks on tenure, and the Hidaka case). Recently, there has been the apparently unprecedented situation where the federal government took back part of a salary increase that had been awarded through its own machinery of an industrial tribunal. Although a few voices have been raised in FAUSA, the general academic response has been indifferent. Budget cuts are simply used as an opportunity to punish dissidents or get ride of untenured staff, rather than to curb waste. In contrast, in the UK academics have shown much more solidarity — and have been more effective in dealing with the Thatcher Government, a government with far more serious economic problems than the Australian Government has.

PREJUDICE IN GRANTING RESEARCH GRANTS

PEER REVIEW AND THE AUSTRALIAN RESEARCH GRANTS COMMITTEE: A CAUTIONARY TALE

Richard Davis

In his well-documented article* Clyde Manwell not only questions the validity of anonymous peer review in general, but describes in detail his own experience with the Australian Research Grants Committee (ARGC) which in 1971 abruptly terminated his grant for a zoological project, and refused to renew it on two subsequent applications. Professor Manwell offers three hypotheses for his failure: (1) Natural selection: poor research; (2) Random drift: the uncertainties of the system; (3) Unnatural selection: deliberate prejudice. He allows readers to draw their own conclusions, presenting in fact compelling reasons for the third hypothesis. His story is so frightening in its implications for the future of higher education in this country that it behoves all academics who have had similar experiences to publicise them in the hope of reform.

Most academics are reluctant to admit such failures or difficulties, which might be used against them in subsequent applications for grants or promotion. It is, as Professor Manwell points out, difficult to present an objective statement of experiences highly damaging to morale or self-respect. I believe, nevertheless, that the documents in my own case are worth citing. History at first sight appears more subjective than the sciences, and more likely to be influenced by non-academic factors. But, interestingly enough, most criticism of peer review seems to come from scientists. There is a clear need for more humanities-based statements on peer review.

As an historian I have specialised on Irish overseas influence in the nineteenth and twentieth centuries. This topic is inextricably linked with state aid for private schools, a particularly contentious contemporary problem. In the late 1960s, while I was completing my research on the Irish in New Zealand, state aid achieved a breakthrough in Australasia as state and national governments vied in increasing subsidies to private schools. Opponents of state aid, like the subsequent Defence of Government Schools, were generally portrayed as cranks or bigoted extremists. Unfortunately — perhaps because of my lack of church affiliation — it seemed to me that the anti-state aid arguments, generally accepted in the nineteenth century, were not inevitably ridiculous. Meanwhile, the increasing sectarian violence in Northern Ireland led to widespread debate there on the dangers of denominational education. Some of the tactics adopted by private school supporters appeared to me highly dubious. I felt obliged to publicise some of the old controversies before the decisions on state aid in Australia were finalised.

My situation, though tenured as a lecturer in Tasmania, was thus a little precarious. Nevertheless, before the end of the 1960s, I established a satisfactory reputation as a researcher. I published several articles in Ireland, New Zealand and Australia, plus a short book on the politics of state aid in Tasmania. My Ph.D. thesis on Irish and educational controversies in New Zealand was, however, savagely attacked by an anonymous referee (later found to be a member of a church education society) when submitted to the Melbourne University Press. The anonymous referee complained that I had ignored vast quantities of archival material, but much of this I demonstrated to be non-existent. Another publisher was found. In 1971, after returning from leave in Ireland, I was promoted to senior lecturer.

By this time several members of my department had been awarded ARGC grants. As my publication record was superior to many, I anticipated no difficulty in obtaining finance for a study of Irish influence in the old Commonwealth countries during the Irish revolutionary period, 1916–22. The work had clear contemporary relevance in that it sought to analyse the methods of overseas pressure groups, simultaneously justifying Irish guerrilla action and state aid for local private schools. I had already written on Irish and educational issues in Australia and New Zealand; an article on the Irish in a Canadian province, where I had spent some of my 1970 leave, was about to appear; comparative imperial studies had long been my interest. Moreover, when lecturing in New Zealand in the 1960s I had obtained, after interview, a small grant for local travel from the New Zealand ARGC; in 1970, the University of Manitoba gave me a research fellowship worth about A$5600, with no teaching required.

My Australian ARGC application in 1971 simply cited two or three articles directly connected with my proposed comparative study; I did not mention other writings with marginal relevance. I was very surprised in October when my application was rejected without interview. Other colleagues who had published little or nothing were sometimes embarrassed by the continuation of grants after their research efforts had petered out. I assumed that there had been some flaw in my mode of application; it was after all a period when funds were flowing relatively freely. Perhaps I should have cited all publications? Maybe I had failed to itemise my financial requirements with sufficient precision?

In 1974 I was granted six months' leave by the University of Tasmania. My original project still interested me. I hoped by concentrated research to accumulate sufficient material, when combined with my previous work, to write a short comparative volume on Irish support groups in the British Dominions during the Irish Revolution. With a grant from the University of Tasmania and cheap accommodation in Ireland, provided by a relative, I could afford to spend my leave in that country. My comparative study, however, required some time in Ottawa, and possibly a short visit to South Africa to track down some elusive material. I calculated that with $1000 from the ARGC — precious little by the requirements of scientific research — the book might be written.

This time I took no chances. My application cited everything already published, plus all my forthcoming work. I had then to my account one book and twelve reasonably substantial articles. Three other articles, including a 22,000-word chapter on Tasmania for D. J. Murphy's *Labour in Politics*[12], were on the way. Three full-length books[1, 2, 3] were in the press in Ireland, New Zealand and Tasmania. All these publications touched in some way on my comparative project. I also nominated two personal referees, both former supervisors of my research and now sympathetic advisers on my current projects. One was Emeritus Professor W. P. Morrell, author of a number of classic studies of British colonial policy and comparative Commonwealth development. The other was Professor F. S. L. Lyons, soon to be elected to Ireland's most prestigious academic position, the provostship of Trinity College, Dublin, and without doubt the most eminent Irish historian of his time. It seemed appropriate that a comparative study of the Irish in the Commonwealth should be supported by such a distinguished Irish historian and so outstanding an analyst of the Commonwealth.

My precautions were in vain. Without even an interview, the ARGC secretary, Mr K. E. Creech, again regretted on 26 October 1973 that my request for support had not been successful. The cyclostyled letter informed me as usual that the committee had "a long-standing policy of not discussing the reasons for the failure of an application" to preserve anonymity and because there was insufficient money to finance all worthy projects. But, it suggested, don't be downhearted, read the Chairman's *Advice to Australian Research Grants Committee Applicants* and try again.

I was, however, already acquainted with this document, especially the section suggesting that if a disappointed applicant wrote nicely to the Chairman, asking what was wrong with his work, the Chairman would endeavour to explain. I accordingly wrote nicely to the Chairman, asking what was wrong with my work. A few weeks later I received a roughly typed letter, signed for Secretary Creech. The letter invited me to "appreciate that these assessments must remain confidential to the Committee". As consolation, however, he enclosed a copy of . . . the Chairman's *Advice to Australian Research Grants Committee Applicants*!

My reply of 29 November was not quite so nice. I requested Mr Creech to refer to the Chairman's *Advice*, p. 12, and read: "If the unsuccessful applicant writes to me in a spirit of bewilderment rather than belligerence, I try to be as helpful as I can". I referred to the specific examples of the sort of help the Chairman was prepared to give. If policy had changed, I argued, the current *Advice* should be withdrawn immediately and future applicants informed that they would be at the mercy of a committee "which issues no explanations of any sort". In the present context Creech's reply and enclosure seemed "not only unsatisfactory but positively insulting". I again requested "*some* explanation".

My 29 November retort achieved results. A letter from Creech informed me tartly that there had been no policy change and that the *Advice* still reflected the committee's policy. He then proceeded to do what he had previously declared impossible — summarise the conclusions of "independent assessors":

> Each of the assessors recognised that the project you proposed to complete presented the possibility for an interesting and original study. However, they were in agreement that a comparative approach coupled with considerable insight and organising ability would be required to make the project worthwhile. The comments made by the assessors indicated that they were not convinced that you had appreciated the intrinsic demands of the project and consequently they were quite unimpressed with the research proposals that you outlined in your application.

What can be made of this? First, it is interesting to note that despite the enormous difference between Professor Manwell's projected study of genetic variation of proteins in Australian native and imported animals and my comparative study of Irish influence overseas, the ARGC response to both had common elements. There was an initial reluctance to supply any information — in my case a Kafka-like bureaucratic stalemate based on patent self-contradiction — followed by a report whose damning conclusion was offset by initial admissions as to the value of the project. As in Manwell's case, there was the implicit double standard: despite the failure of numerous ARGC projects to bear fruit, we were both condemned on the assumption that our good projects might not be successfully completed because of our lack of ability as researchers.

Let us look more closely at the report on my comparative Irish influence project. The "interesting and original study", the assessors argue, would require "considerable insight and organising ability". One would surely expect this of any academic, no matter how lowly. To deny their existence in the case of a candidate with a number of publications would surely require some extremely hard evidence — harder, it is hoped, than the evidence of the Melbourne University Press referee for my New Zealand book who cited non-existent archives. On the former occasion I saw the original report and was able to make what was conceded by the deputy director of the Melbourne University Press (18 February 1969) to be an effective reply, necessitating another opinion (ultimately not granted). I had of course no guarantee that the MUP referee had not been employed by the ARGC. Presumably, the "independent assessors" considered my publications in detail. How did they receive my highly critical article on state aid in the *Australian Humanist*? Were they invariably better qualified to demonstrate the inadequacy of my writing than those who had reviewed it or accepted it for publication? Is it just to deny a grant on the evidence of published work when many grants are awarded to those who have published nothing?

The only stated justification for denying me finance was a belief that I had failed to appreciate "the intrinsic demands of the project". Yet the assessors admitted that the project was original in that no one had attempted anything like that before. How then could they, who had not worked on the project, know in advance "the intrinsic demands" better than myself? Is there indeed any way of convincing an anonymous and unaccountable assessor that anyone knows the "intrinsic demands" of their subject when previous publications and the opinion of the most respected scholars can be dismissed as worthless or irrelevant, without any possibility of a reply? What sort of "academic" procedure is this? In history, at any rate, the anonymous citation of a bogus archive or two can apparently sink any applicant without trace. If ever an interview were justified, it was here: a little cross-questioning would soon have discovered my understanding of the "intrinsic demands" of my chosen field.

So that was that. My experience in 1974 convinced me that I had been black-listed by a rival and could expect no ARGC grant at any time in my subsequent career, unless, of course, I moved to some entirely different field of study. This was, no doubt, the precise objective of the "independent assessors". Professors Lyons and Morrell, who repudiated the ARGC explanation as completely opposed to their recommendations, advised me to battle on without the grant. In late 1974 I took study leave in Ireland with sufficient money to research there, but not enough to visit Canada or South Africa. Before leaving, however, I attempted to force the issue into the open by a direct challenge to the academic whom I believed responsible for my double rejection by the ARGC. Though supplied with a pre-publication copy of my article[7] criticising his methodology and published work in detail, the pundit turned down a request from the editor to write a reply for the next issue.

My six months' leave in Ireland was not quite as productive as I had hoped. Lacking the necessary source material from South Africa and Canada, instead of a book I could publish only a 6000-word article on Irish support groups in the Dominions during the Irish Revolution. I did, however, prepare papers on other aspects of the Irish question, published in England[15, 17], Bangladesh[16], the United States[19], and Australia.[14, 18, 20] More significant was the Dublin Historical Association's publication of my 48-page pamphlet[13], summarising my earlier research on Sinn Fein founder, Arthur Griffith, and incorporating the results of Irish research of 1974. All in all, a lengthy pamphlet and seven or eight papers seem a reasonable return for six months' study leave, despite my lack of ARGC funding. How many ARGC grantees do better? But who cares about the actual writings of an academic who has been proved anonymously to be inappreciative of "the intrinsic demands of the project"?

Between 1974 and 1975, I also published four books whose research had been completed in previous years. Reviews appeared in Ireland, England, Canada, Australia and New Zealand. Some were very good, many were satisfactory, but a few were disappointing. My *Irish Issues in New Zealand Politics*[3], nearly aborted in its early stages, was satisfactorily received by the *Times Literary Supplement* and excellently reviewed in a local journal by the head of a New Zealand university education department. In acclaiming the book as "a masterly and lucid treatment", Professor Rollo Arnold praised the "researches which have ranged through Ireland, North America and Australia, as well as New Zealand, to give depth and perspective" — a view hard to reconcile with the ARGC assessors' complaint that I was unaware of the comparative implications of my subject. Even the New Zealand *Marist Messenger*, despite some reservations, concluded that *Irish Issues* should be studied in all Catholic seminaries. But the pundit who had refused my direct challenge gave it an atrocious but quite unspecific review in an Australian periodical whose editor obligingly refused to publish my reply. With mates like this, who needs anonymity? Book reviews, demonstrating the wide range of academic opinion on most academic issues, are one of the strongest arguments against the current system of anonymous "peer" review which enables one or two "faceless men" to destroy potential rivals without any risk to themselves.

Early in 1976 I was promoted to Reader for the "excellence" of my research in Irish history. For once the academic game of Russian roulette had worked in my favour: instead of blasting my reputation to tatters, the anonymous assessors clicked their chambers benignly.

"Excellent" in 1976, I was inappreciative of "the intrinsic demands" of my chosen field in 1973, judgement in both cases being based on precisely the same work. As for money, my request for a single grant of $1000 was dismissed with ridicule in 1973 by the ARGC; three years later the taxpayer was called on to pay an annual increment of twice that sum for the rest of my career. The original $1000 might have produced a book to enlighten the general public; the continuing increment simply raised my personal standard of living.

Like Professor Manwell, I leave it to the reader to decide whether my disgrace at the hands of the ARGC was the product of natural selection (my incompetence), random drift (my bad luck), or unnatural selection (calculated dishonesty). The decision must be based on the question: how independent were the assessors? My own view comes through strongly in the foregoing pages, but my experience may have made me neurotic or paranoid. My departmental juniors, almost invariably successful in their applications, seek my unprofitable advice on the completion of ARGC forms: simultaneous with my second failure in 1973, a Ph.D. candidate, then under my supervision, obtained a most satisfactory ARGC boost. Should I apply again? Until some reforms are made in the system, my time, financed by the taxpayer, could clearly be spent more profitably.

What sort of reforms? First, the abolition of anonymity. Assessors' reports must be sent to applicants, and an appeal system, headed by an academic ombudsman, can easily be established.[21, 22] Second, actual research needs to be monitored and the results published after five years. If these suggestions are considered too time-consuming and expensive, why not draw the names of applicants out of a hat? Though far from ideal, it would be an improvement on the present system.

References

*C. Manwell, "Peer Review: A Case History from the Australian Research Grants Committee", *Search*, vol. 10, no. 3, March 1979, pp. 81–6.

Books and articles published in 18 months after refusal of second ARGC application:

BOOKS

1. *The Tasmanian Gallows: A Study of Capital Punishment* (Hobart: Cat & Fiddle Press, 1974), pp. xv, 119.
2. *Arthur Griffith and Non-Violent Sinn Fein* (Dublin: Anvil Books, 1974), pp. xxi & 253.
3. *Irish Issues in New Zealand Politics, 1868–1922* (Dunedin: University of Otago Press, 1974), pp. x, 248.
   (Reviews mentioned: (i) *Times Literary Supplement*, 13 February 1976; (ii) *ANZHES Journal*, vol. 5, no. 2, Spring 1976; (iii) *Marist Messenger*, NZ, December 1975; (iv) *Journal of Religious History*, vol. 9, no. 2, December 1976, pp. 216–17.)
4. *A Guide to the State Aid Tangle in Tasmania* (Hobart: Cat & Fiddle Press, 1975), pp. viii, 118.

ARTICLES

5. "New Zealand Liberal Legislation and Manitoba Labour, 1894–1916", *W. P. Morrell: A Tribute — Essays in modern and early modern history presented to William Parker Morrell, Professor Emeritus, University of Otago*. Edited by P. S. O'Connor and G. A. Wood (Dunedin: University of Otago Press, 1973), pp. 169–83 and 289–94.
6. "Irish Catholics and the Manitoba School Crisis, 1885–1921", *Eire–Ireland*, St Paul (USA), Autumn 1973, pp. 29–64.

7. "Patrick O'Farrell and Irish Secular Nationalism — a Reconsideration", *Tasm. Hist. Res. Ass. Papers and Proceedings*, December 1973, pp. 221–38.

8. "General Histories of Ireland published in the 1970s", *Historical News*, Christchurch, May 1974, pp. 9–11.

9. "Tasmania and the Irish Revolution, 1916–22", *Tasm. Hist. Res. Ass. Papers and Proceedings*, June 1974, pp. 69–88.

10. "C. S. Parnell, Cecil Rhodes, Edmund Dwyer-Grey and Imperial Federation", *Tasm. Hist. Res. Ass. Papers and Proceedings*, September 1974, pp. 125–32.

11. "Arthur Griffith and the Decline of Secular Nationalism", *Church and State*, Dublin, Autumn 1974, pp. 6, 36–40.

12. "Tasmania", in *Labour in Politics: The State Labor Parties in Australia 1880–1920*, D. J. Murphy (ed.), University of Queensland Press, 1975. pp. 387–444, 464–6.

Books, articles and papers published as a direct result of the six months' leave in Ireland; refused ARGC funding on grounds of lack of appreciation of "intrinsic demands" of my field:

BOOK

13. *Arthur Griffith* (Dublin Historial Association Pamphlet, 1976), pp. 48.

ARTICLES

14. "The Self-Determination for Ireland Leagues and the Irish Race Convention in Paris, 1921–22", *THRA Papers and Proceedings*, vol. 24, no. 3, September 1977, pp. 88–104.

15. "The Advocacy of Passive Resistance in Ireland, 1916–1922", *Anglo-Irish Studies*, III, Cambridge, 1977, pp. 35–55.

16. "India in Irish Revolutionary Propaganda, 1905–1922", *Journal of the Asiatic Society of Bangladesh*, vol. XXII, no. 1, April 1977, pp. 66–89. (Also given as Conference paper, New Zealand Historical Association, Dunedin, August 1975.)

17. "Arthur Griffith: Architect of Modern Ireland: Part II: 1916–1922", *History Today*, London, vol. 29, no. 4, April 1979, pp. 248–56.

18. "Bertrand Russell and Ireland", *Australian Journal of History and Politics*, vol. 26, no. 2, August 1980, pp. 279–83.

19. "Ulster Protestants and the Sinn Fein Press, 1914–1922", *Eire–Ireland*, St Paul (USA), Winter, 1980, pp. 279–83.

20. "Catholic Education and Irish Nationalism: O'Connell to Community Schools", *ANZHES Journal*, Adelaide, vol. 10, no. 1, Autumn 1981, pp. 1–12.

Articles advocating a higher moral code for academics:

21. "Anonymity: The Cancer of Academia", *Education Research and Perspectives*, Perth, vol. 6, no. 2, December 1979, pp. 3–11.

22. "A Hippocratic Oath for Academics?", *Vestes*, vol. 24, no. 2, 1981, pp. 155–9.

THE AUSTRALIAN
RESEARCH GRANTS SCHEME
— REPLY TO A
CAUTIONARY TALE

Peter W. Sheehan, Chairman
Australian Research Grants Scheme

Dr Davis has applied twice for support from the ARGS and has been unsuccessful, but it is not my intent to engage in personal debate as to the reasons for the denial of funding. I am unable to agree, however, on a number of inferences that are offered about the scheme in relation to his case. It is untrue, for example, that grants are not given "on the evidence of published work when many are awarded to those who have published nothing" (p. 52). ARGS grants are very competitive and publication records play an important part in guiding the committee to decide whether or not the research that is planned is likely to be successful and communicated in major publication outlets. Second, I have seen no evidence that people who publish little are embarrassed by the continuation of their grants when their research efforts have petered out (p. 51.) The scheme monitors its grants through progress reports, interviews and peer assessment and evidence of this kind of situation is very likely to surface. And if it does, a grant would not be awarded.

ISSUES RAISED

There are a number of specific issues raised by Dr Davis's case that are important and worthy of comment. These relate to the strengths and weaknesses of the peer review system, confidentiality of reporting, the function of nominated versus committee-selected assessors, procedures available for requesting feedback, the intent of the scheme's interview mechanism, and suggested reforms.

Peer review, confidential reporting and nominated assessors The peer review mechanism is not perfect and much has been written about chance and consensus in peer review. It is possible, for instance, for experts in a field to disagree among themselves about the same proposal and questions can certainly be raised about the reliability and validity of the assessment. Peer assessment, however, does provide critical evaluation by those familiar with the issues and the science that is being used. Such comment can "drive" research, isolate the "cutting edge" of a research field, and highlight the best proposals.

Dr Davis is too extreme when he talks about faceless men destroying rivals without any risk to themselves (p. 53). Destructive comment of this kind is likely to be detected by the committee which acts as impartially as it can to interpret the evidence and assess its relevance to the proposal that is being considered. The issue of whether that comment should be confidential or not is another matter. Confidential assessment is requested in order to guarantee that frank and honest comment will be given. Obviously there are assessors who, for whatever reason, would make quite different comment when offering it anonymously than when offering it when identified. It is my experience, for example, that nominated assessors can readily convey excessive enthusiasm to support an applicant.

Requesting feedback The account Dr Davis gives of requesting feedback sounds unfortunate and I can only comment on what I know now to be the case. Unsuccessful applicants can write to the committee and request feedback and the committee when giving that feedback attempts to give as detailed a response as possible. Rather than summarise what has been said by the assessors, the committee tries to cite directly from assessors' reports.

The interview mechanism   It is impossible for me to assess in the present instance whether "if ever an interview were justified, it was here (p. 53)" but it is important to reinforce the value of the interview in clarifying doubts in the committee's mind about the adequacy of the research. An interview serves many purposes. It would be conducted if clarification was needed from applicants but not if the committee thought it would add nothing to their case as stated by themselves and judged by the assessors.

Suggested reforms   Reforms, of course, should be considered in the system, and Dr Davis suggests two that require comment. First, the suggestion is made that anonymity be abolished, but Dr Davis's paper begs the question of whether identified comment will be entirely frank. Second, it is suggested that actual research needs to be monitored and results published. The committee, however, does monitor its grants closely. It requests regular and detailed progress reports from all grantees, who also have to submit a final report and state the benefits of their research. The committee considers it important that the people it funds are accountable for whatever support they have received.

Concluding Comment

Grant writing is a frustrating exercise, especially when the application is unsuccessful, and it is of course likely that some proposals funded by the scheme have been judged incorrectly. But the scheme operates as fairly and as objectively as it can to use peer assessment to help it reach a decision about the worth of the research. "Calculated dishonesty" (p. 54) is a judgement that is just not appropriate.

Reply to Professor Peter W. Sheehan

Richard Davis

Professor Sheehan adds little or nothing to the debate. He produces no evidence to back the implication that all is for the best in the best of all possible academic worlds. His picture of a splendid body of men and women operating justly in conditions of perfect secrecy is charming, if naive. Professor Sheehan expects us to believe that a biased assessor would be immediately exposed by his peers. Unfortunately, life isn't that simple.

Two of Professor Sheehan's points are worth considering. First, he denies, albeit with a non sequitur assertion about *future*, not *past*, results, that applicants without publications obtain grants. Evidence of grants to unprolific researchers is readily available. An interesting case was the successful applicant in 1972 who had not published for five years and has produced nothing since. Some monitoring! No one wishes to point the bone at colleagues, but the government should require a detailed public statement, after a suitable interval, juxtaposing each individual's grant and his or her subsequent publications.

Second, Professor Sheehan believes that I beg the question on anonymity. Could anyone be frank if anonymity were removed? Of course they could. Most professional people, even academics, are forced to make unpopular public decisions. What anonymity does is to provide excellent cover for academic factions to manoeuvre undetected. With organisations like the National Civic Council boasting of their academic operations and potential assessors asserting openly that "faith has, of its nature, the special status of offering extra and clearer knowledge, a situation not applying to unbelief"[1] the federal government must act to ensure that justice is seen to be done.

[1] P. J. O'Farrell, "Historians and Religious Convictions", *Historical Studies*, Melbourne, vol. 17, 1976–77, p. 289. Such views, while stimulating in open debate amongst equals, are dangerous in secret committees.

Professor Sheehan carefully skirts my suggestion of an academic ombudsman. Yet an ombudsman of sufficient credibility could easily be appointed to guarantee that public money would always go to active researchers and not to the nominees of aggressive interest groups.

ACADEMIC EXPLOITATION

Brian Martin

For academics, credit for research work is important. It serves as a form of currency for obtaining jobs, promotions, grants and prestige. Not surprisingly, credit for original ideas as well as for the end result of painstaking experimentation, data collection and mustering of arguments, is zealously guarded.

Plagiarism is the most blatant example of stealing credit. It is much more common than is usually recognised.[1] Closely related to plagiarism is faking of results, which in effect claims credit for work not done. Faking is also more common than is usually recognised.[2]

What I call here academic exploitation is the taking of credit for work done by a person in a subordinate position. A variant is pressure on the subordinate to do work of a type or in a way which allows the superior to obtain undue credit. The exploiter's greater power in the relationship is used in establishing and retaining the unfair distribution of credit. An implicit or explicit threat of reprisals, such as a bad recommendation, is used to deter objections.

Exploitation is one of the seamier sides of academia, something which is seldom discussed or even acknowledged. The following examples illustrate some typical forms of exploitation. The examples are some of the ones about which I have received first-hand verbal or written accounts during the past decade. To preserve the anonymity of all involved, names and some other details have been altered.

1. Paul had recently completed his Ph.D. and had written several papers based on his thesis, in collaboration with his supervisor. They passed one paper to the professor and head of the department for his comments. The professor added one sentence to the paper, and added his name as third author.

2. Wing was a student from a Third World country studying for a Ph.D. in zoology at a major Australian university. Dr Williams, Wing's supervisor, although knowing beforehand of Wing's research interests, had invited Wing to Australia to work on various projects in a different area. These projects were unsuitable in themselves as thesis projects but were closer to Dr Williams's own interests. When Wing found that these projects of Dr Williams were not working out, Dr Williams would not listen to any comments. Eventually a confrontation erupted. After this Dr Williams was very hostile and tried in various ways to sabotage Wing's progress, by complaining to the head of the department and the dean, by interfering with Wing's research, by not carefully reading the draft of

Wing's thesis, and by writing poor recómmendations for Wing's applications for post-doctoral positions.

After considerable difficulty and a very trying time psychologically, Wing received his Ph.D., having obtained valuable support from other members of the department.

3.   Joan worked as an assistant to Dr Smith, the head of an English department at a small Australian tertiary institution. Dr Smith did not bother to keep up with the latest writing in his speciality, but instead had Joan do the reading and write summaries of the material for him. When Dr Smith on occasion did write a paper, Joan would spend long hours with him pointing out inadequacies and bringing him up to date, and also track down references for the paper and sometimes rewrite parts of it. For this contribution she never received any credit.

Dr Smith enjoyed the company of young women, and this was one reason for the long hours of discussion with Joan. He asked her about her private life, used physical expressions of affection, and eventually reached the stage of overt sexual proposition. At this, Joan decided to leave.

Dr Smith had exploited many female assistants and students over the years in a similar way.

4.   Elizabeth worked as a technician under Dr Jones in a chemistry department at a major Australian university. She designed most of the experiments and did all the work, setting them up and running them. Yet Dr Jones attempted to take all the credit: visitors to the laboratory would leave with the impression that Elizabeth only washed the glassware. This continuing exploitative situation greatly aggravated Elizabeth. Dr Jones also made a sexual approach. Postgraduate students under Dr Jones were similarly treated.

Elizabeth insisted on her rights, for example by putting her name on publications, but this overcame only some of the exploitation. Later Elizabeth left the laboratory, the university and science.

5.   Penny was an Australian student working temporarily at a major United States university under Dr Brown, a high-flying sociologist. Dr Brown would toss off ideas, and Penny would go off and research the topics and write papers on them. (Often Penny found that the ideas were useless.) On one occasion Dr Brown wanted to put himself in the good graces of grant administrator Dr King. So Dr Brown used one of Penny's studies for a departmental report. The authors were listed as Brown and King.

6.   Alex was a researcher in biochemistry at a major scientific institution. Dr Wilson, Alex's superior, was an eminent scientist who sat on many panels and advisory boards. In one report prepared for circulation to members of such a panel, Alex did almost all the work and writing, but modestly omitted his name from the paper, thinking that Dr Wilson would surely list him at least as co-author. But Dr Wilson without comment used the paper as his own.

How common is academic exploitation? It is impossible to say precisely because there have been few investigations of the phenomenon. Some types of academic exploitation seem to be quite common:

- Informal comment plus a few published accounts[3] suggest that many academics in positions of power obtain joint or sole authorship of research papers to which they have contributed little or nothing. I have been informed of numerous examples of this practice.

- A frequent special case of obtaining undue credit for the work of subordinates is when supervisors of advanced degree students become joint or sole authors of what is meant to be original work by their students. In 1973 an article by Ron Witton about this form of exploitation was published in the *Australian and New Zealand Journal of Sociology*. But the explicit examples included by Witton to illustrate this practice were deleted due to a threat of legal action from one of the writers mentioned.[4]

• The wives of many male academics contribute to their husbands' research work by literature searches, critical comment and discussion, provision of ideas, writing papers and typing. Probably in only a minority of cases do these contributions receive formal credit.[5]

Robin Morgan has noted the particularly extreme case of Aurelia Plath who in the book *Letters Home* "writes movingly of having done all the reading and note-taking for her husband's book, then having written the first draft, and at last having put the manuscript into 'final form' for the printer. At some point in this process Otto Plath revised a bit and inserted a few notes — including adding his name on the title page as sole author, which is, regrettably, not an uncommon practice. Yet another instance of appropriation of the wife's writing by the husband (in this case, F. Scott Fitzgerald) was explored by Nancy Milford in her absorbing book *Zelda: A Biography*.[6]

Why is academic exploitation so little studied? One reason is that it is not in the interests of the exploiters to expose the phenomenon, and the exploiters are usually in positions of power and able to prevent exposure by the implicit or sometimes explicit threat of bad recommendations or defamation suits. Second, exploitation contradicts the genteel, professional image of academia which is promoted for public consumption; even academics who oppose exploitation are hesitant to disrupt the smooth running of the system. Third, studying exploitation does not nicely fit in any academic discipline or specialisation: no one sees it as their professional duty to investigate it. Finally, some forms of academic exploitation are so common that even the exploited accept them as part of the natural order of things.

Outside academia, not giving credit for the work and ideas of subordinates is certainly widespread. Most letters and speeches of parliamentarians are written by their assistants, and articles and reports ostensibly authored by senior bureaucrats are usually written in part or whole by subordinates. Indeed, wherever power or status differences exist in intellectual work — and these are particularly acute in corporations and state bureaucracies — then exploitation becomes a strong possibility.[7]

If academic exploitation is reasonably common, this has several implications for an understanding of academia.

a. Professional responsibility and standards are not enough to keep academia running on a sound ethical course. But because academics are assumed to behave properly, there are insufficient informal and formal avenues for exposing exploitation and obtaining justice. If such avenues existed, they would act as a deterrent to exploitation.

b. Tenured academics have some protection against exploitation, since they cannot be easily dismissed as a reprisal for opposing it. But tenure provides no protection for those who apparently constitute the bulk of those exploited — students, assistants and wives.

c. Exploitation is clearly tied up with hierarchy in academia. Most of those exploited are in junior positions. Scholarly discourse is supposed to take place on the basis of the quality of scholarly contributions, not on the basis of the formal positions or other characteristics of those who make the contributions. But in practice there are strong political power differences in academia which belie the relevance of the model of egalitarian scholarly interaction.[8] Exploitation is one symptom of these power differences. Exploitation also reinforces power differences, by providing credit for work done to those who already have a relative surplus, and removing credit from those who have the least opportunity of getting ahead.

d. Exploitation, as a symptom of academic hierarchy, is closely tied up with sexism and racism. The top levels of academia are predominantly male, white and middle class. Women and racial minorities, when found in academia, are usually at the lower levels. The hierarchical distribution of power in academia allows sexual and racial discrimination to occur in a covert manner: the work of women and minorities is used to further the careers of those already in privileged positions, thus maintaining and justifying the hierarchy.[9]

e.   The vaunted image of many academics who have a high research output, especially those academics with many subordinates, should not be accepted uncritically. How many famous scholars made their greatest breakthrough on the basis of ideas or work of wives, assistants or students? It is impossible to know. But until more information is available, it would be unwise to uncritically accept publication and citation counts as reliable indicators of research capability.

Acknowledgements

I am deeply indebted to the individuals whose cases are described here and who gave me much advice on properly describing their experiences. In addition, Ann Baker, Clyde Manwell and Cedric Pugh offered useful comments on the text.

References

An edited version of this chapter was published as "Exploiting the academic peons", *Australian Society*, vol. 2, no. 9, pp. 28–9 (1 October 1983).

1.   Clyde Manwell and C. M. Ann Baker, "Honesty in science", *Search*, vol. 12, no. 6, pp. 151–60 (June 1981); Brian Martin, "Plagiarism and responsibility", *Journal of Tertiary Educational Administration*, vol. 6, no. 2, pp. 183–90 (October 1984).

2.   William Broad and Nicholas Wade, *Betrayers of the Truth: Fraud and Deceit in the Halls of Science* (New York: Simon and Schuster, 1982); Manwell and Baker, note 1; Michael J. Mahoney, "Psychology of the scientist: an evaluative review", *Social Studies of Science*, vol. 9, pp. 349–75 (1979).

3.   See for example an anonymous letter in *Drug Intelligence and Clinical Pharmacology*, vol. 11, p. 244 (1977). (I thank Clyde Manwell and Ann Baker for pointing out this reference.)

4.   Ron Witton, "Academics and student supervision: apprenticeship or exploitation?", *Australian and New Zealand Journal of Sociology*, vol. 9, no. 3, pp. 70–3 (1973).

5.   Hanna Papanek, "Men, women, and work: reflections on the two-person career", *American Journal of Sociology*, vol. 78, no. 4, pp. 852–72 (January 1973); Martha R. Fowlkes, *Behind Every Successful Man: Wives of Medicine and Academe* (New York: Columbia University Press, 1980).

6.   Robin Morgan, *Going Too Far: The Personal Chronicle of a Feminist* (New York: Random House, 1977), p. 192.

7.   Charles Goodell, *Political Prisoners in America* (New York: Random House, 1973), p. v (Acknowledgements): "I wish to pay special tribute to Michael Smith, without whom this book would not have taken its form or substance. He faithfully and arduously transmuted into type the ideas evolved from our long discussions, as well as contributing many of his own . . . he literally gave a year of his life to this book." Then why was Michael Smith not at least a co-author? Perhaps because he was "only" a New York attorney, whereas Charles Goodell had become well known as a member of the U.S. Congress.

8.   Brian Martin, "The scientific straightjacket: the power structure of science and the suppression of environmental scholarship", *Ecologist*, vol. 11, no. 1, pp. 33–43 (Jan/Feb 1981).

9.   Revealing case studies of sexism in academia and science include Joan Abramson, *The Invisible Woman: Discrimination in the Academic Profession* (San Francisco: Jossey-Bass, 1975); Anne Sayre, *Rosalind Franklin and DNA* (New York: Norton, 1975).

Professors, Promotions and Politics

A Victory for Academic Freedom

Deborah Smith

Reprinted from the National Times, *18–24 October 1981, p. 47.*

Dr Cedric Pugh, an economics lecturer at the South Australian Institute of Technology, has recently won a long battle for promotion — and academic freedom.

Pugh claims that since 1973 he was repeatedly denied promotion to senior lecturer although he had superior academic qualifications to others promoted before him.

Pugh has been publicly critical of the institute's policies and practices and believes he was passed over for promotion for political reasons.

His promotion to senior lectureship was finally conceded at a meeting of the SAIT Council late last month after Pugh had amassed considerable support from parliamentarians and academics both here and overseas. Many had contacted the institute with references or asking for assurances that Pugh's promotion was being denied on scholastic grounds only.

Most colleges of advanced education in Australia have had to make decisions about job losses, staff tenure and the non-renewal of staff contracts because of funding cutbacks.

They face further staff economies following the imminent amalgamation of some colleges with universities and other colleges.

Pugh claims there is not enough scrutiny of the decisions leading to retrenchment of staff.

"CAEs lack the mechanisms to ensure that these decisions will be carried out using fair and proper procedural standards where academic principles prevail — not who has the power in the institution," Pugh told The National Times.

As a result of Pugh's case the South Australian Shadow Minister for Education, Lynn Arnold, raised the question with the Minister for Education, Harold Allison, and the governing body of SAIT, of the establishment of an independent committee to assess promotions at SAIT and other tertiary institutions.

This type of committee, with nominees from South Australian universities, might "further the cause of academic appointments being decided on scholarship rather than on internal politics that may be involved within the institute concerned", said Arnold.

Other parliamentarians were canvassing the idea of legislative amendments to the Ombudsman Act and the SAIT Act which would write external review of staff decisions into the legislation.

Pugh is concerned that situations similar to his own could be experienced by academics at other CAEs when staff are made redundant following college amalgamations.

"It is clear in my mind that those people who lose their jobs will not always be chosen, perhaps in a majority of cases, on scholastic and academic criteria," said Pugh. "They will be determined by who has the power.

"Unless CAEs begin to take some remedial action now my case remains only a bit of personal history in Australian academia. But if more academics in CAEs become aware of the problem, the institutes can start planning to get their machinery for staff assessment and appeals in order before the real crunch hits."

Pugh's problems at SAIT began in 1972. He was outspoken on urban issues — his specialty is economics — and particularly active in leading opposition to a State Planning Authority development in his local area. He had always been a vocal social critic through the Vietnam era.

In November 1972 the Premier, Don Dunstan, invited Pugh to join the Board of the South Australian Housing Trust, a position he held from 1973–76 and again from 1977–80.

Disagreement later arose about Pugh's appointment and whether the approval of the Director of SAIT had been given. Public appointments were a sensitive issue with the institute administration at the time.

In 1974 Pugh was eligible for promotion to senior lecturer but his application was rejected. Pugh was told that his criticisms of the institute administration were weighed against his candidature. He believes his academic performance, with support from eminent referees, was competitive with others who were promoted.

Since 1970 Pugh has been openly critical of some SAIT administration decisions and of CAEs in general.

He objected to the planning of "The Levels" campus, a section of SAIT built on the periphery of Adelaide. As an academic in urban studies he argued that it was poorly sited to serve students; its buildings had no corporate identity; and access was difficult by public transport.

In in-service conference papers he criticised what he saw as the inequality of the administration's allocation of resources in favour of the technologies above the social sciences, administrative sciences and humanities.

He was also openly critical of the creation of a professoriate at the institute in 1977. "My argument was that scholarship and research at SAIT had been set at a lower priority than was acceptable in the general academic community," said Pugh.

"To have a professoriate you have to have demonstrated to the academic community that scholarly values are important."

Pugh believes CAEs "occupy a sort of a no-man's land between scholarly purposes associated with universities and the definite vocational and cultural purposes of Technical and Further Education establishments.

"In reality the CAEs — especially the older ones — have inherited a staffing and seniority structure where scholarship and research has not been significant in appointments and promotions."

Pugh's promotion battle was long and heated. In 1978 the institute council refused to consider any further recommendations for Pugh's promotion on the grounds that he was uncooperative, obstructive and incompatible within the institute's organisation.

Pugh canvassed support and the institute began to receive correspondence from parliamentarians and Australian and overseas scholars giving reasons why Pugh should be promoted. The British Council for Academic Freedom and Democracy and the Council for Science and Society became involved.

In late 1980 Pugh's promotion, this time to principal lectureship, was denied. He was informed that this was not on academic grounds, but because he had not fulfilled criterion (g) among criteria for promotion.

Criterion (g) refers to the advancement of the institute's objectives.

Later he was officially informed that promotion was denied because he had criticised the institute's policies and administration; the case had generated time-consuming and unproductive correspondence; his contacts with the elected members of council amounted to harassment; and his writing was immoderate.

In April this year three South Australian MPs — Robin Millhouse, Stan Evans and Greg Crafter — asked Education Minister Allison to investigate allegations of discrimination against Pugh.

The council finally conceded Pugh's promotion to senior lecturer on September 22.

Critical to the council's change of mind was their request for, and receipt of, a retraction and apology from Pugh for the statements he had made about some members of the council and review committees, SAIT director Professor Eric Mills told the *National Times*.

"Pugh came to believe he was being penalised by council because he made critical remarks about policy. It wasn't what he said, but the way he said it," Mills said.

"No-one really cared if he criticised The Levels campus, or whatever. But when he was younger and less careful about his wording, he made remarks about a number of people involved on the council and committees which were extremely pejorative."

ACADEMIC CAT AND MOUSE

Clyde Manwell

There can be no cooperation between classes whose real interests are opposed . . . The cat cannot cooperate with the mouse; and if the cat does suggest cooperation and the mouse is fool enough to agree, in a very little while the mouse will be disappearing down the cat's throat. But it is always possible to cooperate so long as it is upon a basis of common interests.

George Orwell[1]

Cat-lovers generally, and students of animal behaviour in particular, are well aware that cats play with their mice. The purpose of play in the behaviour of many carnivores is to practise and to refine the skills of predation. This is especially noticeable when a mother cat brings live mice back to her kittens. However, the mouse is not without some anti-predator "evolutionary strategies". If caught, it may feign death, or at least lie still, thereby depriving the predator of the stimuli needed to maintain vigilance. If the cat is careless, the mouse may suddenly dash off, perhaps successfully evading the cat. Another "evolutionary strategy" is for the prey to shriek when caught. This not only warns relatives (and others) but may also attract enemies of the predator itself, thereby allowing the prey some chance to escape.

Having observed the case of the South Australian Institute of Technology (SAIT) versus Dr Cedric Pugh for ten years, I cannot help but note the aptness of Orwell's quotation and the analogies between animal behaviour and administrator behaviour (no value judgement implied). In essence, this case shows the consequences of class stratification, both within a hierarchical institution (administrators versus staff) and within the larger society (universities versus institutes of technology).

Management, caught by times of tight resources, is trying to reduce costs. Promotion (followed by "incremental creep") adds significantly to the increase in recurring salaries. Individual staff members, however, see an unfair delay in recognition of their contributions; they may observe that others have been promoted faster and on less merit. This is not to say that the opinions on each side need be entirely accurate. Rather, it is that the situation has become visualised as a zero-sum game, each side being put in the position of losing both money and reputation if the other side wins.

Deborah Smith's[2] article suggests that the mouse finally evaded the cat, and even got a bit of cheese. However, there are signs that at least one administrative cat was not pleased. Pugh, having waited nearly ten years for his first promotion (and, in the meantime having written a major book and acquired "an international reputation in urban studies"[3]) requested consideration for promotion to Principal Lecturer. His application, in 1980, was not approved and the 1982 review of that decision was also unfavourable. Pugh criticised the procedures and sought advice from scholars outside SAIT. He received, in 1982, the following letter from the Director, Professor E. W. Mills:

The Council views with grave concern your apparent refusal to accept the procedures prescribed by and decisions of the Council. It considers your correspondence as a refusal to be bound by the terms and conditions of your contract with the Institute and to amount in law to a repudiation of them, such as would entitle the Institute to discharge you from its service.

Whether that view be right or wrong, in the light of your past attitude to promotion and the promotion process within the Institute and your protracted and counter-productive correspondence in relation thereto, the Institute is no longer prepared to employ you unless you unreservedly give in writing the following undertakings by 4.30 p.m. on Friday, 30th April, 1982 and unless in future you adhere to the undertakings so given.

The undertakings required are:

1. That you accept the decision on your application for promotion to the senior academic staff dated 8th June, 1980 and the review of that decision conveyed to you by letter dated 23rd February, 1982.
2. That you will enter no further correspondence or public debate regarding the matter.
3. That you will accept and abide by all recommendations and decisions of those bodies charged with considering future applications for promotion for you.

If you do not give these undertakings within the time specified the Institute will have no option but to terminate your services. Alternatively, if you are not prepared to give the undertakings but wish to tender your resignation from the staff, the Institute would be prepared to accept that resignation without insisting on the strict notice required by Clause 2 of Schedule 1 of the Industrial Agreement between the Council of the Institute and the Academic Staff Association.[4]

Pugh was in a difficult position. He had already received a leave of absence without pay from SAIT to take up a temporary position in the Department of Economics and Statistics at the National University of Singapore, so that he could extend his comparative studies on housing economics to South-East Asia. After an exchange of correspondence involving legal advisers, Pugh gave the required undertakings.

However, before the cat could consume the mouse, larger predators entered the scene. Four members of the South Australian State Parliament wrote a letter, addressed both to the Director and to the SAIT Council:

We have recently seen a copy of a letter written by you to Dr Pugh, a member of the staff of S.A.I.T. We are most concerned at some of its contents, as it appears to us that undertakings are being required of Dr Pugh which are not required of other members of the academic staff of the Institute.

The Institute, as a tertiary institution, surely supports the principle of academic freedom for its academic staff. It should not therefore contemplate censorship or gagging of a staff member, or interfere with his or her right to speak freely on any topic, subject only to the general laws of libel. The suggestion that Dr Pugh will be summarily dismissed unless he agrees to this censorship is surely not compatible with academic freedom.

We are also concerned that summary dismissal on such a pretext, even if legally possible, would have disastrous results for the reputation of the S.A.I.T. Academic institutions throughout Australia and indeed throughout the English-speaking world are likely to react most adversely to an attempted dismissal related to a censorship matter. The damage to the good name of the S.A.I.T. could affect recruitment of staff, recognition of graduates, the standing of the Institute's courses and cause untold damage to the high esteem the Institute currently enjoys.

The undertakings requested of Dr Pugh imply that freedoms he and all academic staff currently have are to be removed from him, and him alone. Such discriminatory action seems unjust and unnecessary to us. We would ask that you reconsider this matter and that the Council of the Institute be informed of this correspondence and of our concern.[5]

I do not know how the Director and the Council responded to these views, but the exchange in Parliament reveals that the then Minister for Education still accepts the Director's allegation: the Minister said, "... the staff member concerned was considered to have been acting in breach of his contract with the council of the Institute".[6] It is not explained how Pugh's actions breached his contract and, to my knowledge, the parliamentarians have not pursued the issue further. Nor can I understand how Pugh was supposed to have been "acting in breach of his contract". Why did the administration of SAIT react so strongly?

A clue lies in the nature of the issue: Pugh has questioned the procedures used in deciding upon promotions, not only in his own case but earlier, when in 1977 the SAIT administration decided to confer the title of professor on some of its senior staff. Pugh supported the basic idea, of building up SAIT by offering highly qualified applicants Chairs, but he argued: "... if the Institute would prefer the normal criteria for professorial positions, then the membership arrangements for the selection committee should provide for relevant external membership. The procedures should also include provisions for independent appeal and rigour in following academic principle".[7]

The basic idea, of professorial positions in Australian institutes of technology, is certainly commendable. Australian institutes of technology have been treated as second-class cousins to the universities.[8] Had Pugh's criticisms been taken seriously, there would have been less strident objection from the universities about the SAIT's professoriate.

There is also, as Orwell understood so well, the matter of class. This is not just the two classes of Marxist writers, but the subtleties of multiple stratification. While the SAIT Council has some very capable individuals in its ranks, most of the local establishment members (for example three Supreme Court justices) are on the Council of the University of Adelaide. SAIT and other Australian institutes of technology have not been able to build themselves up like their equivalents in the USA, UK, Netherlands, France, West Germany or Switzerland. Massachusetts Institute of Technology rivals Harvard; "Cal-Tech" rivals UCLA.

Besides this "underdog" position (quite unfair in a number of respects), there has been a related point of conflict with the federal government. The poorer status of Australian institutes of technology became enforced by the 1978 ruling of the Academic Salaries Tribunal. This federal body, which oversees all higher education, set separate salary scales for universities and institutes of technology. SAIT was alleged later to have negotiated a "sweetheart" contract with its Staff Association in the Industrial Court of South Australia so that it paid slightly higher salaries than the level set by the (federal) Academic Salaries Tribunal.[9] In 1984 Senator Susan Ryan claimed that SAIT had overpaid its academics by $175,000, and that she was taking steps to recover that money.

All this "class warfare" on salaries and titles has resulted in considerable erosion of staff morale within SAIT. The situation has pitted universities against institutes of technology, senior staff against junior staff, and administrators against academics.

Thus, it may well be that, despite the good sense and moderation of Pugh's criticisms of SAIT's administration, the issues of professorial status and the alleged overpayment of staff have sensitised administrators at the Institute. Perhaps it is easier for them to displace their aggression on Pugh than to react appropriately to the merit of his criticisms and to put a better case to the federal government to end their second-class status.

In other words, returning to the quote from George Orwell, "it is always possible to cooperate so long as it is upon a basis of common interests", let me look constructively at the situation. The fragmented and demoralised state of higher education in Australia today benefits no one, neither the staff and students, on the one hand, nor the public at large, on the other. Barry Jones, in his book *Sleepers Wake!*[10], made a compelling case for the necessity for Australia to catch up in technology. As Minister for Science and Technology in the federal government, Jones has pressed his case as well as he can — but the trouble is that he lacks help from the leaders representing higher education. In the last federal budget, both science and higher education did relatively poorly. Jones has become so demoralised by the "wimpish lobbying" from the academic and scientific communities, and the consequent poor slice of the budget, that he has considered resigning his ministerial post.[11]

The case of SAIT versus Pugh illustrates well the divisiveness of the issues of rank and promotion. I believe that only quite radical solutions will solve such problems. All systems of higher education should have similar systems of rank, if rank is really needed at all. For many years some American universities have run fairly automatic promotion systems, with mandatory periods in each rank, for example, the University of California, by a number of criteria considered the best university in the United States. Individuals who fail to meet certain minimal standards are not given tenure, nor are they promoted to higher ranks — but that is rather unusual.

While it is recognised that the institutes of technology have a somewhat different purpose, it is also recognised that times are changing. The relationship of knowledge to commerce has been transformed as a result of the Second Industrial (or Information) Revolution. Discoveries, even in seemingly *pure* fields, are *applied* so much more quickly than occurred when the separate institutes of technology and universities were created. The lag-times between invention and commercialisation have also correspondingly shrunk. Thus, the apartheid of institutions of higher education is no longer defensible. Furthermore, research — and social criticism — are responsibilities to be shared throughout higher education.

Independent-minded teachers and researchers, like Pugh, are a valuable commodity which SAIT should treasure. A good critic is a good friend, even if a bit uncomfortable at times.

There have been some changes in the composition of the SAIT Council, and a new Director will be in residence soon. The opportunity is there for the cats and the mice to cooperate and to share the cream and the cheese.

References

1. George Orwell, *The Road to Wigan Pier* (Harmondsworth, Middlesex: Penguin Books, 1962 printing, originally published in 1937), p. 200.

2. Deborah Smith, "A Victory for Academic Freedom", *National Times*, 18–24 October 1981, p. 47. Reprinted on pp. 63–65.

3. Andrew Symon, "Letter threat to dismiss lecturer", Adelaide *Advertiser*, 15 June 1982, p. 11.

4. Letter from E. W. Mills (Director of SAIT) to Cedric Pugh, dated 20 April 1982, two-page document. All of the body of the letter is quoted except the first (introductory) paragraph.

5. Letter from Anne Levy, Lynn Arnold, Greg Crafter and Peter Duncan to the Director and Council of SAIT, dated 27 April 1982. Two typing errors have been corrected.

6. M. Allison, in *Parliamentary Debates (South Australia)*, 10 August 1982, p. 474.

7. Cedric Pugh, "Guide to the Institute: an excursion into off limits territory", *Ego* (SAIT newspaper), 24 March 1978, pp. 6–7.

8. Colin Field, "Time to scrap archaic approach to role of institutes of technology", the *Australian*, 27 June 1984, p. 11.

9. Helen Trinca, "Ryan set to trim waistlines of the 'fat cats' of academe", the *Australian*, 7 March 1984, p. 11; Jane Dargaville and Helen Trinca, "Universities face $80,000 slug for overpaying senior staff", the *Australian*, 2 March 1984, p. 2.

10. Barry Jones, *Sleepers, Wake! Technology and the Future of Work* (Oxford University Press, 1982).

11. Jane Ford, "Angry Jones may quit over budget cuts", the *Australian*, 24 August 1984, p. 2. After the 1984 election, Barry Jones lost the "Technology" part of his portfolio.

Postscript by Brian Martin

On 2 September 1984 I sent a copy of the two contributions in this chapter to the South Australian Institute of Technology inviting a response from someone representing SAIT, or anyone else appropriate, to be included in this book. As of February 1985 I had received no reply.

THE "FIGHT FOR THE FORESTS" AFFAIR

Richard Routley and Val Plumwood

Title and Contents

The book *The Fight for the Forests* (first edition 1973, 290 pages) looked at the situation of Australian forests, especially proposed and progressing industrial development of the forests such as in pine and woodchip schemes; it discussed economic, ecological and social aspects of these schemes and of the planning which underlay and justified them, as well as associated issues in the foundations of economics and environmental decision-making.

Authors

The book's authors were Richard Routley and Val Routley (now Plumwood). Richard Routley has been since 1971 Senior Fellow in the Department of Philosophy, Research School of Social Sciences (RSSS), Australian National University; the position is tenured with a five-year bar, at that time passed more or less automatically. Val Plumwood is the author of a number of published papers on philosophy and environmental subjects.

Qualifications to Write the Book

These were of a reasonable generalist kind. As philosophers we were well acquainted with the theory of scientific methodology, probability and decision theory; as environmentalists and keen amateur naturalists we had a reasonable general knowledge of the biological and ecological aspects involved. The foundations of economics is also an area of academic research and interest. The local forestry literature is neither very copious nor very specialised, so that it is fairly easy to become more or less completely acquainted with it. Most of it is fairly easily understood by people without professional forestry training. *The Fight for the Forests* laid major emphasis on reasoning, on methodological considerations in planning and prediction, and on bringing out underlying or hidden assumptions — especially value assumptions — in these areas. This is an area in which we were well qualified to write. Given the very large range of areas involved in discussing forestry as a social phenomenon, ranging from scientific methodology and decision theory through sociology, social science, economics and many areas of biology and ecology, our own special areas of academic interest and in-depth knowledge were at least as generally relevant to the issues concerned as most of those involved in a conventional forestry training. Care was taken to provide full references to background work in cases where specialist areas of knowledge were involved, so that no one had to rely simply on our authority for claims made. The book attempted then to present an integrated picture of the forestry situation in Australia on the basis of detailed knowledge of some areas relevant to the field, as the work of foresters themselves often does*, and much of it consisted of what is now known as "applied philosophy".

Character of Book

The Fight for the Forests was not a very radical book politically but apparently offended mainly because it attacked cherished programs and because of its strong emphasis on the control of forests by the large forest industries, the close connections of these industries with state forest services, who were allegedly employed in the public interest, and the role of professional foresters in promoting ecologically destructive forestry developments which were in the interests of industry. At that time the forestry profession was a sacred cow, virtually beyond criticism, and the book, rather predictably, was the object of intense hostility from professional foresters (including academic foresters). Its main specific contentions, concerning the excessive nature of the pine program and overestimation in planning for this program, the destructive environmental effects and, for the public, the uneconomic nature of pine and woodchip schemes in public forests, were at the time controversial but have been subsequently vindicated by events and by a number of later studies by others. The book tended to receive unfavourable reviews from foresters, but received many favourable, often highly favourable, reviews from non-foresters.

What Happened

Funds for printing the book were obtained, more or less by chance, from the RSSS, which at that time had a substantial end-of-triennium surplus, without going through any refereeing system After final typing for photo-offset printing was completed, and just a few weeks before the book was due to go to the printer, professional foresters and sympathisers within the Australian National University appear to have got wind of its likely contents. (An article on pines published the previous year, in *Australian Quarterly* 1972, had a substantial impact** and provided a good idea of the book's general stance.) The *then* Vice-Chancellor, Professor R. M. Williams, suggested *that printing should not proceed unless the book was given to the head of the Forestry School at the ANU, to be revised in accordance with his comments.* (Given the attitudes, beliefs, and connections of professionals in general and this Head of Department in particular, this would almost certainly have crippled or destroyed the book.) Fortunately, the Acting-Director of RSSS at the time was Professor G. Sawer, who resisted this suggestion, and was also kind enough to read through the manuscript to check on liability to legal action. (In the fuss preceding publication it had been suggested also that publication should not proceed because of possible liability to such legal action). He suggested a few minor changes of a few lines at one or two points to safeguard against this.

* These points should help to dispel the professionalist myth, propagated commonly by foresters, that only people with professional forestry training are qualified to write about the forests. Often such foresters also advocate a closed decision-making system in which they, as the "relevant professionals", have sole rights of decision. However, forestry issues raise many questions of social values which are of general concern and should be widely discussed. As well, as noted, a very wide range of discipline areas are involved, and some of the most important for the fate of the forests lie right outside conventional forestry training. For example, the major and most influential papers underlying the original planning for the pine program in the late 1960s (papers which were heavily criticised in our work) were the product of a botanist, Dr M. R. Jacobs, although they were primarily concerned with questions of planning and decision. But when considering these questions (e.g. the popular planning methodology of overestimating future demand and population to "play safe"), it is more helpful to understand, say, methodology and decision theory than it is to understand, say, the patterns of seeding of various eucalypts. No one complained about Dr Jacobs going outside his "area of competence", nor was his work suppressed or subjected to censorship on this ground, because he was covered by the professional umbrella. There are many similar cases, which reveal the arbitrariness with which field restrictions are commonly applied to restrict inquiry.

** After the article appeared there was, for the first time, parliamentary questioning of the pine program, with some strong speeches against it, and an increasingly critical attitude was taken in the press.

Publication proceeded. The first edition of the book in 1973 sold out within a few months, and two further editions, revised and updated (1974, 1975), also sold out shortly after printing, making it one of the best selling books ever distributed by ANU Press.

But harassment from irate professionals and their sympathisers within the University was not over. We were left in no doubt that the book had been "an embarrassment to the University". In 1974 the author with library rights was prevented on order from the Acting Head of the Forestry School, Professor Carron, from using the Forestry School Library. As the library contains most forestry publications and material, the order constituted a direct attempt to block further work. The ban was later overturned as a result of intervention from the Biological Sciences Library Committee.

Later, RSSS, apparently in response to criticism of certain school publications, set up a committee to review publications procedure. Shortly afterwards we were informed that no funding would be available for a further edition of the book or for a reprint of the book. No reasons were given. We were not informed that the book was the subject of a review (as there were at that time no proposals by us for a further edition). We were given no opportunity to nominate referees, to supply relevant information, or to influence the outcome of the review in any way. Subsequently the school adopted a different procedural system in which the departments and authors concerned nominate suitable referees. There is little doubt that, had we been given the opportunity to follow the regular system, suitable referees could have been found to provide favourable reports. Meanwhile, orders for the now out-of-print book continue to arrive, and it continues to be favourably reviewed and mentioned, both in Australia and overseas. There is little doubt that a further edition or reprint could have been sold.

General Comments

The situation in the forestry profession showed, at least at the time we were working in the area, a very high degree of suppression and professional cohesiveness, and an exceptional degree of conformity and absence of critical voices. This probably is so pronounced because of the great control and influence exerted by a highly restricted body of employers, namely, a few large forest industries and the state forest services. For the same reasons, perhaps, there was a high degree of secrecy and control of information.

We encountered many severe cases of suppression in the forestry profession (applying in academic, research, bureaucratic and state forest service areas) and in related biological areas. This included action by state forest services to terminate the research projects (in state forests) of those who made public statements unfavourable to them, or who supplied information or were associated with those who did, and many other adverse effects on the careers or prospects of potentially critical professionals. The influence of state forest services extended to within the ANU. Suppression was so regular and pronounced that we believe it is probably true that no one inside the profession or discipline could have, at that time, written a book similar to *The Fight for the Forests*. Such criticism could only appear where it slipped past the usual professional control and suppression mechanisms, as our book did.

The general suppression mechanism illustrated by this case, then, appears to be: a combination of indoctrination and intimidation, plus well-developed professional loyalty, ensures that significant criticism does not originate from *inside* the profession or discipline itself, or does so only in a rare, muted and easily overlooked form; at the same time the professionalism mystique and the dicipline system is invoked, as it was in our case, to ensure that no one *outside* the profession can make such criticism *in a way which needs to be treated seriously* (for example through publication in a university series), and even to ensure that such criticism by potentially dangerous outsiders is silenced altogether. The fragmentation of knowledge, like the fragmentation of work, is thus used as a method of control. It's a neat system, which nicely protects a particular set of doctrines and interests.

Postscript by Brian Martin

On 26 July 1983 I sent a copy of this chapter to the Australian National University inviting a response from someone representing the University, or anyone else appropriate, to be included in this book. On 15 August the Secretary of the ANU replied saying that the University itself did not wish to comment, but that a copy of the chapter had been sent to Professor Griffin, Head of the Department of Forestry, who had given a copy to Dr Carron, and that it was likely that Dr Carron would respond. On 9 September I wrote to Dr Carron inviting a response to be included in this book. As of February 1985 I had received no reply.

FOR THE FREEDOM TO COMMENT BY SCIENTISTS

P. H. Springell

Reprinted from Arena, *no. 44/45, 1976, pp. 28–33.*

The proportion of Australian research and development (R&D) effort by government agencies (53 per cent) is second only to the Soviet Union, and other communist-bloc countries.[1] Of the rest, 37 per cent of performance is derived from industry, and only 10 per cent from universities, and other tertiary institutions. By contrast, over one quarter of Canadian R&D is associated with places of higher learning, while a fifth of American R&D comes from this source.

Traditionally academics in tertiary institutions have a much greater degree of freedom than their industry or public servant counterparts. Scientific comment on controversial issues is therefore severely restricted in Australia, compared to most other industrialized western countries. Speaking out of turn could lead to discrimination when it comes to promotion, or transfer, or at the worst to dismissal and difficulty in securing another job elsewhere.

The announcement by the then Prime Minister Whitlam on 3 June, 1974 that public servants were free to publicly criticize their own departments, therefore seemed a step in the right direction. Whitlam could not guarantee that an outspoken public servant would avoid subtle victimization later, but he was able to eliminate the more blatant reprisals in the form of instant dismissal or demotion. Predictably, there have been few major revelations from conscience-stricken public servants.

There are of course plenty of scientists, and others, in the public service who know on which side their bread is buttered. They tell unashamedly to Ministers what they want to hear, and they withhold adverse comment on what their political masters want to remain ignorant about.[2] Such activities can earn one meteoric promotion, if applied at the right time and place. There is also the so-called "silent majority", who by their silence condone anti-social government activities, and [it was] presumably of these that Abraham Lincoln so aptly said: "To sin by silence when they should protest, makes cowards of men".

Of course I was aware of the lack of safeguards when I first publicly criticized CSIRO for its lack of involvement in environmental research.[3] At that time I had been prevented from publishing two papers on environmental topics[4,5] through the Organization. While CSIRO claimed that they had no objection to my publishing privately, such papers are generally less readily acceptable to scientific journals, while the readership also regards them with some suspicion, particularly if the author's place of work is well known.

It is of interest that the then Science Minister, Mr Morrison, was making statements to the effect that CSIRO should get more involved in the environment.[6, 7] It appeared therefore, that by discouraging me, CSIRO was in fact defying the Minister.

I had taken my fight about the first paper[4] only as far as my Divisional Chief, but I confronted CSIRO Chairman, Dr Jerry (now Sir Robert) Price with the second one.[5] Subsequently, I wrote a third paper[8], which I eventually ended up bringing to Morrison's attention. I pointed out that, in view of his earlier remarks[6, 7], he should overrule CSIRO. Needless to say, he did no such thing[9].

In the meantime, the Labor Government set up the Royal Commission into Australian Government Administration, and this turned out to be an ideal opportunity to air my grievances with CSIRO.[10] Our submission got good publicity[11], which did little to further endear me to the Organization. The contents of the submission were pre-circulated, and thus well known to anyone who was interested enough to read it.

The Industries Assistance Commission (IAC) was holding an Inquiry into Financing Rural Research shortly afterwards, and it was suggested to me by the IAC secretary[12] that I give evidence there as well. I sought CSIRO's permission to prepare a submission in their time in view of Morrison's earlier statement[13] to the effect that it was the duty of scientists to contribute. This request was predictably turned down by CSIRO[14], and belatedly also by the Minister[15], but the evidence was presented just the same.[16]

The submission, which was also pre-circulated, contained criticism of CSIRO's approach to agricultural research, and as such, caused CSIRO further irritation.

The situation was evidently also aggravated by a series of disagreements with my former chief. He did not like my constructive criticism of the aim of the Laboratory in Rockhampton[17], nor did he take kindly to my successfully publishing material[4, 5, 8] he had dismissed out of hand. Furthermore, I had previously expressed objection to the implicit support he gave as Committee member over the years to the continuation of French nuclear tests in the atmosphere.[18] Finally, he was obviously embarrassed[19], when I exposed[20] the fact that he himself had published a paper totally unrelated to his CSIRO duties under the Organization's auspices[21], while objecting to my publishing on environmental topics with CSIRO's blessing. Predictably, there was to be no reprimand[22], thus establishing that rank and file scientists operate under a different set of rules from chiefs.

CSIRO had by this time decided to get rid of me. When attempts failed to dismiss me on grounds of inefficiency[23], because my publications record was better than that of most of my colleagues, it was decided to try and have me transferred to Melbourne.[24]

The Organization went as far as to admit that my work at Rockhampton was quite satisfactory.[24] I therefore concluded that the move was politically, rather than scientifically motivated, and I refused to go.[25, 26]

Despite initial opposition[27], long-service of 10 weeks was granted[28], before the recommendation for dismissal[29] was eventually received. I immediately appealed against the recommendation.

The hearing of the Committee of Inquiry in Canberra was a complete farce. CSIRO should have sought Ministerial approval for the transfer, because my salary was above the level specified by the Science and Industry Research Act. The then Minister (Clyde Cameron) had evidently been advised rather than asked.[30] My case was widely reported throughout the country[31], and this resulted in bad publicity for the Organization.

Initially one might have suspected that this could have been an easy out for the Organization, because my position was very strong. Witnesses at Royal Commissions are protected by Section 6N of the Royal Commissions Act 1902–1973 against victimization. The onus rests with the employer to prove that an employee witness claiming immunity was not being victimized. If prejudicial actions against an employee cannot be disproved, this then constitutes an indictable offence carrying a penalty of $1000, or imprisonment for one year. CSIRO did decide to try and transfer me again.[32] It must have been a difficult decision, since the Executive would obviously be most anxious to avoid further bad publicity, particularly while an Inquiry was being held into CSIRO.[33]

Since the previous CSIRO case against me largely rested on an exchange of letters between the Secretariat and me, my new tactic was to minimize the volume of correspondence, and restrict myself to one-sentence replies. However, when a new job eventuated, I decided to take it, and hand in my resignation to CSIRO.

In the meantime, my attention had been drawn to an initiative of the US National Academy of Sciences designed to guarantee the freedom of Inquiry and Expression for scientists, both at home, and abroad.[34] The Academy drew up a five-point declaration, which it asks scientists everywhere to sign, and remit to Washington. I asked the CSIRO Chairman, and members of the Executive to sign the document.[35] It will be interesting to see what they will do. If the document is not signed, then this would reflect badly on CSIRO, and it would invite curtailment, or even termination of combined US–Australian research projects.[34] In absence of a reply[36], I had to get a question asked in Parliament[37] to ascertain the response. The final decision will be publicized by me in the right quarters.

Throughout my 23 years with the Organization, I have belonged to the CSIRO Officers' Association, indeed I served on the Victorian Committee for a year in the 50s. From the start, the Association's reaction ranged from cool and cautious[38], to outright hostile[39], particularly from the more distant south. My strongest support came from the State Branch in Brisbane, but my own colleagues in Rockhampton felt themselves threatened. They resented the disturbance being created in a backwater to which they had hoped to retire peacefully.

I have strong reasons to suspect that certain senior people in the CSIROOA were unwilling to rock the boat on my behalf for fear of tarnishing their own image and thus adversely affecting their own chances of advancement within CSIRO. The Association was obviously interested in the outcome of my battles, since precedents were being set, which would ultimately affect other members. However initial involvement at the official level had been disappointing, and minimal. However, nothing begets success more than success. The union recently promised to pay costs for any legal representation I might have sought at a future Inquiry into my dismissal. Presumably they will be relieved to know that the offer will not now be taken up because of my resignation.

The CSIROOA seems to be out of touch with its membership, largely because of the latter's apathy. The body actually made a submission of its own to the Royal Commission into Australian Government Administration, but it failed to consult members like me, who might have been interested in contributing.

I feel in this connection that there is a growing body of members who reject the union's preoccupation with salary-related matters, and who would prefer the Association to concern itself more with such things as directing CSIRO's work to socially and environmentally more beneficial purposes.[40] For this reason, I feel also that the CSIROOA should fight for the right of members to speak up on issues of public interest, and it should have shown much more concern when the new Minister deprived staff of a say in the running of CSIRO by suspending the election of an employee onto the Executive.[41]

References

1. Johnson, R. (1974). Down under science policy. *New Scientist* 61 (881): 140.

2. Springell, P. H. (1973). Social irresponsibility of scientists. *Search* 4 (10): 409.

3. Henningham, J. (1974). CSIRO 'stifling research into environment'. The *Australian*, 7 Aug.

4. Springell, P. H. and Seifert, G. W. (1974). Australian beef production to the year 2000 in the world context. *Proceedings of the Australian Society of Animal Production 10:* 351.

5. Springell, P. H. and Blake, J. D. (1975). Water hyacinth problems in the Fitzroy Region of Central Queensland. *Hyacinth Control Journal 13: 3.*

6. Morrison, W. L. (1973). CSIRO and the National Science effort. CSIRO Officers' Association Bulletin No. 147, June, p. 7.

7. Anon. (1974). Charter may be changed. *Coresearch* No. 180, May, p. 4.

8. Springell, P. H. (1975). Dangers of leaded petrol. *Medical Journal of Australia I:* 220.

9. Morrison, W. L. (1975). Letter to Dr. P. H. Springell, 11 Feb.

10. Hundloe, T., Dow, G. and Springell, P. H. (1974). Submission to the Royal Commission into Australian Government Administration. Presented in Brisbane, 3 Feb. 1975.

11. Anon. (1975). CSIRO rule 'withholding information'. The *Australian,* 4 Feb.

12. Davey, A. E. S. (1975). Letter to Dr. P. H. Springell, 18 Feb.

13. Morrison, W. L. (1974). Press release: "Minister at CSIRO Conference", 9 Oct.

14. Wilson, L. G. (1975). Letter to Dr. P. H. Springell, 3 March.

15. Morrison, W. L. (1975). Letter to Dr. P. H. Springell, 20 May.

16. Springell, P. H. (1975). Submission to the Industries Assistance Commission Inquiry into Funding Rural Research. Presented in Brisbane 7 Aug.

17. Springell, P. H. (1973). Some thoughts on the future role of the CSIRO in Rockhampton. Internal memorandum, 23 Jan. Quoted in ref. 10, p. 25.

18. National Radiation Advisory Committee (1972 and earlier). Biological aspects of fallout in Australia from French nuclear weapons explosions in the Pacific.

19. Rendel, J. M. (1975). Letter to Dr. P. H. Springell, 28 Oct.

20. Springell, P. H. (1975). Letter to Dr. J. R. Price, 25 Oct.

21. Rendel, J. M. (1961). Consciousness. *Australian Scientist* April, p. 149.

22. Wilson, L. G. (1975). Letter to Dr. P. H. Springell, 2 Dec.

23. Rendel, J. M. (1974). Letter to Dr. P. H. Springell, 6 Nov.

24. Wilson, L. G. (1975). Letter to Dr. P. H. Springell, 2 Sept.

25. Springell, P. H. (1975). Letter to Mr. L. G. Wilson, 17 Sept.

26. Springell, P. H. (1975). Letter to Mr. L. G. Wilson, 13 Dec.

27. Wilson, L. G. (1976). Telegram to Dr. P. H. Springell, 20 Feb.

28. Wilson, L. G. (1976). Telegram to Dr. P. H. Springell, 27 Feb.

29. Scott, T. W. (1976). Notice of charge and recommendation for dismissal, 26 Feb.

30. Edmunds, K. S., Muncey, R. W. R. and Thornton, R. F. (1976). Appeal against a recommendation of dismissal from the service of CSIRO, 27 July.

31. Anon. (1976). CSIRO scientist wins appeal on sacking. The *Australian,* 28 July.

32. Coombe, J. (1976). Letter to Dr. P. H. Springell, 24 Aug.

33. Fraser, M. (1976). Ministerial Statement: Independent Inquiry into CSIRO. *Hansard* Representatives 5 Oct., p. 1463.

34. Norman, C. (1976). Human rights guidelines adopted. *Nature, London 261* (5556): 89.

35. Springell, P. H. (1976). Letter to Sir Robert Price, 14 Sept.

36. Springell, P. H. (1976). Reply-paid Telegram to Sir Robert Price, 15 Oct.

37. Colston, M. (1976). Question without notice: United States National Academy of Sciences Statement *Hansard* Senate 19 Oct., p. 1210.

38. Radoslovich, E. W. (1976). Letter to Dr. P. H. Springell, 31 May.

39. Coogan, C. K. (1975). Letter to the *Australian*, 14 Feb.

40. Springell, P. H. (1976). Submission to the Inquiry into CSIRO, Nov.

41. CSIRO (1976). Policy circular 76/2, 6 Jan.

Postscript by Brian Martin

On 29 September 1980 I gave a talk to the National Science Forum in which I mentioned a number of suppression cases, including the CSIRO–Springell case. On 3 October, K. J. Thrift, Secretary (Personnel) of CSIRO, wrote to me asking to see details of the evidence behind my claims about what had happened to Dr Springell. In my reply of 13 October I cited Peter Springell's article from *Arena* which has been reprinted here, and noted that to my knowledge there had been no public response to his highly documented article. I also wrote: "If you have any information relevant to the case, I would be pleased to know about it." I received no reply to my letter.

Science Policy under the Whip

Brian Martin

In academia, the standard myth is that advancement is directly related to scholarly performance. Unfortunately performance and position are all too often unconnected. But the myth persists because it is useful in legitimating the power and privilege of those in high places.

There are all sorts of ways in which people can fall from grace on the path to academic success, such as lacking a patron or working in an unfashionable area. For the discussion here the following three factors are relevant:

1. Being a highly talented person. Although brilliance, hard work and scholarly output should enable a person to get ahead in academia, sometimes the opposite occurs. Highly talented and high performance individuals may be resented precisely because they are so good. If those already in positions of power are mediocre in scholarship, then they may be threatened by a talented person. From the point of view of the mediocrities, opposition to high-fliers may be rationalised by perceiving them as arrogant, conceited and overrated. There is a tradition of this in Australia, known colloquially as "cutting down tall poppies".

Opposition to talented people may also come from other talented people who want all the power and glory for themselves. Some eminent scholars prefer sycophants to potential challengers. Safe mediocrities are chosen for positions, given grants, and invited into coteries of the powerful.

Opposition to talented people must be rationalised on some other grounds than their talent, of course. This is often done by denigrating the value of their teaching or research, for example by disdaining the importance, rigour or difficulty of their area of specialisation. Another rationalisation is that the talented person has an "unacceptable personality", an allegation that is often so subjective that it is impossible to refute.

2. Obtaining publicity. Academics who gain publicity for their work are often suspect, especially when they are not in official positions of eminence. When intellectual dissidents gain publicity, this is a direct threat to the power of academic elites. But even those who gain publicity for quite normal academic pursuits may face antagonism: somehow it is not the scholarly thing to be well known outside one's narrow speciality. The main reason for this is that public attention and acclaim is a form of success that is not readily under the control of academic elites, and therefore is distrusted by them.

Another reason for antagonism to those who gain publicity is envy and jealousy. Success in the eyes of others is a valued commodity in academia, and those who achieve high visibility may be resented because of this. In my opinion, one reason why Harry Messel, Head of the School of Physics at Sydney University and for many years the academic best known to the Australian public, has been looked down upon by some academics is because of his success in gaining publicity.

3.   Being a woman. Discrimination against women is deeply entrenched in academia.[1] For many years, women aspiring to be academics were not treated seriously: they and their contributions were not seen to provide any status for a department or discipline. With the rise of the second wave of the feminist movement since the 1960s and the increased assertiveness of many women, the more blatant forms of discrimination have become harder to sustain, though they still occur. It still remains widely true that women, to obtain jobs and recognition on the basis of their scholarship, must be twice as good as male competitors.

One of the most difficult problems faced by women is common social expectations, or rather lack of expectations. Women are not expected to be in desperate need of a job, to deserve the most rapid promotions, or to gain the best opportunities. Women are not expected to be as aggressive as men in personal style, for example in academic debate, and when they are this is seen as objectionable and an affront.

Put together these three factors, and a potent combination results: a highly talented woman gaining lots of publicity for her efforts, thereby upstaging academic elites. That is what the case of Ann Moyal is about. But before describing the case, some of the context is worth describing: Griffith University and science policy.

Griffith University in Brisbane was one of several universities set up in the mid-1970s in the last years of the Australian boom in higher education. Like others of its type, such as Murdoch and Deakin Universities, Griffith was established to be different from the usual university divided into disparate disciplines. Its organisation was based around schools, whole areas of intellectual discourse combining several disciplines in which scholarly interaction was to be encouraged. Many recently established universities, drawing on the University of Sussex model, have aimed at problem-oriented, multi-disciplinary education and research. But the realities have seldom lived up to the plans.

Many academics prefer working in narrow disciplines because this provides a safe power base. Only the other "experts" in the discipline, it is alleged, are able to judge research and teaching in the area. This protects academics, especially elite academics, from outside scrutiny. La Trobe University, in Melbourne, established with a non-disciplinary structure, soon reverted to the traditional form as the professors built up disciplinary empires. Significantly, it was staff with previous academic experience who promoted this process, whereas staff drawn from government and industry were more satisfied with the non-disciplinary structure.[2]

At Griffith, the pattern was different from this.[3] The University had been established with a decision-making procedure based largely on committees rather than the usual structure with professors in positions of dominance. At Griffith, much more power than usual was given to the Vice-Chancellor and to the heads of the schools of which the university was composed. As one of the last new universities before the government funding squeeze began, Griffith has never reached its planned size. This has meant that there is insufficient size for professors or others in key positions to build up positions of power in particular subject areas. In effect, the committee system plus the small size of the University has meant that more power than usual has flowed to the Vice-Chancellor and a few other key people at the top.

One of the innovations at Griffith was the Science Policy Research Centre. Science policy[4] is a relatively new area for academic study. Its importance expanded greatly after the Second World War, during which heavy government funding of, and involvement with, scientific research developed. Nuclear weapons, nuclear power, space programs, defence, agricultural research, industrial research and development: in these and many other areas science was increasingly interlinked with political and economic policy-making. Science policy is the study of such interactions. Sometimes science policy is seen to be "policy for science", namely allocating monies and resources to various branches of science. Another perspective is "science for policy", namely formulating general social goals and then mobilising scientific resources to achieve these goals. "Policy for science" assumes that scientists and especially scientific elites are best equipped to decide the best directions for scientific research, whereas "science for policy" puts government in this role.

Ann Moyal was and is an eminent science policy researcher. She received a First Class Honours B.A. in history at Sydney University, and then worked at the Royal Institute of International Affairs in London, at the South Pacific Commission, as a research assistant to Lord Beaverbrook, and in the early 1960s jointly as Research Fellow in history at the Australian National University and Research Associate of the Australian Academy of Science studying the history of Australian science. In 1972 she became a senior lecturer in the School of Humanities and Social Sciences at the New South Wales Institute of Technology. She taught in the fields of science and government, technology and society and the history of technology. She was known as a researcher of formidable critical abilities, as illustrated by her penetrating study of the Australian Atomic Energy Commission.[5] She was author of the landmark study *Scientists in Nineteenth Century Australia*[6] and in 1976 was a visiting fellow at the University of Sussex, in the Department of History of Science and the Science Policy Research Unit. Beginning in 1973 she received Australian Research Grant Committee grants on science and technology policy in Australia. Her reputation as a historian of Australian science and as a science policy analyst was recognised overseas and she became the key reviewer on these topics of international science policy for the prestigious United States journal *Science*.

Of course, many scholars can boast an impressive sounding background of degrees, jobs and publications. Ann Moyal's career has been more than this. In essence, she has been a pioneer in two fields of study: the history of science in Australia, and Australian science policy.

The Science Policy Research Centre (SPRC) at Griffith had been founded in December 1975 by a recent arrival from Manchester University, Jarlath Ronayne. But he left to become a professor at the University of NSW. Ann Moyal applied for the vacated position. There was some stiff competition for the post. In December 1976 Ann Moyal was offered the post of Director of the SPRC in Griffith's School of Science, and Senior Lecturer in the School. She took up the position in February 1977.

Officially the job entailed 70 per cent teaching and 30 per cent Centre activities, but it became clear that this was unrealistic. When she took up the post, nothing had been done about research or policy for the SPRC: there were no records or correspondence. Ann Moyal saw her foremost job as establishing the activities and reputation of the SPRC, especially since its existence was to be reviewed at the end of 1979, and because it lacked much overt support from the traditional discipline-oriented scientists in the School of Science.

To accomplish this aim, she proceeded on a punishing round of activities to establish a viable research centre in addition to teaching undergraduate courses in science and society and in science policy, supervising honours students and heading the masters degree course in science, technology and society. To promote the SPRC, she made numerous grant applications to funding bodies, made overtures to Commonwealth government departments and other bodies, developed contacts with a variety of relevant Commonwealth ministers and parliamentarians, published papers, invited distinguished Australian and international visitors to give papers at the SPRC, and launched the SPRC Occasional Papers Series.

There can be no doubt that Moyal was a conspicuous person of talent who gained widespread publicity. She was active in giving invited talks on science policy, budgetary issues and other topics on the Science Show on the ABC, and gave an ABC talk on technological change in late 1978 on the program "Encounter". She also appeared on the Queensland ABC and commercial radio stations. During 1978 she became a member of the Science Advisory Committee of the ABC. Minutes of an SPRC Management Committee in July 1978 noted that "a major part of media coverage of Griffith University for 1977 had originated from the Science Policy Research Centre".[7]

The attention bestowed on Ann Moyal and the SPRC may have left senior academics at Griffith feeling upstaged. During 1977, the Vice-Chancellor of the University of Queensland, Sir Zelman Cowan, held a special lunch party for Mrs Moyal, to which he invited his science deans and major science professors. But at Griffith no such welcome was made. In 1978 Senator John Button, then Shadow Minister for Education and Science, made a weekend visit to Griffith, for which the Vice-Chancellor and the Professor of Asian Studies made themselves available. Their cold response when Senator Button asked to see Ann Moyal and complimented them on having someone so outstanding, led him to make a point of visiting her at home. In late September 1978, the then Minister for Science and the Environment, Senator J. J. Webster, rang to ask if he could visit the SPRC, and at Ann Moyal's invitation addressed a large body of students, making himself available for questions on science policy issues. Both the Vice-Chancellor and the Head of the School of Science entirely ignored this visit.

The Vice-Chancellor, Professor F. J. Willett, showed hostility to the SPRC as early as November 1977, when a letter of his appeared in the *Great Griffith Gazette*. In an earlier issue, both the editor of the *Gazette* and Ann Moyal had written about science policy and discussed the views of Alvin Weinberg, a prominent United States science administrator who has often commented on the relation of science and society. Professor Willett's reply is reproduced here in full:

> In a field notable for its portentious [sic] clap trap, the work of Weinberg — if you [the editorial contributor] and Mrs Moyal have dealt with him fairly — will be remembered for a richness of platitude and some tautology.
>
> Questions about decision frameworks for the allocation of scarce resources, especially ways of recognising, evaluating and incorporating value judgements are of venerable antiquity.
>
> They are treated in depth — and sometimes with elegance — in the administrative literature of Rome, China and the industrial West.
>
> Weinberg's codswallop could be discussed for its intrinsic worth if it did not reflect a larger, and questionable premise; that somehow and for some reasons Science is different.
>
> Maybe one reason for the often distasteful standard of literacy in this field is that much is necessary to obfuscate that false premise.[8]

Although Professor Willett later claimed in a private letter[9] that this letter to the *Gazette* was an attempt to put ginger in the *Gazette*'s correspondence columns, and that it paid a compliment to Moyal, others might prefer to infer an underlying hostility to science policy studies.

It is also true that Ann Moyal did not behave obsequiously to those in positions of power above her. Her style has been to pull no punches and to refuse to put up with hectoring or condescension. For many elites who are used to obeisance or toadying, such independent behaviour by a person in a lesser position may be seen as insubordination, or worse — especially if the person is a woman.

In January 1978 Ann Moyal spent a week in Canberra negotiating possible grants for the Centre with the Department of Science, CSIRO, the Australian Institute for Nuclear Science and Engineering, and the Australian Science and Technology Council. The Vice-Chancellor revealed antagonism to these efforts.

At the end of 1978, matters came to a climax. Teaching in the Science, Technology and Science group had increased due to reduced tutorial help. Ann Moyal was working a seven-day week to keep up with her teaching, SPRC activities and research undertakings. Three further commitments added to the pressure. She accepted an invitation from the Joint Academies of Science, Technology and Social Sciences to be one of several major participants in a workshop in April 1979 on "Science and Technology for What Purpose?". She was invited to prepare a paper for the January 1979 Congress of the Australian and New Zealand Association for the Advancement of Science, to be held in New Zealand. She also was under pressure to complete a longstanding research study of the Australian Academy of Science which had been promised for the journal *Search*, but which had been held up by her various duties. A special place was reserved for the paper on this in the March 1979 issue, which coincided with the Academy's 25th anniversary.[10]

With these deadlines and important commitments, Ann Moyal sought cooperation from the Chairman of the School of Science, Dr David Doddrell, to reduce her load of marking some of the first-year essays. This was refused. She then refused to mark more than 18 essays.

The Chairman sent her a letter "suspending" her from the University. Moyal sought legal advice. Letters from her solicitors to the University received no satisfactory answer, but the notice of "suspension" was waived by the University as if it had never been sent. The next week, the Vice-Chancellor requested Moyal to visit him. She took a representative of her solicitors along with her, but he was refused entry to the room. The Vice-Chancellor indicated to Mrs Moyal that there was a prima facie case for her dereliction.

Shortly afterwards, she received notice that a staff Conduct Committee acting as a Tribunal had been set up to hear four allegations against her. It was a remarkable Tribunal. Made up of three members of the University Council including the former Treasurer of Queensland, the Honourable Sir Gordon Chalk, plus a member of the University and the Administration, it was chaired by Queensland Supreme Court judge Mr Justice J. D. Dunn. A member of the University administration assisted the Committee as "prosecutor". The four allegations involved her refusal to mark a certain number of essays and to undertake the invigilation of one of three examinations allocated to her by the Chairman of the School of Science.

The hearing, on 21 December 1978, which dealt with only one of the four allegations, that of refusing to mark some first-year essays, found this allegation proved and decided that no penalty should be imposed. The Tribunal found that Ann Moyal was "a valuable and enthusiastic member of staff" and suggested that the University not carry the matter further.[11] However, this was not satisfactory to "the University". At the administration's insistence, a second hearing before the same tribunal members was held on 27 February 1979, at which all four allegations were found proved and a reprimand was administered concerning two of them. In the light of this experience, Ann Moyal decided to free herself from Griffith University and resigned in April 1979.

The first thing to note about the tribunals is that the charges were trivial in every instance. For example, one charge was that a third-year student's oral examination had been assessed by a research assistant instead of by Moyal. In fact, the assessment was done by Moyal based on a written essay. And is it really so heinous for a research assistant to help out occasionally in teaching?[12]

For every charge there were highly persuasive extenuating circumstances, based on other commitments, which any reasonable person would have accepted and which were raised at the time. For example, in one case a change in plans was required to accommodate a sudden request from the Minister for Science. In normal circumstances the charges laid would never have been brought against a valued member of staff. In most cases, arrangements are willingly made for a high-performance researcher with extra commitments. As it was, the minor breaches of regulations were used as a pretext for formal procedures which had the net effect of severe harassment.

The second important aspect of the tribunals is that they highlighted objectionable features of the University regulations and their implementation. These matters are dealt with in a report, inspired by the Moyal tribunals, by the Executive of the Griffith University Faculty Staff Association (GUFSA), dated 12 June 1979. The points raised include[13]:

> The Statutes laid down for Griffith University give the Vice-Chancellor an extraordinary amount of power. For example, clause 10 of Statute 4.1, Conduct of Staff, permits the Vice-Chancellor to summarily dismiss a staff member if in the Vice-Chancellor's opinion the member has committed a gross breach of the conditions of employment. This is highly unusual for a university statute, and appears to override the whole principle of tenure statutes.[14]

> The Vice-Chancellor has the power to refer a matter to a Staff Conduct Committee, and is also empowered to appoint a person to act in the role of Prosecutor (as happened in the Moyal case). Furthermore, the University, through the Council, also appoints the Staff Conduct Committee which acts as judge. Thus the University may act as both prosecutor and judge.

> Although in the Moyal tribunals the prosecution case was presented in a highly legalistic fashion, no legal advice was allowed to Ann Moyal, who had to present her own case. The tribunal may refuse to allow an open hearing, as happened in the Moyal tribunals. In the second tribunal for Ann Moyal, the Registrar, Mr Topley, presented the University's case. The Executive of GUFSA noted that this "created a strong implication of deliberate connivance between the person laying the complaint and the University who, through the Registrar, took upon itself the burden of prosecution as well as, through the Council and the Staff Conduct Committee, the right to judge. In the case of the Registrar, with his privileged access to documents beyond the reach of most members of staff, he was in a position to prejudice Mrs Moyal's presentation of her case in ways which would not withstand outside judicial scrutiny, particularly as the first hearing had suggested that the further three charges be not proceeded with".

The third important point raised by the tribunals is the implicit double standard inherent in their application. Neither Griffith nor most other universities make regular reviews of staff and use the findings to take formal disciplinary action against staff for poor teaching, poor or nonexistent research, or failure to follow all administrative regulations. Universities have their share of people — at all levels — who are incompetent, do little work, or flout regulations. If such people are so seldom disciplined, why was a talented and hard-working person like Moyal singled out for minor violations?

Ann Moyal calls herself a survivor. Other members of staff at Griffith had been victimised and there was a history of nervous breakdowns and divorce among the staff. Moyal had come to see Griffith as an institution deficient in moral and educational standards and totally lacking in integrity. "I was very lucky to get out", she said. "Others, including some very good members of staff, are trapped there."

Returning to Sydney, she became Visiting Fellow in the Department of Government at the University of Sydney and later Visiting Fellow in the Research School of Social Sciences at the Australian National University. She kept up her science policy research, and can be considered one of the leading members of that field. She was commissioned by Telecom Australia to write a history of telecommunications in Australia[15], was appointed to the National Committee on the History and Philosophy of Science, and in 1983 became Honorary Editor of the new journal of issues in technological change, science policy and innovation, *Prometheus*, and Honorary Editor of the Australian scientific journal *Search*.

There are several lessons which may be drawn from the Moyal case. Among them are the following:

• Harassment concerning apparently the most trivial matters can be a potent form of suppression.

- Violation of the narrow letter of regulations provides leverage for those in positions of power to act against a person. Minor violations that can be formally substantiated can be blown out of all proportion and so outweigh major contributions to scholarship.

- There is no penalty for administrators who fail to accommodate the research needs of staff.

- Regulations, although they may seem innocuous when they lie unused for years, are nevertheless dangerous if they permit the arbitrary use of power.

Acknowledgements

I thank Ann Baker, Clyde Manwell, Ann Moyal, Cedric Pugh and others who prefer to remain anonymous for useful advice in writing this chapter.

References

1. For an analysis of this in Australia see Bettina Cass, Madge Dawson, Diana Temple, Sue Wills and Anne Winkler, *Why so Few? Women Academics in Australian Universities* (Sydney: Sydney University Press, 1983).

2. Miriam Henry, "The La Trobe concept: an idea for a new university?", in: Donald E. Edgar (ed.), *Social Change in Australia: Readings in Sociology* (Melbourne: Cheshire, 1974), pp. 563–82; Neil Marshall, "La Trobe University: the vision and the reality", in: Stephen Murray-Smith (ed.), *Melbourne Studies in Education* (Melbourne University Press, 1981), pp. 1–41.

3. On Griffith and also on the Moyal case, see Adrian McGregor, "The end of the god-professor", *National Times*, 1 December 1979, pp. 59, 61, 63.

4. On science policy see the major international work Ina Spiegel-Rösing and Derek de Solla Price (eds), *Science, Technology and Society: A Cross-disciplinary Perspective* (London and Beverly Hills: Sage, 1977).

5. Ann Mozley Moyal, "The Australian Atomic Energy Commission: a case study in Australian science and government", *Search*, vol. 6, no. 9, September 1975, pp. 365–84.

6. Ann Moyal, *Scientists in Nineteenth Century Australia* (Cassell Australia, 1976).

7. Griffith University School of Science, Science Policy Research Centre Management Committee, Minutes 1/78, document SC/414/78, 20 July 1978, p. 1.

8. F. J. Willett, "Is science different?" (letter), *Great Griffith Gazette*, November 1977, p. 2. See also the letter in reply by Ann Moyal on the same page.

9. F. J. Willett, letter to R. D. Guthrie, Chairman of the School of Science, 16 February 1978.

10. This appeared as Ann Moyal, "The Australian Academy of Science: the anatomy of a scientific elite", *Search*, vol. 11, nos 7–8, July/August 1980, pp. 231–9, and no. 9, September 1980, pp. 281–8.

11. "The decision of the tribunal of 21 December 1978" as dictated to Ann Moyal by the Acting Registrar, Mr Hoult, on Wednesday afternoon 4 p.m., 21 December 1978. See also letter from C. B. Hoult, Acting Registrar, to Ann Moyal, 21 December 1978, which did not include the statement about her being "a valuable and enthusiastic member of staff".

12. I find this charge rather extraordinary since, as a research assistant myself, I have taught and assessed four entire third-year courses with full support by my department. The Dean of Science certainly has not brought charges against the Head of the Department for allowing this.

13. "Some comments on the operation of 'Statute 4.1 — Conduct of Staff' by the Executive of the Griffith University Faculty Staff Association", 12 June 1979.

14. On this see the comments by Les Wallis of the Federation of Australian University Staff Associations in McGregor, op. cit. note 3, p. 61.

15. Ann Moyal, *Clear Across Australia: Telecommunications 1854–1983* (Melbourne: Thomas Nelson Australia, 1984).

Postscript

On 3 April 1984 I sent a copy of this chapter to Griffith University inviting a response from someone representing the University, or anyone else appropriate, to be included in this book. On 18 May the Acting Vice-Chancellor, Professor Robert Segall, replied as follows:

Dear Mr Martin,

I read your article with interest. I can say personally that I endorse your comments on Ann as a highly talented historian. I very much admired her scholarly study, "Scientists in Nineteenth Century Australia".

She was a colleague of mine in the School of Science as you may know and I greatly enjoyed her company and was extremely sorry when she left.

As to the content of your article, I feel obliged as Acting Vice-Chancellor to say that I think you need to be cautious as to what you publish.

Yours sincerely,

(signed) R. L. Segall

Acting Vice-Chancellor.

Fruit Fly, Free Speech and Academic Justice in Adelaide

The Fruit Fly Papers

C. M. Ann Baker

Introduction

This case history describes the attempt to dismiss my husband, Professor Clyde Manwell, from the University of Adelaide, and the aftermath. The case history is presented in two parts: an updated version of the original *Fruit Fly Papers*[1], and the then Vice-Chancellor's *Statement* on the evidence relating to the dismissal charges, together with his view of a number of controversial events.[2] The case has also featured in other published items.[3-9]

At times we were critical of the way the Vice-Chancellor handled matters. However, in updating this case history, it is now possible to say that it is greatly to his credit that he finally admitted that the charges contained "a number of errors"[10] and that, without being asked, he attempted to ameliorate the damage by providing funds for our research.[11]

I am aware that the Vice-Chancellor was under pressures which made it difficult for him to find a fair solution quickly, before local gossip, intrigue and publicity had resulted in polarisation. The problem was that the author of the dismissal complaint, Professor H. G. Andrewartha, was then (and still is) an eminent Australian scientist with great influence, both locally and nationally. For many people at the University of Adelaide it was expedient to assume that the dismissal complaint was correct. Had more of our colleagues within the University provided the Vice-Chancellor with the kind of information which was placed before the Committee of Three in 1972, or which came out in the Supreme Court case in 1975, the situation could have been settled with far less acrimony and damage. Instead, after an initial approach to the Staff Association made it clear that no significant help could be expected from that quarter[12], and after learning the extent to which the complainant was able to influence the investigative processes within the University, it became necessary to use the laws on defamation.

Accordingly, in re-examining this case history I am interested not only in presenting the historical development, together with some discussion of the issues that arose along the way; I am even more interested in making observations that will help others. Since the sacking attempt in 1971 we have received many requests for assistance from other academics or scientists whose jobs have been threatened.

In analysing this case history the former Vice-Chancellor's *Statement*[13] is especially important. First, it provides an administrator's-eye view of the case. Second, it provides a model for how an administrator should report the facts relating to a set of sacking charges that had been officially received. Such a statement might be unnecessary where an administrator refuses to receive a complaint, although that is debatable, especially where any gossip or publicity has occurred. But, once a complaint is officially received, then the reputation of the person against whom the complaint has been made becomes clouded in the eyes of at least part of the university community. Sacking complaints are rare in scientific and academic institutions. Some episodes in our case histories reveal examples of where other staff have committed serious offences without being considered for dismissal. Thus, the very fact that a sacking complaint is considered at all by the higher administration is grievously damaging. The highly competitive nature of the intellectual professions means that an individual's reputation is a major determinant of his or her livelihood. This is *not* to inhibit valid criticism, either of inadequacies in teaching or in research. Indeed, it is precisely because it is necessary in scholarship to engage occasionally in critical comments that it is so important to protect the jobs of academics and scientists from unfair or inaccurate allegations. For everyone, whatever his or her occupation, unfair attacks on the reputation violate a fundamental human right.[14]

Fruit Fly in South Australia

Since 1947 it has been realised that outbreaks of Mediterranean Fruit Fly ("Med-fly") and Queensland Fruit Fly occurred occasionally in Adelaide and in some other parts of South Australia.[15] In 1947 the attempt to eradicate fruit fly began, with some 1300 people employed in removing fruit and in spraying.

Part of the problem is that fruit fly outbreaks may arise in three different ways, and expert opinion is not in agreement as to their relative importance. First, fruit fly can be brought in by people transporting contaminated fruit from interstate. There have been complaints that the fruit fly inspection stations at state borders (and at airports) are not fully effective. Second, fruit fly, like many other insects, can be carried long distances by winds; the prolonged periods of northern or eastern winds may help to disperse fruit fly, especially Queensland Fruit Fly. Third, on occasion some low-level breeding populations of fruit fly become established in South Australia, although the extremes of hot and cold weather in this state probably eliminate most of these populations eventually, or at least keep fly numbers low until favourable weather allows enough successful reproduction to reach outbreak levels.[16]

Since the 1950s, the South Australia Department of Agriculture has maintained a fruit fly detection system consisting of a grid of several thousand traps baited with what is hoped to be a suitably attractive lure for the two species of fruit fly. Although secrecy surrounds much of the fruit fly program, I have been informed by sources within the Department of Agriculture that, if five or more flies are found in a single trap upon the periodic inspection, an outbreak is declared. There are good reasons for attempting to eradicate fruit fly: they attack many species of commercially valuable fruit, and also some vegetables; they often damage 10–50 per cent of the crop in other states, and many countries will not import fruit from other parts of Australia because of widespread infestations.

In South Australia the attempts to eradicate fruit fly have involved a varying combination of two approaches. On some occasions the emphasis has been placed on "denying the enemy resources". Gangs of men came around and stripped all the fruit from residents' trees. It has been argued that only ripe fruit should be removed and that green fruit should be left so as to prevent the dispersal of egg-laying fruit fly.[17] However, much of the emphasis is placed on pesticides. Usually the immediate outbreak area is cover-sprayed. Adjacent areas are bait-sprayed. The latter involves placing about a cupful of a bait-plus-pesticide solution on a few trees or bushes on each property.

As so often happens in pest control or eradication programs, the situation becomes ruled by the interests of professional pest-controllers (including scientists in the employ of the government), pesticide manufacturers, and politicians.[18] Inspection of the Parliamentary Debates for South Australia, or letters to the editors of local newspapers, reveals that the eradication measures have had adverse effects on non-target organisms; for example, cows have died after being sprayed for fruit fly and a funeral procession was disrupted by the rowdy behaviour of a spray gang.[19]

The fruit fly program, with its repeated attempts at eradication, has become a major bureaucracy in the South Australia Department of Agriculture, a source of funds and favours for a few South Australian academics, and a dependable solution to periods of local unemployment (except in recent years when the program's costs had to be contained).

It was in 1971, when a fruit fly outbreak occurred near our residence, that Professor Manwell and I learned at first hand some of the abuses of the program. As the Department of

Zoology had poor facilities for keeping animals, we kept at home a collection of ducks and chickens to supply eggs for research and teaching, including studies on the effects of low levels of pesticides on the developmental appearance of certain molecular markers. Although we were supposed to be in an area that received only the bait-spraying, on two occasions fruit fly gangs not only invaded our animal pens and drenched some of the poultry, nests and plants with pesticide, but also broke down the fencing and trampled many plants. On one occasion the supposed supervisor of the spray gang was caught peeping in a window when the shower was running.

When Professor Manwell complained about such behaviour, he received more than the usual bureaucratic runaround. A letter from Manwell to the Department of Agriculture, asking for information about the fruit fly program, was not answered but was turned over to the Head of the Department of Zoology, Professor H. G. Andrewartha.

After consulting various experts about the local fruit fly program (and finding that some of them were even more critical about it than we were), and after reading the relevant literature, we made a number of public criticisms about the program, which can be summarised as follows[20]:

1. Privacy and safety of residents cannot be ignored in programs of pest control or eradication.

2. Spraying, if necessary at all, should be confined to spraying the combined bait-pesticide mixture in small quantities on *street* trees. As the object in the *bait*-sprayed areas is to attract fruit fly *to* the poison, it is not necessary to enter people's property at all. This procedure, of spraying pesticide-bait combinations on street trees has been adopted with considerable success (and public approval) in parts of New South Wales. It is also a more efficient method. Instead of gangs of men entering each property, a single spray operator (often mounted on the back of a vehicle) can place the small shot of pesticide-bait spray on each street tree, thus allowing a wider area to be covered in a given time. A modification of this procedure involves spraying a sex-attractant-and-pesticide mixture on a piece of fibre-board and hanging up pieces of this impregnated fibre-board at suitable locations. The advantages of these New South Wales techniques are that less pesticide is used, the risks to pets and people are greatly reduced, and invasion of privacy is unnecessary.

3. Alternative methods of eradication should be considered. In particular, the sterile male method of eradication had been claimed to be effective in dealing with localised outbreaks of fruit fly.[21] It was also suggested that research should be done to find more effective attractants, for while the yeast protein hydrolysate bait is attractive to many fruit flies, even better results might be obtained by using sex pheromones.

4. The quarantine to prevent fruit fly infected fruit from being brought into South Australia from other parts of Australia should be made more effective. The inadequacies of the checkpoints, often unmanned and easily evaded, had been a subject of complaint in the state Parliament.

Reaction to Criticism of Fruit Fly Spraying

Our criticisms were quite ordinary. Most of them had been made before. However, it appears that this was the first time any scientists had publicly expressed doubts about the local program. No longer could the South Australia Department of Agriculture fob off complaints with the excuse that the program was scientifically sound.

From the public, including, quite surprisingly, some in the lower ranks of the fruit fly sprayers, we received a number of horrifying examples of the abuses that had occurred. While many in the spraying gangs had behaved themselves, others had caused unnecessary damage to gardens and property. There was also dissatisfaction with the expense of the program. In particular, in recent years fruit fly outbreaks were becoming more common.

Clearly, the programme had not eradicated fruit fly, despite some success in curbing individual outbreaks.

After our public comments, the initial attack in the state Parliament came from the political right, notably D. N. Brookman and H. K. Kemp, both good friends of Professor H. G. Andrewartha, at that time Head of the Department of Zoology at the University of Adelaide. Brookman's attitude is exemplified in the following quotation:

> I should like to be assured that firm action will be taken against people who have such wrong ideas as to set themselves up as interpreters of civil liberties.[22]

A week after the initial attacks in the South Australian Parliament, and the day after a second attack on the fruit fly criticisms, Professor Andrewartha sent a letter to the then Vice-Chancellor. That letter, as well as much subsequent correspondence, was published later in full in *On Dit*, the student newspaper. Professor Andrewartha's first letter of complaint dealt *only* with Manwell's fruit fly criticisms; for example, he says:

> ...Manwell is a physiologist and cannot claim professional expertise in population ecology. Population ecology is my specialty and I think that the University should inform the Minister of Agriculture...[23]

Professor Andrewartha referred to Manwell's criticisms as "intemperate", an adjective the Vice-Chancellor repeated in his letter to the Minister for Agriculture, written three days after Andrewartha's letter. The Vice-Chancellor's remarkable letter is quoted below in full:

> You will be aware that a member of the staff of our Zoology Department, Professor C. Manwell, has been in the "news" with some frequency over the last few weeks. In view of this I am enclosing for your information a copy of a letter to me from Professor H. G. Andrewartha, who is the Head of the Department.
>
> Professor Manwell is of course entitled to his views; but I want you to know that his *often intemperate remarks*, and criticisms of your staff, are not supported by the University. The University would not wish Professor Manwell to be treated differently from any citizen. [emphasis added]

Professor Manwell only received a copy of this letter a year after it was sent. When he challenged the Vice-Chancellor to present examples of "often intemperate remarks", the Vice-Chancellor did not reply to the challenge. This is hardly surprising, for Manwell, a newcomer to the University of Adelaide, had not been involved in any other controversy, public or private, and had met the Vice-Chancellor on only two brief and pleasant occasions.

The last sentence in the Vice-Chancellor's letter probably refers to Manwell's request to the Department of Agriculture not to spray in the immediate vicinity of the experimental animals. Such an "exception" would have been entirely compatible with even the existing program, for the animals were confined to the back part of the yard and, normally, the bait-pesticide spray was delivered to only one or two fruit trees on a property. There had been far more damaging exceptions to the fruit fly spraying reported in Parliament, for example, commercial growers in fruit fly areas who avoided spraying entirely or who shipped fruit out of the area of the "outbreak".

On 19 April 1971, Professor Andrewartha again wrote to the Vice-Chancellor. This time he alleged that Manwell had flouted "the scholarly precept that one should teach within one's area of professional competence", that for four lectures in Zoology 1, Manwell had "placed much emphasis on the sociological, political and technological aspects of contraception"; that he "lacks judgment and perspective" because "he distributed to the class 12 quarto pages containing 49 references to books and articles"; that he set fifty "true or false" questions in Zoology I examinations; that the book *Molecular Biology and the Origin of Species*, written by Manwell and Baker, contains some errors in statistics, and that:

Manwell's public statements about the Department of Agriculture's campaign to eradicate fruit fly...included statements that were unscientific. These statements embarrassed me because, from their form, it was far from clear that Manwell was speaking only for himself. He gave the University as his address and his status as Professor of Zoology...

Professor Manwell first learned of the nature of the charges on which dismissal from the University was sought when a reporter from the *Advertiser*, a local newspaper, telephoned me. A year later a member of the University Council revealed that he too had been asked by a newspaper reporter about the planned sacking long before the news finally broke in *On Dit*.

Vice-Chancellor's Response

By the middle of May 1971 the Vice-Chancellor sent Manwell a copy of Andrewartha's second letter of complaint, as required by the University Statutes on dismissal. Manwell wrote a reply denying the charges and pointing out significant errors. He also showed the Vice-Chancellor certain evidence, such as the carbon copy of the original letter to the newspaper about the fruit fly spraying, proving that, contrary to Andrewartha's allegation, the letter had been written from a private address. Indeed, the possibility of unauthorised editorial alteration of the address on the published letter should have been apparent to any reader, for the editor had left the name of the suburb of the residence (St. Peters) below the inserted "Professor of Zoology, University of Adelaide". The University is located in the city proper and not in St. Peters, or any other suburb.

The Vice-Chancellor wanted a "preliminary investigation" of the charges, chaired by a Supreme Court Justice and with two academics as the jury. Manwell agreed to the general procedure but strongly objected to the restricted selection of four academics nominated by the Vice-Chancellor, all close friends of the originator of the complaint. Details of the procedure in selecting academic jurors by the Vice-Chancellor deserve careful description. The Vice-Chancellor maintains that Professor Manwell agreed to two Professors of biological sciences: Professors *Bennett* (Genetics) and *Elliott* (Biochemistry) (written statement by the Vice-Chancellor to the Commission of Inquiry, dated 10 September 1971). Professor Manwell maintains that he did not agree to those names and had insisted that the jurors should be further removed from the individual who had originated the complaint. Whether or not there was agreement is now immaterial, in the light of other aspects of the times and names. At the meeting between the Vice-Chancellor and Manwell, early on 4 June, the Vice-Chancellor had already obtained approval from Andrewartha of the academic jurors selected to investigate his complaint and had already received a letter from Andrewartha, dated 1 June, which contained the following passage:

> ...I...wanted to remove Manwell and Baker from the list because I am thoroughly convinced that this is a most unsuitable textbook for undergraduates. I sought the advice of Professor *Bennett* and Professor *Elliott* on this specific point and they reinforced my own opinion. [emphasis added]

It seems remarkable that of all the academics available, the Vice-Chancellor would nominate as academic jurors the two people that Professor Andrewartha stated were in agreement with him.

Also remarkable are the dates of various occurrences: Manwell's copy of Andrewartha's letter of 1 June bears the following record from the office of the Vice-Chancellor: "Copy sent to Professor C. Manwell 4 June 1971". In other words, it was sent in the campus mails on the same day that Manwell had a 9 a.m. meeting with the Vice-Chancellor. Thus, the crucial information — that Professor Andrewartha had already consulted Professors Bennett and Elliott and had already received what he, Andrewartha, interpreted to be a reply favourable to that portion of his complaint — was not made available to Manwell at the time he was asked to agree to the limited choice of jurors (already approved by the originator of the complaint), although the Vice-Chancellor was already in possession of that information.

It is easy enough to prove that in academic discipline procedures the selection of jurors is expected to conform to the typical procedures of law. For example, we quote from the "Rights and Responsibilities" document, prepared under the Chairmanship of the Deputy Vice-Chancellor of the University of Adelaide at about the same time as this episode occurred. Under the heading of "Impartiality", that document states:

> No one should sit as a Chairman or member [involved in disciplinary proceedings] if he is subject to any bias in favour of or against the person charged with misconduct, or if the circumstances are such as to be likely to lead fair-minded persons to suppose that he might be so biased... the principles governing a challenge for cause to a juror in a case before the Supreme Court of South Australia should apply to a challenge to the Chairman or a member of a Board.

The Committee of Concerned Scholars assumed that these aspects of the "preliminary investigation" were all unfortunate mistakes and did not assign blame to individuals; however, the Committee understood why Professor Manwell then sought legal advice outside the University.

The Commission of Inquiry

On 3 September the University Council set up a Commission of Inquiry under Clause 10 of Chapter IV of the Statutes on dismissal. Originally it was planned to hold the entire proceedings in secret. Peaceably, but firmly, four hundred students and some staff members, after hearing Professor Andrewartha's letters of complaint read to them by student leaders, opened the "star chamber" to the public. By December 1971 the Council of the University of Adelaide accepted the Commission of Inquiry's dismissal of the complaint, quoting from the Commission's report:

> The complaint against Professor Manwell, in the form in which it has been referred to us by the University Council, does not appear to have been formulated with close attention to the wording of the University Statutes and the vagueness, in this sense, of the complaint has caused the Commission some difficulty and concern...
>
> ...we cannot find within that letter [of complaint] allegations which if proved true, would show that Professor Manwell had grossly or persistently neglected his duties or that he had been guilty of serious misconduct in or about the performance of his duties such as would constitute grounds for dismissing him under clause 9 of Chapter IV of the University Statutes.
>
> Accordingly, we see no reason for us to proceed further with this inquiry and we recommend that the University Council should not regard or treat this complaint as a basis for dismissing Professor Manwell.

Academic Justice at Adelaide?

Judging from the above passage, one might assume that academic freedom and justice were returning to the University of Adelaide after some initial difficulties. That view would, however, be overly optimistic.

There are other ways of removing an academic besides sacking. The most effective method is to try to drive him out by interfering with his research and teaching, and to submit him to other types of harassment. The University Council had little alternative but to accept the judgement by the Commission of Inquiry, which it had itself appointed. However, the Council left Professor Manwell under the authority of the Department Head who had attempted his dismissal. In effect, this was the administration's way of passing a guilty verdict against Manwell.

Leaving the victim under the jurisdiction of the Head of Department who had sought dismissal on inadequate charges generated intrigue and ill-feeling, which is still evident years later. The Council's attention was drawn to a similar case which occurred at about the same time at the University of Lancaster in the UK. In that situation the governing body of the University of Lancaster resolved the problem sensibly and fairly by removing the staff member from the authority of the Department Head who had initiated an inadequate dismissal complaint.[24] At the University of Adelaide, there had apparently been a similar conflict involving the very same Head of Department who had attempted to get Manwell sacked, and that conflict had been resolved by transferring the staff member in question to another part of the University. However, this information, although known to some members of the administration, was withheld from us at the time. This matter will be discussed more fully later in this chapter.

After the Commission of Inquiry rejected the dismissal complaint, the Council appointed the "Committee of Three" (which was later called the "Committee on Residual Problems in Zoology" or "Committee to Resolve Residual Problems in Zoology"). The committee consisted of the then Deputy Vice-Chancellor, the then Chairman of the Education Committee, and a third individual who was simultaneously the President of the University of Adelaide Staff Association and a Member of the University Council (and who subsequently was promoted to Reader and who also became Deputy Chancellor).

Rather than resolve residual problems in zoology, the actions of the Committee of Three exacerbated them. Manwell's legal advisers led him to believe that the Committee of Three would clear his name of the errors in the dismissal complaint. Without fully informing Manwell, the legal advisers lifted the libel writ so that, presumably, the Committee of Three would not be violating a possible *sub judice* situation.

The Committee of Three, reporting to the University community through a widely circulated document, failed to report on the accuracy of the charges (although Manwell and I presented much of the evidence, which was ultimately accepted by the Vice-Chancellor) and failed to report on the variety of subsequent harassments Manwell endured, some of which were contradictory to the original sacking charges (discussed later). Furthermore, before the sessions held by the Committee of Three, Andrewartha was allowed carte blanche in introducing new charges. Although there was supposedly an agreement that both sides would receive copies of all documents involved in the charges, despite repeated requests Manwell was not given copies of certain documents referred to by Andrewartha.

The Committee of Three's report attempted to explain the situation as simply a personality clash arising as a consequence of "a difference in background" between Manwell and Andrewartha. The Committee of Three produced no evidence to support that conclusion — and ignored a not inconsiderable amount of evidence to the contrary. The upshot was that, by its failure to report on much of what was placed before it, plus some very revealing testimony, the Committee reinforced the University establishment in judging Manwell guilty. Furthermore, by failing to probe the examples of the harassment of Manwell, his wife, his students and his prospective students, the committee allowed a tacit understanding that these people were "fair game" for subsequent victimisation.

Manwell's situation was made more precarious by the fact that his legal advisers did not pursue the failures of the Committee of Three more strongly. Again without fully informing the client, there was an unexplained delay of nearly a year in the reintroduction of the libel writ. As a result, the accuracy of the charges could not be tested in such a way as to clear Manwell's name until four years after the original sacking attempt. In South Australia, at the same time, other defamation cases (including one brought by another academic) had reached the Supreme Court within nine to twelve months. Indeed, had the delay not occurred, and had the case been pursued more vigorously, it is likely that it would have been settled out-of-court, for much of the evidence against the charges rested on documents (although, as will become evident later, the testimony of witnesses brought some interesting facts to light).

There can be no doubt that the harassment of Manwell reached a low level after the frustrated sacking attempt. Manwell was denied honours students and was not allowed to give his advanced course — in spite of the fact that the Department Head who had sought dismissal had admitted in correspondence to the Vice-Chancellor that Manwell's advanced teaching was "well received".

A student with a first-class honours degree from another Australian university was turned down for a Commonwealth scholarship at the University of Adelaide. He had made it clear that he had wished to do research under Manwell's supervision. Normally a student with a first-class honours degree is automatically given a Commonwealth scholarship.

A Question of Madness?

Roy and Zhores Medvedev, in a book bearing this title, have documented how dissenters in the Soviet system can be defined as "insane" and can thus be removed or discredited.[25] There is evidence to suggest that this policy is used in some Australian universities. Perhaps the most sordid aspect of the dismissal of Professor Sydney Sparks Orr from the University of Tasmania was that the administration based much of its evidence on Orr's dreams, recorded in psychoanalysis, to indicate that he was mentally unbalanced.[26]

A few weeks after the Council of the University of Adelaide accepted the report of its Committee of Three, a member of the University Council, who was attached to the Department of Zoology as a Reader, stated that Manwell or his wife needed to see a psychiatrist, and presented them with a list of three names, including the Professor of Psychiatry at the University of Adelaide. Later the same member of the Council wrote Manwell a letter to that effect, using the official stationery of the Department of Zoology, University of Adelaide.

Although Manwell brought this matter to the attention of the Council of the University of Adelaide, no disciplinary action was taken. In terms of professional qualifications in psychiatry there is no evidence that that particular member of Council, who was, as already mentioned, a Reader attached to the Department of Zoology, was within his professional position in querying the mental health of a colleague and his wife.

One cannot help but note the contradiction: one of the major charges against Manwell incorrectly alleged that he had written a letter to the editor of a local newspaper from his official University position. In contrast, a member of the Council (and of the local establishment) can use official University stationery when attempting to refer a colleague and/or his wife to a psychiatrist.

Academic Intrigue as an Expression of "Personality Conflict"

As in another South Australian case — the Institute of Medical and Veterinary Science versus Coulter, discussed elsewhere in this book — the fundamental question must be asked: Why "the paralysis of conscience" which allows the tolerance for suppression, victimisation on false charges, and indifference to questionable behaviour? In this section evidence is presented for the role of personality conflict, and the consequent general demoralisation, as a contributing cause. In the next section evidence is presented for the role of vested interest, the desire to suppress criticism of possible sources of patronage.

The data available on intra-university personality conflict do not allow one to prove conclusively that the situation at the University of Adelaide is worse than at most other universities. However, there is evidence that there has been serious conflict and demoralisation quite apart from this episode.

First, the very fact that the Committee of Three chose to explain the sacking attempt as a petty personality squabble, despite contrary evidence, suggests that either such an explanation readily came to their minds as a result of their knowledge of other cases within the University or that such an explanation would be readily accepted by the majority of Adelaide academics, presumably on the basis of their own experiences. In arguing the case for a University Ombudsman, a former Registrar of the University of Adelaide mentioned that staff grievances imposed "a heavy burden of work on the Vice-Chancellor".[27] That former Registrar provides no data as to the number of complaints, or the percentage resolved satisfactorily, but does present information indicative of serious staff demoralisation in terms of alcoholism, and states: "The Director of the Health Service will confirm that this is not a negligible problem among University staff (as, no doubt, among the staff of any large employer)."

Since the frustrated sacking attempt, a powerful group within the University Council has sought to make dismissal easier — and finally achieved those aims in 1983. Quotations from the Council's own document provide evidence of the prevailing authoritarian attitudes.[28] The reason for changing the tenure statutes is given as " . . . that the Council should not be unduly restricted in its governing of the University". Especially revealing is the following passage: " . . . Statutes and Regulations . . . bind not only the University community *but also the Council* . . . Rules are promulgated by Council alone and, while binding on the University community, can be changed *or over-ridden* by Council . . . " (emphasis added). However, perhaps the most striking aspect of this Council document, announcing that the dismissal statutes would be changed, was a section dealing with "ineffective academic staff" suffering from "drug dependency (including alcohol dependence)". Although, as in the Registrar's document, no data are presented to show how serious the problem is, the fact remains that drink and other drugs are perceived by the University Council as being such an important problem among the academic staff they govern that this problem is discussed extensively in such a document, whereas all other problems of academic misconduct, whether sexual harassment, lack of publication, poor teaching, or plagiarism, are ignored.

Few would deny that the abuse of alcohol and other drugs is evidence of poor morale, as well as that the presence of drug-abusing staff is likely to affect the morale of more temperate staff (and students).

Like other closed professional groups, academics rarely criticise their colleagues before the general public, however much they might argue in private or in the columns of some professional journals. For academics to use the newspapers as a means of protest about university conditions is a sign of total frustration. Around the time of the attempt to sack Manwell, two senior academics made public their dissatisfaction with university conditions.

The Head of the Department of Microbiology, Professor Derrick Rowley, was quoted extensively in an interview with a reporter from a local newspaper.[29] Rowley complained of the "intolerable" state of medical education and the "run-down morale" of staff at the University of Adelaide, adding:

> The better staff tend to go elsewhere, and the poorer ones tend to stay and hasten the decline.

At about the same time, the Professor of Philosophy, John Smart, who held one of the two existing Foundation Chairs at the University of Adelaide, resigned to take a Readership elsewhere, blaming "the intrigues of university politics" and saying:

> University administration is not as gentlemanly as it was and people are suspicious about each other.[30]

Other writers, including a former Vice-Chancellor, provided evidence of staff conflict and dissatisfaction.[31] In a sense, such comments can give a misleading picture, and there is a need for a quantitative survey of staff opinion about a number of different aspects of their work environment. In terms of publication and citation the University of Adelaide ranks well above most other Australian universities.[32] Nevertheless, the above quotations do show that there is serious dissatisfaction and demoralisation among some staff at the University of Adelaide. In any organisation where there is rivalry and authoritarianism, the resulting intrigue means that it is easy for a crisis to be precipitated accidentally. The escapism, whether into drugs and drink, or into productive research, means that there is no effective protest against unfairness in procedures or victimisation using false charges.[33]

Suppression of Criticism of Possible Sources of Patronage

The South Australia Department of Agriculture, which runs the fruit fly eradication program, is a source of research funds and facilities for certain members of the University of Adelaide. The Department of Agriculture and the University of Adelaide are closely linked by statute, although this linkage has been reduced in recent years. In 1950 the Waite Agricultural Institute of the University of Adelaide received £33,000 for research on fruit fly. At the same time as the dismissal attempt was being made, the South Australia Department of Agriculture was offering, through Parliament, research funds for one of Professor Andrewartha's supporters in the Department of Zoology.

Staff members soliciting research support from agricultural interests might be worried about our public criticisms of the South Australia Department of Agriculture. Such statements might also worry staff members obtaining funds from questionable sources; for example military organisations — and another of Andrewartha's supporters was doing research involving burning and maiming large numbers of rats in a project funded by the military.

Interaction of the research support and personality conflict explanations is apparent. The privileged position of the Waite Agricultural Research Institute vis-a-vis the rest of the University of Adelaide is a source of resentment. For example, the Waite Agricultural Institute, quite apart from extra research funding from other sources, receives more than 10 per cent of the annual budget for the University of Adelaide but only carries 2–3 per cent of the actual teaching load. With the exception of two staff members known to us, the Waite Institute were staunch supporters of the South Australia Department of Agriculture and Professor Andrewartha.

Another type of interaction between research support and personality conflict may have contributed to the situation. When Manwell was on the staff of the University of Illinois he had occasion to report to the federal and state governments the misuse of his grant funds by two senior academics: an unauthorised payment of $933.32 to a pregnant, unmarried student. No doubt those individuals felt some resentment over the fact that Manwell reported this to the authorities. In correspondence placed before the Committee of Three, Andrewartha made a vague allusion to this situation and mentioned having "confidential letters from two prominent American scientists". Although Manwell requested that the Committee of Three investigate this connection and, in particular, compel Andrewartha to produce this correspondence, the Committee did not do so. The dates and the nature of that correspondence would be important in ascertaining to what extent pressure for dismissal came from academics entirely unconnected with the University of Adelaide.

The corrupting effects of sources of patronage is the one common theme to be found in the diverse criticisms by radical[34] and conservative[35] academics: research funds, consultantships, and other forms of patronage bias the views and behaviour of some academics.

"Dear Professor Manwell, Rats in This Department Are Gassed"

For many academics who have sought assistance in contesting unfair dismissal attempts, blocked promotions or other administrative actions, there is the problem of shifting charges. The following pair of examples suggest that the shifting of charges might depend upon the nature of the audience. The first example is of a charge brought before the Committee of Three, which held a secret academic court. The second example is of a charge brought before the Supreme Court of South Australia, an open court attended by many members of the public.

As an example of Manwell's "misconduct", a letter from Manwell to Andrewartha, dated 24 August 1971, was produced before the Committee of Three. In that letter Manwell complained to Andrewartha about the Zoology Department's use of an unnecessarily cruel method of killing rats, which were then given to first-year students for dissection. Manwell's letter was largely a quotation from the Universities Federation for Animal Welfare's Handbook, which opposes the use of gas and recommends an injection of barbiturate instead.[36] The fact that a staff member in the Department of Zoology had sought to use Manwell's supply of carbon monoxide for rat gassing suggests that the usual procedures involving town gas were not satisfactory. Indeed, a technician complained to Manwell about "the rodent Auschwitz". The response to Manwell's letter was an ultimatum: "Dear Professor Manwell, Rats in this department are gassed".

This example, presumably of a charge of insubordination on the part of Manwell, could actually be brought up within the University with complete impunity. However, this example was not brought up before the Supreme Court — even though Manwell had wanted it. Was this because Manwell's opposition to cruelty to animals, backed by the anti-gassing comments of the Universities Federation for Animal Welfare, might have received a more sympathetic hearing from the general public?

In the Supreme Court case, instead, a different charge appeared. This is described in Manwell's article in the student newspaper which detailed a number of the difficulties he encountered in giving a course on comparative biochemistry and pollution:

> A major point of attack was my third year course. On two occasions that course was cancelled unilaterally by the then Head or a successor. In neither case was I presented with any academically valid explanations. Each time higher authority in the University did suggest that the course be reinstated. However, on both occasions the secret cancellation and subsequent appeal took sufficient time that the immediate objective, removing the course, was effected. On one occasion the attempt to delete the course from the Calendar, presumably at the galley proof stage, was bungled: the entry was deleted in one place and left in another, causing considerable confusion for students.
>
> When in 1975 the defamation action reached the Supreme Court, we learned of a new tactic towards the environmentally-oriented course. After failing to establish the validity of any of the more specific allegations of a serious nature in the original sacking complaint, the defence attempted to make a new charge that I had allowed my wife to work in the third year course for a time greater than allowed in the conditions of her appointment (which was a temporary, hourly paid one). It was claimed that the students had received too much attention.
>
> For "evidence", the defence presented a carbon copy of a document, purported to have come from the Registrar's Office. This document included both the official announcement of my wife's temporary appointment, followed by a passage limiting the hours to be worked.
>
> I was asked in court if I had ever seen that letter. I had not. Fortunately, my wife kept the *original* of that letter from the Registrar. The original was presented by us in court. It simply announced the appointment. It did not bear the incriminating typed passages on what was purported to be the carbon copy of the same document. We were also fortunate in that there had already been placed in evidence a letter from the then Head of Department who had admitted that the third year course had been well received by students. The former Head had attributed the success of the course to my wife's efforts (a statement with which I fully agreed). She had, after all, come in to work at the last minute at the former Head's request when the regular demonstrator left in mid-year to accompany her husband.[37, 38]

Neither during the Supreme Court case, nor when Manwell's article was published, were we given any explanation for the discrepancy between the top copy and the carbon copy of what was supposed to be the same letter. It seems such a state of affairs is acceptable in South Australia. The nature of the charge, presumably corruption involving money, was likely to be considered more impressive in a public hearing. The facts that I was working at Andrewartha's request, when the demonstrator he had appointed left with virtually no notice, and that he had never complained about the amount of time I spent preparing materials for the teaching of a revised course for which the Department of Zoology was poorly equipped, were further contradictions to this charge.

Contradictions

These are not the only contradictions for which a final answer needs to be given. Other contradictions in the treatment Manwell received at the University of Adelaide need to be explained.

In the sacking complaint Andrewartha had criticised Manwell's first-year teaching. However, as mentioned in the previous section, Andrewartha had later admitted that Manwell's advanced teaching was well received. Why then did the administration of the University allow Andrewartha to remove Manwell's advanced teaching and to assign Manwell to much more first-year teaching? Andrewartha even attempted to assign Manwell to teaching statistics — despite the complaints about the use of Chi-square statistics in the book. Did the administration really believe the accuracy and importance of Andrewartha's complaint? Was the administration prepared to tolerate any sort of victimisation after the failed sacking attempt, even if it was in direct contradiction to the sacking complaint? Why did the administration fail to give Manwell any relief from his teaching duties in order to prepare his defence before the Commission of Inquiry and the Committee of Three?

Of particular interest is the fact that, despite the Committee of Three's report, which was not favourable to Manwell, Professor Andrewartha was still not satisfied. I quote from Andrewartha's letter of 1 May 1972 to the Council of the University of Adelaide:

> I ask the Council not to receive the Report on Residual Problems in the Department of Zoology...
>
> On reflection I do not now believe that the Committee's denigration of me was malicious. I think that it may have been a mere consequence of the pre-established need to whitewash Professor Manwell and that it may have crept in almost unnoticed by the Committee while it was absorbed in this task...
>
> I urge the rejection of this Report but at the same time I have a constructive alternative which I would like the Council to consider at the appropriate time. I have written the details of my proposal to the Vice-Chancellor, leaving it to his discretion to bring the matter forward at the appropriate time.
>
> I believe that the solution which I have proposed to the Vice-Chancellor is practicable and has a reasonable chance of success; I hope that it may be accepted. But I do not believe that it is the most moral solution to the problem. I believe that the most moral solution to the problem... would be for the Council to acknowledge frankly that the abortive "Inquiry" that was held in 1971 was no inquiry at all, and to take steps to conduct a proper inquiry under Chapter IV of the Statutes. If I were invited by the Council I would be prepared to present a complete complaint technically worded and fully documented.
>
> In this connection I would remind the Council that on April 19th, 1971 I wrote a short 4-page letter to the Vice-Chancellor which I thought (and I believe that the Vice-Chancellor held the same opinion) would serve to open a full Inquiry into Professor Manwell's relations...

Andrewartha's letter to the Council of the University of Adelaide is a surprising document, to say the least. Nowhere in the Committee of Three's report can I find any passage that would qualify as "denigration" of Andrewartha. As discussed previously, the Committee of Three's report did not "whitewash" Manwell.

In one sense the report was unfair to Andrewartha as well as to Manwell. Had the Committee of Three's published report included a verbatim transcript of all the testimony, as well as copies of all documents, it would have been much clearer to the Council and to the remainder of the University community that *other* staff members of the University of Adelaide had misinformed Andrewartha. The failure of the Committee of Three to report what actually took place allowed those who had supplied the misinformation to get away with it — and in some cases to continue to cause trouble.

Andrewartha's letter to the Council of the University of Adelaide, quoted above, shows that he did not accept the judgement of the Council's Commission of Inquiry or the Council's Committee of Three. For the Council to ignore such apparent insubordination is revealing. It was also grossly unfair to Manwell. The Council's act, of leaving Manwell under the administrative control of Andrewartha, branded Manwell as guilty, both to the remainder of the University community and to the international community of scholars.

And, some at least in the University administration were aware of an important precedent — which only became public knowledge during the court case in 1975: Manwell's predecessor, the previous Second Professor of Zoology, a distinguished Australian, testified in court that he had had a serious conflict with Andrewartha and that this was resolved fairly by the University administration when they transferred him from the control of Andrewartha to a personal Chair in the Waite Agricultural Institute of the University of Adelaide (although he continued to do some teaching in the Department of Zoology).

Without access to the secret records of the University administration, it is impossible to know who in the administration was aware of this precedent, or whether or not there was any opposition to the victimisation of Manwell. As the previous Second Professor of Zoology came from an almost identical background to Andrewartha, the reason for that conflict cannot rest in the Committee of Three's attempt at explanation: "a difference in background". As the conflict between Andrewartha and the previous Second Professor of Zoology took place before Manwell arrived, not even in the University of Adelaide was it reasonable to blame him for the situation.[39]

There is also evidence, which only became public in 1977, that the University Council may not have been in agreement over the victimisation of Manwell. A member of the local establishment, who was then a member of the University Council, made an unprecedented critical analysis of the Council's inadequacies in an article in a local newspaper:

> Urgent matters going to the true heart of university interests, such as the dispute involving the Zoology Department (which scandalously, was allowed to drag on for four or five years) and the way a certain chair was filled recently after two years of politicking, tend to be swept under the carpet due to pusillanimity and the workings of the committee system.[40]

That member's central theme is of vital importance, for it suggests that the problem is more the fault of the system than of individuals: the University Council "never has enough time to make well informed, well debated decisions" because a few special interest groups have ways to get their business before the Council.

The Standard of Discipline — or the Double Standard?

As discussed elsewhere (Introduction; Charges and Cross-Examination) it is difficult to prove suppression. Even if personality conflict (a common occurrence in some academic institutions) is not a significant factor prior to the attempt to discipline a dissident, it is certain to occur after any unfair attempt at discipline. An important complicating factor is that often there are a number of individuals involved in a sacking attempt. The author of a sacking complaint may really believe that he is honestly describing grievous and accurate charges against the work performance of the dissident. The problem is that other individuals, often keeping discreetly in the background, have given the author of a dismissal complaint information that is slanted. Such inaccurate information from other individuals can arise in at least four different ways:

1. A motive of suppression, to discredit the dissident.
2. A motive of personal dislike for the dissident — or a motive of personal dislike for the author of the sacking complaint. In the latter situation the motive for supplying

misinformation against the dissident is to entrap the author of the dismissal complaint into bringing incorrect charges, with the possibility of subsequent exposure.

3. A desire to please some vested interest. This might be in order to obtain research funds, or to advance in the hierarchy.

4. Just sheer incompetence in bringing incorrect information to the attention of a superior.

Suppression motives can show finer distinctions. There may be the desire to protect some specific agency or individual. There may be a more generalised dislike of criticism, or "boat-rocking". In a provincial institution there is often a dislike of any critic, although tolerance may be extended on the basis of local connection or on the basis that the criticisms are not really a threat which might effect reform.

Providing certain criteria for suppression are met, the existence of a double standard in discipline adds credibility to the interpretation of events as being *suppression*. Let us now look at certain features of this case history, and then let us compare it with other examples of the standard of discipline at the University of Adelaide:

1. Complaints about the dissident act are made to the dissident's superiors, not to the dissident himself. In this case, Manwell's letter to the fruit fly section of the Department of Agriculture was not answered — but was turned over to Professor Andrewartha, Manwell's immediate superior. Note also that neither the South Australia Department of Agriculture, nor the parliamentarians who criticised our public comments on the fruit fly program, deigned to provide unpersonalised and reasoned criticisms of our comments for the media. In addition, the South Australia Department of Agriculture has been involved in other suppression cases.[41]

2. In the official letters of complaint, alleging unsatisfactory performance, certain activities which had occurred *before* the act of dissidence were not complained about until *after* the act of dissidence. In this case, Andrewartha complained in his second letter to the Vice-Chancellor, dated 19 April 1971 (and used by the Commission of Inquiry as the sacking charges), that Manwell had lectured on Human Biology instead of Mechanisms of Evolution in the previous years in the first-year course — although the Vice-Chancellor's *Statement*[42] makes clear that this situation had been accepted, and presumably approved, by Andrewartha in official Zoology Department documents. Indeed, in the court case in 1975 it was brought out that another staff member, from the Department of Genetics, had lectured upon Mechanisms of Evolution, had set reading in a book with that very title, and had set examination questions on that topic. At the University of Adelaide such a fundamental contradiction was apparently entirely acceptable.[43]

3. Charges laid against the dissident are inadequate in substance or are erroneous in specific examples of alleged misconduct. In this case, the Council's own Commission of Inquiry considered the charges to be inadequate by the standards set in the dismissal statutes. The Vice-Chancellor's *Statement*[44] reports that the specific allegations of any significance are erroneous.

4. Supporters of the dissident, or even neutral parties whose comments do not support victimisation, are themselves harassed. In this case, two of the three academic witnesses for Manwell at the court case complained to us of being threatened by other academics. Manwell's students, or prospective students, complained to us on numerous occasions about harassment. At one stage in the affair, a group of students attempted to get matters aired before the Faculty of Science — but that attempt too was suppressed. A letter from a victimised prospective student was shown to the Committee of Three, apparently without effect.[45] As the dissident's wife, I have been repeatedly subjected to victimisation within the University, except for the period when the then Vice-Chancellor, after the publication of his *Statement*[46] was still in authority within the

University. During that time the pledge that he made — "I will do all I can to help everyone in the University to work harmoniously together" — was kept.[47] His example kept those who had benefited from Andrewartha's sacking attempt in their proper place. When the then Vice-Chancellor left the University of Adelaide, the harassment returned.

5.   Violence and threats of violence are used; "frame-up" situations are created. The situation at the University of Adelaide has some remarkable parallels with the Orr case at the University of Tasmania[48] and with the O'Brien case at the University of Western Australia.[49] Manwell received repeated threats of violence from unidentified individuals. On several occasions in the University, situations were encountered which appeared to be set up — with violence having an unanticipated outcome in one instance. While the general climate of victimisation revealed in this case history is such as to induce a feeling of paranoia, certain incidents involving known supporters of the sacking attempt, or individuals who profited from the sacking attempt, cannot be interpreted as being innocent. It is important to emphasise that we have no evidence that Andrewartha himself was involved in any of these situations; indeed, most of them occurred after he had retired from the University. Furthermore, we believe that he would strongly disapprove of the behaviour of certain of his supporters. The use of violence seems to have become necessary to cover up for the original error and suppression. If the matter were simply one of a mistaken belief that justifiable charges for sacking existed, then as soon as evidence against the charges was accepted by the higher administration, that should have been the end of it. Instead, there is an obsessive desire to destroy the dissident, a desire that knows no limits. This overreaction is one of guilt — guilt from having been revealed as having profited from the promulgation of falsehood.

6.   There is selective violation of privacy; information about an intended sacking becomes circulated as a means for discrediting the dissident. In this case, the first indications of the sacking attempt and our first knowledge of the charges came via a reporter from a local newspaper — hardly the proper procedure for handling sacking complaints as specified in the University's statutes. It is not known who was responsible for the leaking of this information.[50] It contrasts with the effective secrecy imposed by the University administration in other instances where the University community had much more right to the information, as in an example provided below. The selective use of privacy is shown by the fact that the Commission of Inquiry was to be a "star chamber" affair, until the threat of a riot in the Council chamber caused a change in the original decision.[51] Clearly, privacy would have been very much to Manwell's advantage in the initial stages of the affair. However, once the gossip started, then a public hearing, with the charges and the evidence, would always be to the benefit of an innocent individual. As the criticisms Manwell made about the fruit fly spraying could not be easily countered, the news of the sacking attempt, and the *lack* of news about the inadequacies of the charges, would be the most effective strategy for suppression.

Finally, what about comparative standards of discipline at the University of Adelaide? Can the affair be explained as a result of an attempt "to run a tight ship"? Given the concern over discipline expressed in some of the Council's communications, such as the examples given earlier in relation to attempts to make dismissal easier[52], can the situation be explained as a consequence of the desire to impose the highest standards of behaviour?

One of the more disillusioning aspects of the entire episode was the number of occasions when other staff members, or students, told us of serious misbehaviour occurring in the University. It is not, however, necessary to divulge these allegations, some of which may well have been incorrect or exaggerated. It is sufficient to mention two publicised examples where the offenders have had the opportunity to deny the allegations.

Inadequacies in the teaching of another staff member in the Department of Zoology were such as to provoke a revolt by the normally docile students of Zoology II, most of whom signed a petition alleging "the inability of the Department of Zoology to mount a course of adequate quality".[53] There is no evidence known to us that Andrewartha or anyone else took any disciplinary action over a situation which gave the Department considerable bad publicity. Was that because Manwell had nothing to do with the Zoology II course at that time?

The other example is more recent. It did not involve the Department of Zoology in any way. It supplies, however, an important counter-example to the high-standards-of-discipline hypothesis. This second example is best presented in the words of aggrieved students:

> Late last year a woman student at Adelaide University had a harrowing experience when a male lecturer followed her through the campus at night.
>
> In spite of her attempts to fend him off, the lecturer involved put his arm around her and tried to kiss her. The woman had just separated from the friends with whom she had spent the evening and she, and the academic involved, were completely alone.
>
> To protect the identity of the woman student neither she nor the lecturer will be named, but for her it was a terrifying experience which she will not easily forget.
>
> This lecturer had for a long time taken an interest in a student club connected with his department. On the night when the woman was harassed he had arranged for the club members to hold a function in the University Staff Club on the Hughes Plaza.
>
> . . . as the evening drew to a close, the staff member began talking about her grades. He tutored her in one of her subjects and he mentioned a possible discrepancy in her marks.
>
> She took this seriously and as she left with her friends she was worried about her academic performance. She separated from the group to go to her car and was followed and harassed by the academic.
>
> When she reached her car she let herself in, believing that the worst of it was over.
>
> However, he stood in front of her car preventing her from driving off. She wound down the window to tell him to go but he seized the opportunity to open the car door and force his way in. He made her drive to the Law School car park where he had left his vehicle. He was persistent. Even then he was still trying to kiss her.
>
> Eventually she succeeded in pushing him out and was left distraught and upset and very worried about her marks . . .
>
> It is instructive to consider what happened to the harasser whose episode was described above. He is still teaching in this University. Although complaints were made and some form of admonition was eventually delivered to him, he has not had to pay for the degrading way in which he treated one of his students.
>
> Liz Burdon and
> *On Dit* staff[54]

There has been no denial of any part of the description of this case of violent sexual harassment, coupled with an attempt to manipulate the student's grade. Furthermore, it has been impossible to obtain an official statement explaining the case and justifying the way it was handled. The students reported that the sexual harasser "is still teaching in this University". However, an "off-the-record" comment from an administrator (who does not wish to be identified) was that the offending staff member had been allowed to resign for reasons of "health". That suggests that resignation did not come until *after* students "blew-the-whistle" in the newspaper. Even worse, there are persistent rumours that this staff member was paid handsomely to take early retirement. The excuse is that he had a "drink problem".

The combination of carefully calculated secrecy and the failure to invoke the dismissal statutes is a blow, whether to student morale, to the high-standard-of-discipline hypothesis, or to many Australian academics. The failure to let justice be *seen* to be done has meant that *all* staff members who have recently left the University in early retirement, or to go elsewhere, are among the candidates for the inevitable speculation and gossip.

"Another Entomological Vietnam"

What then of the issue that precipitated this case, the fruit fly problem in South Australia? In 1972, the year following our public criticisms of the fruit fly eradication program, there were four outbreaks, including one in the affluent suburb of Burnside. The South Australia Department of Agriculture began using a more toxic organophosphate pesticide in some of the cover-spraying.[55] There were not only reports of extensive bird kills, but also complaints of cats being taken ill or found dead. In an upper-middle class suburb there was no shortage of vocal opponents to the "overkill" aspects of the fruit fly program. Another staff member of the Department of Zoology, and his wife, experienced fruit fly "eradication" at first hand and made their opinions, which were similar to ours, a matter of public record:

> Mr Dunstan's [the then Premier of South Australia] views on fruit fly spraying... are inconsistent with his alleged concern for the environment, which apparently only extends to trivialities.
>
> As pointed out in leaflets now being distributed by the Stop the Spraying Campaign (which bear the name of the Campaign and its address and are therefore not anonymous, as he claims), the present fruit fly eradication programme is destroying birds and beneficial insects, and is exposing householders to a poison...
>
> We fully agree with Mr Dunstan and the Department of Agriculture in their insistence that fruit fly must be controlled.
>
> On the other hand, we deny that the present eradication programme is the most suitable for SA [South Australian] conditions.
>
> There is a perfectly unobjectionable alternative — the sterile male method — which does not involve the use of poisons, or any risk to human health or the environment and which is being used in other parts of the world.[56]

Also in 1972, the Environmental Interdisciplinary Committee, a group of individuals who represented different South Australian professional bodies, including medicine, chemistry, engineering and other sciences, held its own investigation of the fruit fly program in Adelaide. Its report [57] reached almost identical conclusions with those written by us a year earlier, although we were not involved in preparing the report, nor in its approval by the Ecological Society of South Australia.

As the years have passed, it has become gradually apparent that the fruit fly situation in Adelaide is getting worse, not better. In the period 1947 to 1971, before we went public on fruit fly, outbreaks occurred in fewer than half of the years. Since 1971 outbreaks have occurred in every year but one. The repeated claims by politicians and by the South Australia Department of Agriculture, that they are winning the war against fruit fly, do not agree with the facts. What is especially ominous is that the overall trend in outbreaks-per-year seems to have risen in the 1970s despite the increasingly unfavourable weather for fruit fly: prolonged droughts, cold winters and hot, dry summers.

A few of the South Australian politicians are beginning to realise that there is "no light at the end of the tunnel". One of the parliamentarians who had been so eager to attack Manwell in 1971 complained in 1974 that the outbreak was "the largest ever" and then even advocated biological control (if in a form that was inappropriate to the problem!):

> I have been interested in the biological control of fruit fly for many years. Officers can get bugs to do the work for them, and the bugs enjoy doing it. The method is cheaper than spending much money on chemicals, which pollute the air.[58]

But, worse was to come. By 1979–80 there were 11 outbreaks in one fiscal year, including, for the first time, winter outbreaks. Thus, our 1971 predictions, of more pesticide resistant fruit fly and more climatically tolerant fruit fly, were confirmed. Although not yet recorded from South Australia, and, hopefully outside its range of temperature adaptation, Oriental Fruit Fly, a species that attacks over two hundred different varieties of fruit and is a major pest in many parts of the world, had been reported as having invaded over one-third of the Northern Territory. The need for action against fruit fly at a federal level, to develop sterile male eradication programs, and the prediction of "another entomological Vietnam" continued to be ignored.[59]

Further cracks in the monolithic local fruit fly dogma appeared when one Member of Parliament found that "a delicious and attractive peach" was "a mouthful of maggots" and complained of:

... the shocking indifference of both Ministers of Agriculture in this Labor Government for the way in which they have ignored my request for information and reassurance about the retention of our road-block system during the time that this Government has been in office.[60]

Lynn Arnold, representing the Labor government, replied rather facetiously:

As to whether or not they [road block inspections] are very effective technically, it is not absolutely convincing... it is more the perceived effectiveness on those who pass by... It is a difficult thing to assess short of interviewing fruit flies coming through and asking them whether they are deterred by the road block.[61]

However, the Labor government appeared to reverse its earlier decision to drop the road-block inspections at the borders. Certainly, with the present understanding of the fruit fly problem, it would be extremely unwise to stop the border inspections. In fact, the rather lax standards should be tightened up. Nor need one begin "interviewing fruit flies" to monitor the effectiveness of the road-block inspections. It is likely that molecular markers can be used to tell where fruit fly immigrants are coming from.

The lax standards for fruit fly inspection at the borders (and the airport) are not the only signs of a poor attitude towards the fruit fly problem in South Australia. The failure to cope with fruit fly has had the unfortunate consequence that some people take the program as a joke. In 1981 a beer company was using fake fruit fly inspectors in a television commercial. The Minister for Agriculture admitted that such a humorous advertisement could damage the fruit fly program because: "We do have some credibility problems in this area..."[62] However, the Labor government, ready enough to tolerate, if not condone, the suppression of academic critics, was not prepared to suppress such powerful vested interests as local advertising agencies or breweries.

The reader may wonder why South Australia did not follow the trend and use sterile males to eradicate fruit fly, a method that has been successful in other places since the 1960s.[63] The South Australia Department of Agriculture began to raise sterile males, but, for reasons which have not been fully explained, the programme was a failure:

Unfortunately, the sterile males that were bred in captivity under sheltered conditions could not survive when turned out into the wild and they could not excite their wild sisters sufficiently to be of any use.[64]

Yet, in Western Australia sterile males have been successfully produced with sufficient libido to, in the first field trials, almost eradicate a vigorous and long-standing population of Med-fly.[65]

Why have the politicians, public servants and scientists in the South Australian government been unable to accomplish what others in many countries, and now Western Australia, have been able to do: eradicate isolated populations of fruit fly?

The answer rests in our case history: in South Australia it has been easier to suppress discussion and dissenting views than to suppress fruit fly populations. In Western Australia residents were able to get compensation through the courts for damage done in overly enthusiastic pesticide-based eradication programs; accordingly, there has been a more effective drive to reduce pesticide usage and to adopt the highly specific sterile male method.

Although the Council of the University of Adelaide accepted the report of its Committee of Three (or Committee on Residual Problems in Zoology) it declined to accept one suggestion by its Committee which was the essence of scholarly responsibility:

> We [the Committee of Three] believe, from the several interesting discussions we had, that the fruit fly problem is of considerable scientific importance and interest. We feel it would be useful to arrange a discussion on this topic in the University under the aegis of the Department of Adult Education.

Why should the University Council suppress such a proposed discussion? Why did the University community accept such censorship without any visible signs of protest?

Such is the march of folly into "another entomological Vietnam". But, the consequences of the acceptance of suppression extend far beyond the politics of pest control and eradication. The pattern of suppression and scapegoating in an institution of higher education, run by the cream of local society, has grievous implications for the entire society. It is to the information-processing leadership, the scholars, the judiciary and the politicians, that the community looks for the standards of justice.

References

1. C. M. Ann Baker (ed.), *Fruit Fly Papers* (Committee of Concerned Scholars, privately published 24-page document, 1973). The updated version of the *Fruit Fly Papers* keeps intact approximately one-quarter of the original document. Some general sections discussing academic problems have been deleted because they overlap material presented elsewhere in this book. With the passage of time additional information became available, both on the fruit fly problem in South Australia and on the sacking attempt. The 1975 court case was settled before judgement, when the University administration finally agreed to publish the facts concerning the dismissal charges (and to publish those facts *without* the previous condition that Manwell resign in order to have his name cleared of false charges!). The 1975 court case provided important insights not available at the time the original *Fruit Fly Papers* were prepared. I express my gratitude to the original members of the Committee of Concerned Scholars. I thank the then editors of *On Dit* and the members of the University community who opened the "star chamber" trial to the public and who liberated (or violated, depending on your point of view) documents which helped to prove my husband's innocence. I thank also the members of the international community of scholars who wrote to the University, or to newspapers, protesting the treatment we received.

2. G. M. Badger, "Statement concerning the complaint by Professor H. G. Andrewartha against Professor C. Manwell", *Lumen* (University of Adelaide), 3 June 1975, pp. 3–6, reproduced in this volume on pp. 113–120.

3. Judy Chase, "Fly in funding ointment", *Times Higher Education Supplement,* 26 April 1974, p. 13.

4. G. M. Badger, "The fruit fly papers", ibid., 21 June 1974, p. 22.

5. C. Manwell, "The fruit fly papers", ibid., 18 October 1974, p. 23.

6. A. E. Shields, "The fruit fly papers", ibid., 3 January 1975, p. 8.

7. Clyde Manwell, "Peer review: a case history from the Australian Research Grants Committee", *Search* 10, pp. 81–6 (1979).

8. Clyde Manwell, "An open letter to the president of FAUSA", the *Australian* (*Higher Education Supplement*), 27 May 1981.

9. Clyde Manwell, "How to get rid of environmentally oriented teaching", *On Dit* (University of Adelaide student newspaper), vol. 50, no. 9, Fifty Year Memorial Issue (7 June 1982), p. 16.

10. See note 2 above.

11. This was not only a generous act by the former Vice-Chancellor, it was good administrative policy. It made it clear to certain of the supporters of the sacking complaint that they should behave, for the victim was not without some influential support within the institution. At the same time, it meant that the supporters would not have their own access to funds within the Department squeezed. It should not be forgotten that where a Department Head (or Chairman and his clique) have control of departmental funds it is not difficult to find reasons to reduce the shares given to disfavoured individuals; worse, if some get less, others will get more and, accordingly, easily rationalise (or exacerbate) the situation. The use of more "statutory" means for allocating resources, i.e., that each staff member gets an equal share, and that expenditures for teaching are set on a per student basis, would reduce the prizes to be gained by scapegoating and intrigue, and thus would reduce the tensions within some universities.

12. It is important to distinguish between the actions of some of the members of the executive of the Staff Association in 1971–75 and some of the earlier members of that executive. One official of the Staff Association at the time Professor Manwell asked for assistance told him: "Sorry, there is little we can do for you as we have never had a case like this before". Later we learned that another prominent official of the local Staff Association was a consultant for the Department of Agriculture's fruit fly program and also a protégé of the author of the sacking complaint! However, a distinguished academic who had earlier been a Staff Association official not only correctly predicted the response of those who were at that time members of the "inner circle" of the local Staff Association, but also warned: "Get a lawyer. You do not realise your danger". He then went on to point out how the smugness of Adelaide provincialism would not be bothered by the fact that the charges were false and that others had been driven out of the University of Adelaide in a similar way.

13. See note 2 above.

14. Article 12 of the Universal Declaration of Human Rights reads: "No one shall be subjected to arbitrary interference with his privacy...nor to attacks upon his honour and reputation. Everyone has the right to the protection of the law against such interference or attacks." A. H. Robertson, *Human Rights in the World* (Manchester University Press, 1972), p. 187.

15. Several species of fruit fly (Tephritidae) are serious pests in Australia, with the introduced "Med-fly", *Ceratitis capitata*, and the native Queensland Fruit Fly, *Dacus tryoni*, being the major pest species. See R. A. I. Drew, G. H. S. Hooper and M. A. Bateman, *Economic Fruit Flies of the South Pacific Region* (Queensland: Plant Quarantine and Entomology Branch, Department of Primary Industries, 1978; a second edition with a few changes was published in 1982). For the first discussion of fruit fly in South Australia, see H. G. Andrewartha, *Fruit Fly* (South Australia Department of Agriculture, eight-page pamphlet, 1947) and D. C. Swan, *Fruit Flies* (South Australia Department of Agriculture Bulletin 409, February 1949).

16. Queensland Fruit Fly have a relatively limited temperature tolerance: see A. Meats, "The bioclimatic potential of the Queensland fruit fly, *Dacus tryoni* in Australia", *Proceedings of the Ecological Society of Australia* 11, pp. 151–61 (1981). A few days at 35°C is sufficient to sterilise adults and immatures; summer temperatures in South Australia can exceed 40°C. Nevertheless, there is evidence to suggest that in the last

hundred years Queensland Fruit Fly have extended their range into much of eastern New South Wales and the extreme eastern part of Victoria; thus, presumably, there has been some evolution of tolerance to greater extremes of temperature, possibly as a consequence of hybridisation with another member of the genus *Dacus*: see C. E. Birch and H. G. Andrewartha, "Queensland fruit fly: a study in evolution and control", *New Scientist* 28, pp.204–7 (1966).

17. M. A. Bateman, "Area control as a tool in integrated pest management systems", in P. J. Cameron, C. H. Wearing and W. M. Kain (eds), *Proceedings of the Australasian Workshop on Development and Implementation of Integrated Pest Management* (Auckland, New Zealand: Entomology Division of DSIR, 1982), pp. 162–72.

18. Robert van den Bosch, "The pesticide Mafia", *Ecologist*, vol. 10, March issue, pp. 78–82 (1980); Mary Louise Flint and Robert van den Bosch, *Introduction to Integrated Pest Management* (New York: Plenum Press, 1981). See also: Paul Ehrlich and Anne Ehrlich, *Population/Resources/Environment* (San Francisco: Freeman, 1972, second edition); and David Pimental (ed.), *World Food, Pest Losses, and the Environment* (American Association for the Advancement of Science, Selected Symposium No. 13, 1978). These more recent publications basically confirm the politics of pest control as claimed by earlier environmentalists, who were often the targets of suppression, e.g., Rachel Carson, *Silent Spring* (Boston: Houghton-Miflin, 1962); Frank Egler, "Pesticides in our ecosystem", *American Scientist* 52, pp. 110–36 (1964); Frank Egler, "Pesticides in our ecosystem: communication II", *BioScience* 14, pp. 29–36 (1964); Richard Rudd, *Pesticides and the Living Landscape* (University of Wisconsin Press, 1964); Harry Rothman, *Murderous Providence: A Study of Pollution in Industrial Societies* (London: Rupert Hart-Davis, 1972). A meeting of the Entomological Society of America censured not only Frank Egler for his *BioScience* article but also the editorial board of *BioScience* for publishing it. Many members of the Entomological Society of America receive research funds from pesticide companies or the US Department of Agriculture, a bureaucracy captured by agribusiness interests. It was later revealed that the issue of *BioScience* containing Egler's excellent paper only arrived at subscribers' addresses at the time the Entomological Society of America was having the meeting at which it passed the vote of censure: thus, it is doubtful if most of those voting had the opportunity to read the article before voting: see C. L. Judson, "Pesticides, politics and peace" (letter), *BioScience* 15, p. 159 (1965).

19. Baker, op. cit.

20. Some of the local news-reporting of our comments was incomplete or distorted. A detailed description of our criticisms was published in *On Dit*: Clyde Manwell and C. M. Ann Baker, "Use and abuse of science. I. The fruit fly programme in South Australia", *On Dit*, 17 March 1971, pp. 10–12.

21. An American authority on fruit fly eradication recently concluded: "The medfly has been eradicated from the continental U.S. six times — with applications of pesticides. However, such applications are undesirable in urban areas. Fortunately, the SIRM [Sterile Insect Release Method] against medflies has been well developed and tested in Hawaii, Cyprus, Spain, Italy, and Central America". He then describes how Med-fly were eradicated by the use of sterile males when an outbreak covering 100 square miles in Los Angeles County occurred in 1975 (an area much larger than any Adelaide Med-fly outbreak I know of): see L. E. LaChance, "Genetic strategies affecting the success and economy of the sterile insect release method", in: Marjorie A. Hoy and John J. McKelvey, Jr. (eds), *Genetics in Relation to Insect Management* (New York: Rockefeller Foundation, 1979), p. 9. The sterile male method is not a panacea. A later outbreak in California turned into a disaster when inadequately sterile males were released. That, however, was not the fault of the method itself but inadequate "quality control",

which should always check radiation dosage and percentage sterility (as well as mating competitiveness). I have been informed of the fact that one fruit fly outbreak in Adelaide went temporarily out of control because of an error in diluting the pesticide. For theoretical reasons which need not be discussed here, the sterile male method is intrinsically much more suitable for complete eradication than is pesticide application: see, for example, the classic paper by E. F. Knipling, "Sterile male method of population control", *Science* 130, pp. 902–4 (1959); also, T. P. Bogyo, A. A. Berryman and T. A. Sweeny, "Computer simulation of population reduction by release of sterile insects, I", *International Atomic Energy Authority Panel Proceedings*, pp. 19–25 (1971).

22. D. N. Brookman, in *Parliamentary Debates* (South Australia, 3 March 1971), p. 3721. For other attacks, see C. R. Story, ibid., 3 March 1971, p. 3701; H. K. Kemp, ibid., 11 March 1971, p. 3963. Brookman and Kemp were then well-known ultra-conservatives. Kemp had attempted to introduce legislation to broaden the grounds for dismissal of academics. Brookman had also been a member of the Council of the University of Adelaide.

23. This quotation reveals more than just the cult of the expert. It reveals how misinformation flows through the University bureaucracy. Some individuals persuaded Andrewartha that Manwell's (and my) criticisms were an attack on his expertise. First, as the discussion of fruit fly in the text and the notes of this chapter show, no single expertise, including "population ecology", is the whole story. If any specialty is important in understanding problems such as the emergence of resistance to pesticides, or the emergence of pre-mating isolation (which can cause the breakdown of a sterile male eradication program), it is mechanisms of evolution together with molecular biology. Second, my own expertise involved agriculture, including working for the Ministry of Agriculture, Fisheries and Food (England and Wales). Manwell had specific expertise with orchard pests and had done research over many more zoological topics than just "physiology". As the Vice-Chancellor was ultimately to admit, "Professor Andrewartha did not give detailed particulars of any allegedly unscientific statement either in his formal letters of complaint or with me in correspondence" (quoting p. 4 of his *Statement*: see note 2 above). Thus, Andrewartha never particularised his objections to our criticisms, despite having had every opportunity to do so — including four weeks of examination and cross-examination in the Supreme Court of South Australia in 1975. In fact, there was little difference in even the details of the scientific views by Manwell and Andrewartha on fruit fly. In our presence Andrewartha had made some strong criticisms about the way the South Australia Department of Agriculture carried out the fruit fly eradication program. Andrewartha had been co-author of an article recommending the use of the sterile male method against Queensland Fruit Fly (see Birch and Andrewartha, note 16 above). Although it was popular in Adelaide to ascribe the cover-spraying to Andrewartha's advice to the Department of Agriculture, that is incorrect; Andrewartha did not advocate cover-spraying in his original article (see note 15 above). The cover-spraying appears to have been the idea of Sir Thomas Playford, a former Premier of South Australia: C. R. Story in *Parliamentary Debates* (South Australia, 14 August 1974), p. 447.

24. This refers to the attempted sacking of Dr David Craig from the University of Lancaster, basically over allegations of Marxist bias in teaching and examining in 1971–72. When it was found that the Head of Department's allegations were not such as to warrant dismissal, the administration of the University of Lancaster protected Craig's research and teaching by removing him from the authority of the Head of the Department, thus defusing further conflict. The University of Adelaide administration could not easily have been unaware of this case, for it received widespread publicity in

academic circles. See, for example, *The Craig Affair* (London: Council for Academic Freedom and Democracy, 1972); Roger Grinyer, "Craig affair moves to climax", *Times Higher Education Supplement*, 28 April 1972, p. 1; "The Craig affair — documents from the CAFD file", ibid., p. 7; Roger Grinyer, "Uneasy peace follows Craig compromise", ibid., 5 May 1972, pp. 1, 24; E. J. Hobsbawm, "Accepting new facts of life in the universities", ibid., 12 May 1972, p. 1. Several factors appeared to have contributed to getting fairer treatment for a victimised staff member at the University of Lancaster when compared with the University of Adelaide. Even though the Vice-Chancellor tended to support authority, he was prepared to admit that the administration was not without error: "Among the purposes of the college system was to prevent the university becoming soulless and monolithic, aloofly ruled by faceless bureaucrats. We have slipped too far in that direction". (Mr Charles Carter, Vice-Chancellor, quoted by Brian MacArthur, "Carter defends decision to force confrontation with students", *Times Higher Education Supplement*, 21 April 1972, p. 5). Although the AUT branch at the University of Lancaster let Craig down, the academic group of the ASTMS (Association of Scientific, Technical and Management Staff trade union) "struggled to the bitter end on behalf of myself and my victimized colleagues", quoting David Craig, "The solidarity of university teachers" (letter to the editor), *Times Higher Education Supplement*, 12 October 1973, p. 12.

25. Zhores Medvedev and Roy Medvedev, *A Question of Madness* (London: Macmillan, 1972). See also: Sidney Bloch and Peter Reddaway, *Russia's Political Hospitals: the Abuse of Psychiatry in the Soviet Union* (London: Gollancz, 1977); and, Amnesty International, *Prisoners of Conscience in the USSR* (London: Quartermaine House, 1980). For examples of the use of psychiatry to suppress dissent in the "free world", see: Thomas S. Szasz, *The Manufacture of Madness: A Comparative Study of the Inquisition and the Mental Health Movement* (New York: Harper and Row, 1972). Not too surprisingly, Szasz's views have not been popular with some politicians and professionals. Szasz himself describes one response to his earlier book, *The Myth of Mental Illness*: "Within a year of its publication, the Commissioner of the New York State Department of Mental Hygiene demanded, in a letter . . . , that I be dismissed from my university position because I did not 'believe' in mental illness". Quotation from pp. 11–12 of Thomas S. Szasz, "The Myth of Mental Illness: three addenda", *Journal of Humanistic Psychology* 14, pp. 11–19 (1974).

26. W. H. C. Eddy, *Orr* (Brisbane: Jacaranda Press, 1961). See also, in the present work, the chapter "Not Merely Malice".

27. A. E. Shields, "Report on University Personnel Officer/Ombudsman" (four-page document, dated 27 March 1981), pp. 1, 2. Not only have the former Registrar's cogent arguments for an Ombudsperson been ignored, but there appears to have been an attempt to keep the issue from being openly debated on campus. The document itself was distributed to us amongst material from the Staff Association but there is no indication on the document itself as to what its official status or sponsorship is.

28. "Proposed changes to tenure statutes", *University of Adelaide Bulletin*, vol. 8, no. 5, pp. 1–16 (7 May 1982). See also: Clyde Manwell, "Comments on proposed changes to tenure statutes", a six-page document circulated among staff at the University of Adelaide. Earlier, the University of Adelaide Staff Association opposed the proposed weakening of the dismissal statues, e.g., ". . . the changes would achieve nothing except possibly provide a new vehicle for the pursuit of academic vendettas", quoting E. C. Semple, M. Peay, P. Gill and J. F. Keeler, "UASA comments on Report of the Council Committee on Statute IV" (University of Adelaide Staff Association document, 1981), p. 5. The drink and drugs problem was also mentioned by an academic administrator from the University of Adelaide in testimony before the Senate

Standing Committee on Education and the Arts: proofs of the Official Hansard Report, hearings on *Tenure of Academics*, Adelaide, 11 February 1982, pp. 1757–8. Even FAUSA, in discussing "action taken on personal cases" claims that it is working "on a number of longer term projects, including the development of grievance procedures, . . . and the provision of alcohol rehabilitation schemes": *Federation of Australian University Staff Associations Newsletter*, 10 September 1984, p. 4. Might not "the development of grievance procedures" reduce the need for "the provision of alcohol rehabilitation schemes"?

29. Derrick Rowley in an interview with Stewart Cockburn, "S. A. medical education intolerable", Adelaide *Advertiser*, 20 October 1972, p. 5.

30. John Smart, quoted in "Philosophy professor resigns", the *Australian*, 30 December 1971, pp. 1, 3.

31. A. P. Rowe, *If the Gown Fits* (Melbourne University Press, 1961); for a brief description of Rowe's contributions to the University of Adelaide and the antagonistic response he ultimately generated, see the chapter "Paralysis of the Conscience". A number of the quarrels among staff are described in W. G. K. Duncan and R. A. Leonard, *The University of Adelaide 1874–1974* (Adelaide: Rigby, 1975); interestingly, this reference does not examine the attempt to sack Manwell, nor does it mention earlier quarrels among staff in the Department of Zoology which occurred before Manwell arrived in 1969 to take up the second Chair of Zoology.

32. Clyde Manwell and C. M. Ann Baker, unpublished studies.

33. The key word here is "effective". Members of the original Committee of Concerned Scholars interviewed a number of staff members and found that some claimed to have complained privately to members of the administration about the treatment Manwell received. In addition, over thirty individuals from outside Australia wrote letters complaining about the unfairness of the case. None of this had any apparent effect on an administration convinced that might was right. In contrast, there stands the reversal of the decision to hold a "star chamber" trial. Manwell's requests that the Commission of Inquiry be open were refused by the administration. Nor was the Staff Association prepared to fight on Manwell's behalf for this fundamental principle of natural justice. When, to everyone's surprise, several hundred students opened the "star chamber", the Commission of Inquiry quickly adjourned and voted that the trial would be open after all, as Manwell had originally requested. Thus, private appeals for fairness were not effective — but a mass show of solidarity, with the potential for violence, was. In other words, for protest to be effective, it must be public and command sufficient force to get a hearing — a sad reflection on an institution supposedly devoted to truth, fairness and rational argument.

34. Thorstein Veblen, *The Higher Learning in America: A Memorandum on the Conduct of Universities by Business Men* (Stanford: Academic Reprints, 1918, 1954 reprinting); N. Chomsky, "The responsibility of intellectuals", in Theodore Roszak (ed.), *The Dissenting Academy* (London: Chatto and Windus, 1969), pp. 254–98; Ian Yates and Andrew McHugh (eds), *Roger Russell and Australia's Universities: the Pentagon's Trojan Horse?* (Melbourne: Australian Union of Students, 1974); David N. Smith, *Who Rules the Universities?* (New York: Monthly Review Press, 1974).

35. Robert Nisbet, *Degradation of the Academic Dogma* (London: Heinemann, 1971); Frank Knopfelmacher, "University reform", *Quadrant*, December 1969, pp. 41–50; Richard J. Barber, *The American Corporation: Its Power, Its Money, Its Politics* (New York: Dutton, 1970), especially chapter 7; Edward Shils, *The Intellectuals and the Powers* (University of Chicago Press, 1972).

36. Universities Federation for Animal Welfare, *Handbook on the Care and Management of Laboratory Animals* (London: UFAW, second edition), especially p. 367.

37. Manwell, "How to get rid of environmentally oriented teaching", op. cit.

38. In spite of harassment and a lack of support over the past twelve years, Manwell's comparative biochemistry and pollution course has, on average, trebled its enrolment. This has occurred over a period of time when interest in the environment has waned, and other environmental courses and programs have had declining numbers of applicants.

39. The full details of the conflict between Professor Andrewartha and the previous Second Professor of Zoology are not known to me. While the "personality conflict" or "difference in background" theory is popular locally, it should be stated, in fairness to all parties, that prior to the fruit fly incident and the sacking attempt, Manwell and Andrewartha got on well together, both professionally and socially. Manwell accepted his position as subordinate to the Head of the Department and did not contest the running of the Zoology Department. This is not just my opinion. The evidence for this statement rests in the absence of any specific allegations of earlier conflict in Andrewartha's letters of complaint.

40. Walter Crocker, "Hour on hour of petty detail", Adelaide *Advertiser*, 27 October 1977, p. 5. Crocker was the Australian ambassador to a number of countries and a career diplomat with the United Nations; he has written several important books on the problems of Asian and European countries. He was also Lieutenant-Governor of South Australia for many years.

41. For example, a representative from the S. A. Department of Agriculture complained about Coulter's criticisms of pesticide use: see "Paralysis of the Conscience" (p. 129).

    In 1974 residents in an area of the Adelaide hills were subjected to extensive spraying of phenoxy-herbicides by the S. A. Department of Agriculture (and other government agencies). Some residents approached Manwell for help in terms of analysing samples for 2,4,5-T and the TCDD ("dioxin") contaminant. In turn, Manwell approached a knowledgeable organic chemist, who was much better equipped for such difficult assays. That organic chemist replied to Manwell (letter dated 11 March 1974):

    > I appreciate your views that it would be desirable to have independent tests on water and plants in the area to see if residues of 2,4,5-T are present.
    >
    > Regretfully, however, I feel that I should not at any price undertake such tests, or indeed direct anyone in the Department at present under my care to conduct such tests.
    >
    > My reasons for this stem from my complete lack of faith in certain government people who, in conjunction with their confraternity in the commercial sphere, tried very hard in a thoroughly despicable way last year to bring discredit upon me, following my criticisms of spraying activities in SA [South Australia] with 2,4,5-T and with amitrole.
    >
    > If any tests conducted by me or anyone in my Department yielded positive results of an embarrassing nature to the same people, I fear that another smear campaign would be implemented and that rumours would be concomitantly circulated to the effect that we had "cooked" our findings.

42. See note 2 above.

43. Manwell had been placed in an especially delicate situation, for shortly after he arrived in Adelaide he was specifically warned by Andrewartha, who knew that Manwell had published some work in genetics, not to intrude on the territory of the Department of Genetics. Manwell, who was (and is) interested in population genetics and evolutionary theory, had, in fact, respected Andrewartha's warning. Certain students — and a staff member — from the Department of Genetics frequently came to Manwell (and to me) for advice and assistance in the use of electrophoresis to measure gene frequencies of biochemical markers in populations. They freely confessed that they did not dare admit to certain senior staff in the Department of Genetics that they had to seek advice from us.

44. See note 2 above.

45. I quote from the letter written by a student to Manwell (published later in *On Dit*, see note 9 above):

> As you doubtless know by now I shall not be coming to work with you. I was refused a Scholarship by your University despite my first class honours...I venture to suggest that forces within your Department set out to deprive you of a student...I had earlier exchanged some rather bitter correspondence with [name of staff member deleted] which left me with no delusions as to the reception I could expect should I go to Adelaide. Fortunately, I was offered a scholarship to...
>
> To close, I must admit to regret that I won't have the opportunity to work with you...The issues you chose to make a stand on are those which also concern me deeply...

46. See note 2 above.

47. See note 11 above.

48. Eddy, op. cit. See also the chapter "Not Merely Malice".

49. Roger Gale, "A new 'Orr case' brewing in the west?", the *Bulletin* (Sydney), 17 March 1983, p. 41; see also the chapter "Archives of Suppression".

50. See note 2 above.

51. See note 33 above.

52. See note 28 above.

53. See note 1 above.

54. Liz Burdon and *On Dit* staff, "Sexual harassment on campus", *On Dit*, vol. 51, issue 5, 11 April 1983, p. 11.

55. Around this time the S.A. Department of Agriculture began to use fenthion as a replacement for malathion in some of the spraying. More recently, there has been the admission of using the toxic, and highly persistent, organochlorine pesticide chlordane "to kill maggots in the soil": see "Fruit fly eradication — what happens in home gardens", South Australia Department of Agriculture Fact Sheet 45/81 (1982 reprinting). Chlordane has been banned from many uses in the USA because it is carcinogenic: Samuel S. Epstein, *The Politics of Cancer* (New York: Anchor/Doubleday, 1979, revised edition). The relatively low acute toxicity of malathion, or the somewhat higher toxicity of fenthion, is only part of the situation. Certain of the milder organophosphate pesticides, mild in terms of short-term toxicity tests, can give rise to dangerous long-term delayed effects: Ronald L. Baron, "Delayed neurotoxicity and other consequences of organophosphate esters", *Annual Reviews of Entomology* 26, pp. 29–48 (1981). Thus, the absence of major acute effects upon exposure is no guarantee that weeks or months later severe symptoms will not develop. Recent World Health Organisation statistics estimate that pesticide poisoning throughout the world seriously injures approximately one million people a year, with 5000 deaths. In South Australia pesticides and other agrichemicals are the second commonest cause of childhood poisoning. Such figures underestimate the role of delayed neurotoxicity and other symptoms whose onset occurs only long after exposure, for the morbidity and mortality statistics are based on observations of immediate acute toxicity.

56. D. A. Duckhouse and Sylvia Duckhouse, "Fruit fly poison", Adelaide *Advertiser*, 6 June 1972, p. 5. Earlier, Dr Duckhouse wrote: "It is high time that this costly programme, the product of a more poison-happy generation of scientists, was updated in line with current concern for conservation of the environment". Adelaide *Advertiser*, 29 April 1972, p. 5.

57. Environmental Interdisciplinary Committee, *The Fruit Fly Problem in Adelaide* (The Report to the Special Committee on Pesticides and Weedicides, 1972). The summary of its views is reprinted in its entirety in the reference in note 1 above.

58. C. R. Story, quoted in *Parliamentary Debates* (South Australia, 14 August 1974), pp. 447–8. This quotation suggests that Story does not understand the problem: the object is eradication, not control; predators or parasites may reduce a population but they almost never eradicate it, in contrast to the sterile male method: see the references by Knipling and by Bogyo and colleagues at the end of note 21 above.

59. Clyde Manwell, "Urgent", the *Australian*, 9 April 1976, p. 8.

60. N. Lewis, quoted in *Parliamentary Debates* (South Australia, 21 September 1983), p. 985.

61. Lynn Arnold, quoted in *Parliamentary Debates* (South Australia, 19 October 1983), p. 1184.

62. B. A. Chatterton, quoted in *Parliamentary Debates* (South Australia, 19 November 1981), p. 2068; and 10 December 1981, p. 2618.

63. See notes 16 and 21 above.

64. C. R. Story, quoted in *Parliamentary Debates* (South Australia, 14 August 1974), p. 448.
    It is true that South Australia has a special problem in that it is repeatedly invaded by two species of fruit fly (see note 15 above). Thus, sterile male cultivation would require raising colonies of both species. This would not be very difficult. The entire situation, however, argues strongly for assistance from the federal government. After all, "Med-fly" are probably coming from Western Australia and Queensland Fruit Fly are probably coming from the eastern states.

65. Kingsley Fisher, Research Officer in charge of the Fruit Fly Eradication Program, Carnarvon, Western Australia, personal communication to Clyde Manwell, 1984. The initial suppression of 98 per cent of the breeding population after three months' flooding with sterile males is expected to be followed by complete eradication. These results are especially good when one considers that the population in Carnarvon is not completely isolated, for there is no way to ensure that people do not bring infected fruit from the large region of south-west Western Australia where Med-fly are numerous. Thus, there is the continuous risk of reintroduction. Planning for this program was first publicised in 1980: Robert Bennett, "Sterile flies may be the final solution", the *Australian*, 30 April 1980, p. 2; see also: K. Fisher, "Fruit fly under attack from the sterile insect technique", *Western Australia Journal of Agriculture* 22, pp. 51–2 (1981).

STATEMENT CONCERNING THE COMPLAINT BY PROFESSOR H. G. ANDREWARTHA AGAINST PROFESSOR C. MANWELL

G. M. Badger

Reprinted from Lumen, *3 June 1975, pp. 3–6.*

On the 19th April 1971, Professor H. G. Andrewartha, Professor of Zoology and Head of that Department, wrote to me to make a formal complaint about the work of Professor C. Manwell of the same Department. At my request, Professor Manwell commented on the complaint in a letter dated 13th May 1971, and Professor Andrewartha commented on his reply in a letter dated 1st June 1971.

There was no suggestion either in the letter of complaint or in subsequent material that Professor C. Manwell has been involved in any matter involving moral turpitude. The complaint related entirely to teaching, research and administration and included a criticism of

Professor Manwell's public statement on the South Australian Department of Agriculture's fruit fly eradication programme.

In due course, the letter of complaint came before the Council of the University and later before a Commission of Enquiry established by the Council and set up in accordance with the provisions of the Statutes of the University. The Commission met in formal session and had before it the letter of complaint, together with certain documents which had originally accompanied it. The Commission had the assistance of Counsel who had been instructed by the University, and the two professors concerned were each represented by Counsel.

It was necessary for the Commission of Inquiry to consider whether the matters which had been alleged by Professor Andrewartha in his letter of complaint, assuming for the purpose of argument that they were in every case well founded in fact, amounted to such conduct on the part of Professor Manwell as was contemplated by the relevant Statute. After hearing argument from all Counsel, the Commission ruled that the matters alleged against Professor Manwell in the letter of complaint were not such as would justify any action under the Statute, even if proved. The Commission of Inquiry therefore made no investigation into nor finding about the matter which had been alleged.

The finding of the Commission of Inquiry, which was adopted by the University Council on 3rd December 1971 and subsequently published throughout the University was as follows:

"We cannot find within that letter" (referring to Professor Andrewartha's letter of complaint) "allegations which, if proved true, would show that Professor Manwell had grossly or persistently neglected his duties or that he had been guilty of serious misconduct in or about the performance of his duties such as would constitute grounds for dismissing him under Clause 9 of Chapter IV of the University Statutes. Accordingly we see no reason for us to proceed further with this inquiry and we recommend that the University Council should not regard or treat this complaint as a basis for dismissing Professor Manwell under Chapter IV of the University Statutes."

The Council recognised that there were problems in the Department, and it asked a small committee consisting of the Deputy Vice-Chancellor, the Chairman of the Education Committee and the President of the Staff Association "to hold discussions with both Professor Andrewartha and Professor Manwell, with a view to advising the Council on the most suitable course of action to be taken". This Committee has been variously referred to as "The Committee on Residual Problems in Zoology" or "The Committee of Three".

After receiving a copy of the letter of complaint by Professor Andrewartha, Professor Manwell wrote to me on 13th May 1971 setting out his version of the matters in the complaint. This letter went before the Commission of Inquiry. As the Commission had not found it necessary for the reasons they gave to enquire into the accuracy of the complaint, Professor Manwell wrote to me on the 3rd December 1971 requesting that he be given an opportunity of demonstrating what he claimed was the factual inaccuracy of the complaints made against him by Professor Andrewartha, and this letter was before the University Council. Professor Manwell did not challenge the right of Professor Andrewartha to hold and express opinions concerning his, Manwell's, scientific work and general capacity, nor did he seek that the University should investigate these matters but that there should be a finding upon the strictly factual allegations upon which the letter of complaint was based.

The Committee of Three held that it was impossible to find fully and finally on the whole body of facts as this would require invoking judicial powers including the power to subpoena and cross examine witnesses.

The report of the Committee of Three was received by the University Council on 9th June 1972 and subsequently published throughout the University along with a number of resolutions by the Council following its consideration of the report.

There has been a great deal of comment on the letter of complaint and related matters since that date. These are widely varying personal opinions on the factual merits, the quality and the relevance of the complaint itself and of the subsequent material generated and of the report.

It appeared to me from information given to me by the Committee of Three that Professor Manwell had been able to establish that a *prima facie* case existed that there were some inaccuracies with regard to factual material in the original letter of complaint. At the request of Professor Manwell, I therefore resolved to carry the investigation of factual material further, and, with the help of the University's solicitors and his solicitors, I made considerable progress. However, as will be explained later, the letter of complaint had become the basis of a libel action by Professor Manwell against Professor Andrewartha. In these circumstances, it was not possible to publish results of my own investigations while the matter was *sub judice*. The libel action did indeed come before the Supreme Court of South Australia on 13th May 1975; but after some days the parties agreed to a settlement out of Court, this settlement to involve the publication by me of my assessment of the matter. I understand that Professor Manwell believes that much of what he sought to achieve by his action was in fact achieved by the evidence presented in defence of his scientific work by scientists of repute and integrity.

The following comments are made in an attempt to correct the record as far as it seems possible to do so regarding the letter of complaint. I will then comment on some of the other matters.

Broadly, the complaint concerned itself with:

a.   specific allegations relating to Professor Manwell in teaching and administration;

b.   the book *Molecular Biology and the Origin of Species* (written by Manwell and Baker and published after the arrival in Adelaide of the authors);

c.   an allegation that in a private letter to a daily newspaper on the subject of the South Australian Department of Agriculture programme for the eradication of fruit fly in South Australia, Professor Manwell had embarrassed the Zoology Department by expressing some views that were unscientific and by giving his University address and title, thus suggesting (it was complained) that the views expressed might be taken to be those of the Zoology Department.

As to (b), both Professors agree that it is the function of the scientific community, and not of the University, to decide the scientific merit of scientific work. Professor Andrewartha has made his criticism and has pointed to an unfavourable review of the book. Professor Manwell has pointed to some commendatory letters from overseas scientists and to some favourable reviews of the book. Such differences of opinion are not uncommon in scholarly work. Professor Andrewartha, whilst maintaining that the book is unsuitable for use as an undergraduate textbook (as to which point there has been a contrary view expressed by another professor of the University), says that Professor Manwell's research and publications, including the book, are stimulating and of considerable value to scientists.

As to (c), Professor Andrewartha did not give detailed particulars of any allegedly unscientific statement either in his formal letters of complaint or with me in correspondence. As to the publication of his University address and title, I can only say that it is not uncommon for academics in this University to write to the Press upon matters of moment giving their academic address and title and that Professor Manwell has produced prima facie evidence in the form of a carbon copy of the letter to the Press that his University address was not used in the correspondence to the Editor and was apparently added in the newspaper office.

I turn now to the complaint insofar as it related to teaching and administration and deal with each specific complaint in turn.

As a background, I set out the scope of Professor Manwell's teaching duties. Professor Manwell was not assigned any duties by Professor Andrewartha, as Head of the Department, for the part-year of 1969, but as appears below he delivered in that year four lectures in the Zoology I Course by informal arrangement between the academic in charge of that Course and himself.

For 1970 his teaching duties were:

a. Four lectures in Zoology I and participation in tutorials.

b. A series of six lectures in Zoology II and certain practical sessions.

c. A series of 24 lectures in Zoology III and certain practical sessions.

d. Certain work with postgraduate students.

e. He was required to set examination questions relating to his lectures in each of the above units and to mark the students' answers in Zoology II and Zoology III.

The letter of complaint was written in April 1971 before Professor Manwell had undertaken any of his lecturing duties for that year.

The letter of complaint made a number of specific allegations relating to a series of four lectures delivered by Professor Manwell in the Zoology I Course. The first was: "Having been asked to give four lectures in Zoology I on 'mechanisms of evolution' he chose instead to teach 'human biology', addressing himself chiefly to the 'population explosion' and its sociological consequences. He seems to have placed much emphasis on the sociological, political and technological aspects of contraception, and also on the psychological and sociological consequences of crowding." At the Commission of Inquiry, Professor Andrewartha stated that he was referring to lectures in the year 1970.

The history of this course of lectures is that it was first delivered late in 1969 after the arrival of Professor Manwell in Adelaide and following a verbal arrangement made between the Lecturer in Charge of the Zoology I Course and Professor Manwell. There was some discussion between them and it was understood that four lectures would be given but with some emphasis on the way in which man is affecting his own evolution. The course of lectures and assigned reading was the subject of a question (see below) set by Professor Manwell in the 1969 final examination paper.

In 1970, the series of lectures was incorporated into the official course programme, published within the Department, from which it is clear that Professor Manwell was to and did lecture upon Human Biology and not upon Mechanisms of Evolution. In 1971, the subject matter of the lectures was incorporated into tutorials in which Professor Manwell participated with others and at the request of Professor Andrewartha, Professor Manwell lectured on Mechanisms of Evolution.

Professor Manwell denies that the description of the subject matter of his lectures in the complaint is accurate; he has provided an outline of his lectures as he says they were delivered. This outline did not include items dealing with the "sociological, political and technological" aspects of contraception or any other aspects of contraception. Professor Manwell says he referred the students to portions of the textbook by Peel and Potts, *Text Book of Contraceptive Practice*, and told them that they would be examined on those portions of that textbook. He asserts that his lectures as given were within his area of competence. Professor Andrewartha does not purport to rely upon direct knowledge, or upon any first-hand account of the content of the lectures, but he holds the view that it was reasonable for him to infer the topics lectured on from the examination question. Professor Manwell, however, says that the examination question related both to the lectures given by him and to the set reading in Peel and Potts. There is, as far as I am aware, no documentary evidence to substantiate the description of the lectures contained in the complaint.

Professor Manwell maintains that he did not teach outside his area of competence, and I have no reason to doubt his judgment.

The next allegation is that Professor Manwell in choosing how much to teach "lacks judgment and perspective" in that in providing for four lectures in Human Biology in Zoology I he prescribed three substantial textbooks and he distributed to the class twelve quarto pages containing forty-nine references to books and articles. The three textbooks referred to by Professor Andrewartha are *Text Book of Contraceptive Practice, Population, Evolution and Birth Control* and *Population Resources and Environment*.

The situation as to textbooks is as follows. None of these textbooks appeared in the 1969 University Calendar Outline of Courses because the four lectures were not planned until about August 1969 in that year. Professor Manwell assigned part of the book by Peel and Potts *Text Book of Contraceptive Practice* as reading. The outline of courses in the 1970 Calendar did not include any of the three textbooks mentioned by Professor Andrewartha; but the Course Outline given to the students by the Lecturer in Charge included Peel and Potts as assigned reading.

The Outline of Courses in the 1971 Calendar included only two of the textbooks mentioned by Professor Andrewartha, namely Peel and Potts, and Hardin's *Population, Evolution and Birth Control — a Collage of Controversial Ideas*. Of these, only Peel and Potts had been suggested by Professor Manwell. Hardin had been suggested by the Lecturer in Charge of the Course. The four lectures in Human Biology were not delivered by Professor Manwell in 1971 due to the request by Professor Andrewartha referred to above.

Early in 1971, Professor Manwell spoke to Professor Andrewartha about using Ehrlich and Ehrlich's *Population/Resources/Environment*. Professor Andrewartha agreed that this textbook should be considered when the syllabuses for 1972 were being reviewed. Professor Manwell immediately instructed Professor Andrewartha's secretary to telephone the bookshop and tell them that Ehrlich and Ehrlich would be included among the reading for Zoology I in 1971; but Professor Andrewartha over-ruled these instructions. The Course Outline for Zoology I for 1971 did not include this textbook.

In summary it appears that Professor Manwell personally prescribed only part of one of the three textbooks mentioned by Professor Andrewartha and had suggested one other.

The allegation as to the distribution to the class of twelve quarto pages, containing forty-nine references to books and articles is correct. This was done as early as 1969. As to that, Professor Manwell says that he instructed the students that the books listed were not required reading and would not be examined upon (which does not seem to be in dispute) and that the purpose of the document was to stimulate interest by illustrating the scope of the available material.

The next complaint in relation to the Zoology I lectures was that Professor Manwell "flouted scholarly precepts of scientific method" in that for the final examination upon his lectures he set a question consisting of fifty statements each requiring a true/false answer. Professor Manwell did set such a question for the 1970 examination, but he says that he set precisely the same sort of question in 1969 without any criticisms or suggestion for alteration. I understand that true/false questions have previously been used in Zoology I. Professor Andrewartha expressed the view that some of the questions set could not be satisfactorily answered without qualification.

Professor Manwell tells me that this type of question is not generally approved by him, but was adopted in this case for special reasons and that he used quite different and traditional methods in Zoology II and Zoology III (as is the case).

Professor Manwell has pointed out that no student had to answer his question. The lecturer in charge of the course specified that students should answer either Professor Manwell's question or Professor Andrewartha's question on Ecology. Over half of the class opted for Professor Manwell's question.

The next allegation in the letter of complaint was a second instance of what was said to be teaching "outside his area of professional competence". The allegation was that in putting forward six subjects as suggestions for essays for Honours students, Professor

Manwell offered topics which were outside his area of competence and were an invitation to polemics. The background to this complaint is that all staff-members in the Department were asked to submit topics, the students being assigned three or four essay topics from a large number of topics which had been suggested to the Lecturer responsible for the Honours year by all the staff-members. Professor Manwell maintains that the topics suggested by him were not outside the area of his competence.

The list of topics enclosed in the letter of complaint in fact contained eight topics, two of which were used, one in a slightly modified form. There were fourteen Honours students. One student wrote an essay on the first topic in the list and two students wrote an essay on the second topic. These two students also wrote an essay on another topic suggested by Professor Manwell which was not contained in the list. Four other students wrote on topics suggested by Professor Manwell which were not contained in the list. All the topics upon which students wrote essays were approved by the Reader in Charge of the Honours Programme.

I certainly think that some of the topics suggested by Professor Manwell may have lent themselves to polemics, but this would doubtless be true of a large number of topics in many departments and it does not constitute a criticism of the topic if it is otherwise valid.

The next allegation was that Professor Manwell "does not collaborate well with his colleagues in academic matters", and three specific instances were given together with a general statement. The first of these specific instances is the same as the first allegation in relation to Zoology I lectures, namely that the lectures were delivered upon "Human Biology" rather than "Mechanisms of Evolution", and this has already been discussed above. The other specific instances given by Professor Andrewartha concerned a discussion at a staff meeting and the treatment of a request made by a staff-member to Professor Manwell. Professor Manwell has given his account of these matters. The allegations involve people other than the main protagonists and I can make no comment.

The next general complaint relates to "administration" and to Professor Manwell's membership of the Faculty of Science. The actual allegation was that during 1970 he was a member of the Faculty of Science and attended only two meetings; and that when asked to continue his membership during 1971 he declined "with some uncomplimentary remarks about the Faculty". The letter of complaint added that Professor Manwell had an unsympathetic attitude towards administration and was not well informed about it.

The facts as to the Faculty are as follows. Professor Manwell was appointed to the Faculty of Science by the Council of the University at its meeting on 5th December 1969. The Faculty records show that he attended meeting on 12th May 1970, 15th May 1970 (adjourned meeting), 9th June 1970 and 14th July 1970. There is no record that Professor Manwell was informed of his appointment and Professor Manwell says that he was first informed by Professor Andrewartha of his appointment on the day before the May meeting in 1970. Professor Andrewartha agrees that he spoke to Professor Manwell in May 1970 about his membership of the Faculty after having noticed that he had not attended earlier meetings.

Professor Manwell says he did not attend meetings in the third term because (as is the case) Faculty meetings were held at 2 p.m. on Tuesday afternoons and the time-table for his third term unit in Zoology III (approved by the Head of the Department) prescribed lectures and practical work from 2 p.m. to 5 p.m. on that day each week. The Faculty records indicate that Professor Manwell did not attend the meetings in August, or in November and December (after practical work for the year had been completed). In fairness, it should be added that many academics are irregular in their attendance at Faculty and other committee meetings.

Finally, as to membership of the Faculty of Science in 1971, Professor Andrewartha alleged that Professor Manwell declined membership and Professor Manwell says that he did not. On this there appears to be no way of making a finding.

I now turn to some of the other material which has been published over the last four years. Many of the published comments have been ill-informed. The letter of complaint itself was confidential and remained so as the matter was *sub judice* with respect to the University procedures and *sub judice* with respect to the libel action. It was not therefore possible for me, or for the University, to correct some of the misunderstandings.

In March 1971, Professor Andrewartha told me that he intended to submit a complaint about Professor Manwell's work and, early in April, he sent me a draft of his proposed complaint. I discussed this with him on 8th April 1971 in the presence of the then Deputy Vice-Chancellor and the then Registrar. In my view, the complaint even if proved was not sufficient to get Professor Manwell dismissed, and I said something to this effect to Professor Andrewartha. I also told him that if he did decide to send it to me I would send a copy to Professor Manwell to seek his comments; and that if the matter could not be resolved in this way I would endeavour to have it investigated as a complaint not involving dismissal. I returned the draft to him.

The letter of complaint was dated 19th April 1971 and was accompanied by a number of documents and other papers. I was absent interstate for most of the latter part of April and I did not send a copy of the complaint to Professor Manwell until 6th May 1971. In the meantime, Professor Manwell had heard from Professor Andrewartha that the complaint had been sent and he wrote me a note dated 5th May 1971 asking for the details and stating that he heard about the complaint from a reporter.

I do not know how this could have occurred. All I can say is that no reporter heard it from me. Professor Andrewartha and Professor Manwell have assured me that no reporter heard it from them.

Professor Manwell's reply to the letter of complaint was dated 13th May 1971; and Professor Andrewartha's reply to this was dated 1st June 1971. Both letters are referred to in the earlier part of this Statement.

The complaint was not resolved by this exchange of letters and I sought to find a procedure to resolve the matter. In view of the seriousness of the allegations, I asked a member of the University Council, who is also a Judge in the Supreme Court, to adjudicate — with the help of two biological assessors. I consulted Professor Andrewartha about the procedure and suggested two names for the assessors. He agreed. I consulted Professor Manwell in the same way. He agreed to the Judge. He specifically objected to one of the two assessors, and had some general reservations. I suggested several other possibilities. Two names eventually emerged. Unfortunately, Professor Andrewartha's letter of 1st June had not at that time been copied or sent to Professor Manwell. Accordingly, he did not then know that both persons had been mentioned in Professor Andrewartha's letter of 1st June as having been consulted about one aspect of the complaint. I did not myself see this as a difficulty as both proposed assessors have the highest integrity. Nevertheless, I later learned that Professor Manwell was indeed worried about this. Had he pointed this out to me immediately after receiving the copy of Professor Andrewartha's letter, I would have had no hesitation is seeking two alternative assessors who would have been acceptable to him. In the event, I did believe that the proposed committee was acceptable to both Professors and I wrote to the Judge and to the two biologists asking them to serve.

One of the proposed assessors wrote to say that he had once criticised Professor Manwell to a colleague. This letter has been seen by Professor Manwell's solicitors. In view of this, I decided that this particular staff-member could not be one of the assessors and sought to find another. I mention this because it has subsequently been alleged that I attempted to establish a biased Committee.

I attempted to consult Professor Manwell again about the composition of the Committee, but despite repeated efforts between 16th and 18th June I was unsuccessful. However, in view of the fact that Professor Manwell was upset by the content and tone of the complaint and believed that he stood in serious risk of being dismissed, I can understand that he felt that he needed legal advice. On the 21st June he told me that he had in fact consulted his solicitors. On the 22nd June I wrote to Professor Manwell again asking for consultations, but by this time there had been a break-down in communication.

I was told much later that, on about the 16th June, Mrs. Manwell had been advised that her grandfather had died and Professor Manwell says that for some time thereafter he was pre-occupied with that bereavement.

On 2nd July 1971, I received a letter from Professor Manwell's solicitors. This letter asked a number of questions about the procedure I was proposing (all of which could, I believe, have been satisfactorily answered); but it went on to say that they had been instructed to issue proceedings against Professor Andrewartha for libel. On the same day, 2nd July 1971, Professor Manwell's solicitors also wrote to Professor Andrewartha requesting a withdrawal and apology, failing which, by the end of the week, a writ would be issued. The letter from Professor Manwell's solicitor, simultaneously seeking comments on the proposed procedure and declaring that instructions had been given for a writ to be issued, was the first communication from Professor Manwell's solicitors to the University. Published statements that the solicitors telephoned and wrote to me about the procedures are not correct. Nor is it correct to claim, as has been published, that "recourse to the laws of defamation" was considered only after attempts by the legal advisers "to effect investigations under fairer conditions" had failed.

I now come to the problem of a postgraduate student who wished to work with Professor Manwell. There has been a dispute over the possible acceptance of and awarding of a scholarship to this student. The then existing situation in the Department undoubtedly influenced the eventual result which was that the student did not come to the University to study.

I am convinced that there was no interference with the due processing of the application for the scholarship and the problems arose solely out of the situation in the Zoology Department.

In this statement, I have tried to set out the facts relating to the letter of complaint, and about some of the other material, as fairly and as accurately as I can. It is now published as a settlement to the dispute and I wish to record that settlement has been effected without payment to either side (except for legal costs). Professor Andrewartha, Professor Manwell and Miss C. M. Ann Baker (Mrs. Manwell) do not necessarily agree with all the comments I have made; but they do agree that the publication of this Statement and the discontinuance of the libel action, concludes the matter. Their signatures hereto confirm that agreement. For my part, I hope that those involved will try to put the dispute behind them. I will do all I can to help everyone in the University to work harmoniously together.

Postscript by Brian Martin

On 11 October 1983 I sent a copy of an earlier version of this chapter to the University of Adelaide inviting a response from someone representing the university, or anyone else appropriate, to be included in this book. On 21 October the Registrar of the University of Adelaide replied with some comments which were not for publication. On 29 November I sent a letter enquiring about a statement in the Registrar's reply. On 2 December the Registrar replied concerning this point, requesting that the information remain confidential. A year later, on 11 October 1984, I sent the Registrar a revised and enlarged version of this chapter, again inviting a response. The comments opposite were contained in the Registrar's reply dated 29 October.

COMMENTS ON THE FRUIT FLY PAPERS

F. J. O'Neill, Registrar, The University of Adelaide

There are two matters on which I wish to comment, firstly on safeguards for the proper management of research projects and secondly on the nature of our now suspended Early Retirement Scheme.

The University has two Committees which impinge on the nature and procedures for research as outlined in the article. The Outside Grants Committee was established in 1970 and has as its primary purpose to ensure that research work financed from sources outside the University should be appropriate to a University, be broadly acceptable to the University community and be unlikely to infringe the general freedom of enquiry of the University and of the staff concerned, and should not distort the normal teaching and research functions of any Department.

The Committee on the Ethical Use of Animals for Experimental Purposes was established in August 1973 and ensures *inter alia* that:

(i) Care of all animals shall be in accordance with generally accepted laboratory practices, with appropriate consideration for bodily comfort, humane treatment, and sanitary environment.

(ii) Experiments using animals should be designed to keep numbers to a minimum. Every effort must be made to avoid any unnecessary discomfort to animals. Procedures subjecting animals to discomfort shall be conducted only when such discomfort is unavoidable and is justified by the objectives of the procedure.

(iii) Surgical procedures must be done under appropriate anaesthesia. Generally acceptable techniques to avoid infection and minimize pain must be followed throughout. The postoperative care of animals must minimize discomfort in accordance with generally accepted practices. If an animal has, in the course of an operation, been so injured that its recovery would involve serious suffering, it must be destroyed while still under the anaesthetic. The disposal of animals must be done in a humane manner.

(iv) The use of animals by students shall be under the supervision of a qualified teacher and shall be in accordance with these principles. The qualified teacher is responsible for ensuring that these principles are followed, and shall have acknowledged them in writing.

In the light of the foregoing I am sure that you will agree that those insinuations regarding research mismanagement in this University cannot be substantiated.

I now turn to the nature of the suspended Early Retirement Scheme. This Scheme was established in order to encourage some tenured academic staff who were aged 55 years or more and who had more than ten years service to retire early in order that the University could operate within its reduced budget. All applications received were considered openly within the various committees of the University and those approved were publicly reported. Further applications under this particular scheme have now ceased, since the amount set aside has been fully committed to meet payments under the Scheme.

I refer you to my previous letter of 2/12/83 on the question of a retirement of a staff member due to ill health. This staff member *did not* participate in the Early Retirement Scheme outlined above.

REPLY TO THE REGISTRAR

C. M. Ann Baker

The Registrar's comments on "The Fruit Fly Papers" are, in a number of ways, most interesting. He does not deny the facts concerning the unfair treatment of a staff member at his institution. The Registrar's response is academic: "The University has two Committees..."

In regard to mistreatment of animals the Registrar has made an error where he refers to my comments as "insinuations". I did not make "insinuations". I presented *facts*, such as the existence of the exchange of correspondence concerning the gassing of rats in the Department of Zoology and the military-financed project by a supporter of the author of the sacking complaint (the project involving the burning and maiming of large numbers of rats). Perhaps the Registrar, out of fairness to the present Chairman of the Department of Zoology, should have mentioned that he was not involved in any way with the situations which were described. It is my understanding that, now, the RSPCA can investigate the animal facilities at any time it wishes, unannounced.

In regard to the University of Adelaide's standards of discipline, I am glad to see that the Registrar has *finally* made some sort of a statement for publication, however incomplete and inadequate, about the case of the sexual harasser whose actions were interpreted as attempted bribery over grades.

In his more recent letter the Registrar writes: "This staff member *did not* participate in the Early Retirement Scheme outlined above." I *did not* state that he did. My sentence in *The Fruit Fly Papers* is: "Even worse, there are persistent rumours that this staff member was paid handsomely to take early retirement." The Registrar can hardly deny that (a) the sexual harasser was allowed to retire early and (b) there are rumours that he was paid handsomely to leave quietly. Perhaps the Registrar will ultimately inform the public as to why the dismissal statutes were not invoked. Indeed, given the use of force, why did not the University assist in seeing that criminal charges were brought? There seems to be one law for outsiders and another law for insiders.

Given the Registrar's concern about the mistreatment of animals and the early retirement of sexual harassers, perhaps he could explain what action the University administration has taken over a seminar announced in the 30 July 1984 University of Adelaide Diary of Events, entitled "Acid-base regulation in *Crocodylus porosus* that are buggered"?

PREVENTING PREVENTIVE MEDICINE

MUTAGENS AND MANAGERS

Brian Martin

(Note: This article was originally written in 1980 to publicise the IMVS–Coulter case, and was revised in 1981. The text has been left unaltered).

Dr John Coulter has been a leading environmentalist in South Australia since the 1950s. His research, advice and public statements have helped workers and citizens challenge health hazards on the job and in the community on numerous occasions. Not surprisingly, this activity has been most unwelcome in the top levels of chemical corporations and their allies in government and the scientific community.

On 30 June 1980 John Coulter was sacked from his job at the Institute of Medical and Veterinary Science (IMVS) in Adelaide, and the environmental mutagens testing unit which he headed was closed down. There are many cases of suppression of scientists who speak out or do research on issues affecting the public interest, thereby posing a threat to corporate and bureaucratic vested interests.[1] The Coulter case is the most serious of such cases in Australia to be publicised in recent years.

Background

After receiving his M.B., B.S. degrees and practising general medicine for a few years, John Coulter joined the IMVS in 1959 at the age of 28. His position was a surgical research officer. His early work included research into staphylococcal hospital cross infection, purification, properties and mode of action of staphylococcal alpha toxin, gas chromatographic separation of amino acids and the levels and medical effects of chlorinated hydrocarbon pesticides and cadmium. In about 1967 he was promoted to the position of specialist pathologist.

During his time at the IMVS Dr Coulter was outspoken on numerous environmental and health issues, including water fluoridation, uranium mining, the proposed petrochemical plant at Redcliff in South Australia, the consequences of nuclear weapons tests at Maralinga, South Australia, in the 1950s, and the health hazards of drugs and industrial chemicals. Because he has been willing to write articles and speak at public meetings and rallies on such topics, Dr Coulter has often been called upon by environmental organisations, trade unions and other organisations. In all this activity he has been careful to emphasise that he speaks in his private capacity only.

Often Dr Coulter has been willing to speak out when others with the same knowledge have kept quiet. At one stage in the proposal for a petrochemical plant at Redcliff, it was planned to produce and export ethylene dichloride, a toxic intermediate product, rather than the usual final product polyvinyl chloride. The ethylene dichloride was to have been taken out of Spencer Gulf in 30,000 tonne tankers. Dr Coulter publicly pointed out that ethylene dichloride is highly toxic and a potential cause of cancer. Health Commission staff were aware of this hazard, but no one said anything publicly. No doubt they felt vulnerable due to their position in a government department. It is now accepted by the US National Cancer Institute that ethylene dichloride does cause cancer.

Epichlorhydrin is a bonding agent, one of numerous chemicals used in the pulp and paper industry. About two years ago, Dr Coulter provided information to workers in the Amalgamated Metal Workers' and Shipwrights' Union at Mount Gambier, South Australia, about the health hazards of epichlorhydrin. The workers knew what chemicals were being used in the manufacturing process, but could not obtain information about their hazards through normal channels.

In speaking out about risks to environment and health it is easy to offend corporate and government interests which have a financial or bureaucratic stake in products, practices or policies linked with the risks. Research institutes such as the IMVS depend on government money provided through government bodies and individuals sensitive to corporate interests, and to some extent on direct grants from corporations. As a result, those who speak out about risks to environment and health may experience pressures to keep quiet. This has happened to Dr Coulter on a number of occasions.[2]

In 1978 the Bayer company brought an action against the Australian Broadcasting Commission, partly over remarks Dr Coulter had made on a television program regarding one of its products containing the mutagenic pesticide dichlorvos. The action was subsequently dropped about two years later but in the interim pressure was brought to bear on Dr Coulter through the Agricultural Chemical Trade Association and the Director of the IMVS. Dichlorvos is currently under urgent review by the National Cancer Institute in the US, as some animal tests have suggested that dichlorvos may be carcinogenic.

In 1979 Velsicol Australia complained to the Director of the IMVS about a lecture Dr Coulter had given, in a private capacity, to a Melbourne seminar on pesticides. Dr Coulter had mentioned the way the parent company in the US had handled information on the carcinogenicity of two of their products, chlordane and heptachlor.[3]

Perhaps more threatening to the management of the IMVS was Dr Coulter's mutagenicity testing. In the late 1970s Dr Coulter, on his own initiative, set up in the IMVS a unit for testing the mutagenicity (capacity to cause mutations) of substances, using the Ames test. This test uses bacteria to look for mutagenic potential, and is considered one of the best available ways to obtain a cheap, quick and fairly reliable (80 to 90 per cent accuracy) assessment of the cancer-initiating potential of substances. This environmental mutagens testing unit (EMTU) provided a service for the testing of chemicals, and was found useful by many groups.[4] A more reliable assessment of carcinogenic properties would require experiments with large numbers of animals over a period of years; no testing of this sort takes place in Australia.

Some of the samples submitted for testing came from groups outside the scientific and medical communities, in particular from workers' health organisations. Dr Coulter on occasion provided results directly to the groups or workers involved as well as to the IMVS. Such action escapes the control over the dissemination of scientific information typically exercised by the management in government scientific organisations.

A few years ago, workers who were coating steel pipes with pitch for the South Australia Engineering and Water Supply Department were concerned about possible health risks from fumes. Dr Coulter investigated for the workers and found that levels of polycyclic hydrocarbons in the atmosphere were very high. Each 100 kilograms of pitch used in the coating process released 1.2 kilograms of benzpyrene. In terms of total mutagenic activity, this was equivalent to four million cigarettes, released in a fairly closed area.

After the workers protested, the job was contracted out to private industry. The South Australia Health Commission then inspected the work conditions. Unlike Dr Coulter, the Commission provided figures on benzpyrene levels to the employer but not to the workers.

On 16 April 1980 Dr Coulter submitted a report to the Fire and Safety Committee of the IMVS on the mutagenic and potentially cancer-causing properties of ethylene oxide, which was being used in an IMVS laboratory as a sterilising agent.[5] At the same time that he released the report to the IMVS Committee, Dr Coulter provided copies to the workers at the laboratory using the chemical. The Director of the IMVS rebuked Dr Coulter for releasing the report to the workers.[6] But the significance of the findings was not disputed: the use of ethylene oxide was immediately discontinued, and $40,000 is being spent on the construction of an alternative sterilising apparatus.

As a result of stories circulating in the IMVS about the ethylene oxide report, Dr Coulter posted the report and related correspondence on noticeboards of the IMVS.[7] The Director of the IMVS then instructed Dr Coulter not to make available to any staff member of the IMVS any material dealing with the affairs of the IMVS without his, the Director's, express approval.[8]

Earlier, in March 1980, Dr Coulter was informed that on 30 June the EMTU would be closed and that he would be transferred and demoted with a drop of $10,000 in annual salary.[9] But instead of being transferred and demoted, on 30 June Dr Coulter was sacked outright, having been informed of this a few days earlier.

The Arguments

The Director of the IMVS, Dr J. A. Bonnin, has said that the decision to dismiss Dr Coulter was based not on his environmental activities but on financial and professional considerations.[10] Such claims are usual in suppression cases, and do not rule out the role of deeper underlying reasons. In any case it is instructive to evaluate the stated reasons for the dismissal and the closure of the EMTU.[11]

1.   Dr Bonnin has said that the IMVS cannot afford the $85,000 per year needed to support Dr Coulter, his ancillary staff and laboratory.[12] In reply, Dr Gouldhurst[13] noted that "On March 26, 1980 the IMVS had a credit balance $882,000 above its budget expectations for this point in the year, despite Dr Coulter's laboratory having been funded in the present year". Dr Bonnin has not responded to this point. Nor has any note been made by the IMVS Council of the public value of Dr Coulter's work. The ethylene oxide case yields a minimum figure of $10,000 per worker to remove a mutagenic risk to young fertile workers. A similar costing of some of the EMTU's findings might well yield a net positive value for its efforts in South Australia alone, apart from the wider scientific benefits.

2.   Dr Bonnin has said that "Many drugs and chemicals are now tested by, or for, their manufacturers and there is little need for this work in Adelaide which manufactures almost none of these substances".[14] However, it is well known that results of such testing by or for manufacturers are often unavailable, poorly publicised, inadequate or misleading.[15] Whether or not the chemicals are manufactured in Adelaide appears irrelevant if workers and consumers are being exposed in Adelaide.

Work at the EMTU showed the mutagenic properties of the drug tinidazole.[16] Unknown to Dr Coulter at the time, two earlier researchers[17] had obtained the same results using samples provided by the pharmaceutical producers Pfizer. Whether or not the earlier work had existed, a case for the EMTU can be made. Showing the mutagenicity of tinidazole was itself important. But if it is objected that this had already been done[18], the question remains as to why this work was not mentioned by the pharmaceutical company in its promotional literature when tinidazole was launched on the Australian market.[19] This case illustrates the necessity for independent testing facilities.

3.   Dr Bonnin has said that mutagen testing would better be done elsewhere, such as in the chemistry division of the Department of Services and Supply.[20] While this may be true, it does not justify the termination of an existing unit before any alternative is available.

Similarly, the South Australia Minister for Health, Mrs Jennifer Adamson, has said that the SA government regards testing of potentially carcinogenic materials "as a matter of utmost importance", that a national testing laboratory should be set up and that "there is no useful purpose in individual States duplicating aspects of the work which will be carried out effectively and on a comprehensive basis by a national laboratory".[21] There are two flaws in this rationale for the shutdown of the IMVS unit. First, there is no guarantee that a national testing laboratory will be free from political and economic pressures and that it will be responsive to the public interest. Part of the effectiveness of any testing process is its independence, and a set of separate laboratories may be more effective in achieving this than a single large facility.

Second, the Minister's statement talks about a national laboratory which *will* carry out effective work. The establishment of such a laboratory could easily take several years. The promise of future efficacy, even if kept, is no excuse for terminating a current program.

4. Dr Bonnin has said that Dr Coulter had not been successful in attracting research grants from appropriate bodies such as the Anti-Cancer Foundation or the National Health and Medical Research Council.[22] Apart from the scarcity of grant funds even for well-qualified applicants[23], the role of the IMVS management must be questioned here. Since it is obvious from statements by Dr Bonnin published in the Adelaide *Advertiser*[24] that there is much personal discord between Dr Bonnin and Dr Coulter, it is doubtful that Dr Coulter would have received the wholehearted support of the IMVS Council necessary for the success of most grant applications.[25] Also to be taken into account is the possibility of political or personal bias in the allocation of research grants.[26]

5. In justifying the decision to demote Dr Coulter, Dr Bonnin has said that Dr Coulter was prematurely promoted to the position of specialist pathologist, since the position now requires that the recipient hold a higher degree or qualification.[27] However, this requirement postdates Dr Coulter's promotion by ten years or so and does not apply.[28] In any case, the decision to sack rather than demote Dr Coulter invalidates this argument.

6. Dr Bonnin has written that Dr Coulter has had "markedly low productivity as a full-time research worker", and noted that Dr Coulter "has published only three papers in recognised journals in more than two years".[29] Dr Bonnin has not provided sufficient evidence to justify this point.[30] First, Dr Bonnin has not provided any evidence concerning publication rates of other IMVS staff. Mean publication rates for scientists are of the order of one or two papers per year, with the median considerably lower. Second, the IMVS has no official policy or requirements for publication by research staff. Nor is demotion or dismissal specified as a penalty for failing to publish. Nor have other IMVS staff with poorer publication records than Dr Coulter been sacked. Third, no mention has been made of the practice by which senior staff in many scientific organisations have their names attached to papers to which they have contributed little or nothing, so distorting even further the formal data on publications which supposedly reflect research productivity.

A related point is raised by Dr Bonnin's statement that "I really respect both Dr Coulter and his views but the point is that if he is going to do that at the expense of his official duties I have got to be responsible for this".[31] This implies that spending one's time doing esoteric research of interest to only a handful of specialists is acceptable, while evaluating environmental hazards to the community at best counts for nothing professionally. For the manager of a research organisation to take this view is to take a narrow official charter for his organisation. Dr Coulter's view is the contrary one — that scientific knowledge should be used for the benefit of the community, and that public knowledge and awareness is the best way to ensure that this occurs.

7. Dr Bonnin has said "It is not the role of this institute to establish a large routine testing service for the testing of chemical substances for cancer-producing properties".[32]

In a sense this is the key point. Who makes the decisions about the direction of scientific research, and who benefits from the particular decisions made? The Council of the IMVS obviously believes that it should be making these decisions. Dr Coulter and his supporters believe that the IMVS actions are serving the interests of chemical and drug companies at the expense of the public interest: "As a public institution the responsibility of the IMVS is to defend the public — not to defend the private interest of drug and chemical companies... This is the fundamental difference between us".[33]

Since the closure of the EMTU, there are only two mutagen testing facilities in Australia. Only one is truly independent — the one run by Dr Don MacPhee of the Microbiology Department at La Trobe University in Melbourne. Dr MacPhee, like Dr Coulter, has done testing for unions. The other laboratory, headed by Dr Robert Baker in Sydney, is under the control of the Commonwealth Department of Health, and therefore is subject to the same sorts of pressures as the IMVS.

Responses

Many individuals and groups have expressed their concern about the sacking of Dr Coulter and the closing of the EMTU at the IMVS. Many letters have been written to newspapers, to the South Australian Minister for Health and to parliamentary leaders in South Australia. Trade unions, led by the United Trades and Labor Council of South Australia[34], have expressed concern about the removal of a service which frequently benefited their members. The opposition Labor Party in South Australia has called for a public inquiry into the IMVS[35], and questions have been asked in the South Australian Parliament by members of the Australian Labor Party and the Australian Democrats. An inquiry into the IMVS has been held, though this was mostly concerned with issues besides the Coulter case.[36] Dr Coulter has mounted a challenge against his dismissal in the South Australian Industrial Conciliation and Arbitration Court.

The Coulter–IMVS dispute illustrates clearly the type of conflict that can arise where there is the possibility of pressures on the direction and use of scientific research exerted by corporate and bureaucratic vested interests on the one side and by workers and the general public on the other. Usually such conflict is muted. It is precisely because Dr Coulter has been outspoken about issues of public concern that his dismissal is also a public issue.

The issue is also a public one because there are no formal avenues for appeal or adjudication within the IMVS or the South Australian government for those opposed to the closing of the EMTU or the sacking of Dr Coulter. It remains to be seen whether public pressure will be sufficient to change the decision of the IMVS Council which is backed by the present South Australian government. But it is certain that this struggle will not be the last one of its kind.

Postscript

Early in July 1980 Dr Coulter initiated a case against the IMVS in the South Australian Industrial Court, alleging wrongful dismissal. Such cases often require two years to complete. After 18 sitting days in court and 1237 pages of evidence, the hearing was adjourned *sine die* when the IMVS undertook to certify that Dr Coulter had been retrenched for the reason that there was no longer work available for which he was suitable and qualified. The IMVS also undertook to support an application by Dr Coulter for superannuation on the basis of this certification. In other words, the court case was suspended while Dr Coulter tried to obtain superannuation, in the hope of a quick settlement, with support from the IMVS which now said that he had been retrenched rather than dismissed.

The Superannuation Board initially rejected Dr Coulter's application. This decision was appealed to the Superannuation Tribunal, which in December 1981 ruled that Dr Coulter had been retrenched under section 67.1.D of the *Superannuation Act*.

The resolution of Dr Coulter's case raises several points. First, the court procedure is heavily weighted against the victim of dismissal (or retrenchment). Dr Coulter, without income, was legally pitted against the IMVS, with, by comparison, virtually unlimited financial support, and whose executive members had nothing at risk financially. Nor indeed did they risk anything morally, since the dismissal (or retrenchment) was the responsibility of a corporate body, namely the IMVS.

Second, the court is not a forum for getting at the truth. Anything that did not apply specifically to the issue of whether the alleged dismissal was harsh, unjust or unreasonable was not considered. Once the case was taken before the Superannuation Board the underlying issues were submerged even further.

One interpretation of the events is that Dr Coulter was in fact wrongfully dismissed, but that the IMVS later found it preferable to interpret its action as retrenchment. This of course is not the official interpretation, which can be presented thus. Officially, the South Australian government could not afford to spend $33,000 per year to pay Dr Coulter to work on mutagenicity testing, hence his retrenchment. But the South Australian government can afford to pay over $50,000 in legal and other costs to obtain Dr Coulter's retrenchment, and henceforth to pay Dr Coulter $22,000 per year in superannuation to do nothing.

Dr Coulter now no longer has access to IMVS facilities. He is however free to carry out research on his own and to speak freely on environmental and health issues.

References

1. Brian Martin, "The scientific straightjacket: the power structure of science and the suppression of environmental scholarship", *Ecologist*, vol. 11, no. 1 (January/February 1981), pp. 33–43; Ralph Nader, Peter J. Petkas and Kate Blackwell (eds), *Whistle Blowing: The Report of the Conference on Professional Responsibility* (New York: Grossman, 1972); Samuel S. Epstein, *The Politics of Cancer* (San Francisco: Sierra Club Books, 1978); Robert van den Bosch, *The Pesticide Conspiracy* (Garden City: Doubleday, 1978).

2. Bill Guy, "Does Dr. Coulter have to go?", Adelaide *Advertiser*, 17 June 1980, p. 5; Anonymous, "One man's work under fire", *Canberra Times*, 27 June 1980, p. 2; Deborah Smith, "Labor promises an inquiry into SA medical institute", *National Times*, 20–26 July 1980, p. 36.

3. Epstein, op. cit.

4. Bill Rust, "Unions irate at 'sacking' of scientist", Adelaide *Advertiser*, 8 April 1980, p. 6; Richie Gun, letter, Adelaide *Advertiser*, 12 April 1980, p. 5.

5. J. R. Coulter, "Memorandum to Fire and Safety Committee, IMVS", 16 April 1980.

6. J. A. Bonnin, letter to J. R. Coulter, 23 April 1980.

7. J. R. Coulter, "Memorandum to staff of the I.M.V.S.", 8 May 1980.

8. J. A. Bonnin, letter to J. R. Coulter, 9 May 1980.

9. Barry Hailstone, "Sacked for speaking out — scientist", Adelaide *Advertiser*, 31 March 1980, p. 12.

10. Barry Hailstone, "Director gives reasons for scientist's move", Adelaide *Advertiser*, 1 April 1980, p. 8.

11. ibid.; J. A. Bonnin, letter, Adelaide *Advertiser*, 12 April 1980, p. 5; Guy, op. cit.; Anonymous, op. cit.; Smith, op. cit.

12. Hailstone, op. cit. (note 10).

13. P. R. S. Gouldhurst, letter, Adelaide *Advertiser*, 10 April 1980, p. 5.

14. Hailstone, op. cit. (note 10).

15. Epstein, op. cit.; Paul Brodeur, *Expendable Americans*, (New York: Viking Press, 1974); Rachel Scott, *Muscle and Blood* (New York: E. P. Dutton, 1974); R. Jeffrey Smith, "Creative penmanship in animal testing prompts FDA controls", *Science*, vol. 198 (23 December 1977), pp. 1227–9.

16. John R. Coulter and John V. Turner, "Tinidazole (TNZ) (Ethyl [2-(2-methyl-5-nitro-1-imidazolyl)ethyl]sulphone) is mutagenic in a *Salmonella typhimurium* assay", *Mutation Research*, vol. 57 (1978), pp. 97–101.

17. D. G. Lindmark and M. Müller, "Antitrichomonal action, mutagenicity and reduction of metronidazole and other nitroimidazoles", *Antimicrobial Agents and Chemotherapy*, vol. 10 (1976), pp. 476–82.

18. Bonnin, op. cit. (note 11).

19. P. R. S. Gouldhurst, letter, Adelaide *Advertiser*, 22 April 1980, p. 5.

20. Hailstone, op. cit. (note 10).

21. Jennifer Adamson, "Mutagen testing" (news release) (Adelaide: Office of the Minister for Health, 4 July 1980); Smith, op. cit.

22. Hailstone, op. cit. (note 10); Bonnin, op. cit. (note 11).

23. Michael Ross, letter, Adelaide *Advertiser*, 18 April 1980, p. 5

24. Hailstone, op. cit. (note 10); Bonnin, op. cit. (note 11).

25. Gouldhurst, op. cit. (note 19).

26. Clyde Manwell, "Peer review: a case history from the Australian Research Grants Committee", *Search*, vol. 10, no. 3 (March 1979), pp. 81–8.

27. Hailstone, op. cit. (note 10); Bonnin, op. cit. (note 11).

28. Gouldhurst, op. cit. (note 19).

29. Bonnin, op. cit. (note 11.)

30. Gouldhurst, op. cit. (note 19).

31. Guy, op. cit.

32. Bonnin, op. cit. (note 11).

33. Smith, op. cit.

34. Rust, op. cit.

35. Smith, op. cit.

36. Barry Hailstone, "Clash of views", Adelaide *Advertiser*, 9 October 1980, p. 8; A. G. McGregor, letter, Adelaide *Advertiser*, 27 October 1980, p. 4; Report of the Committee of Inquiry into the Institute of Medical and Veterinary Science (December 1980).

PARALYSIS OF THE CONSCIENCE

Clyde Manwell and C. M. Ann Baker

Introduction: Professionalism versus Conscience

The previous chapter, "Mutagens and Managers", examined the more immediate events associated with the attempt to remove Dr John Coulter, a leading Australian environmentalist, from his position in the Institute of Medical and Veterinary Science (IMVS) in Adelaide.

This chapter probes the *background*, including the behaviour of other scientists, their attitudes towards the removal of a colleague under unusual circumstances, the responses by various groups within the wider community, and the recent history of intellectual conflict in

South Australia. Thanks to the Parliamentary Debates, to official documents arising from investigations of the IMVS, to news reporting, and to transcripts of legal proceedings, there is a wealth of material available for the case of the IMVS versus Coulter.

We are seeking to understand how intellectual conflict arises, how attempts are made to bias information flow (especially for socially significant matters such as the environment and public health) and how such problems might be avoided in the future, or at least how the damage done to people might be reduced as much as possible.

In the previous chapter Brian Martin presented evidence that the case of the IMVS versus Coulter contained elements of suppression and of unfairness. *When a case of this kind occurs, why do scientists, academics or other professionals fail to protect intellectual freedom and fail to protest injustice?* We circulated a rather bland petition (calling for an investigation into the attempt to dismiss Dr Coulter) to more than a hundred South Australian scientists and academics. We found that only five were willing to sign. Yet, several hundred members of the wider community were willing to sign similar, or stronger, petitions. *Is there any connection between the paralysis of conscience in intellectual organisations and the low morale within those organisations?*

Gerald Holton, physicist and historian of science at Harvard University, has reached what he himself acknowledges to be a "more pessimistic" conclusion: the "pursuit of science as currently fostered and understood" and "societal concerns" are "possibly even antithetical traits — antithetical both in terms of the psychodynamics of the majority of individual scientists and in terms of the social structure of science as a profession".[1] Holton, surveying data on the psychology of scientists and some case histories, builds up a composite picture of the average scientist as indifferent to human problems. Holton emphasises the need to encourage and to protect the tiny minority of scientists who are willing to speak out. These are our only hope to curb the evils arising from the misuse of science and technology.

If Holton is correct — and our own reading of the relevant literature supports his conclusions[2] — then we must look very closely at the wider background of suppression cases, seeking what roles other sections of the community, such as the mass media, the legal system and the general public, might play in providing feedback on abuses. We must also look at the interactions among different elites, representing the professions, politicians, bureaucrats and corporate interests — what collectively, if vaguely, can be called the *establishment*. Within various groups individuals differ in their values, some being more *cosmopolitan* and others more *local* in their latent social roles.[3]

We note the similarities among suppression cases, even when the dissenters are from different walks of life and the issues, too, are different. As described in the introduction to this book, there are certain basic similarities between cases, similarities which allow one to consider suppression as the most reasonable explanation for the events. However, we are also looking at something deeper: the non-independence of suppression cases, a reflection of the climate of community attitudes and the effectiveness (or lack thereof) of feedback mechanisms, with, of course, the attitudes of the establishment often dominating the outcome. Is it possible that there is a hypocrisy factor: *the more strongly an establishment believes in its own innate superiority, the more difficult it becomes to rectify wrongs?* A certain pattern of behaviour becomes apparent in cases of intellectual dissent in South Australia. It does not mean that every example results in suppression and victimisation, but it does mean that these outcomes are more common than one would expect and that details of cases, which on the surface appear to be different, are remarkably similar.

In this chapter we do not consider the accuracy of the charges themselves that were used to justify the dismissal of Dr Coulter from the IMVS. The evaluation of the information available to us pertaining to the specific published allegations is set off in its own chapter: "Charges and Cross-examination".

The Charges Against Coulter Are Published in a Local Newspaper

Initially, the then Director of the IMVS, Dr J. A. Bonnin, a member of a prominent Adelaide family, gave the impression, in an article written by a reporter, that financial reasons were paramount in the decision to demote Dr Coulter, which would have meant a loss of one-third of his salary, and to close the mutagen-testing laboratory (as described in the previous chapter).[4] It was claimed that the IMVS had to find an extra $85,000 a year to support Coulter and his research. From the beginning of the publicity, however, Coulter maintained that he was being victimised because of his outspoken views on a variety of local environmental and medical matters.[5]

However, the financial reasons looked less compelling when another medical doctor[6] revealed that in the same year the IMVS "had a credit balance $882,000 above its budget expectations" — a sum ten times that said to have been needed by the then Director for Coulter and his laboratory.

The Director himself wrote to the *Advertiser*, stating that the reasons for downgrading Coulter "have become confused with finance"[7] and proceeded to list the charges against Coulter (which are quoted in "Charges and Cross-examination").

The publication of the Director's letter to the editor, attacking the competence of Coulter, seems surprising, to say the least. Most newspapers would be hesitant to publish such obviously defamatory material. We do not know what evidence, if any, the Director of the IMVS provided to the editor of the *Advertiser* for the accuracy of the charges. Less damaging allegations made against local politicians or other individuals of prominence have been the subject of successful libel actions. One can only speculate as to why the newspaper was willing to publish such charges — and why, then, for balance, it did not also report the details about those charges when the case finally came before the Industrial Court at the end of 1980 (and when the testimony of witnesses could have been reported verbatim).

But more than one force was at work. As will be described later, the *Advertiser* in October 1980 published the results of investigative news-reporting on the problems within the IMVS. We cannot recall any other recent situation where the *Advertiser* has published anything quite so critical of a local institution that has several prominent local names associated with it.

There was evidence that relations between the IMVS and certain newspaper reporters were not good. In the transcript of the first court case involving Coulter, the Director, under cross-examination, said: "I said that Mr Halestone [presumably Barry Hailstone, now a senior reporter with the *Advertiser*, who wrote several articles on the IMVS] should not come into the [IMVS] building, nor should other press or people without approval".[8] The December 1980 Report of the Committee of Inquiry into the IMVS concluded that "the Institute's relations with the public media have become unsatisfactory, and it is important for the Institute to improve them".[9]

We do not know what were the causes of the IMVS–reporter conflict. We do not presume to know who was right and who was wrong. The conflict may have had the effect that the *Advertiser*, if unfair to Coulter over the charges themselves, was at least willing to publish several letters in support of Coulter (although it refused to publish two letters from a scientist who could comment professionally on certain of the charges). The *Advertiser* also published an article by Bill Guy which provided the pros and cons concerning the closing of Coulter's mutagen testing laboratory.[10]

In examining cases of this kind we must consider historical factors. It would be unwise to assume that a local newspaper will always ferret out the facts behind an unfair dismissal case. Controversy may help to sell newspapers — but too much criticism of powerful local figures can lead to repressive action. For example, only a few years earlier Rohan Rivett, then editor of the *News* in Adelaide, was charged with seditious libel, a criminal offence punishable by a long gaol sentence. Rohan Rivett had the audacity to question the fairness of the handling of the Stuart case, where an Aboriginal had supposedly "confessed" to raping and murdering a child.[11] Several people claimed that the "confession" was obtained by torture. Rohan Rivett, as a courageous editor, found himself charged in 1960 for the same crime William Cobbett was persecuted for in early nineteenth century England. The charge of seditious libel is reminiscent of the "slander of the state"[12] charges commonly used against Soviet dissidents, at least before the Soviets discovered the use of psychiatry. Although the jury failed to convict Rohan Rivett of seditious libel, Rivett found it necessary to leave South Australia. The message, of state-sanctioned repression, had made its mark.

Not only do the local newspapers tread carefully where the establishment is concerned. There is evidence that some individuals in the local establishment can use reporters for their own ends. In comparing the personal experiences of South Australian dissidents, in five cases (including the authors of this chapter: see "The Fruit Fly Papers" chapter) the dissidents or their wives first learned of the dismissal attempt from a reporter on the *Advertiser*. Even the same reporters are used in different cases. This example of where the media are manipulated is most simply explained as "softening up" the dissident or his wife. It may be perceived necessary in cases where the charges themselves lack substance or accuracy.

The Hidden Phase of the Controversy

Before discussing the hidden phase of the Coulter case, it must be stated, in fairness to both Dr Coulter and the IMVS administration, that there had not always been antagonism over Coulter's interests in preventive medicine and the environment, nor objections to his public appearances and activities in community organisations. An earlier senior administrator of the IMVS, Dr Earle Hackett, supported Coulter. Hackett's own ABC radio programme contributed to public discussion of a number of scientific and medical controversies. For more than fifteen years Coulter worked in the IMVS and made public forays without conflict with the IMVS administration.

Problems arose in 1978 when Coulter appeared on a television program, warning of the dangers from the mutagenicity of dichlorvos, a commonly used household pesticide. A member of the IMVS Council, who was also a representative of the South Australia Department of Agriculture, wrote a letter of complaint to the Director. We have not seen that letter and can only guess its nature from comments in the transcript of the court case. We find it difficult to understand what concern the matter was of the SA Department of Agriculture. Bayer, the offended chemical company, brought a "gag writ" for $10,000,000 damages against the ABC — but did not pursue it in court.

In October 1979 the Caulfield Institute of Technology, in Melbourne, held a seminar under the general title "Plants, Pesticides and People: Where Are We Going?". The seminar included several speakers with pro-pesticide views, as well as Coulter, who spoke on the genetic hazards of pesticides. Coulter's talk was important. Not only did he review the use of bacterial mutagenesis in assisting in the search for carcinogens (see "Mutagens and Managers"), Coulter also pointed out the long-term dangers arising from any substance that is mutagenic.[13]

During that talk Coulter discussed the difficulties in effecting adequate control of toxic substances. He presented a slide which summarised the situation for two organochlorine pesticides: chlordane and heptachlor. These substances first became commercially available around 1950. Only around 1965 did it become realised that these substances were carcinogenic in certain experimental animals. The first legal proceedings to restrict the use of chlordane and heptachlor did not occur until 1974. Coulter's slide also included, as evidence for the delay in effective action, the following comment, based on Samuel Epstein's *The Politics of Cancer*[14]: "December 1977, six senior executives of Velsicol found guilty of conspiring to conceal information on carcinogenicity of chlordane/heptachlor".

The contents of this talk were rapidly relayed back to the Velsicol corporation for action. That company sent a letter of complaint, not to Coulter but to Coulter's boss.

It is important to examine in its entirety the reply from the Director, Dr J. A. Bonnin, to the Marketing Manager of Velsicol Australia Ltd, dated 16 November 1979:

> Thank you for your letter of 24th October, 1979, which you wrote to me for the attention of Dr J. Coulter, concerning the paper he presented at a seminar entitled "Plants, Pesticides and People — Where are We going", held in Victoria in October, 1979.
>
> I have discussed this matter with Dr Coulter and sent him a copy of your letter. Dr Coulter has made it quite clear to me that he was acting as a private individual on this occasion and did not give this talk as a member of the staff of this Institute. He claims to have made a clear announcement of this fact at the lecture.
>
> Although I regret that this should have happened and I will be considering the matter further with Dr Coulter, I feel that this Institute should divorce itself from this whole matter and that any further correspondence should be addressed to him as a private individual.

The Director appears to have accepted the fact that Coulter appeared at that seminar in a private capacity. (Recall that this allegation also figured in other South Australian cases — see the chapter "The Fruit Fly Papers"). Indeed, quite properly in our estimation, the Director suggests that any further correspondence from Velsicol should be sent directly to Coulter.

Why then should the Director "regret that this should have happened"? Presumably he is referring to the subject of Velsicol's complaint, that Coulter had mentioned that six of its executives, or former executives, had been convicted of conspiring to withhold evidence. It was true. The following passage appears in Epstein's *The Politics of Cancer*:

> On April 4, 1977, it was reported that a special grand jury in the Federal Court of Chicago was investigating Velsicol on charges that the company had criminally conspired to conceal information on the carcinogenicity of C/H [chlordane/heptachlor]. Specifically, Velsicol was charged with withholding the findings of carcinogenicity arrived at by its own consultants in 1972...
>
> In December, 1977, the federal grand jury handed down an eleven-count felony indictment, naming six present or former company executives, all of whom face prison terms, charging: "From August 1972 to July 1975 the defendants... conspired to defraud the United States and conceal material facts from the United States Environmental Protection Agency by failing to submit data which tended to show that Heptachlor and Chlordane induced tumors in laboratory animals and thus might pose a risk of cancer to humans."[15]

Nor is this the only example of suppression that Velsicol has been involved in. Frank Graham, in *Since Silent Spring*[16], details how Velsicol attempted to suppress the publication of Rachel Carson's *Silent Spring*, the book that alerted millions to the dangers of the abuse of pesticides.

It is also true, as the letter from Velsicol to the Director of the IMVS pointed out, that in April 1979 a higher court reversed the grand jury indictment. But this was on a legal technicality, not on the merits of the case — withholding of information on carcinogenicity. This reversal of the grand jury's indictment appeared in a small news item in the *Chicago Tribune*, and Coulter could hardly be expected to know of it in Australia, where even more internationally prominent newspapers are difficult to obtain. Anyway, it is irrelevant to Coulter's basic point, the long delay in getting effective action to limit the use of carcinogenic pesticides.

Neither Bayer in 1978, nor Velsicol in 1979, complained about the substance of Coulter's comments: there are inadequacies in controlling pesticides for adverse effects on non-target organisms, including humans.

"Infinitely Squalid Local Politics"

Readers may wonder why the relative innocuousness of Coulter's activities should provoke such a reaction from the Director of the IMVS. After all, if it is accepted that Coulter's comments were both correct and made in a private capacity, why should the Director write in his letter to the Marketing Manager of Velsicol Australia Ltd: " . . . and I will be considering the matter further with Dr Coulter . . . "? That has an ominous ring to it, especially when viewed in the light of what happened later.

To understand Coulter's situation more fully, it is necessary to examine briefly other recent South Australian cases of suppression and personality conflict in a historical perspective.

South Australia had at one time such a degree of tolerance for religious and intellectual diversity that it was widely known as "the Athens of the Antipodes" and "a paradise for dissenters". South Australians have always regarded themselves as better than the rest of Australians, for the state was settled by free men: "no convicts here" is an unofficial state motto. South Australia had much to be proud of in the early days. It gave women the right to earn university degrees and the right to vote long before these rights were given to women in the rest of Australia.

However, the isolation of South Australia meant that its local establishment received few intellectual challenges. The original tolerance of diversity slowly metamorphosed into hypersensitivity towards any sort of criticism, into factional fighting within the establishment, and into sporadic episodes of scapegoating outsiders. In certain of the recent cases of conflict, outsiders were punished in unnecessarily nasty ways.

An example is provided by the case of the former Vice-Chancellor of the University of Adelaide, A. P. Rowe.[17] After his distinguished service during the Second World War, when he administered the large group of scientists involved in the development of radar, Rowe was invited to become the Vice-Chancellor of the University of Adelaide. Rowe made many improvements in the University, including a study leave program, greatly improved salaries, and the initiation of surveys of students' problems and performance. In the official history of the University, written to commemorate its centenary, Rowe is considered one of the two best Vice-Chancellors.[18]

Gradually, Rowe fell out with some of the senior staff. He realised this and indicated that he would not be seeking reappointment. Thus, Rowe had provided the perfect opportunity to be allowed to leave gracefully and without open hostility. Instead, the major academic committee of the University of Adelaide, the Education Committee, drove Rowe out with a vote of no confidence.

Rowe himself phrased the basic question which applies not only to his own case but to others: " . . . how could the few persuade the many to act so swiftly and ruthlessly?"[19]

South Australia was the first Australian state to establish a festival of the arts, in 1960. The festival has been very successful, both locally and internationally. However, in recent years it has been plagued by conflicts between some members of the local establishment and the cosmopolitan talent brought in to direct the festival or to perform.[20] The local–cosmopolitan conflict involving the festival reached a peak in the same years as the attempt to sack Coulter from the IMVS. It was when the noted English festival organiser Christopher Hunt left that his play-directing colleague Peter Brook complained of Adelaide's "infinitely squalid local politics".[21]

Some of the sackings in South Australia have had a more sinister element — the covering up of dubious activities. "Jock" Marshall, then Professor of Zoology at Monash University, Melbourne, when reviewing the causes for the decline or extinction of many species of vertebrates in Australia, wrote the following:

> Three years later came a sordid and much publicised affair involving the Adelaide Zoo. This is a
> poor-class institution: nevertheless, it is run by a group of socially-acceptable Adelaidians who

always include the "Lord Mayor of Adelaide for the time being". A gentleman, described as the son of a former Lord Mayor, but who was nevertheless a bird dealer and at the same time the appointed agent of the Zoo, was convicted of making false customs declarations in the attempted export of birds. A local bird-dealing firm with whom he did business was convicted at the same time. According to press reports, this gentleman bought birds from Zoo officers as well as from dealers in the course of his allegedly illegal exports. In the year 1961–62, 75% of all birds sent abroad went from Adelaide Zoo, and 24% were despatched from Taronga Park, Sydney. These birds were consigned to foreign zoos, great and small, but how many ever went on public display is conjectural. From February 1961 to June 1963, nearly £12,000 was got by the Adelaide Zoo from the sale of fauna but, as an official inquiry found, the *"financial transactions were dealt with through a separate account and did not form part of the Council's income and expenditure statement as published"*. At the same time, however, no evidence was found that any of the money received had found its way into the pockets of Councillors. It was during this unsavoury affair that the Adelaide Zoo found itself the centre of a second scandal concerning its dismissal of a new and universally respected director . . .[22] (emphasis added)

We have been informed from several sources that the director, to whom "Jock" Marshall refers, had made himself unpopular with certain powerful people because he blew-the-whistle on the animal smuggling (and this resulted in the call for a Royal Commission). Local–cosmopolitan conflict still is manifested at the zoo. Although the reasons behind the conflict have not been made public, recently one zoo director was sacked and the present zoo director has had his position threatened, despite the fact that many members of the public, and the zoo staff, feel that he has made many improvements.[23]

The sacking of the highly regarded Police Commissioner, Harold Salisbury, drew widespread local and international protest. He was dismissed by the then Premier of South Australia, Donald Dunstan, for allegedly failing to inform the government fully about the existence of secret files on certain citizens. Although the government defended its actions in terms of concern about citizens' right to privacy, there is evidence from one of our case histories ("The Fruit Fly Papers") that the government had little if any concern about unnecessary invasion of privacy. Information contained in two books dealing with recent political events in South Australia suggests that the primary concern was about the *kind* of information the police had on certain local establishment figures.[24]

Police Commissioner Salisbury had nothing to do with the secret files, which had been organised under a predecessor, with help from ASIO and the CIA. Salisbury, originally distrusted because of his overseas origin, had quickly become popular with both the police and the people of South Australia. He introduced a variety of reforms, rather along the lines of "community policing". During his period in South Australia there were no allegations of police corruption, as have occurred subsequent to his sacking and are an endemic problem in some other Australian states. Salisbury had on a number of occasions spoken out against lax standards of discipline, inaction on corruption, overly lenient convictions for crimes of violence, and against child pornography. Salisbury's public comments had brought him into conflict with certain important politicians. The situation has been summarised by Max Harris:

It soon became apparent that Mr Salisbury belonged to an alien and exotic breed. His presence was a continuing culture shock. He ran the cleanest and most respected police force in Australia. He also represented a totally non-political conservativeness which ran quite counter to the libertarian trendiness which was the pride and joy of the Government and its surrounding Establishment.[25]

Far from favouring secret dealings, Salisbury had been one of the few individuals in authority in South Australia who favoured publishing a secret document about the death of a lecturer at the University of Adelaide. This lecturer was alleged to have been a homosexual.

He was killed when thrown into the Torrens River, adjacent to the University of Adelaide campus. Three members of the police force resigned after refusing to answer questions about the death of the lecturer. Salisbury had brought in overseas investigators to prepare a report on the case and he had wanted that report, known to be critical of the police, to be published. The local establishment has successfully kept that report secret and the police officers were never indicted — although the Police Commissioner believed that there was a good case against them. We have been told that an important local establishment figure was also at the scene of the crime, though not an active participant; there appears to have been a desire to spare his feelings about why he was present at a place where it was known that homosexuals congregated.[26]

Salisbury's sacking resulted in considerable public disquiet. There was also a statement from the former Governor of South Australia, Sir Mark Oliphant, who believed that Salisbury had been unfairly treated. Although estimates of the numbers vary, some 7000–15,000 people demonstrated in Victoria Square on behalf of the sacked Police Commissioner, as compared with only 100–200 supporters for the Dunstan government. While the government made a series of attempts to excuse its handling of the situation, it decided (*after* the popular protest) to pay the remainder of Salisbury's salary, plus expenses and pension.

These recent cases, ranging from the arts to the zoo, from academics to the police, represent a minority of South Australian cases in the sense that only these cases have been the subject of published disapproval. There are other cases known to us where there has not been protest to expose unfairness.

The existence of so many cases in a relatively small community must raise questions about the nature of those who rule in South Australia — the establishment. This is not to say that all members of the establishment are in agreement about such cases. It is not to say that most members of the establishment would participate in such unfair means of suppressing dissent. But the existence of such a series of cases (and the unpublished ones are as bad) does raise the question of why certain members of the establishment do not keep their colleagues in better order. Also, why have establishment members so rarely spoken out against such abuses? There has been a poor showing in attempts to rectify wrongs. Differences in opinion, personality clashes, even public rows, occur everywhere. What is special about these South Australian cases is a consistent pattern of behaviour:

1. The victim is an ''outsider'', often from overseas.[27]

2. There are many who feel that the victim had performed well in his job.

3. The allegations to justify the sacking (or equivalent) have often been vague, insubstantial or erroneous.

4. Although the opportunity exists to allow the victim to leave quietly, it is deliberately ignored by those in charge. For example, the Police Commissioner was sacked almost one year before he would have had to retire. Elsewhere, the humane and sensible way to settle such differences is to offer a fair ''golden handshake'', allowing the individual to leave with a minimum of acrimony. Instead, there is an obsession to destroy the individual and his reputation, regardless of the cost (which is passed to the taxpayer).

5. The establishment is extremely reluctant to admit that a mistake has been made, or to admit that the procedures used to get rid of some dissident were unfair. Some partial measure of compensation for a damaged reputation is given begrudgingly only for the minority of cases where the establishment must quiet an outraged public.

With these other recent examples in mind, the reader can perhaps understand Coulter's position a bit better. For Coulter was more than the average dissenter. He is widely regarded as an extremely effective public speaker. A Western Australian in origin, Coulter converses in a pleasant and direct Australian manner. While he has an encyclopaedic knowledge of medical and environmental matters, he never forces this learning down the listener's throat. He has been an elected official in a number of community organisations and has often appeared as their representative at governmental enquiries. Coulter is a formidable adversary for government bureaucrats and industrial witnesses: patient but quick, and just aggressive enough not to be intimidated. He is probably the opponent most feared by a variety of local vested interests. He must have been at the top of any local "hit list".

Local Conscience: Parliamentarians and the Politics of Preventive Medicine

Coulter's popularity with many local groups meant that there was quite widespread public support for him. Many petitions on his behalf were sent to parliamentarians. Coulter also received strong support from part of the trade union movement, notably a delegation from the United Trades and Labor Council. The Environmentalists for Full Employment, a group with links to the trade union movement, also supported Coulter.

However, the Australian Labor Party (ALP) itself appeared less interested in the case. Certain ALP politicians in South Australia (who were then in opposition to the government in power) did a splendid job on behalf of Coulter (and the public) by bringing to light a number of deficiencies within the IMVS. In particular, Terrence Hemmings raised issues in the state Parliament involving the IMVS. This ALP politician was joined by Robin Millhouse, then representing the Australian Democrats (and later appointed to the Supreme Court of South Australia).

Why was the overall support from the ALP rather weak? Three explanations are worth considering:

First, in South Australia there are some establishment members who are in the ALP, although there are more in the Liberal Party. The two main parties differ little in their political positions.

Second, the ALP has strong representation from professional elites, notably lawyers and academics. Politicians recruited from these professions may not be really establishment — but some strongly seek to become establishment. There are often tensions between ALP politicians representing the professions and those who are from the more traditional Labor base, namely the trade unions.

Third, the ALP, both nationally and locally, has been ambivalent over many environmental issues. Nothing makes this clearer than the recent contortions over uranium mining. The last traces of credibility were lost when the South Australian ALP delegates pushed for a platform that excluded uranium mining except for Roxby Downs, to which the state ALP is strongly committed.[28] Surely, if there are ethical and environmental reasons to oppose uranium mining, these apply with equal force across state boundaries. There is a feeling among some ALP members that cleaning up the environment means a loss of jobs. We will not pursue here another inconsistency, that the ALP (with the exception of Barry Jones) has been passive to the inroads on employment arising from automation and computerisation. Accordingly, one can see how an intelligent environmentalist would be viewed as a threat to the policy manoeuvrings of some influential ALP politicians.

The issues Coulter has raised over the years have a strong unifying theme. The emphasis on a healthy lifestyle and a clean environment, both at home and at work, raises the issues of individual independence, local control and accountability of elites. This threatens corporate, bureaucratic and professional interests. Preventive medicine, largely in the form of better sanitation, better nutrition, and less pollution, has been more effective than curative medicine in improving the health of the community.[29]

But, curative medicine is more profitable to many medical doctors and to the entire "medical-industrial complex". Coulter made a cogent case for restoring the balance between preventive and curative medicine in his 1980 submission to the Committee of Enquiry into the Provision of Pathology Services in South Australia. Coulter pointed to the exponential rise in the cost of IMVS services to consumers (gross payments to the IMVS went from $2,000,000 in 1970 to $17,000,000 in 1980 and are still rising). He contrasted this with the nearly static morbidity and mortality patterns in South Australia during the same period. Others have called attention to the contrast between the rapidly rising cost of medical care and the failure to improve the health statistics of the population, or even the decline in health for certain occupational groups.[30] In the United States the "medical-industrial complex" consumes fully 10 per cent of the gross national product, though there have been only minor improvements in health statistics in the last twenty years. Where improvements have occurred, notably in the reduction of cardiovascular mortality, it is believed that the improvements have come from encouraging people to adopt a healthier lifestyle (for example, by cessation of smoking, taking moderate exercise, and reducing the amount of saturated fat and salt in the diet) rather than by new developments in curative medicine (for example, coronary bypass operations).[31] At the same time, certain forms of cancer are increasing in frequency. Some of these cancers are associated with exposure to carcinogens, such as asbestos and chlorinated hydrocarbons, in the work environment.[32, 33]

There is a significant group of medical doctors who support Coulter's position on the importance of preventive medicine. There is probably a healthier state of dissidence within the medical profession than among other professional groups — witness recent public criticism by surgeons of the examples of "overservicing" (unnecessary operations) by their colleagues. Both the Doctors' Reform Society and the Australian Society of Microbiologists were groups who protested to Members of Parliament about the removal of Coulter from the IMVS.

However, Coulter's views would be less attractive to those professionals whose profits and prestige come from curative medicine. This includes not only many practising medical doctors *but also a large portion of the biomedical research community*. Research involving cures gets more rewards than research devoted to prevention. In terms of vested interests, the one exception proves the rule: preventive medicine based on vaccines has often been rewarded (as indeed it should be in most cases). Vaccines are highly profitable to drug companies, for they are given to large numbers of healthy people and, thus, represent a proportionately larger market.

Coulter's proposed restoration of a better balance between preventive and curative medicine has important implications for elites outside the "medical-industrial complex". Preventive medicine would focus on both alcohol and the motor vehicle as major causes of death and disability. Motor vehicle accidents are not only a major cause of death, especially for young males, but account for nearly half of the patients in long-term care in neurologic wards (the paraplegics and quadriplegics). The motor vehicle is also the source of much profitable litigation for the legal profession and has spawned a massive "captured bureaucracy" within the government. Preventive medicine poses a direct challenge to the many intellectuals who staff the custodial services, dealing with the debris left by drink, drugs, unsafe working conditions, and the chronic unemployment characterising the modern "welfare state". Thus, perhaps it is not too surprising that there was not strong support among many professionals, including politicians, for Coulter's right to free speech and a fair trial in the IMVS.

Conflicts-of-Interest: "I'm Not Suggesting Everybody Would Do That"

Although they were only a minority in Parliament, Terrence Hemmings and Robin Millhouse were effective in raising a number of issues about the IMVS. After the sacking of the dissident came the deluge. There had been warning signs: an earlier investigative committee had criticised the management and accounting procedures in the IMVS. There were widespread rumours of staff dissatisfaction — and several of these cases involved actions in the Industrial Court.

On 17 September 1980, nearly six months after the announcement of the Coulter sacking, Terrence Hemmings put before the South Australian Parliament the results of his detailed investigations into a number of problems at the IMVS. He concentrated on the desirability of accurately accounting for the sources of funds for travel expenses:

> ...the Deputy Director [of IMVS] was Dr R. G. Edwards...[and] he had been overseas 17 times in the last 10 years...the cost of his travel had been borne as follows: from Dr R. G. Edwards' personal funds, or by international professional organisations, 70 per cent; by I.M.V.S. funds, 6 per cent; and by private companies, 24 per cent. The companies contributing to the 24 per cent were Pfrimmer, $1504; *Technicon*, $7720; and Hoffman-La Roche, a Swiss [-based drug transnational], $400.
>
> The Deputy Director had taken 17 trips in 10 years, at a total cost of $38,000, representing a little more than $2000 a trip. One would suggest either that the Deputy Director is a frugal traveller and possibly a future contributor to *See Europe on $15 a day*, or that the answer given to the Minister was not correct.

Hemmings went on to compare those numerical figures with what appeared in the transcript of "...a case held before the Industrial Court on 19 February 1979. This case dealt with an action taken by Dr R. G. Edwards, who wanted to carry on private practice as well as being a public servant":

Question:	Have the I.M.V.S. in the time you've been in your situation benefited at all from that sort of work [attending meetings and taking trips]?
Answer:	Yes. Best illustrated by placing a direct cash value on it of approximately $400,000.
His Honour:	Question: Sorry, who has put the cash value on this?
Answer:	That is cash received by the institute in the form of various grants or other direct support from —
Question:	Overseas?
Answer:	Industry overseas, industry local, other funding bodies.
Question:	How do you say that's directly related to your trips overseas?
Answer:	It's derived, well I could illustrate it point by point if you wish, but it's been derived much of it from specific conferences that I've held with people overseas. For example, I will be going to Sydney tomorrow to receive $25,000 which is derived directly from a meeting held in Basle, Switzerland.
Question:	Do I draw the inference from that that if someone hadn't gone to that conference in Basle, Switzerland, you wouldn't have got the $25,000?
Answer:	That in that instance is absolutely correct, yes, sir. I have a somewhat unusual role, shall we say, in an unusual expertise. *I'm not suggesting everybody would do that.* [emphasis added]

Mr Hemmings then emphasises the discrepancies in the IMVS accounts:

> That organisation was called Hoffman La Roche, which is a drug company. We have not been able to find in any reports a reference to $25,000; nowhere have we been able to find, in past reports, a figure of $400,000. This is the kind of thing which we want to know and which a public inquiry could bring out, but up to now, the Government and the Minister [for Health] have chosen not to give any form of answer to our request.[34]

A week later Lynn Arnold raised in Parliament another problem: the IMVS had purchased a number of very expensive medical testing machines, including some from Technicon, which may not have been satisfactory:

I do not know what these machines do, but I have been informed that in fact some of these machines do not do very much, that they have been sitting at the institute for substantial periods of time in some cases without being used at all, or at least without being used until questions were raised in this place [Parliament] earlier this year. Suddenly, I am informed, some of these machines got their first usage to try to justify the purchase of that equipment. I think that a public inquiry could very usefully find out not only the relationship of the purchase of these items of equipment with donations to the institute but also whether that equipment was necessary to the operations of the institute.[35]

"Suffer the [Aboriginal] Children"

Also in the parliamentary debates Hemmings refers to where Coulter (not mentioned by name but readily identifiable) and a colleague had sought to publish in the *Medical Journal of Australia* on the mutagenicity of Flagyl and other 5-nitroimidazole drugs.[36]

A critical point to know is that G. D. Searle and Co., which manufactures Flagyl, had been in trouble with the US Food and Drug Administration (FDA) over inadequacies in its testing for safety. The journal *Nature* published the following comments about G. D. Searle and Co.:

A relatively unremarkable scientific paper, published early in 1972, has touched off a major scandal over the testing and regulation of drugs in the United States. It has led to allegations that some drug companies have conducted sloppy animal tests, faked results and presented misleading toxicity reports to the federal government...

The concern over the quality of drug testing was triggered by a study published in the Journal of the National Cancer Institute by Mario Rustia and Philippe Shubik of the Eppley Research Institute. The study indicated that a commonly prescribed drug, *known as Flagyl*, increases the incidence of pulmonary and lymphoid tumours in mice. The paper raised eyebrows in FDA because the agency had in its files reports of two studies submitted by the drug's manufacturer, G. D. Searle and Co., which claimed to show that Flagyl is not carcinogenic in rats.

A thorough check on Searle's study was then conducted by Adrian Gross, an FDA scientist. Gross concluded that Searle's study did indeed show evidence of carcinogenicity, but the company's report didn't reflect all the data. FDA officials took the matter up with Searle, and two years later the company re-submitted its report. This time, Gross said in an interview last week, the summary agreed with the data, which would have been fine except that it was the data, not the summary, which had been altered.[37]

Coulter and his colleague had wished to include in their manuscript sent to the *Medical Journal of Australia* part of this quotation from the article in *Nature*. Hemmings, in his 17 September 1980 contribution to the South Australian parliamentary debates, describes what he believed then happened:

On 14 July 1977 Professor V . . ., who was, I think, the head of the tissue pathology unit at the I.M.V.S., came into the office to discuss the paper with the two gentlemen [Coulter and colleague?] from the I.M.V.S. I want to quote what was given to me, because I feel that it is important that we have it down correctly. Professor V . . . said he wanted a quotation from *Nature* removed and also any reference to, or use of, the terms "drug company" or "drug firm", and he made a statement as follows:

"This institute gets money from drug companies to carry out research."[38]

At that point in the debates Hemmings was interrupted by a question from a fellow parliamentarian: "Was a transcript taken of the conversation?" Hemmings replied: "Both gentlemen were present when this was said, and I understand that statutory declarations will be forthcoming if required." He then continued:

The purpose of Professor V . . .'s demand was quite clear. A higher priority was being set on the protection of one of the institute's sources of funds than on the protection of the public by making relevant information more widely available. It was also protecting the interests of the drug companies. The gentlemen concerned became extremely angry over this request and even the morality of such a request. Professor V . . . made it perfectly clear that he was acting on instructions from a higher authority, and he stated that he was not going to involve his own ethical standards to disagree with an instruction from a higher authority.

The following week a similar request was made by Dr E . . ., then head of the Division of Clinical Chemistry and the Acting Deputy Director. The same reasons were given, namely that the I.M.V.S. received money from drug companies and chemical companies [,] and that a paper such as that proposed could have had adverse effects on that kind of money coming into the organisation.

Hemmings then goes on to describe the alleged act of suppression itself:

The two gentlemen were forced to delete this passage [the original quotation from *Nature* commenting on the drug companies' inadequacies] and any references to drug companies or chemical companies. I maintain that that is direct suppression of information which could be of value to the public and to medical practitioners, and one would have thought that it was the duty of the I.M.V.S. Director and his Deputy Director, and the council, to make sure that that kind of information was forthcoming to the general public, but it was suppressed.[39]

At this point we turn to the paper by Coulter and Turner[40] which was published in the *Medical Journal of Australia*. Coulter and Turner pointed out the medical significance of their earlier work on the mutagenicity of 5-nitroimidazole drugs. Medical doctors and researchers had been giving 5-nitroimidazole drugs to Aboriginal children. This was not just for the treatment of *diagnosed* protozoan gut infections. There were also instances where these 5-nitroimidazole drugs were being given to Aboriginal children as a prophylactic — or just as part of the "control" in an experiment. In these latter situations there is a question of medical ethics: *individuals who are not suffering from a disease are being given a treatment which carries an unknown but potentially serious risk.*

One might also wonder if some of these medical doctors and researchers (to whom Coulter and Turner had addressed their article) had obtained informed consent from these human "guinea pigs". Probably they needed decent sanitation and better nutrition more than a prophylactic drug or to be experimented upon. Drug companies, and compliant medical researchers, have long used the disadvantaged in society as experimental objects, even though their disadvantages may invalidate the scientific conclusions from the experiments.

The fact that a drug company involved in producing these 5-nitroimidazole drugs had recently been in trouble with the US Food and Drug Administration in regard to the suppression of results indicating carcinogenicity of a 5-nitroimidazole compound, was then (and still is) of paramount importance. It should have been mentioned in the *Medical Journal of Australia* paper; and Coulter and his colleague had endeavoured to do so. The fact, that there had been inadequacies in the information flow concerning possible toxic side effects, was something that medical doctors needed to know in making their own cost/benefit decisions as to whether or not to prescribe these drugs. The thalidomide disaster is only the most conspicuous of a number of examples of where inadequate drug testing, combined with suppression of information, has had tragic human consequences.[41]

Report of the Committee of Inquiry into the IMVS

After successfully preventing a full inquiry into the IMVS and the Coulter dismissal for several months, the then Minister of Health, the Honourable Jennifer Adamson, M.P., announced on 28 October 1980 that there was to be a wide ranging inquiry into the IMVS.

Three individuals were appointed: Dr Ronald Wells, a medical practitioner, Professor Neville F. Stanley, a biomedical researcher, and John E. Burdett, an accountant.

After the delay of almost a year, the government wanted results fast. The committee conducted its inquiry between 17 November and 19 December and its report was published in the latter month. The committee stated that it believed "a full and frank report was sought in our terms of reference"[42] — but the Coulter case received only the briefest possible mention. We cannot find any discussion about the alleged suppression incident raised by Terrence Hemmings in the parliamentary debates, although he claimed he had two witnesses prepared to give statutory declarations.

The report does dwell on "weaknesses in the recording and reporting of financial transactions".[43] On the question of private firms financing overseas trips by senior staff, the report said the following:

> Of particular concern has been the financing of trips by potential suppliers for Institute staff to test or view equipment. The Institute of Medical and Veterinary Science Act requires that the Institute conform with the requirements of the Public Service Supply and Tender Act in its acquisition procedures. The Public Supply and Tender Act has been framed to ensure fair and equal competition for all tenderers and while there is no evidence to suggest that the Institute has contravened the spirit of the Act, it has left itself open to criticism. The Committee considers that the Institute should discontinue accepting financial assistance from private companies to view or test equipment either prior to or during a tender call.[44]

The committee also suggested:

> . . . the Institute revise its procedures for approving overseas travel to ensure that travel funded by a Specific Research Grant is referred to the [State] Overseas Travel Committee for approval.[45]

We find the longer quotation given above to be ambiguous. If the overseas travel practices were within "the spirit of the Act", what about the letter of the Act? If everything was satisfactory, why the proposed changes mentioned in the shorter quotation? Was the Public Service Supply and Tender Act actually breached by the examples given in Parliament by Terrence Hemmings and Lynn Arnold? If not, why didn't the committee defend the Deputy Director openly? Surely, if Hemmings and Arnold were wrong, and the situation capable of misinterpretation, should this not have been clearly stated, with the evidence presented to Parliament and the public? And, if the Public Service Supply and Tender Act had been violated, why weren't the appropriate individuals in the IMVS prosecuted?

Another serious deficiency in the committee's report was its failure to acknowledge how one of its recommendations corresponds exactly to the position that Coulter (and Earle Hackett) had argued for years; quoting from the report:

> Increasing awareness of and concern about environmental pollution, including the contamination of food [,] and the abuse and iatrogenic effects of drugs [,] is likely to cause an increased demand for testing and monitoring by the Institute.[46]

Closing Coulter's mutagen testing laboratory runs counter to the committee's recommendation.

On other matters the report is more explicit. To see this better we now go back two months in time.

The Advertiser *Wades in on the IMVS: "a Web of Intrigue, Tension and Unrest"*

In October 1980 the *Advertiser* "tipped the bucket" on the IMVS, to use an Australian colloquialism. Barry Hailstone, the medical writer for the *Advertiser*, alleged that:

> Behind the sedate, white-coated, cool professional appearance of the SA Institute of Medical and

Veterinary Science on Frome Road is a web of intrigue, tension and unrest . . .

An interplay of temperament, blended with innuendo, allegation and spite is shaking the foundations of the institute, often regarded as an SA bastion of professional standards and discrimination . . .[47]

Seven members of the higher administration of the IMVS wrote a letter to the editor stating that "morale within the divisions is generally good".[48] Their letter did not deal with the other allegations raised in Parliament and in Barry Hailstone's article.[49]

A longer letter to the editor, from A. G. McGregor, Chairman of the Council of the IMVS (and a well-known local lawyer, cattle-breeder, and patron of the arts), replied as follows:

It would be idle to pretend that in an organisation the size of the IMVS there are not a few disaffected individuals or disagreements over organisation or professional and scientific matters from time to time . . .

The heads of the divisions of the institute wrote to you recently stating that morale within the divisions was generally good.

As they are the senior officers in charge of the staff in their divisions they would know the attitudes of their staff well.[50]

It is thus of interest to read what the Report of the Committee of Inquiry into the IMVS concluded:

There is a strong body of opinion within the Institute, which has been supported in a significant number of well documented submissions to the Committee and in discussion with Institute staff, that there is . . . a lack of confidence in, and hostility to senior management, with staff hostility extending in some instances to a questioning of the integrity and fairness of senior management . . . [There is] a degree of unrest and low morale existing within the Institute.[51]

"Suffer the Animals"

No sooner had the Minister for Health finally allowed an inquiry into the IMVS than a new scandal broke out. Robin Millhouse announced in the House of Assembly that he had received documents from a previous Acting Director of Veterinary Pathology at the IMVS. The new allegations were that experiments on animals were not properly supervised in some instances, and that "the 'bioethics' committee was a ghost committee" whose function "was simply to deceive any inquisitive animal welfare organisations into believing that the welfare of animals was adequately protected".[52]

This prompted yet another official investigation into the IMVS. Professor Bede Morris, an immunologist from the Australian National University, was brought in to investigate the treatment of animals at the IMVS, and at other research institutions in Adelaide. His report, *Enquiry into the Use of Laboratory and Experimental Animals*, deserves a wider readership than most such government reports get. Bede Morris's report is an excellent statement of the various perspectives and practices on animal welfare. The report also ranges out into other subjects that are relevant; for example:

The present system of funding much of medical research in Australia leads to research grants being given to so-called Senior Investigators who are only prepared to devote minimum periods of time to the research. Grants are given to them to fund salaries of relatively junior Research workers and Technicians who actually do the work. The 3 to 4 days a month devoted to the research by the Senior Investigator is questionably adequate for the science but unquestionably inadequate for the animals.[53]

Professor Bede Morris makes no attempt to whitewash what went on in the past at the IMVS:

There are no satisfactory excuses for the circumstances that were allowed to develop in the Institute over a period of several years prior to 1978. The administration of the operating theatres and the supervision of the post-operative care of animals were just not good enough. A major part of the problem seemed to rest with the Institute administration allowing a contumacious technical staff to exploit their position in the operating theatres in a quite outrageous way. The people who were using the operating theatres at this time appeared to be unable, unwilling or indifferent to reporting an unsatisfactory situation that was working against their own individual best interests and against the corporate interests of the Institute. There was no adequate supervisory arrangement to ensure that malpractice would be quickly detected and eliminated, and as a consequence the operating theatre complex acquired a shady reputation among some Institute staff as a place where unsavoury arcane operations were being done to animals.[54]

Professor Morris drew attention to the problem that was also mentioned in at least two other inquiries into the IMVS: the awkward position of the veterinarians vis-a-vis the medical doctors.

The public criticisms of the incidents with experimental animals led to press reports which referred to the maltreatment of animals at the "Vet Institute" and it was suggested subsequently that members of the Institute's veterinary staff were to an extent responsible for allowing these misdemeanours to occur. This was quite wrong and these suggestions should have been corrected by the Institute's administration. As a consequence the delinquency of medical practitioners resulted in obloquy for the veterinarians which further alienated the Institute's veterinary staff.[55]

The IMVS had been founded around 1938 with the high hopes that medical doctors and veterinarians could work together in research and in practical problems. This was a sensible plan from at least two standpoints: a number of diseases are transmitted between man and animals; and, farm livestock are especially important to the economy of South Australia.

Unfortunately, the plan did not take into account the sociology of complex research organisations dealing with biomedicine. Medical doctors are among the most highly paid professionals, rivalled only by lawyers. Medical doctors tend to take a condescending view towards other scientists. The IMVS is not alone in having serious tensions between medical doctors and non-medical research staff, which includes veterinarians. Medical doctors insist on, and get, higher salaries, more research money, and more perks.

The arrogant treatment received by non-medical researchers in medical institutes drives many highly trained and competent scientists out of medical research. Yet, the nature of modern research is such that neither medical doctors alone, nor any other single group, have a monopoly on expertise. Each needs the others. These social-structural problems, manifested in conflict between different professional groups, ensure that the non-medical researchers, the taxpayers, and the animals, all suffer. At least it can be said in fairness to the IMVS that when, in the following year, Professor Bede Morris returned to inspect the animal facilities he was impressed with the improvements in the physical plant and with the high standard of care provided by the animal attendants.

Is the Setting Responsible for the Paralysis of Conscience?

This background on both the community setting and the institutional setting helps to provide an understanding of Coulter's plight. Within the general community Coulter received widespread support. There is no paralysis of conscience in many sections of the South Australian community; quite a number of ordinary citizens were prepared to protest, to sign petitions, and to provide support for Coulter in other ways. Where the paralysis occurred was among the powerful local establishment and among certain professional groups.

The dissident from outside a community brings in new ideas and refers his observations to broader international standards. This is resented and resisted by locals who are intolerant of any kind of criticism, as well as by that certain class of cosmopolitans whose major aim in life is the pursuit of fame or profit.

The background to the Coulter case reveals how he was caught in "a web of intrigue, tension and unrest"[56], to quote one of the newspaper items on the IMVS. Even though ultimately some attempt was made to investigate some of the problems at the IMVS, the individual who had the courage to speak out on issues of preventive medicine and the environment was considered expendable in the "infinitely squalid local politics".

It is the long-suffering patient who carries a double burden for this "web of intrigue, tension and unrest". The fees charged for medical testing by the IMVS are expensive. This has facilitated the growth of what Terrence Hemmings terms "the millionaire pathologist" and various "empire-building exercises".[57] This is all part of the uncontrolled inflation of the "medical-industrial complex".

The point has been reached where many patients must forgo adequate medical testing and treatment because of the money consumed by petty squabbles among bureaucrats, consumed by equipment which is either unnecessary or inadequate, or consumed for research which is irrelevant to the task of reducing human suffering.

We now pass to the questions about the substance and the accuracy of the charges laid against Coulter by the then Director of the IMVS.

References

1. Gerald Holton, *The Scientific Imagination: Case Studies* (Cambridge University Press, 1978), especially chapter 7. The quotations are from p. 235 with some italicised sections in normal type.

2. The authors have sampled over three thousand references dealing with the history, sociology and psychology of scientists, and are in the process of preparing a more general review of the evidence for Holton's conclusions and the consequences for man of unchecked abuse of science and technology. The basic point, the lack of altruism among scientists, the result of some combination of intrinsic personality characteristics and of the pressures from within and outside the scientific community, is evident in many studies. For the interested reader we recommend the following, chosen to show how similar conclusions are reached by individuals taking quite different analytic approaches: Joseph Haberer, *Politics and the Community of Science* (New York: Van Nostrand-Reinhold, 1969); Daniel S. Greenberg, *The Politics of American Science* (originally published as *The Politics of Pure Science*) (Harmondsworth, Middlesex: Penguin Books, 1969 edn.); Bernice T. Eiduson, *Scientists: Their Psychological World* (New York: Basic Books, 1962); Jerome R. Ravetz, *Scientific Knowledge and Its Social Problems* (Oxford: Clarendon Press, 1971); Brian Martin, *The Bias of Science* (Canberra: Society for Social Responsibility in Science, 1979).

3. We are using the terms *local* versus *cosmopolitan* rather along the lines of A. W. Gouldner, "Cosmopolitans and locals: toward an analysis of latent social roles — I". *Administrative Science Quarterly* 2, pp. 281–306 (1957). As with all dichotomous classifications it is an oversimplification, but nevertheless a useful one, upheld in further studies: E. V. Morse and S. Gordon, "Cognitive skills: a determinant of scientists' local–cosmopolitan orientation", *Academy of Management Journal* 17, pp. 709–23 (1974). Although these references discuss refinements, the terms local and cosmopolitan are basically self-explanatory. Locals are committed to immediate organisational values. Cosmopolitans are individuals who are committed to a broader set of values; these values may be those of a particular profession, such as medicine or science, or they may be those of a particular dissenting movement, either within a profession (for example, preventive medicine versus curative medicine) or uniting a number of different community groups, i.e., cutting across other social boundaries (for example the

environment movement, peace movement, or, of course, political parties, right or left). Our discussion of local versus cosmopolitan does not imply any value judgement. Local values may be fine and fair, or so supportive of self-interest and hierarchy within an organisation as to be destructive of broader community interests. Cosmopolitans too may become overly committed to self-interest and this can be expressed in their private ideologies and in their "pressure group" actions vis-a-vis the broader community interests. However, commitment to cosmopolitan values does allow greater possibility for identification with broader community concerns, and reference to more time-tested ideals.

4. Barry Hailstone, "Director gives reasons for scientist's move", Adelaide *Advertiser*, 1 April 1980, p. 8.

5. Barry Hailstone, "Sacked for speaking out — scientist", Adelaide *Advertiser*, 31 March 1980, p. 12.

6. P. R. S. Gouldhurst, "Cancer research" (letter to the editor), Adelaide *Advertiser*, 10 April 1980, p. 5.

7. J. A. Bonnin, "Cancer research work" (letter to the editor), Adelaide *Advertiser*, 12 April 1980, p. 5.

8. Coulter v. IMVS and Public Service Board, South Australia Industrial Court 4 December 1980, p. 913 of transcript.

9. R. Wells, N. F. Stanley and J. E. Burdett, *Report of the Committee of Inquiry into the Institute of Medical and Veterinary Science*. 207-page printed document, dated December 1980, but with no other identification. Obtained from the South Australian government publications outlet. (Quotation on p. 25).

10. Bill Guy, "Conservation campaigner in crisis: does Dr Coulter have to go?", Adelaide *Advertiser*, 17 June 1980, p. 5.

11. Peter Ward, "The trial of journalism", *Australian*, 23 April 1981, p. 11. A summary of the Stuart case is provided by Ward McNally, *Aborigines, Artefacts and Anguish* (Adelaide: Chi Rho, Lutheran Publishing House, 1981), Ch. 9.

12. Peter Reddaway (ed. and trans.), *Uncensored Russia: the Human Rights Movement in the Soviet Union* (London: Jonathan Cape, 1972).

13. There has been a mistaken belief in some epidemiological circles that genetically caused diseases are totally separate from environmentally caused diseases. Many genetically based diseases originate as a consequence of mutagens, which may occur either naturally or by human intervention in the diet, from other aspects of the environment, or even produced by metabolic activation of natural substances brought into the body. Increasing the human mutation rate, either by exposure to increased amounts of radiation or by exposure to mutagenic chemicals, poses both short and long term threats. Deleterious genes are removed by the death of individuals, or their failure to reproduce. A sizeable body of expert opinion regards somatic mutation as involved in both ageing and in the genesis of certain cancers. Even for some cancers of known viral causation, exposure to low levels of radiation, or to certain chemicals, can activate the latent virus and start the oncogenic process (see Natalie M. Teich and R. A. Weiss, "Beware the lurking virogene" in: R. F. Beers, Jr. and E. G. Bassett (eds), *Recombinant Molecules: Impact on Science and Society* (New York: Raven Press, 1977) pp. 471–83; and reviews in *Comprehensive Virology*).

14. Samuel S. Epstein, *The Politics of Cancer* (San Francisco: Sierra Club, 1978), p. 280. The interested reader will find the following articles useful: Samuel S. Epstein and Joel B. Swartz, "Fallacies of lifestyle cancer theories", *Nature* 289, pp. 127–30 (1981); and Samuel Epstein, "Polluted data", *Ecologist*, vol. 9, issue 8/9, pp. 264–72 (November–December 1979).

15. ibid.

16. Frank Graham, *Since Silent Spring* (London: Hamish Hamilton, 1970), see especially p. 49.

17. A. P. Rowe, *If the Gown Fits* (Melbourne University Press, 1960); see also Sir Mark Oliphant, "Book reviews: the quality of Australian universities", *Vestes*, vol. 3, pp. 45–9 (1960).

18. W. G. K. Duncan and R. A. Leonard, *The University of Adelaide 1874–1974* (Adelaide: Rigby, 1975).

19. Rowe, op. cit., p. 222.

20. For reports on some of these incidents see: Christopher Hunt, interviewed by James West, "The arts: a hunt in the sun", *National Times*, 2–8 March 1980, p. 44; Christopher Hunt, "Festival must satisfy an establishment", Adelaide *Advertiser*, 24 March 1980, p. 3; Anne Chisholm, "The martyrdom of St Christopher the unwise," *Observer* (London), 23 March 1980, p. 37; Bernard Levin, "Adelaide, as an Englishman sees her", *The Times* (London), 2 April 1980, p. 16; Lance Campbell, "Director to leave festival", Adelaide *Advertiser*, 28 March 1983, p. 1; Peter Ward, "Why Sharman quit as shaman", the *Australian*, 7 April 1983, p. 14; Sally Gibson, "Exit Moshinsky in festival dramatics", *National Times*, 29 April–5 May 1983, p. 29; Lance Campbell, "Fight to fix SA's festival", Adelaide *Advertiser*, 16 July 1983, p. 7; Lance Campbell, "Resignation call contrived: Earle", Adelaide *Advertiser*, 6 August 1983, p. 13; Shirley Stott Despoja, "Struggle of titans behind centre's best show", Adelaide *Advertiser*, 21 June 1984, p. 7; L. Campbell, "Walking out on controversy", Adelaide *Advertiser*, 18 August 1984, p. 2.

21. Peter Brook, quoted in Sheridan Morley, "Peter Brook quarrying theatre in Australia", *The Times* (London), 7 April 1980, p. 7.

22. A. J. Marshall, editor and part author, *The Great Extermination* (London and Melbourne: Heinemann, 1966), pp. 67–8.

23. Chris Milne, "Society gags zoo staff and director", Adelaide *Advertiser*, 30 March 1984, p. 1; Chris Milne, "Urgent Council meeting considers sacking zoo director", Adelaide *Advertiser*, 30 March 1984, p. 1; Jane Willcox, "Zoo controversy — Council wanted to get director out of the way", *On Dit* (University of Adelaide student newspaper), vol. 52, issue 6, 9 April 1984. This controversy is especially unfortunate as the past and present zoo directors have made many improvements and the zoo is very popular with the public.

24. Stewart Cockburn, *The Salisbury Affair* (Melbourne: Sun Books, 1979); Des Ryan and Mike McEwen, *It's Grossly Improper* (ISBN 0 9595162 0 4, privately published, 1979).

25. Max Harris, "Dunstan sacked God's Englishman", the *Australian* (*Weekend Australian Magazine*), 10–11 June 1978, p. 2.

26. See also the comments by Anne Summers, "New questions in the dossier affair", *National Times*, 30 January–4 February 1978, p. 5, who refers to " . . . a well known and respected Adelaide citizen who had in the past been the victim of police entrapment techniques in public lavatories. He fears giving evidence against police and of having his record disclosed".

27. There is an interesting exception that proves our rule. On p. 132, we mentioned the attempt to convict the editor of the *News*, Rohan Rivett, of seditious libel after he had questioned the fairness of the procedures used to obtain a conviction of the Aboriginal, Rupert Max Stuart. There is another dissenter involved in this case, the well-known scholar of Aboriginal language and legends, T. G. H. Strehlow, at that time a lecturer at the University of Adelaide. Strehlow, one of the few people who could converse with Stuart in his own language, proclaimed that he was innocent. Furthermore, Strehlow

used his knowledge of the language to show that Stuart could not possibly have expressed the kind of thoughts that were in the "confession". This brought Strehlow into a head-on clash with a powerful local establishment figure who also had great influence within the University of Adelaide. Strehlow did not have his university position threatened, perhaps because it would have provoked further protest, especially from non-conformist church groups or the emerging "Aboriginal rights" groups. He was not a member of the local establishment, but he was the son of a respected minister who had worked on a mission in South Australia. However, Strehlow, despite being a world recognised authority on Aboriginal cultures, never received the Chair of Anthropology he had expected the University of Adelaide to provide, although in 1970 he was given a personal professorship in Australian Linguistics. The result was that it was not until Strehlow was close to retirement (and death) that the University created a Department of Anthropology. Was this because the powers-that-be wanted to avoid Strehlow's competition with less accomplished candidates for the job? Thus, while University of Adelaide administrators deny that Strehlow was discriminated against because of his act of dissidence, not only did Strehlow himself believe he was victimised (see the Ward McNally biography in note 11 above), but others have told us of a similar interpretation. It is difficult to evaluate these claims, but it is otherwise hard to explain why the University waited so long to set up a Chair of Anthropology, especially given the proximity of the University to several important Aboriginal tribes. However, our point here is that, as a local and not an "outsider", Strehlow was at least partly protected from the kind of vindictive treatment others have received.

28. See: "Uranium — the split widens", the *Australian*, 12 June 1984, p. 1; Peter Logue and Greg Sheridan, "Hawke gives in on uranium to save Roxby", the *Australian*, 13 June 1984, p. 1. Of one South Australian politician, originally a vocal opponent to uranium mining on both ethical and practical grounds who switched to supporting the big Roxby Downs project in South Australia, the political reporter on the Adelaide *Advertiser* commented that he had "castrated his effectiveness and credibility in the anti-uranium debate": Matt Abraham, "Survival sparked a glow", Adelaide *Advertiser*, 21 July 1984, p. 28.

29. T. McKeown, *The Modern Rise of Population* (London: Arnold, 1976); A. J. Culyer, "What do health services do for people", *Search* 10, pp. 262–8 (1979).

30. Douglas Black, J. N. Morris, C. Smith and P. Townsend, *Inequalities in Health* (Department of Health and Social Security, UK, 1980). This report, obviously unpalatable to the Minister, was not actually suppressed but its release made without publicity and without adequate numbers of copies being distributed: "so grudgingly made available by DHSS", as an editorial in the *British Medical Journal*, 20 September 1980, p. 762, puts it.

31. Editorial, "Why has stroke mortality declined?", *Lancet*, 28 May 1983, pp. 1195–6. In a single year in the USA $3,250,000,000 was spent on 160,000 coronary bypass operations: see Eugene Braunwald, "Editorial retrospective: effects of coronary-artery bypass grafting on survival", *New England Journal of Medicine* 309, pp. 1181–4 (1983).

32. See note 14 above.

33. For information on asbestos, see: International Agency for Research on Cancer, *IARC Monographs on the Evaluation of the Carcinogenic Risk of Chemicals to Man*, vol. 14, *Asbestos* (1977); B. K. Armstrong et al., "Epidemiology of malignant mesothelioma in Western Australia", *Medical Journal of Australia*, 21 July 1984, pp. 86–8.

For information on carcinogenesis by chlorinated hydrocarbons see the appropriate IARC monographs, and C. Heidelberger, "Chemical carcinogenesis", *Annual Reviews of Biochemistry* 44, pp. 79–121 (1975).

Among the most powerful pieces of evidence for the importance of anthropogenic chemicals in the environment in causing cancer are the data from geographical differences in the incidence of certain types of cancer: see W. J. Blot, T. J. Mason, R. Hoover and J. F. Fraumeni, Jr., "Cancer by county: etiologic implications", in: H. H. Hiatt, J. D. Watson and J. A. Winsten (eds), *Origins of Human Cancer*, Book A, *Incidence of Cancer in Humans* (Cold Spring Harbor Conferences on Cell Proliferation, vol. 4, 1977), pp. 21–32.

It would be misleading to give the impression that all types of cancer have risen in incidence. A marked decline in gut cancer in Western countries has been observed in recent years; the reasons for this are not known with certainty but have been suggested to be the result of people eating less food preserved with nitrates.

34. Terrence Hemmings, *Parliamentary Debates* (South Australia: 17 September 1980), p. 880.

35. Lynn Arnold, *Parliamentary Debates* (South Australia: 24 September 1980), p. 1089.

36. Terrence Hemmings, *Parliamentary Debates* (South Australia: 17 September 1980), p. 881. The 5-nitroimidazole drugs include Flagyl, also called Metronidazole. These compounds are used to treat infections such as amoebic dysentery and vaginal trichomoniasis. Some of the individuals' names in Hemmings's quotation are deleted.

37. Colin Norman, "Where lies the test?", *Nature* 264, pp. 308–9 (1976).

38. Hemmings, op. cit.

39. ibid.

40. John R. Coulter and John V. Turner, "Treatment of amoebiasis and giardiasis", *Medical Journal of Australia*, 9 September 1978, p. 268. See also: John R. Coulter and John V. Turner, "Tinidazole (TNZ)...is mutagenic in a *Salmonella typhimurium* assay", *Mutation Research* 57, pp. 97–101 (1978).

41. Phillip Knightley, H. Evans, E. Potter and M. Wallace, *Suffer the Children: The Story of Thalidomide* (London: Andre Deutsch, 1979). See also John Braithwaite, *Corporate Crime in the Pharmaceutical Industry* (London: Routledge and Kegan Paul, 1984); and, Stanley Adams, *Roche versus Adams* (London: Jonathan Cape, 1984).

42. Wells, Stanley and Burdett, op. cit., p. 1.

43. ibid., p. 45.

44. ibid., p. 47.

45. ibid., p. 48.

46. ibid., p. 13.

47. Barry Hailstone, "Clash of views: intrigue at the Institute", Adelaide *Advertiser*, 9 October 1980, p. 8.

48. D. J. Cook, T. W. Steele, D. E. Gardner, D. W. Thomas, R. J. Kimber, B. Vernon-Roberts, and B. P. Marmion, "Chiefs defend institute", Adelaide *Advertiser*, 20 October 1980, p. 5.

49. Hailstone, op. cit.

50. A. G. McGregor, "IMVS council replies to criticism", Adelaide *Advertiser*, 27 October 1980, p. 4.

51. Wells, Stanley and Burdett, op. cit., p. 35.

52. "Illegal surgery at vet institute", Adelaide *Advertiser*, 9 October 1980, p. 1.

53. Bede Morris, *Enquiry into the Use of Laboratory and Experimental Animals* (Report to the Minister for Health, dated March 1981, 57-page document), quoting from p. 37.

54. Morris, op. cit., p. 33.

55. ibid., p. 39.

56. Hailstone, op. cit.

57. Terrence Hemmings, in *Parliamentary Debates* (South Australia: 24 February 1982), quoting p. 3098.

CHARGES AND CROSS-EXAMINATION

C. M. Ann Baker and Clyde Manwell

Introduction

Here we confine ourselves to a brief examination of the charges laid against Dr Coulter. The administration of the Institute of Medical and Veterinary Science, Adelaide, considered that these charges were sufficiently *serious* to warrant first demotion and then dismissal. The administration of the IMVS was, we presume, convinced of the *accuracy* of the charges.

For many case histories it would be difficult to publish this kind of analysis of the charges. Usually there are no court transcripts or equivalent verbatim records of where witnesses are examined and cross-examined.

This chapter has three main objectives: first, to present the facts available to us that are related to the charges the Director laid against Coulter in the local newspaper. Fair play demands that the charges be answered in at least as conspicuous a place.

Second, to provide a model for individuals who must defend themselves against certain types of charges.

Third, to integrate the results of the study of the IMVS versus Coulter, and to seek to understand how information flow within an organisation becomes biased. It is an oversimplification to think that, if A brings charges against B, and those charges are shown to be wrong, that A was entirely at fault. Are there C, D and E in the background who provided misinformation to A about B? Is the bearing of tales within an organisation a mode of adaptation to survival, or advancement, in a demoralised institution?

We consider only the first court case. The second court case did not concern the charges, or Coulter's competence, in any way. After the settlement had been agreed upon by Coulter and the IMVS, it was then necessary for Coulter to fight a second court case to obtain his pension rights. We do not know the reasons behind this second court case. It may have been simply a harassing tactic on the part of the South Australian government. It was an exercise in naked bureaucratic power, symptomatic of the scene as reviewed in the chapter "Paralysis of the Conscience".

Particularising the Charges

For the person who wishes to understand such a dismissal case — or needs to organise a defence against administrative action — the first problem is to decide just what are the charges. Administrations often use a multiplicity of charges. Is this in the hope that at least some of the charges will stick, or at least find a sympathetic resonance of disapproval in the organisation itself or in the wider community? A multiplicity of charges can conceal the fact that, individually, each charge lacks substance. It is helpful to distinguish between two categories of charges: those that are just general allegations and those that are illustrated with one or more specific allegations.

In some cases the charges are shifted around. New charges are brought in when old ones are found to be unsatisfactory. This situation is summarised in W. H. C. Eddy's exhaustive study of the sacking of Professor Orr from the University of Tasmania: "Charges were not only many; they were mobile".[1]

The Coulter case typifies these problems, but the situation is simplified by the fact that the then Director of the IMVS could use the local newspaper as a vehicle to list his complaints. It is to these published charges that primary attention is drawn. A few additional charges crept in by the time the case reached the court. The nature of these additional charges was like their predecessors. An example is dealt with by quoting the Director under cross-examination. Some general allegations in regard to obtaining research grants were reviewed by Brian Martin in "Mutagens and Managers".

Charge 1: Degree Qualifications

Barry Hailstone's first reporting of the reasons the Director gave for Coulter's demotion, in the 1 April 1980 news item, focused largely on matters of the supposed expense and value of Coulter's mutagen testing laboratory. These matters have been dealt with in preceding chapters. However, Bonnin also levelled a specific charge: "Dr Coulter had been prematurely promoted to medical specialist status and salary on his undertaking to write up earlier work in the form of a thesis for his degree of doctor of medicine".[2]

This charge is also the first listed in Dr Bonnin's letter of 12 April 1980 to the editor of the Adelaide *Advertiser*:

> His broken agreement to submit his work for an appropriate postgraduate qualification. It was on the basis of this agreement that he was promoted. Senior research workers are required to obtain such qualifications, which he could easily have done. He has for many years been paid as a specialist pathologist for which he has no qualification.[3]

As indicated by Brian Martin[4] this charge is cancelled by the undisputed fact that Coulter was promoted to medical specialist status in 1967 and, at that time (and for a number of years afterwards), there was *no requirement* for any degrees beyond the basic medical degree, which Dr Coulter had. In the court testimony two other facts emerged: there were other staff in the IMVS promoted to medical specialist without any more further-degree qualifications than Coulter had; and, of particular importance, the issue of having further degree qualifications only arose, at the earliest, in 1977, according to the IMVS administration — although the first written documentation appears to be in a letter dated 28 February 1980 addressed to Coulter.[5]

We cannot determine whether or not Coulter gave some special "undertaking" involving a specific commitment by some given date. We can find no claims for the existence of any special contract; presumably the "undertaking" was verbal. "Undertaking" might well have been understood differently by different parties. We would be surprised if anything more than a vague arrangement would, or could, be "undertaken". First, the requirements for such advanced degrees are usually stated imprecisely, leaving the interpretation of pass or fail to the judgement of senior administrators in the IMVS (several of whom have joint appointments with the University of Adelaide).

Second, given the problems that arose for Coulter, starting in July 1977, discussed in "Mutagens and Managers" and "Paralysis of the Conscience", we can well understand why Coulter would be hesitant to submit his work where the same decision-making superiors would be involved. It must also be realised that such advanced degrees are usually given for a large number of publications and, as explained elsewhere ("Academic Exploitation" and "Evaluation of Performance"), the accumulation of large numbers of publications is sometimes obtained by parasitising the efforts of others. Coulter did all of his work alone, or with one or two colleagues. He covered a broad area of preventive medicine and environmental contamination. At least with the permission of the Director, and on some occasions as a result of specific requests from the Director, Coulter investigated a wide range of topics, often having to learn, or develop, new techniques on each occasion. It cannot be held against Coulter (or any other scientist in a similar situation) that not every one of these investigations resulted in a publication. The necessity to change research topics makes it obligatory to wait much longer to accumulate enough material on a coherent theme to fit the usually narrow requirements of a thesis.

In summary of this charge, contrary to the description in the *Advertiser*, that Coulter "had been prematurely promoted to medical specialist", it would have been fairer to say that, at the time he had been promoted he had all the necessary degree requirements and that any further requirements occurred after — long after — the promotion. The charge itself would basically be an allegation of incompetence in the previous group of administrators who had "prematurely promoted" a member of staff.

Charge 2: Failure to Publish and Low Productivity

The second charge comes in two overlapping forms, quoting from Bonnin's letter to the editor of the *Advertiser*:

> His failure to publish the results of past research. All research workers are expected to publish their work in reputable scientific journals and, despite repeated requests, and written direction, this has not been done.
>
> His markedly low productivity as a full-time research worker, for which he is employed and which has been drawn to his attention. He has published only three papers in recognised journals in more than two years. The institute is criticised for allowing this state of affairs to continue for as long as it has. Several of the institute's routine service personnel are far more productive, fitting in their research studies along with their other duties.[6]

This charge lacks precision in its particularised example: "He [Coulter] has published only three papers in recognised journals in more than two years." "More than two years" allows one to interpret the claim in any way, from three papers in two years and one day to three papers in, say, fifty years.

Inspection of the Report of the Committee of Inquiry into the IMVS reveals a list of staff publications for the period 1977–80. Coulter is first or sole author on two publications in 1977–8 and second author on a third publication in that period. Coulter is first or sole author on three more publications in 1978–9. He has no publications listed for 1979–80, which is hardly surprising, given the circumstances. Considering only first or sole authorship, that represents five publications in something over two years. For the three overlapping year periods, there is a total of 361 publications (including many abstracts) for all of the IMVS staff involved in research. Given that there are more than 100 staff members or equivalent (including temporary appointments, fellowships etc.), this is about one publication per person per year.

We conclude that Bonnin's allegation is in error. Coulter had six publications, on five of which he is first or sole author, not three, over the two-plus year period. The evidence to reach a correct publication count should have been easily available to the Director, or to whomever he delegated responsibility to evaluate Coulter's performance.

Charge 3: Failure to be Cited

In Bill Guy's *Advertiser* article, entitled "Does Dr Coulter have to go?", Dr Bonnin is quoted as follows:

> You assess a research worker's work by reading his published work. If that published work is quoted by others you know that people are accepting that work.
>
> All we know is that Dr Coulter has published very little indeed that is refereed . . . and basically he isn't quoted by other people.[7]

As we explain in more detail elsewhere ("Evaluation of Performance"), the situations with regard to both refereeing of manuscripts and citations of publications are complex. As the papers by Coulter which are listed in the IMVS inquiry report[8] are published in journals like *Mutation Research*, *Medical Journal of Australia*, *Australian Journal of Pharmaceutical Science* and *Lancet*, we will pass to the editors of those journals the essence of Bonnin's allegation of "very little indeed that is refereed". We do not believe that such an allegation would be accepted by the editors of those journals. In any case, certain of those journals, notably *Medical Journal of Australia* and *Lancet*, are places where a number of the staff of IMVS publish.

What about the second part of the Director's allegation, that Coulter's work "basically . . . isn't quoted by other people"? A few minutes inspecting *Science Citation Index* (discussed in "Evaluation of Performance") allows that allegation to be settled. The following table compares the number of citations to papers where Coulter is the first author with two types of convenient "controls". One is the Director himself, J. A. Bonnin, and the other is the average publishing scientist, a figure which is available in the *Science Citation Index*:

Table 1

Year	J. R. Coulter	The Director of IMVS, J. A. Bonnin	Average citations per cited scientist
1970	8	5	6.52
1971	15(1)	0	6.67
1972	14	6	6.65
1973	11	2	6.95
1974	14	3	7.05
1975	9	4	7.05
1976	18	3	7.48
1977	11	4	8.01
1978	10(1)	0	8.12
1979	10	2	8.05
1980	10	1	8.28
1981	9	2	8.48
1982	4	2	8.34

Science Citation Index counts

The numerical data dispose of the Director's allegation that Coulter isn't cited. Coulter is not a prolific publisher, but several of his papers receive a number of citations over the years. This suggests the pattern of a perfectionist, who has a small output but which includes some items which have made an important impact. In every year but the last one Coulter receives more citations than does the average publishing scientist. The sudden drop in 1982 might be the result of the damage done to Coulter by the sacking attempt and the concomitant publicity without the clearing of his name.

As mentioned earlier, Coulter changed research topics, although keeping to the paradigm of preventive medicine. This shows up in his low incidence of self-citation — only two such self-citations in the period sampled. If you publish several papers in a field, you have more opportunities for self-citation and you also attract proportionately more attention to your work, for multiple publication in a specialised topic is often thought to mark the individual as an authority.

As our earlier discussion about preventive medicine and environmental problems revealed, *these topics are under-represented in research effort and in publication outlets*. Thus, researchers like Coulter tend to receive fewer citations than researchers in popular fields, such as curative medicine. Yet, even when these qualifications are ignored, Coulter has a reasonable citation count.

At this point in discussing the charges, a somewhat legalistic matter should be raised. As the Report of the Inquiry into the IMVS says:

It must be accepted that the Institute is not primarily a research organisation, but an extensive array of laboratories designed to carry out diagnostic procedures to assist clinicians in human and veterinary medicine, and to provide health surveillance throughout the State of South Australia.[9]

Thus, there appears to be no official requirement for publication, or for being cited. True, as a nearly full-time researcher, it would be fair to expect some publication and it would be fair to expect that the work is occasionally cited. It is an interesting reflection on priorities and procedures that this requirement for publication (and for being cited) is not officially stated, let alone enshrined in the Statutes, but it can be invoked, if capriciously.

Charge 4: Failure to Have Papers Approved by Higher Authority in the IMVS

This charge appears in the following form in the Director's letter to the editor of the *Advertiser*:

His failure to comply with the Regulations under the Institute of Medical and Veterinary Science Act with respect to submitting any manuscript for approval before sending it for publication.[10]

This appears to refer to an incident which was explored in the cross-examination of the Director.[11] Coulter had taken his holiday leave to attend the ANZAAS conference which, in that year (1979), was held in New Zealand. Coulter delivered a paper on one of his research interests. As to the allegation that Coulter's paper had not been vetted beforehand, consider the following sample of the Director's testimony under cross-examination:

Q. You remember receiving that letter, Doctor.

A. [Bonnin] Yes.

Q. Do you remember reading the last paragraph of the letter which again referred to the copy of the paper that Doctor Coulter was going to read at the A.N.Z.A.A.S. conference *being submitted to Professor Vernon-Roberts*.

A. Yes.

Q. Do you remember now reading that.

A. Not particularly but I note, it has got noted "J.A.B." in my handwriting, so I've obviously read it.[12]

On the following page of the transcript the Director makes an important admission:

Q. Did you read the paper [that Coulter delivered in New Zealand]?

A. [Bonnin] No.

Q. If you had doubts about whether it had anything to do with Institute business, why didn't you ask to read it, doctor.

A. I don't really consider the matter is a major issue...*if it is read by someone to whom I had delegated that authority*... He didn't choose to show it to me as having anything controversial...*I will accept what I am informed on by the people to whom I delegate that work*, and I can't for the life of me remember what I was told about that paper now.[13] [emphasis added]

Charge 5: Not Justified Some of His Statements About Environmental Matters

The remainder of Bonnin's letter to the editor deals basically with Coulter's mutagen testing and the issues are discussed in "Mutagens and Managers". Two issues are not discussed there and are explored briefly here; there is also the general allegation which implies sloppiness and error in his public statements. In the *Advertiser*, Bonnin alleged:

Dr Coulter has not justified, scientifically or practically, some of his statements about hazardous environments.[14]

As there is no specific example given, no example of where Coulter made an erroneous or misleading statement (with his exact words in a quotation), this allegation has little value. It is purely the Director's *opinion*.

Against the Director's *opinion* we place our opinions and the evidence from the case. We have heard Coulter speak publicly on several occasions. He was more careful in qualifying his conclusions and in checking out his facts than are some others who speak on medical or environmental matters. In all the copious testimony, correspondence, and other documentary detail this case has spawned, there are remarkably few allegations of error on the part of Coulter.

At this point we can also clear up an allegation which received some prominence, namely that Coulter had made his talks or articles appear as if they were official to the Institute of Medical and Veterinary Science. This type of charge seems to be popular in Australia (see, for example, "The Fruit Fly Papers" chapter). Yet, those high enough in the hierarchy can have it both ways, for example, "I appear in a personal capacity as well as representing the Australian Vice-Chancellors Committee".[15] For practical purposes it is difficult to avoid providing a work affiliation; indeed, to conceal that affiliation could itself be misleading and thus the object of administrative complaint. In any event, many academics and scientists write letters to the newspapers, or give talks to the public, identifying themselves in terms of their employment address without this being grounds for sacking, or less severe discipline, even though the comments made have nothing to do with either academic business or their professional qualifications. The irony is that, on all the occasions we have heard Coulter talk, he was scrupulous in emphasising that his opinions were being expressed as a private citizen.

This point, that Coulter was talking in a private capacity, has an important bearing on charge number 5. If it is accepted that his remarks were made in a *private* capacity, then the *nature* of those remarks cannot become an *official* matter (except perhaps where the remarks brought conviction on some criminal charge or were a direct attack on the IMVS).

Charge 6: Usurping Priority

The following passage appears in the Director's letter to the editor:

> His claim to be the first in the world to demonstrate the mutagenicity of Tinidazole repeated by Dr Gould-Hurst [*sic*] ("The Advertiser", 10/4/80) is not correct as this observation was made by Drs Lindmark and Muller in a paper published two years earlier.[16]

The specific example given by the Director involves a third person (a Dr Gouldhurst, whose name is not hyphenated), not Coulter. No example is given where Coulter himself has ignored or stolen priority. Accidental or deliberate assumption of priority is a common sin among scientists and there are many examples of where it has led to feuds.

Inspection of Coulter and Turner's paper[17] reveals that they *do* acknowledge priority, writing that "This work confirms that of Lindmark and Müller" and citing the correct reference.

Where Coulter and Turner do have priority is in the very important matter, discussed in the previous chapter, of pointing out the potential dangers in using this widely prescribed compound (and related 5-nitroimidazole drugs) in situations where there is no clear benefit to be gained by the patient.[18]

Charge 7: Using IMVS Facilities for Private Purposes

We have covered all the allegations made by the Director, either in his own letter to the editor[19], or in the comments attributed to him by *Advertiser* reporters.[20, 21] Several similar charges were brought into the Industrial Court hearing, where, in our opinion, none of them stood up well to thorough cross-examination. To avoid making this chapter too long or too tedious, it is sufficient to select one example. Many pages of the transcript are devoted to determining how much of Coulter's xeroxing involved private matters. Basically, we are sympathetic to the Director here — having frequently had important and urgently needed material for teaching or research delayed in the University because of other staff, or outside people, using the xeroxing machines for copying private material, totally unrelated to institutional functions. However, the Director did not prove the offence in Coulter's case. Consider the following passage from the transcript:

Q. [question] Numbered paragraph 7 of the reasons for the resolution to remove Dr Coulter from his previous position is "used the facilities of the Institute for his own private purposes", do you see that.

A. [answer: Dr J. A. Bonnin being cross-examined] Yes.

Q. You signed that document, didn't you.

A. Yes.

Q. Was the use of the photostat machine one of the facilities that he [Coulter] used for his private purposes that you were referring to in that paragraph.

A. Yes.

Q. And the photostating of articles when he could have written off for re-prints.

A. Well that's something that the staff were asked not to do but —

Q. — lots of staff did it.

A. Yes, I'm aware of that.

Q. Well Doctor [Bonnin], how did you know that he [Coulter] was using the photostat machine for his private purposes.

A. How did I?

Q. Yes.

A. *Well it was reported to me.* [emphasis added]

Q. Who by, Doctor.

A. Later on —

Q. Later on, when Doctor.

A. Oh I can't remember. It was pretty well known...

Q. When Doctor.

A. I can't remember when.

Q. You can't remember.

A. No, two years ago I really can't remember — two years ago probably.

Q. *Did you mention that to Dr Coulter at any stage.* [emphasis added]

A. *No,* but he's — I've seen him myself photographing — xeroxing things in the evenings he's —

Q. — well how do you know that was for his private purposes, Doctor.

A. I don't, I didn't say they were...

Q. What you've just told us, Doctor, you just told us that staff have told you that he used the photostat machine to photostat some of his talks, private letters —

A. — I've never taken it up.

Q. And yet you regarded that as a reason for his dismissal.

A. Yes, it's become — it's one of the — it's one of the (what's the word they say) it's one of the facilities of the Institute which he has used for his own private purposes. It's one of them.

. . .

Q. What have you observed, doctor.

A. I have observed Dr Coulter quite extensively using the copying machines.

Q. But you don't know what he was photocopying.

A. No.

Q. Well, then you don't know that he was using it for his private business?

A. —

Q. You just said "No" then didn't you, doctor?

A. Yes. Some of the times when he was copying and I saw him I have no doubt he was using them copying them [sic] for work which concerned his work.

Q. It may well be that every time you saw him photostating he was doing it on work concerning the Institute.

A. It is conceivably possible but in my opinion unlikely.

Q. But you've got no evidence otherwise have you.

A. No, I haven't.[22]

This passage, not atypical of much of the transcript, shows four important points:

1. No hard evidence existed for the alleged offence.

2. The Director got at least some of his information about Coulter from tales told by other staff.

3. No complaint about the alleged offence was made to Coulter prior to the decision to dismiss him.

4. It was well known that other staff in the IMVS were doing what Coulter was alleged to have been doing. During the court case, Coulter's lawyers produced several examples of where other IMVS staff had used the facilities of the Institute for private purposes. There is also a worrying aspect about this allegation against Coulter. Coulter had considerable official responsibility for knowledge about a number of areas of preventive medicine and the environment. At any time he could be called upon (and, indeed, was called upon) by the Director, or other Institute staff, for advice. Xeroxing is often the fastest and most accurate way to keep source material ready for such requests for information. In addition, scientists often keep abreast of developments by exchanging xeroxed material with their colleagues. This has a number of advantages, not least of which is that journals can be kept in the library and are readily accessible to all staff. The use of reprint request forms, instead of xeroxing, is actually uneconomic for short papers, as the cost of postage (which the IMVS has to pay) exceeds the cost of the xeroxing. There are also the possibilities that there will be a delay of months in receiving reprints requested by mail or that the author will not have any reprints for distribution. Thus, we feel that this allegation was, without evidence of the xeroxing of purely personal items, singularly unfair. As came out in the first part of the transcript, "lots of staff did it", and we would add: for good reason.

Evidence for Suppression?

The case of the IMVS versus Coulter has been explored in depth: the setting itself, both the community and the institution, the first signs of conflict between Coulter and certain members of the administration of the IMVS, the closing down of Coulter's mutagen testing laboratory; and, finally, the cross-examination of the Director of the IMVS. Our explorations reveal evidence satisfying certain criteria for suppression, as laid down in the "Introduction". The evidence is summarised below:

1.   As described by Terrence Hemmings in the South Australian Parliament, an alleged direct incident of suppression occurred on 14 July 1977: a senior administrator in the IMVS told Coulter and his colleague to delete a quotation (originally published in *Nature*) from a manuscript Coulter and colleague were submitting to the *Medical Journal of Australia*. The suppressed passage referred to the difficulties that a drug company had had with the US government about inadequate testing for safety. The suppressed passage had direct relevance to the humanitarian object of the paper by Coulter and colleague: the same or closely related drugs were being given to Aboriginal children who had *not* been diagnosed as having the diseases which the drug was intended to combat. The children were being given a drug for which there was no clear medical benefit and for which an unknown but potentially serious long-term risk existed.

2.   Coulter objected strongly to the administrative command to delete this quotation from *Nature* in the manuscript intended for submission to, and ultimately published in, the *Medical Journal of Australia*.[23] From around that time onward certain senior administrators in the IMVS found fault with Coulter's performance.

3.   Further conflict occurred when Bayer in 1978 and Velsicol in 1979 complained about public statements Coulter had made about the inadequacies in the safety tests of certain widely used pesticides (of which Bayer and Velsicol were among the manufacturers). *In both instances the complaints were made not to Coulter but to people higher up in the IMVS hierarchy.*

4.   We cannot claim to know the motives of those senior administrators in the IMVS. We can only point to the information that was revealed in the South Australian Parliament, much of which also appeared in the local newspaper[24], that certain powerful figures in the IMVS received research funds and travel expenses from drug companies and other private organisations — and that these funds were not accurately summarised in the IMVS's reports.

5.   Despite the fact that only a short time earlier Coulter had begun his studies on mutagenic toxicity with the authorisation of the then Director of the IMVS, that Director decided to close down Coulter's laboratory. Yet, considerable evidence existed for the utility of Coulter's testing, both for a number of public and private organisations (including several trade unions), and to the IMVS itself (the ethylene oxide incident described in "Mutagens and Managers"). Furthermore, Coulter's work also complied closely with both the letter and the spirit of the IMVS's charter, which includes monitoring the health of South Australia.

6.   *The charges for which Dr Coulter was first to be demoted, then dismissed, and finally "retrenched", were lacking in substance and in accuracy.* It is especially important to contrast this situation with the examples of behaviour by other staff members — none of whom were considered for such action. Besides the examples mentioned throughout these three chapters on the Coulter case, there were yet other examples: the Director in cross-examination[25] admitted that one IMVS staff member had "smacked one of the girls over the face for inadequate reasons" and another IMVS staff member "had been stealing things from the operating theatre" and "was contravening the Veterinary Practitioners Act".

True, these examples of differential treatment (sacking for Coulter, on incorrect charges, and less severe or no punishment for others on what may well have been correct charges) are not in themselves proof of suppression. It could be that in the IMVS sacking is a random process, unrelated to what you actually do, or don't do. It could be a means of controlling subordinates by demonstrating the *real* power of the elite. This has historical precedents, for example the Inquisition. It can also be the case, as discussed later in "Elites and Suppression" that the grievousness of an offence is judged by its challenge to bureaucratic authority, as in the ethylene oxide incident. This is perceived as a more important "offence" because it is a direct challenge to a hierarchical system — even though one outside observer, the Member of Parliament for Napier, Terrence Hemmings, considered that Coulter's action (of informing the affected workers, the appropriate IMVS committee, and the Director, of the dangers from ethylene oxide, more or less simultaneously) was appropriate under the circumstances.

In any case, when these examples of capricious standards for dismissal are added to the other information, they strengthen our belief that the Coulter case is basically one of suppression.

Misinformation or Disinformation?

There is also a largely unexplored dimension of suppression involving the accidental or deliberate distortion of information flow about individuals within an organisation. The problem is apparent in many places in the Director's testimony during examination and cross-examination. It is so striking that one cannot help but feel some sympathy for the Director, as well as for Coulter. Repeatedly the Director points out how he relied upon other staff members for information about Coulter.

It can be argued strongly that the Director should have taken adequate precautions to ensure the accuracy of his charges against Coulter. However, the Director is entitled to assume that the person to whom he delegates the responsibility in such a matter will obtain full and accurate information. The Director is entitled to assume that information about Coulter, given to him by other staff, is given for no other reason than the welfare of the IMVS and its mission in public health and diagnosis.

Did the misinformation given to the Director by others cause the situation to become unnecessarily complicated by polarisation and personality conflict? Was the Director unwittingly tricked into taking the action he did? Was the Director himself a pawn in the power struggles involving corporate, professional and bureaucratic elites at the local establishment level?

We would have thought that supplying misinformation to the Director was a serious offence and one that would have been investigated fully. Was any of that misinformation really disinformation; that is, a deliberate attempt to bear false witness? Was crucial information deliberately withheld in order to create a false picture? Were easily ascertainable "facts" not properly checked? Evidence for individuals passing misinformation or disinformation about a dissident occurs in several of our cases, especially the Orr case ("Not Merely Malice").

It may be of significance that it was only when the cross-examination of witnesses other than the Director began, that the IMVS suddenly agreed to settle out of court.[26] Thus, unfortunately, the full role of these other witnesses in the spread of misinformation cannot be ascertained.

Organisational intrigues occur in many intellectual institutions, and feuds among academics and scientists are, as Arthur Koestler wrote, carried out "with a remarkable degree of bitchiness".[27] However, it is our distinct impression that interpersonal rivalries and tale-bearing are more common in Australian institutions than in American or English ones. We have had similar opinions given to us, quite spontaneously, by Australian scientists with overseas experience. We suggest that tale-bearing is a mode of adaptation (if a reprehensible one) employed by some to survive or advance in an institution with low morale. Others just "opt out", or "drop out", but do much less harm.

To explore this hypothesis further one would need quantitative data on the level of dissatisfaction within different intellectual organisations in Australia and elsewhere. Few data exist and, to our knowledge, none for the institutions that figure in our major case histories.

However, contrary to the claims made by IMVS administrators, the Committee of Inquiry into the IMVS concluded in its report that there was "a degree of unrest and low morale... within the Institute" and based that conclusion on "a significant number of well documented submissions to the Committee and... discussion with Institute staff...".[28] The only cross-national quantitative study of staff morale we can find establishes clearly that one Australian institution of higher education has a much higher state of demoralisation than the average American university.[29]

Such a situation of extreme demoralisation is loaded with the potential for positive feedback. Once staff learn that one of their colleagues is "fair game", the opportunity is seized. Apparently, a significant number of intellectuals feel that they must release their frustrations, or consider that someone who is a bit different is a threat.[30] In particular, a dissident, known or suspected of having criticised powerful vested interests that might be a source of money or influence for some other academics, is perceived as an enemy.

Paralysis of the Conscience

There is a responsibility to get to the bottom of cases, such as the Coulter one, where the charges are so obviously inaccurate. It is more than just a matter of finding out who said what about whom, although clearly much of the charges was based on hearsay. It is a matter of finding out what went wrong to ensure that it does not happen again.

We can understand the management view, of wishing to let the issue die quietly. However, as is evident from certain of our cases, the obsessive vindictiveness of some intellectuals makes "rehabilitation" of the victim impossible. Indeed, there is often response generalisation so that the aggression is directed at the victim's supporters, wife, and students.[31] Thus, the rather cynical strategy of administrative convenience, of failing to find out exactly what did go wrong and why, is only remotely acceptable if it is combined with adequate protection and compensation for the victim whose reputation was unfairly damaged. If our case histories show nothing else, they show the lack of even this level of pragmatism. The real integrity that is necessary to admit that a mistake has been made, and to make restitution, seems almost absent.

For Coulter, confronted with sheer bureaucratic power, and the indifference or antagonism of many of his colleagues, the consequence of this paralysis of the conscience was that he had to accept a not entirely fair settlement. Had it not been for the protests from the general public, it is unlikely that he would have got even that. He had heavy legal bills and a severely injured child to support. The financial settlement was placed at two-thirds of his 1980 salary. The wording of "demotion" or "dismissal" was changed to "retrenchment". Coulter had to agree not to comment on his case in the future — itself a revealing admission on the part of the local establishment that obtained this settlement.[32]

We conclude by asking a question whose implications spread much wider than this particular case history: *Is the paralysis of conscience a terminal case — terminal for the society that cannot evolve adequate checks on the abuses of science and technology?*

References

1. W. H. C. Eddy, *Orr* (Brisbane: Jacaranda Press, 1961), p. 592. The case history is summarised in the chapter "Not Merely Malice".
2. Barry Hailstone, "Director gives reasons for scientist's move", Adelaide *Advertiser*, 1 April 1980, p. 8.
3. J. A. Bonnin, "Cancer research work" (letter to the editor), Adelaide *Advertiser*, 12 April 1980, p. 5.
4. Brian Martin, "A case of suppression?" (letter), *Search* 13, pp. 59–60 (1982). See also: Brian Martin, "Dismissed Australian scientist" (letter), *Science* 209, p. 1182 (1980).
5. Coulter v. IMVS and Public Service Board, South Australia Industrial Court, 1 December 1980, p. 794 of transcript.

6. Bonnin, op. cit.

7. Bill Guy, "Does Dr Coulter have to go?", Adelaide *Advertiser*, 17 June 1980, p. 5. The deleted part from within the Director's quotation is in the original report by Bill Guy.

8. R. Wells, N. F. Stanley and J. E. Burdett, *Report of the Committee of Inquiry into the Institute of Medical and Veterinary Science*. A 207-page printed document, dated December 1980, but with no other identification. Obtained from the South Australian government publications outlet. The quotation is from p. 64.

9. ibid.

10. Bonnin, op. cit.

11. Coulter v. IMVS and Public Service Board, South Australia Industrial Court, 2 December 1980, pp. 891, 892.

12. ibid.

13. ibid.

14. Bonnin, op. cit.

15. Senate Standing Committee on Education and the Arts, *Tenure of Academics*, proof of official Hansard report, Canberra, 30 April 1982, quoting from p. 2155.

16. Bonnin, op. cit.

17. John R. Coulter and John V. Turner, "Tinidazole (TNZ)...is mutagenic in a *Salmonella typhimurium* assay", *Mutation Research* 57, pp. 97–101 (1978), quoting p. 99.

18. John R. Coulter and John V. Turner, "Treatment of amoebiasis and giardiasis", *Medical Journal of Australia*, 9 September 1978, p. 268.

19. Bonnin, op. cit.

20. Hailstone, op. cit.

21. Guy, op. cit.

22. Coulter v. IMVS and Public Service Board, South Australia Industrial Court, 4 December 1980, pp. 904, 906, 907, 910.

23. Coulter and Turner, op. cit. (note 18).

24. Barry Hailstone, "Clash of views: intrigue at the Institute", Adelaide *Advertiser*, 9 October 1980, p. 8.

25. Coulter v IMVS and Public Service Board, South Australia Industrial Court, 9 December 1980, pp. 1025–6.

26. This situation is remarkably similar to the authors' experiences in South Australia. When the defamation case reached the Supreme Court, we were told by our legal representative that the administration "had declared war to the death". However, just before it was time for the three witnesses to appear for the administration, we received the offer to settle before judgement, the offer being essentially to publish the Vice-Chancellor's "Statement concerning the complaint..." and to pay the costs. A careful reading of the Vice-Chancellor's *Statement* allows one to identity the sources of certain misinformation (disinformation?) which crept into the dismissal complaint.

27. Arthur Koestler, *The Case of the Midwife Toad* (London: Hutchinson, 1971), p. 54. There is another observation by Koestler which is especially appropriate to this case history, and to some of our others. After providing a number of examples of misinformation written about Paul Kammerer by eminent biologists, Koestler concludes (p. 147): "What amazes the layman is that all these University professors, who only had to ask an assistant to look up the data in the back numbers of *Nature*, apparently did not feel impelled to do even that. Polemics apart, such cavalier treatment of facts would hardly be forgiven to a reporter in the popular press."

28. Wells, Stanley and Burdett, op. cit., p. 35. These comments on demoralisation are

especially significant in that, with few exceptions, this report is not critical of the IMVS and, at times, is quite extravagant in its praise. The fact that there have been in recent years at least four different enquiries into parts or all of the IMVS certainly does, however, suggest that *something* is wrong.

29. The Dean of Social Sciences at the Western Australian Institute of Technology (WAIT) surveyed attitudes of 259 staff members, a 60 per cent sample of the total staff at the WAIT. His questionnaire used several statements that were in the American study by J. V. Baldridge, D. V. Curtis, G. P. Ecker and G. L. Riley, *Policy Making and Effective Leadership* (San Francisco: Jossey-Bass, 1978). In response to the statement "They [the administration] understand the needs of academics and try to make this a place where staff can work productively", 58 per cent of staff at American universities said "yes", whereas only 17 per cent of the WAIT staff said "yes". In response to the statement "Communication between staff and administration is open, easy and effective", 61 per cent of staff at American universities said "yes", whereas only 17 per cent of the WAIT staff said "yes". In response to the statement "If faced with a campus disturbance they [the administration] would give in to outside pressure", 33 per cent of staff at American universities said "yes", whereas 72 per cent of the WAIT staff said "yes". See: N. F. Dufty, *Academic Staff Attitudes on Institute Decision-Making* (1979), p. 31 (78-page document from the Dean of Social Sciences, WAIT, Hayman Road, South Bentley, W. Australia 6102). It is a matter of urgency that similar studies be done for other Australian intellectual institutions, asking also "open-ended" questions to find out how staff perceive their work environment. If this trend of pronounced demoralisation is evident in other studies, some far-reaching reforms will be needed. That such demoralisation occurs at another Australian institution is suggested by the observation made by a new Vice-Chancellor: "When I returned to university life two years ago, I was struck by the number of academic staff dissatisfied with their life as academics and suffering from a lack of personal security . . . these impressions . . . crystallise in the view that higher education institutions, even for people with tenure, are frequently lonely places, breeding personal insecurities, cynicism and competitive jealousies . . . ": K. R. McKinnon in: *Tertiary Education in the Eighties: Paths to Reward and Growth*, Research and Development in Higher Education, vol. 6, p. 13 (1983). Another sign of demoralisation is the increasing exodus of young scholars from Australia at a time when, as a result of tight job markets overseas, other "brain drains" have reduced or stopped. For example, in 1976 11 per cent of all new Australian Ph.D.s took jobs overseas; by 1982 that had risen to 28 per cent: M. Powles, *The Role of Postgraduates in Australian Research* (Council of Australian Postgraduates Association, 207 Lygon St., Carlton, Victoria 3053, dated 1984), especially Fig. 12, p. 124.

30. One of the clearest signs of demoralisation within Australian universities is the recent emergence of covert and overt racism. While there are many theories about the causes of racism, for nearly half a century the most popular ones have been some sort of modification of the original frustration–aggression hypothesis, for example, demoralisation and relative deprivation: See, for example: Carl Iver Hovland and Robert R. Sears, "Minor studies of aggression: VI. Correlation of lynchings with economic indices", *Journal of Psychology* 9, pp. 301–10 (1940); G. W. Allport, *The Nature of Prejudice* (Cambridge, Massachusetts: Addison-Wesley, 1954); Reeve D. Vanneman and Thomas F. Pettigrew, "Race and relative deprivation in the urban United States", *Race* 13, pp. 461–86 (1972). Academics are generally considered among the more racially tolerant groups, in part because, like journalists, lawyers and teachers, their expertise with a language and their often middle-class origins protect them from direct competition with ethnically or racially distinct immigrants. However, in the last ten to fifteen years the academic job market has gradually tightened,

increasing competition among Australians, British, Americans and many other groups for university positions. Recently in Australia attempts have been made to stop Australian universities from hiring staff from overseas: "West toughens entry rules for foreign scholars", the *Australian*, 7 December 1983, p. 21; "Stem flow of overseas academics" (report of 54th ANZAAS congress) the *Australian*, 15 May 1984, p. 4. Even FAUSA is pushing for a modified form of this policy of hiring Australians before overseas applicants: "Stricter line urged on overseas staff", the *Australian*, 7 September 1983, p. 18. Among Australian students and staff racism has recently become more apparent, to such a point that there has been a flood of articles on the subject; of particular interest are the following: Errol Simper, "Racism stalks our campuses", the *Australian*, 19–20 May 1984, p. 10; Helen Trinca, "Academics split on foreign students", the *Australian*, 3 August 1984, p. 3; "Foreigners denying Australians tertiary places, MPs told", the *Australian*, 22 May 1984, p. 3. Students and staff, demoralised by their perceptions of their working conditions, conform to the scapegoating pattern of the regular "working class"; it fits well with the idea of a "split labor market": see Edna Bonacich, "A theory of ethnic antagonism", *American Sociological Review* 37, pp. 547–59 (1972). Another sign of acute demoralisation on the Australian academic scene has been the open conflict in FAUSA over attempts to decrease discrimination against women; compare: P. Le P. Darvall, "No proof" (letter), the *Australian*, 26 September 1983, p. 8; Jo Gaha, "Uni battle for women" (letter), the *Australian*, 3 October 1983, p. 6; L. B. Wallis, "Academic stand" (letter) the *Australian*, 20 October 1983, p. 8.

31. The case of Patrick O'Brien at the University of Western Australia (see "Archives of Suppression") has been described: "The harassment of his family, at the same time as his prosecution by the university, indicates that what his political and ideological enemies have been incapable of achieving academically, they are now seeking to do in other ways." Quoting Roger Gale, "The universities: a new 'Orr case' brewing in the west?", the *Bulletin*, 17 March 1981, p. 40. See also, Patrick O'Brien, "Fabian chickens come home to roost", *Times Higher Education Supplement*, 6 March 1981, p. 11.

32. According to the agreement, this arrangement is also supposed to apply to the IMVS administration. However, the situation is unequal in that Coulter's reputation was publicly damaged in the newspaper without the facts about the charges ever being published. Such agreements are no protection for the victim, for they cannot be applied to those other individuals who were not disciplined and who can continue to bear tales.

Postscript by Brian Martin

On 28 February 1984 I sent a copy of earlier versions of the previous three chapters to the Institute of Medical and Veterinary Science inviting a response from someone representing the Institute, or anyone else appropriate, to be included in this book. On 6 April B. J. Kearney, Director of the IMVS, replied, offering no comments for publication.

ARCHIVES OF SUPPRESSION

compiled by Brian Martin

The number of cases of clear or suspected suppression is enormous. The previous chapters have presented a number of cases in some detail, though any one of them could be described at much greater length. To give an idea of the scale and variety of suppression, presented here are some thumbnail sketches.

Because the phenomenon of suppression has not been conceptualised or studied systematically, the available evidence about it is spread far and wide, and difficult to track down. What I have done here is to describe a variety of cases which I or my colleagues have come across in our reading. Non-academic cases are included to show the forms suppression can take in the "free world" and to illustrate the severe consequences that suppression can help to perpetuate, such as exposure of people to toxic chemicals. There are three main criteria for inclusion: first, the suppression or suspected suppression is either major or distinctive in character; second, substantial and accessible documentation is available; third, the case is not described elsewhere in this book.

These criteria, though not rigorously applied, eliminate literally hundreds of cases for which only limited documentation is available, such as in newspaper articles. Even so, due to the large volume of available material, many well-documented suppression cases, including famous cases, are not listed here. The aim here is not to itemise all the most important suppression cases, but rather to give an indication of the variety of material available for the further study of suppression.

Unless otherwise indicated, I have written the sketches presented here. (Two of the sketches were provided by C. M. Ann Baker and Clyde Manwell and edited by me.) Many of the references are ones I have come across or found cited in my reading. Many others have been specifically suggested or provided by a wide range of individuals.

Naturally, the cases here reflect a particular set of interests and reading, and should not be taken as a reliable indication of the actual occurrence of different types or areas of suppression. In particular, only cases from English-speaking countries have been included.

The cases are grouped according to country, and within each country by alphabetical order of the person suppressed or of the author of the account, whichever seemed most appropriate. In only a few non-Australian cases have attempts been made to personally verify the information presented. Only a bare outline of each case is presented, with sources indicated for those who desire more detail.

I am deeply indebted to a large number of people for suggesting references, for providing copies of documents and for offering advice concerning descriptions of cases. Since not all these individuals wish to be mentioned in this regard, reluctantly I have omitted detailed acknowledgements. Needless to say, their contributions towards this compilation have been greatly appreciated. Final responsibility for all the descriptions nevertheless rests with me.

* AUSTRALIA

P. L. Bazeley, Director of the Commonwealth Serum Laboratories (CSL), made statements to the press about the CSL Bill before Parliament. He was suspended and charged with improper conduct in his official capacity. He admitted his guilt and apologised, and was reduced in rank and salary.
Reference: R. S. Parker, "Official neutrality and the right of public comment. I. The implications of the Bazeley case", *Public Administration* (Australia), vol. 20, no. 4, December 1961, p. 291–304; "II. The vow of silence", vol. 23, no. 3, September 1964, pp. 193–211.

Les Bowling worked for General Motors – Holden's from 1972 to 1975, when he was dismissed because of his union activities. By court order he was reinstated in 1976, but then dismissed again in 1978. His case illustrates how a large corporation can use the legal system, with its long delays, to dampen shop floor activism by workers. Even with full financial support from legal aid and with a favourable legal decision, little may be gained for the workers through the courts.
Reference: Anthony Regan, "Fighting the company: sacked workers win... almost", *Legal Service Bulletin*, vol. 6, no. 2, April 1981, pp. 64–7.

Arthur L. Burns was a professor of political science at the Australian National University, and a prominent and vocal anti-communist. In 1981 ANU Council terminated his appointment, citing medical grounds. Burns asked ANU for the reason, in writing, for his dismissal, but this was refused. Burns then applied to the Federal Court for the reasons to be given under the *Administrative Decisions (Judicial Review) Act*. Justice Ellicott, who had been Attorney-General when the Act was introduced in 1977, ruled for Burns, but this was reversed by the Full Federal Court.
References: "The Burns case", *Australian Law Journal*, vol. 57, no. 4, April 1983, pp. 199–200; William Maley, "The Arthur Burns case", *Quadrant*, vol. 27, no. 11, November 1983, pp. 18–21; A. L. Burns, letter, *Quadrant*, vol. 27, no. 12, December 1983, p. 5.

Allan Healy completed his Ph.D. at the Australian National University in 1962. His thesis was a detailed examination of Australian colonial policy in Papua New Guinea, showing many shortcomings. At that time, Australian control over PNG was considered by the Australian government to be vital to Australian security, whereas Healy's thesis presented the case for more rapid political devolution of power to PNG. To gain access to official documents, Healy had to sign forms giving the Department of Territories the right to grant or refuse approval for any publication. Because of the critical nature of the thesis, the Department demanded that the thesis be kept under lock and key at the University, and University officials collaborated in this suppression. Rumours were spread about Healy, who was thereby denied any academic job in the area of his expertise.
Reference: Allan Healy, "Letter from Australia: censorship as a nineteenth century survival", *Index on Censorship*, vol. 1, no. 3/4, Autumn–Winter 1972, pp. 185–95.

The Human Sciences Program at the Australian National University, an environmentally and humanistically oriented series of undergraduate courses with a holistic perspective, was established in 1973. Opposition to the program was voiced by some leading members of the ANU from the time it was first proposed in 1970, and has continued in spite of one favourable external review of the program and many favourable assessments by students and university colleagues. Staff member Jeremy Evans had an average record of publications and an outstanding record of teaching, yet reappointment and review committees recommended in 1979 against granting him tenure. There were protests from students and staff at the ANU. An appeal committee, with Staff Association representation, finally recommended a further two-year period of contract employment. After a 15-month deliberation during 1983–4, the appropriate committee finally recommended tenure. The program has also been subject to cuts in staff – and to threats of further cuts or amalgamations – in spite of strong student support and only moderate running costs per student.

References: Brian Martin, ''The scientific straightjacket: the power structure of science and the suppression of environmental scholarship'', *Ecologist*, vol. 11, no. 1, January–February 1981, pp. 33–43; Ian Hughes, ''Environmental education at ANU — a new dark age?'', *Bogong* (Journal of the Canberra and South-East Region Environment Centre), vol. 4, no. 5, November–December 1983, pp. 8–9.

Frank Knopfelmacher was in the Psychology Department at the University of Melbourne when in 1964 he applied for a senior lecturership in political philosophy in the Philosophy Department at the University of Sydney. Knopfelmacher is a Czech Jew whose entire family was killed by the Nazis. Politically he has long considered himself a social democrat. In addition to his scholarly work, Knopfelmacher was well known as a fierce and vocal opponent of Soviet communism. He took strong and strongly worded stands on current affairs in popular journals. He had also raised charges of undue Stalinist influence among academics at the University of Melbourne.

There were three candidates for the philosophy post. Knopfelmacher's application for the job was discussed with great intensity around the University of Sydney for months before the selection committee made its decision, and numerous highly unfavourable allegations were made about Knopfelmacher's character in private conversation. The selection committee for the philosophy position unanimously (with one abstention) recommended Knopfelmacher. But in April 1965 the Professorial Board rejected his appointment outright, in an unprecedented and since unrepeated move. (The more accepted procedure in such rare cases was for the Board to refer the matter back to the selection committee for further inquiry, offering appropriate criticisms.) The Board's decision was influenced by the circulation of one and only one of Knopfelmacher's articles, which was not one of his academic publications, to the members of the Board. The circulation of this article was especially promoted by Professor Ted Christiansen, who was well known to have pro-Soviet views.

After the Board's decision, more than one Sydney University professor attacked Knopfelmacher's character and political views in several letters to newspapers. Later the political philosophy post was readvertised. There were two applicants, of whom Knopfelmacher was one. The other candidate was unsuitable, and this time the selection committee (essentially unchanged from before) voted against Knopfelmacher's appointment. As a result of the second committee's decision, no appointment was made to the post.

References: ''The Knopfelmacher case, Australia'', *Minerva*, vol. 3, no. 4, Summer 1965, pp. 538–55; A. K. Stout, ''On university appointments: thoughts after Knopfelmacher'', *Minerva*, vol. 4, no. 1, Autumn 1965, pp. 55–72; ''The Knopfelmacher case, Australia'', *Minerva*, vol. 4, no. 2, Winter 1966, pp. 287–99; A. J. Dunston, ''I had never even heard of Dr K.'', *Bulletin*, vol. 87, 25 December 1965, pp. 27–9; Geoffrey Fairbairn, *Revolutionary Warfare and Communist Strategy: The Threat to South-East Asia* (London: Faber and Faber, 1968), pp. 43–7.

Roy J. Kriegler has documented the oppressive working and life conditions at the BHP shipyard and steelworks at Whyalla, South Australia. BHP, as the major employer, has been ruthless in exploiting workers in many ways, especially in relation to working conditions.

The managerial staff are totally compliant in doing anything to help the company. Suppression of intellectual dissent plays a role in maintaining this situation. For example, when on a rare occasion a *Whyalla News* journalist went beyond official sources of information, BHP sought his dismissal by exerting influence on the proprietors of the newspaper.

Reference: Roy J. Kriegler, *Working for the Company: Work and Control in the Whyalla Shipyard* (Melbourne: Oxford University Press, 1980).

Stuart Macdonald, of the Information Research Unit in the Department of Economics at the University of Queensland, studied the information provided by the CSIRO about its research work, and concentrated on that from the Division of Entomology. He concluded that "the arguments publicly presented for the actual deployment of resources are often weak". He was told by senior personnel at the Division that the draft of his article contained serious errors, and that access to Divisional records to reveal these errors would be granted only if he withdrew the article from publication. He was threatened with legal action by a senior member of CSIRO.

References: Stuart Macdonald, "Faith, hope and disparity: an example of the public justification of public research", *Search*, vol. 13, nos 11–12, December 1982–January 1983, pp. 290–9; Ronald Strahan, "Stirrers in science", ibid., p. 271; Stuart Macdonald, "Faith, hope and disparity — an apologia to CSIRO", *Search*, vol. 14, nos 1–2, February–March 1983, pp. 39–41.

George Munster and Richard Walsh in November 1980 published a book entitled *Documents on Australian Defence and Foreign Policy 1968–75*. The documents reproduced in the book were secret memos, briefings and cables prepared by Australian government bureaucrats concerning such defence and foreign policy issues as Australia's involvement in the Indochina War, US bases in Australia, the decolonisation of Papua New Guinea, and events leading to the Indonesian invasion of East Timor. The Melbourne *Age* and the *Sydney Morning Herald* had acquired serialisation rights to the book. On the eve of publication, the federal government served interim injunctions to prevent publication of the book and of excerpts in the newspapers, invoking both the *Crimes Act* and the *Copyright Act*. (Quite a few copies of the book and of the newspapers containing the excerpts were sold or distributed before the interim injunction came into effect.) The High Court decided that the *Crimes Act* did not provide grounds for an injunction in this case but continued the injunctions solely on the grounds that direct and extensive quotation from the documents without permission was a breach of Crown copyright. However, the substance of the documents was later conveyed by means of synopses, short quotations and critical comments when Munster and Walsh published *Secrets of State*.

Reference: George Munster, *Secrets of State: A Detailed Assessment of the Book They Banned* (Australia: Walsh & Munster, an imprint of Angus & Robertson Publishers, 1982).

Patrick O'Brien is a senior lecturer in the Politics Department at the University of Western Australian (UWA). In the 1970s he acquired a substantial reputation both as a scholar and as a public commentator in providing a critique of left-wing political thought and action. He has been a frequent contributor to newspapers and radio programs. Often his criticisms have been greatly resented by those attacked, for example when in 1980 O'Brien made pointed comments about the connection between the UWA Guild of Undergraduates and the UWA branch of the Australian Labor Party, and the use of funds by the Guild.

Following a wine and cheese social held by the UWA Politics Club on 25 July 1980, a number of complaints were made to the Vice-Chancellor about O'Brien's alleged behaviour at the social. These allegations were used as a basis for launching a major campaign against O'Brien, which included organising articles in newspapers, the circulation of a defamatory and inaccurate leaflet, the spreading of rumours and harassment of his family, in particular by obscene telephone calls made anonymously. O'Brien apologised in writing to the complainants — whose identities were not revealed to him for many months — for any offence he may have caused to any individual at the wine and cheese social, but the apology was not accepted.

In early 1981 an article by O'Brien in the *Times Higher Education Supplement* about academic freedom further angered his opponents. Eventually the University brought formal charges in open court against O'Brien for violations of UWA by-laws. In October 1981 the magistrate found him not guilty of striking a student, the only serious charge against him. In dismissing the charge the magistrate, Sir Clifford Grant, saw fit to say: "I was not impressed by the fifth prosecution witness ... Clearly he was incensed by the critical nature of the defendant's radio talks and articles, culminating in an argument which was heated on both sides ... " He added that the bulk of the accuser's evidence was either "fantasy or imagination".

O'Brien was found guilty of using offensive language and urinating behind a pillar on a secluded part of a verandah after dark — an act which O'Brien openly and unashamedly admitted and which was only witnessed by two male colleagues from a distance. These charges were dismissed. Legal counsel on both sides were amazed that such nonsense was brought before the court. Even the magistrate opined that "If every person who behaved in a ribald manner or with less than propriety at a private party were to be charged before the courts, I fear that even the ranks of the legal profession could be so depleted that there would be insufficient counsel left to represent them". Moreover, a double standard was apparent in the UWA administration's lack of action over abusive and offensive language in student publications and in the concerted and scurrilous attacks against O'Brien.

When the court case was reported to the UWA Senate, it was implied that prosecution witnesses had not given coloured evidence, and that it was O'Brien who had induced the University to pursue him in court. These and other statements to the Senate — considered by many to be untrue and in conflict with the findings of the court — have never been corrected, although three members of the Senate requested that an apology be made to O'Brien.

References: Patrick O'Brien, "Fabian chickens come home to roost", *Times Higher Education Supplement*, 6 March 1981, p. 11; Roger Gale, "Patrick O'Brien, victim", *Quadrant*, vol. 25, no. 5, May 1981, pp. 11–13; "University of Western Australia misled", *Facts* (National Civic Council), March 1982, pp. 7, 10–14.

Michael Spautz was a tenured senior lecturer in the Department of Commerce at the Universiy of Newcastle. In 1978 he began questioning the validity and scholarly nature of the Ph.D. thesis of Professor Alan J. Williams, another member of the same department. Dr Spautz alleged that Professor Williams's thesis was based on inverted causality and that it contained spurious statistics and plagiarised passages. Dr Spautz also questioned the legitimacy of Professor Williams's new role as Head of the Management Section in the department. Receiving no response to his criticisms that he felt was satisfactory, Dr Spautz gradually escalated the criticisms into a major campaign. A university committee was established in 1979 and another in 1980 to inquire into the problem. The committees focused on the actions of Dr Spautz rather than on the substance of his allegations, which were never examined more than cursorily. After the report of the second committee, University Council dismissed Dr Spautz from his position, without making formal charges of misconduct or providing him a full and effective opportunity to defend himself against such charges.

Following his dismissal, Dr Spautz launched several court actions alleging wrongful dismissal and alleging that various university officials had criminally defamed him. When some of his actions were lost and costs awarded against him, Dr Spautz refused to pay and as a result began serving a 200-day prison sentence. But after 56 days in prison he was released after a judge ruled that he had been illegally imprisoned.

References: Brian Martin, "Disruption and due process: the dismissal of Dr Spautz from the University of Newcastle", *Vestes*, vol. 26, no. 1, 1983, pp. 3–9; G. C. Curthoys et al. (Executive of the University of Newcastle Staff Association), "Report of the Executive to the members of the Staff Association on the recent dismissal of a tenured member of the academic staff of the University", University of Newcastle Staff Association, 11 July 1980; Michael Spautz, numerous memos under the title *In Vita Veritas*, available from the author at 502/362 Glebe Road, Hamilton, NSW 2303; Brian Martin, "Plagiarism and responsibility", *Journal of Tertiary Educational Administration*, vol. 6, no. 2, October 1984, pp. 183–90.

Struan Sutherland is Australia's leading snake venom expert. Employed at the Commonwealth Serum Laboratories, he has suffered harassment from administrators since 1974, mainly due to petty-minded jealousy over his successes. Actions against him have included cutting of staff, refusing to pay for examination fees, exclusion from meetings and cancelling of projects.

References: Deborah Smith and Bruce Hanford, "A research career is not meant to be easy", *National Times*, 17–23 February 1980, p. 52; Mark Plummer, "Top scientist gagged", *Commonwealth Professional*, no. 278, March 1980, pp. 3–5; Robert Drewe, "How bureaucratic venom threatens your life", *Bulletin*, vol. 101, 12 January 1982, pp. 18–24; Adrian McGregor, "Triumph and tragedy of the spider man", *Weekend Australian*, 27–8 March 1982, p. Magazine 3; Adrian McGregor, "A great day of victory", *Weekend Australian*, 3–4 April 1982, p. Magazine 8.

V. G. Venturini was appointed a commissioner on the Trade Practices Commission in February 1975. Venturini found that the Commission was taking no action against several well-documented violations of the *Trade Practices Act*, such as the cartel in zinc. He made biting criticisms of the Commission's lack of action in this and other areas, and many of his criticisms received wide publicity in the mass media, Instead of launching an investigation into the Commission's failings, the government in June 1977 restructured the Commission. All the commissioners were reappointed except for Venturini. In effect he was sacked.

Reference: V. G. Venturini, *The Administration of the Murphy Trade Practices Act. Malpractice: Antitrust as an Australian Poshlost* (Sydney: Non Mollare, 1980), especially pp. 268, 290–2.

CANADA

Marlene Dixon in the early 1970s taught in the sociology department at McGill University. An attempt was made to deny her reappointment, and also that of Pauline Vaillancourt, in the political science department, due to their participation in radical activities and their Marxist views. The attempt to deny reappointment failed: Dixon's and Vaillancourt's academic records were too good, and they were able to mobilise external pressure from the larger academic community and from the general public against what was clearly a politically inspired action. After their reappointment, a campaign of harassment was waged against Dixon, Vaillancourt and other radical scholars including eminent sociologist Immanuel Wallerstein. Every minor mistake they made was blown out of proportion, their students were harassed, their suggestions were blocked, and their efforts towards the smallest change were sabotaged. The harassment was eventually successful, and Dixon, Vaillancourt and Wallerstein all left McGill.

Reference: Marlene Dixon, *Things Which Are Done in Secret* (Montreal: Black Rose Books, 1976).

Wilson Bryan Key has studied and written popular accounts of the use of subliminal messages in advertisements. Many complaints from advertising companies and other pressures effectively harassed Key out of the University of Western Ontario.
Reference: Wilson Bryan Key, *The Clam-plate Orgy and other Subliminals the Media Use to Manipulate Your Behavior* (Englewood Cliffs: Prentice-Hall, 1980), pp. 112 ff.

David W. Livingstone and Richard V. Mason have documented the way in which informal peer pressure in a formally interdisciplinary environmental studies centre was focused against scientists who pursued research areas outside the mainstream, discipline-based scientific perspectives. Allocations of departmental resources were made selectively to those with the "correct" perspectives.
Reference: David W. Livingstone and Richard V. Mason, "Ecological crisis and the autonomy of science in capitalist society: a Canadian case study", *Alternatives*, vol. 8, no. 1, Winter 1978, pp. 3–10, 32.

David Mandel in 1980 applied for a permanent appointment in the Department of Political Science at McGill University. The departmental appointments committee recommended Mandel, but this was rejected by a vote of the department meeting. Mandel complained about the rejection of his application, alleging political bias against his Marxist orientation, his opposition to Israeli government policies, and his active support of the strike by maintenance staff at McGill, and also alleging procedural defects. A fact-finding committee of the Canadian Association of University Teachers found that Mandel had been unfairly treated, and also made important recommendations concerning procedures for academic appointments. CAUT's Academic Freedom and Tenure Committee recommended that CAUT and McGill establish a joint committee of inquiry, but McGill refused to do this. The detailed public documentation on this case illustrates the extreme difficulty of demonstrating suppression in appointments under present rules and procedures.
Reference: Dale Gibson, André Côté and J. K. Johnstone (CAUT Fact-Finding Committee on Discrimination or Unfair Hiring Practices in Making University Appointments), "Report"; Academic Freedom and Tenure Committee, "Report on the Mandel Case and the Fact-Finding Committee Report"; and responses, *CAUT Bulletin*, April 1984, pp. 49–58.

UNITED KINGDOM

Anthony Arblaster, in presenting the case for academic freedom, has described many cases and types of suppression, including attacks on students (especially radicals), victimisation, attacks on teachers, invoking of "morality" for suppression, and bias in appointments. Arblaster places suppression in the context of political power structures: industry, the state, and academic establishments. He states: "the most direct attacks on academic freedom have come from the academic authorities themselves, and it is their gross and arbitrary power which continues to constitute the most serious threat to educational freedom".
Reference: Anthony Arblaster, *Academic Freedom* (Harmondsworth: Penguin, 1974), quote from p. 94.

John Baldwin and Michael McConville are two sociologists at the University of Birmingham whose book *Negotiated Justice: Pressures to Plead Guilty* was published in 1977. A rare example of critical research on the activities of the legal profession, the book caused controversy, especially from an enraged legal establishment. The Chairman of the Bar reportedly attempted to stop publication of the book and the Vice-Chancellor of the University of Birmingham was persuaded to form an investigating committee, supposedly to determine the academic merits of their study. Although some shortcomings in statistical technique were found in the study, the basic discovery, that plea bargaining was commonly used by the English legal profession and the courts, often with behind-the-scenes negotiations unknown to the defendants, was not refuted.

References: John Baldwin and Michael McConville *Negotiated Justice: Pressures to Plead Guilty* (London: Martin Robertson, 1977); A. P. Sealy and G. Gaskell, "'Negotiated justice': the dynamics of credibility", *Bulletin of the British Psychological Society*, vol. 31, 1978, pp. 261–4 (contributed by C. M. Ann Baker and Clyde Manwell).

Roland Chaplain started work in 1964 at Edgbaston Observatory, which came under the control of Birmingham University. He developed plans for a 24-hour warning service to local clients such as firms, highways departments, market gardeners and public utilities, relying on knowledge of past local weather patterns and information from numerous amateur weather observers. In 1969 Chaplain was sacked from his post. There are several factors behind the dismissal and the collapse of the local forecasting scheme.

- Local weather forecasting — including actually talking with users of the service — is a low-status activity in academia compared to sophisticated computer models favoured by the academics who sacked Chaplain.

- Chaplain was receiving much favourable media coverage about the planned local forecasting service. Most academics look down on publicity.

- Chaplain lacked formal credentials, scholarly publications and a suitably prestigious academic post.

- Chaplain had ambitious plans for the forecasting service, and vocally criticised poor working conditions, low wages and short staffing at the Observatory. These complaints were the immediate cause of his dismissal which was on the grounds that Chaplain had disobeyed instructions from his superiors.

The available documents suggest that due process was denied to Chaplain in his appeal against his dismissal.

Reference: C. M. Ann Baker, Clyde Manwell and Brian Martin, "The University of Birmingham versus Roland Chaplain: academic justice, community service and the professionalisation syndrome", to be published (available from Brian Martin).

Mike Cooley, an engineer working for Lucas Aerospace, was a leading figure in the Lucas Aerospace Combine Shop Stewards' Committee during the period when it developed an alternative corporate plan for switching some of Lucas's production from aerospace components to heat pumps, kidney machines and other socially useful products. In 1981 Cooley was sacked. There was very strong local and international union support for his reinstatement, but individual unions failed to coordinate strike action effectively to this end and the campaign for reinstatement failed.

Reference: Hilary Wainwright and Dave Elliott, *The Lucas Plan: A New Trade Unionism in the Making?* (London: Allison and Busby, 1982), pp. 207–12.

Rodney Fordham, John Taylor, Ross Hesketh and Trevor Brown are scientists who worked in the British nuclear power program. Each of them expressed doubts about some aspect of nuclear safety, initially through normal internal procedural channels. When they made their criticisms public, or threatened to do so, the nuclear industry attacked them in various ways, such as by criticism of their work, transferral or dismissal.

Reference: Rob Edwards, "A new kind of nuclear victim", *New Statesman*, 22 July 1983, pp. 8–10.

David Triesman has analysed the issues underlying the 1973–4 dispute between the

Association of Scientific, Technical and Managerial Staffs and the London University Institute of Psychiatry focusing on differences concerning scientific theory and method, how these differences relate to different political understandings of society, and how these link with industrial relations.
Reference: David Triesman, "The Institute of Psychiatry sackings", *Radical Science Journal*, no. 5, 1977, pp. 9–36.

Peter Watkins directed the film *The War Game*, which portrays the likely physical and political consequences of a nuclear attack on Britain. The film was made for the British Broadcasting Corporation in 1965, but the BBC has refused ever since to allow the film's screening on television anywhere in the world. An experienced film director, Watkins has met stiff opposition in his further efforts to treat the issues of nuclear war and nuclear power on film. Watkins is also quite concerned about the way in which the visual media use audiovisual systems of meaning to induce confusion and passivity in viewers, especially in treating issues relating to nuclear war.
Reference: Peter Watkins, "The nuclear war film", *Thesis Eleven*, nos 5/6, 1982, pp. 125–38.

UNITED STATES

Howard M. Bahr, through a study of official statistics of the American Association of University Professors and interviews with social scientists at universities, concluded among other things that "There are approximately one hundred personally perceived violations of academic freedom for every officially reported violation".
Reference: Howard M. Bahr, "Violations of academic freedom: official statistics and personal reports", *Social Problems*, vol. 14, no. 3, 1967, pp. 310–20.

Morris H. Baslow, a marine biologist, worked for a company of consulting engineers who were studying the effect of thermal effluents from Consolidated Edison power plants on marine life. Baslow questioned the lack of reporting of larvae and fish growth at higher than optimal temperatures to the Environmental Protection Agency. He was fired. Although protected by whistleblower legislation, it took a year of litigation before a settlement was reached.
Reference: Constance Holden, "Scientist with unpopular data loses job", *Science*, vol. 210, 14 November 1980, pp. 749–50.

Jim Benson, in 1976 an employee in the Solar Division of the Energy Research and Development Administration, had contracted for the writing of a study on energy scenarios for the US. The resulting report pointed out the large economic and environmental costs of a high-energy future based on coal and nuclear power, and presented the advantages of a lower-energy solar-based future. Benson was fired, and the report rewritten to remove the support for a solar future.
Reference: Ray Reece, *The Sun Betrayed: A Report on the Corporate Seizure of U.S. Solar Energy Development* (Boston: South End Press, 1979), pp. 107–12.

Tom Brokaw, a news commentator for the National Broadcasting Commission, gave a wide-ranging interview to the magazine *Mother Jones*, published in April 1983, in which he presented some views on politics and economics which were critical of the powers that be. As a result of the interview, many attacks were made on Brokaw by newspaper commentators and considerable pressure was put on Brokaw's boss.
Reference: Deidre English, "Brokaw: seen but not heard?", *Mother Jones*, vol. 8, no. 6, July 1983, p. 5.

The Central Intelligence Agency has on a number of occasions approached major New York publishing houses to try to suppress or alter books about the CIA. (The CIA also had by 1967 produced, sponsored or subsidised over one thousand books in the US and elsewhere.)
Reference: David Wise, *The American Police State: The Government Against the People* (New York: Random House, 1976).

Rosemary Chalk and Frank von Hippel, in the course of making some recommendations about protection of individuals who speak out in the public interest, describe several cases of suppression.
Reference: Rosemary Chalk and Frank von Hippel, "Due process for dissenting whistle-blowers", *Technology Review*, vol. 81, no. 7, June/July 1979, pp. 49–55.

J. David Colfax was denied tenure at Washington University because of political activities. In an article about suppression of radicals in academia in the early 1970s, he notes that an informal survey he conducted revealed several dozen cases of suppression besides the more well-known instances, and that in no case was the professional competence of the person suppressed seriously questioned.
Reference: J. David Colfax, "Repression and academic radicalism", *New Politics*, vol. 10, no. 3, Spring 1973, pp. 14–27.

Hugh DeWitt works at Lawrence Livermore National Laboratory, near San Francisco, which designs nuclear weapons. DeWitt is a theoretical physicist, one of the few at the lab not directly involved with weapons work. Over the years he has spoken out frequently and critically about the role of the lab in the nuclear arms race. In 1979 he served as an expert witness for the *Progressive* magazine; the *Progressive* had been accused by the US Government of revealing secrets of hydrogen bombs. As a result, the lab imposed sanctions on DeWitt. A settlement was reached in October 1980 in which a warning notice was removed from DeWitt's personal file.
References: John Walsh, "*Progressive* case fallout has a long half-life", *Science*, vol. 210, 24 October 1980, pp. 410–11; Marjorie Sun, "DeWitt, Livermore Lab patch up over *Progressive*", *Science*, vol. 210, 14 November 1980, p. 747; Hugh E. DeWitt, "The nuclear arms race seen from within an American weapons laboratory", *Science and Public Policy*, vol. 9, no. 2, April 1982, pp. 58–63.

Marlene Dixon has described the way the ideas of "professionalism" and "academic standards" have been used to suppress dissenting academics and ensure ideological homogeneity in North American social sciences.
Reference: Marlene Dixon, "Professionalism in the social sciences: institutionalized repression", *Sociological Inquiry*, vol. 46, nos 3–4, 1976, pp. 251–62.

Edith Efron wrote a book, *The News Twisters*, published in 1971, which presented an analysis of US network television coverage of various topics in 1968 in which she found massive anti-Nixon bias, anti-Vietnam War bias, anti-"white middle class" bias, pro-"black militants" bias, and virtually no treatment of the Viet Cong or violent radicals. Richard Salant, News President of Columbia Broadcasting System (CBS), organised a campaign to discredit *The News Twisters* by making misleading associations and organising academic refutations.
References: Edith Efron, *The News Twisters* (Los Angeles: Nash Publishing, 1971); Edith Efron with the assistance of Clytia Chambers, *How CBS Tried to Kill a Book* (Los Angeles: Nash Publishing, 1972).

Samuel S. Epstein has documented the role of industry in promoting production practices in the face of evidence of their role in causing or promoting cancer. Scientists who have defended asbestos, certain pesticides, and other cancerous substances have received grants, consultancies, directorships and jobs. Furthermore, grossly inadequate or fraudulent research which benefits industry is frequently encountered. Those who have exposed the dangers have often been suppressed: "Constraints on data, from gross inadequacy, biased interpretation, manipulation, suppression and outright destruction, are commonplace, especially when profitable products or processes are involved".

References: Samuel S. Epstein, *The Politics of Cancer* (San Francisco: Sierra Club Books, 1978), quote from p. 300; Samuel S. Epstein, "Polluted data", *The Sciences* (New York Academy of Sciences), July/August 1978, pp. 16–21.

The Federal Bureau of Investigation's Cointelpro program was designed to suppress and repress political dissent, especially by black activists, anti-war activists and left-wing activists. Methods used included:

- providing derogatory information to university and school administrations in order to encourage firings;
- distributing material to smear or blacklist individuals;
- inciting violence via agents provocateurs;
- encouraging splits in social movements;
- promoting the red-baiting of socialists;
- robbing files.

Nearly half of FBI documents stolen from the Media, Pennsylvania FBI office were devoted to political surveillance, almost entirely of liberal or left groups.

References: Nelson Blackstock, *Cointelpro: The FBI's Secret War on Political Freedom* (New York: Vintage, 1976); Paul Cowan, Nick Egleson and Nat Hentoff, with Barbara Herbert and Robert Wall, *State Secrets: Police Surveillance in America* (New York: Holt, Rinehart and Winston, 1974).

A. Ernest Fitzgerald went to work for the Pentagon as a cost control expert, and soon found that wasteful procedures were standard policy, that cost overruns were justified by after-the-fact accounting procedures, and that enormous pressures were brought to bear against those opposing or exposing the system. After Fitzgerald gave testimony to a congressional committee about cost overruns on the C-5A transport aircraft in 1969, he was vilified by the Air Force and then sacked. In his account of his experiences, he also mentions about 10 other cases in which individuals who questioned military policies or procurements were reprimanded, isolated, demoted, sacked, blacklisted or declared crazy.

Reference: A. Ernest Fitzgerald, *The High Priests of Waste* (New York: W. W. Norton, 1972).

Leslie J. Freeman has interviewed a number of insiders from the nuclear industry, most of whom have been suppressed. For example:

- Rosalie Bertell is a mathematician and medical researcher who has investigated the effect of low-level ionising radiation on health. As a result of speaking publicly about these issues, the nuclear industry put pressure to stop her on the cancer hospital where she worked, critiques of her work were made with the intention of discrediting it, and her research funding was cut. In 1979 while she was driving, an object was dropped out of a car in front of her, causing a blowout, and then people from another car marked "Sheriff" (apparently spuriously) briefly quizzed her about the incident and falsely claimed to radio the local police.
- John Gofman was a highly successful medical physicist working partly for Lawrence

Livermore Laboratory. After doing calculations in 1969 about the expected number of child deaths from fallout, pressure was put on him to prevent publication, rumours were circulated about his incompetence, attacks were made on his work, his funding was cut and even minor grant applications refused. Gofman's colleague Arthur Tamplin had 12 of 13 staff under him taken away. A person from the Public Health Service said that he had been approached by someone from the Atomic Energy Commission and told, "We need you to help destroy Gofman and Tamplin".

- John Everett, a carpenter, in 1979 testified on behalf of a demonstrator at the Shoreham nuclear power plant under construction on Long Island. As a direct result, he lost his union shop steward position and was laid off his construction job.

Reference: Leslie J. Freeman, *Nuclear Witnesses: Insiders Speak Out* (New York: W. W. Norton, 1981).

Robert Justin Goldstein has massively documented political repression and suppression of dissident ideas and groups — especially labour and radical political groups which pose threats to elites — in a century of US history. Goldstein says: "The holders of *certain* ideas in the United States have been systematically and gravely discriminated against and subjected to extraordinary treatment by governmental authorities, such as physical assaults, denials of freedom of speech and assembly, political deportations and firings, dubious and discriminatory arrests, intense police surveillance, and illegal burglaries, wiretaps and interception of mail." Goldstein shows that political repression has helped destroy radical labour and political movements, helped prevent the US labour movement from obtaining major power until the 1930s, and helped discourage the exercise of political freedoms.

Reference: Robert Justin Goldstein, *Political Repression in Modern America from 1870 to the Present* (Cambridge, Mass.: Schenkman, 1978), quote from p. ix.

Frank Graham, Jr. has documented the extremely hostile response of the chemical and pesticide industry and subservient university scientists to Rachel Carson's *Silent Spring* and to others who spoke out about pesticides. Graham mentions, among other cases:

- threats or action against four biologists who spoke out about the Fire Ant Program in south-eastern United States;
- difficulties faced by Robert L. Rudd in getting his key book *Pesticides and the Living Environment* published;
- the condemnation of the journal *BioScience* by the Entomological Society of America (dominated by economic entomologists with links to agribusiness) for publishing an article by Frank Egler.

Reference: Frank Graham, Jr., *Since Silent Spring* (Boston: Houghton Mifflin, 1970).

Carol S. Gruber has described the response of US universities to the First World War. The academic community uncritically rallied in support of war and the state. There was little tolerance of those who doubted the morality of the US cause. Many of those who were vocal in dissent were suppressed: there were many sackings and contract non-renewals. Gruber describes in detail the cases of two dissidents, political scientist William A. Schaper and psychologist James M. Cattell. A great many scholars who held dissenting views remained silent throughout the war. In contrast to those suppressed, those who promoted the war — for example by producing propaganda for the government — were unaffected in their later careers.

Reference: Carol S. Gruber, *Mars and Minerva: World War I and the Uses of the Higher Learning in America* (Baton Rouge: Louisiana State University Press, 1975).

Richard Harris has provided extremely detailed accounts of three cases involving the Bill of Rights, each of which involved extensive legal challenges.

- Charles James was dismissed from his high school teaching position for wearing a black armband.
- Alan and Margaret McSurely, politically committed community organisers in Kentucky, were arrested and many of their papers were seized under the state's sedition laws.
- Ellen Grusse and Terri Turgeon refused to answer questions before a grand jury, invoking the Fifth Amendment. They were sent to prison.

Harris concludes that the freedoms of the Bill of Rights have seldom been upheld, and that those who pursue their rights at great self-sacrifice are the ones who guarantee them for everyone else.

Reference: Richard Harris, *Freedom Spent* (Boston: Little, Brown and Company, 1976).

Holger Hjortsvang, Max Blankenzee and Robert Bruder were engineers working for the Bay Area Rapid Transit System (BART) in the San Francisco region. They voiced technical criticisms of BART and consequently were fired in 1972.

References: Robert M. Anderson, Robert Perrucci, Dan E. Schendel and Leon E. Trachtman, *Divided Loyalties: Whistle-blowing at BART* (West Lafayette: Purdue University, 1980); Robert Perrucci, Robert M. Anderson, Dan E. Schendel and Leon E. Trachtman, "Whistle-blowing: professionals' resistance to organizational authority", *Social Problems*, vol. 28, no. 2, December 1980, pp. 149–64.

David Horowitz has exposed the role of foundations in propping up academic programs to serve US foreign policy, and has also exposed the close links between the CIA, academic programs and university heads, and the government. He describes the squashing of the prestigious and unique Institute of Hispanic American and Luso-Brazilian Studies at Stanford: the Institute's head, Ronald Hilton, resigned after all Ph.D. candidates were withdrawn by the university without discussion or consultation.

Reference: David Horowitz, "Sinews of empire", *Ramparts*, vol. 8, October 1969, pp. 32–42.

Peter Infante, a scientist at the Occupational Safety and Health Administration, routinely argued that the chemical formaldehyde is a potential cause of cancer. After pressure from the Formaldehyde Institute on OSHA, Infante was given notice he was to be fired.

Reference: Marjorie Sun, "A firing over formaldehyde", *Science*, vol. 213, 7 August 1981, pp. 630–1.

Lionel S. Lewis analysed all contested dismissals reported in the *American Association of University Professors Bulletin* between 1916 and 1970, and found that "in only 13 of the 217 dismissal cases was there even a suggestion of incompetence in either their teaching or research". Before 1945, financial and other internal pressures were the main reason for dismissal. From 1945 to 1962, external coercion was more prominent. From 1963 to 1970, pressure from university administrations to get rid of ideological embarrassments played a greater role.

References: Lionel S. Lewis, "Academic freedom cases and their disposition", *Change: The Magazine of Higher Learning*, vol. 4, no. 6, July/August 1972, pp. 8, 77–8. See also Lionel S. Lewis, *Scaling the Ivory Tower: Merit and its Limits in Academic Careers* (Baltimore: Johns Hopkins University Press, 1975).

Michael Miles has described the political dynamics of the suppression of radical university faculty in the early 1970s. The federal government encouraged local initiative by university administrations. Miles gives several examples of left-wing staff who were not granted tenure or, especially when they were involved in "disruptive" actions such as rallies, were dismissed. Student newspapers were censored, and injunctions used to provide summary justice against student militants. Campus disciplinary procedures were modernised by liberalising the forms of due process while strengthening the content of the rules. As a result, protection for left-wing faculty came more from courts than from other faculty or administrations.

Reference: Michael Miles, "The triumph of reaction", *Change: The Magazine of Higher Learning*, vol. 4, Winter 1972–3, pp. 30–6.

Ralph W. Moss gives many examples of how the "cancer establishment" in the United States persists with so-called "proven" methods, namely surgery, radiation therapy and chemotherapy, and uses all sorts of methods to oppose so-called "unproven" methods. He describes the problems faced in studying and promoting anticancer approaches based on Coley's toxins, laetrile, hydrazine sulfate, vitamin C and other nutritional approaches, Burton's immunological method and Livingston's theory of the cancer microbe. Methods used to suppress criticisms of the orthodox methods and to suppress alternative methods include:

- Denying funds. Linus Pauling was repeatedly denied modest grant requests to study the use of vitamin C against cancer (p. 181).
- Cutting off grants. Irwin Bross had grants cut off after he spoke out about the dangers and ineffectiveness of radiation therapy (p. 60).
- Diverting funds to wrong purposes. A $750,000 bequest intended for Livingston's microbial research was diverted for other uses (p. 204).
- Blocking publication of articles. Robert E. Lincoln's clinical results on using viruses to treat cancer patients were denied publication (p. 91).
- Sackings. Moss himself, a former Assistant Director of Public Affairs at the Memorial Sloan-Kettering Cancer Center, was fired after he associated himself with an internal newssheet criticising the Center's stance on laetrile (p. 152).
- Misrepresentation. Positive results for laetrile were ignored or denied (p. 137).
- Blacklisting. Inclusion on the American Cancer Society list of "unproven methods" of cancer management is in effect a form of blacklisting. No investigation had been made of over 40 per cent of the listed methods, the results were contradictory or inconclusive in over 10 per cent of the listed methods, and positive results were found for over 10 per cent of listed methods (pp. 79–94).

Those most often responsible for such suppression often have direct ties with corporations producing cancer-causing environmental chemicals (see especially pp. 67, 228–9, 270, 293–301). The alternative methods are unwelcome to the "cancer establishment" either because they are new, because they use a preventive approach, because they contradict cancer paradigms, or because they use cheap and safe (and unpatentable) chemicals.

Reference: Ralph W. Moss, *The Cancer Syndrome* (New York: Grove Press, 1980).

Ralph Nader, Peter Petkas and Kate Blackwell edited the account of a 1971 conference on professional responsibility, in which they present 10 major case studies, and 20 shorter studies, of individual "whistle-blowers": people who have spoken out about some hazard or other issue of concern to the general public, and who have been victimised as a result. For example:

- Edward Gregory, a safety inspector for General Motors who spoke out about General Motors cars leaking carbon monoxide.

- Jacqueline Verrett of the Federal Drug Administration who told the press about her research which revealed health hazards from cyclamates.
- William Stieglitz who resigned from the National Highway Safety Bureau and criticised federal safety standards for automobiles.
- A. Dale Console who testified to Congress about unscrupulous drug marketing techniques used by pharmaceutical companies.
- Christopher Pyle and Ralph Stein who exposed the Army's surveillance of civilians.
- Charles Pettis, an engineer who opposed and exposed corruption in road-building in Peru by international construction and engineering firms.

Reference: Ralph Nader, Peter J. Petkas and Kate Blackwell (editors), *Whistle Blowing: The Report of the Conference on Professional Responsibility* (New York: Grossman, 1972).

Bertell Ollman, a prominent Marxist scholar, was offered the post of Chairman of the Department of Government and Politics at the University of Maryland in 1978. He was unanimously supported by the 10-member faculty search committee out of 100 candidates for the post. After many Maryland state legislators and several syndicated newspaper columnists protested against the appointment because of Ollman's Marxist views, the President of the University in an unprecedented move rejected the appointment. Ollman brought a civil suit against the University of Maryland over the President's decision. In spite of extensive evidence that political pressure had played a key role in blocking the appointment, the judge ruled against Ollman in 1981.

References: R. M. Frumkin, "Bertell Ollman's struggle", *Zedek*, vol. 1, nos 3–4, May–August 1981, pp. 46–53; "The case of Bertell Ollman", *Critique*, no. 14, 1981, pp. 109–20; Bertell Ollman, *Class Struggle is the Name of the Game: True Confessions of a Marxist Businessman* (New York: William Morrow, 1983).

J. Robert Oppenheimer was a theoretical physicist who during the Second World War directed the Los Alamos laboratory in the development of the first nuclear bomb. After the war he continued to be involved with development of nuclear weapons. But in 1953 he was accused of being associated with communists in the past and of opposing the development of the hydrogen bomb. A security hearing found him not guilty of treason but ruled for the withdrawal of his security clearance. Many leading scientists came to his defence after his trial, and his case became perhaps the best known example of the victimisation of intellectuals in the recent history of English-speaking countries. (Indeed, the Western scientific establishment has virtually canonised Oppenheimer — who suffered no threats to either his employment or his research — while ignoring the plight of thousands of other more deserving cases, such as Haakon Chevalier, who lost his job as a result of false testimony from Oppenheimer.)

Recent revelations of importance are the fact that the FBI bugged pre-trial conversations between Oppenheimer and his lawyers and that the Nobel prize-winning physicist Hans Bethe claims that Edward Teller's technical mistakes, rather than Oppenheimer's opposition, are what hindered work on the hydrogen bomb. John Ziman ably sums up the case itself:

> The charges were trumped up, as a manoeuvre to get rid of him, in the unscrupulous manner of political life at the top...nothing more than a dirty, rotten bit of political trickery, activated by malice and vindictiveness, but without much influence on the actual course of events, for he was not, in fact, standing in the way of some great change of policy, and could have been eased out or bypassed without all the drama.

References: P. M. Stern, *The Oppenheimer Case: Security on Trial* (New York: Harper and Row, 1969); D. J. Kevles, *The Physicists: The History of a Scientific Community in Modern America* (New York: Knopf, 1978); A. K. Smith and C. Weiner (editors), *Robert Oppenheimer: Letters and Recollections* (Cambridge: Harvard University Press, 1976); Herbert

York, *The Advisors: Oppenheimer, Teller and the Superbomb* (San Francisco: W. H. Freeman, 1976); D. Shapley, "Oppenheimer case boils up again", *Nature*, vol. 296, 1982, p. 695; W. J. Broad, "Rewriting the history of the H-bomb", *Science*, vol. 218, 1982, pp. 769–72; John Ziman, *The Force of Knowledge: The Scientific Dimension of Society* (Cambridge: Cambridge University Press, 1976), quote from pp. 144–5 (contributed by C. M. Ann Baker and Clyde Manwell).

Michael Parenti, a political scientist, worked at the University of Illinois in 1970. He was active politically from a viewpoint that was critical of established institutions, and for example spoke at rallies. At the peak of protest against the invasion of Cambodia and other crimes, a student strike was held. In one incident during this time, Parenti was beaten by police, and later judged guilty of aggravated battery in spite of six witnesses who claimed it was Parenti who was attacked. He was staked out by police for weeks. The University administration gave no support to staff and students who were attacked and wrongly charged. Instead, attempts were made to get rid of "radicals" on campus. Philip Meranto, who had been assured of tenure, and who did nothing more than interpose his body between Parenti and police blows, found his position threatened. Graduate students lost their fellowships. Academics who voiced any support for student activism were routinely rejected when making job applications. The university put material about Parenti's activities in his file, which was to be made available to other prospective employers.

Reference: Michael Parenti, "Repression in academia: a report from the field", *Politics and Society*, vol. 1, no. 4, August 1971, pp. 527–37.

Charles Peters and Taylor Branch have written and collected many articles about people who have exposed corruption in industry or government, many of whom have been fired, smeared, or otherwise suppressed. Those who dissent in the public interest often have trouble later in gaining employment, because employers demand loyalty: the whistle-blower might do it again. Some of the cases presented by Peters and Branch involve:

- James Boyd, an office staffer who exposed the financial corruption of Senator Thomas Dodd;
- Adam Hochschild who exposed the uselessness of the Army Reserve and National Guard;
- Jeffrey Record who exposed the use of Cobra helicopter gunships for killing noncombatants in Vietnam;
- Robert S. Benson who exposed excess spending by the Department of Defense;
- Gary J. Greenberg, an attorney with the Justice Department who challenged the Department's reluctance to enforce civil rights legislation;
- Otto F. Otepka who tried to expose communists in government and who leaked classified documents to do so.

Reference: Charles Peters and Taylor Branch (writers and editors), *Blowing the Whistle: Dissent in the Public Interest* (New York: Praeger, 1972).

Geoffrey Rips has documented the extensive campaign against the US independent press in the late 1960s and early 1970s carried out by police, the military, and government intelligence agencies. Measures taken included:

- arresting street vendors of newspapers;
- intimidating distributors and printers;
- banning papers from campuses;
- making arrests for selling obscene literature (while establishment media carrying identical material were not prosecuted);
- illegal surveillance of staff, including opening of mail and tapping of telephones;
- raids of offices, often with confiscation and destruction of documents and equipment;

- sending of anonymous disruptive letters;
- drug arrests and excessive sentences;
- physical attacks and beatings of staff by police and vigilantes;
- bombings of offices and cars;
- arrests of staff or contributors for the purposes of harassment.

Reference: Geoffrey Rips, *The Campaign Against the Underground Press* (with contributions by Allen Ginsberg, Aryeh Neier, Todd Gitlin and Angus Mackenzie, edited by Anne Janowitz and Nancy J. Peters) (San Francisco: City Lights Books, 1981).

Herman and Julia R. Schwendinger have documented the suppression of many important social scientists in the formative years of North American sociology. For example:

- Edward W. Bemis was dismissed from the University of Chicago after saying some calming things about the Pullman strike;
- Edward A. Ross was forced to leave Stanford University after making public comments about Chinese immigration which implicitly criticised Leland Stanford's exploitation of Chinese workers;
- William E. B. Du Bois was starved of funds because he did not acquiesce to the Tuskegee "machine" which apologised for blacks rather than criticising those who attacked them.

Concerning the importance of suppression in the development of sociology in North America, the Schwendingers say: "Political repression, for example, will be regarded as the primary factor in the maintenance of liberal hegemony within academic institutions in the United States. Liberal scholarship never would have dominated the field of sociology, then or now, in the absence of politically repressive conditions."

Reference: Herman and Julia R. Schwendinger, *The Sociologists of the Chair: A Radical Analysis of the Formative Years of North American Sociology (1883–1922)* (New York: Basic Books, 1974), quote from p. xxiv.

Rachel Scott has documented the pressures exerted by industry on their own and outside scientists to come up with results favourable to profits. Established scientists who take pro-industry positions on issues such as the effects of asbestos are respected even if they make outrageous statements. The choice of which work to publish may be dictated by what is useful to industry.

Reference: Rachel Scott, *Muscle and Blood* (New York: E. P. Dutton, 1974), especially pages 174–203.

Karen Silkwood was a laboratory analyst at a plutonium plant in Oklahoma run by Kerr-McGee Nuclear Corporation. In 1974 she became concerned about health and safety at the plant. In July that year she was contaminated by plutonium. Shortly afterwards she became a member of the bargaining committee for the Oil, Chemical and Atomic Workers, assigned to health and safety. She began collecting information on safety violations and on the falsifying of quality-control records on fuel rods. In early November she was again contaminated by plutonium. On 13 November she was killed while driving to deliver documents about falsifying records to a reporter for the *New York Times*. Her documents were not found.

Reference: Richard Rashke, *The Killing of Karen Silkwood* (Boston: Houghton-Mifflin, 1981).

Robert van den Bosch, in his account of the hazards of pesticides and how pesticide companies promote dependence on their products, describes about a dozen cases of suppression of scientists, including himself, who had done research or made statements critical of pesticides. Attacks have included pressure exerted through university administrations, criticisms in newspapers and farm magazines, loss of jobs and funds, and censorship of publications. Van den Bosch describes how the pesticide companies exert pressure through university administrations, by threats of withdrawing grants, by threatening to withdraw advertising from magazines, and by providing to sympathetic researchers grants, gifts and travel funds.

Reference: Robert van den Bosch, *The Pesticide Conspiracy* (Garden City, New York: Doubleday, 1978).

Deena Weinstein has conceptualised the phenomenon of "bureaucratic opposition": opposition movements within bureaucracies. Bureaucracies themselves are conceptualised by Weinstein as authoritarian political systems. Suppression of intellectual dissent is one way in which budding or established bureaucratic oppositions are attacked. Weinstein gives many examples of bureaucratic oppositions and of their two basic methods, informing and direct action, and of the different types of reprisals from bureaucratic elites.

References: Deena Weinstein, *Bureaucratic Opposition: Challenging Abuses at the Workplace* (New York: Pergamon Press, 1979); Deena Weinstein, "Bureaucratic opposition: the challenge to authoritarian abuses at the workplace", *Canadian Journal of Political and Social Theory*, vol. 1, no. 2, Spring–Summer 1977, pp. 31–46.

Alan Wolfe has documented for the United States the use of state power to destroy organisations threatening the power of elites, and the role of the ideological manipulation to win people's support for the capitalist system. Wolfe presents both a history of state repression and suppression and also an analysis of these as part of the democratic state and its ideology.

Reference: Alan Wolfe, *The Seamy Side of Democracy: Repression in America* (New York: David McKay, 1973).

Zedek is the journal of the Social Activist Professors Defense Foundation (19329 Monte Vista Drive, Detroit MI 48221, USA). It began publication in 1980, and has included many articles and news reports on suppression of US academics, especially dismissals and denials of tenure to professors who have taken outspoken radical stands on social issues. Also included is useful material on developing campaigns to oppose suppression. The following cases are among the many described in *Zedek*:

- R. M. Frumkin, an associate professor at Kent State University involved in many radical movements, who was dismissed in 1975 as the culmination of several dismissal attempts and administrative harassment. When Frumkin later exposed plagiarism and misuse of funds by colleagues, the Kent State administration took no action.

- Charles Stastny, an associate professor at Central Washington University and a long-time political activist, who was dismissed from his tenured position in 1980 after a long period of surveillance and harassment from the administration.

- Katherine van Wormer, an assistant professor at Kent State University's Department of Criminal Justice Studies and a feminist, pacifist, Quaker and humanist with an outstanding teaching and research record, who was denied tenure in 1983.

- Scott Nearing, who was dismissed from the Wharton School of Economics in 1915 due to his opposition to child labour in Pennsylvania. Nearing, a famous US radical, suffered suppression on several occasions. He was charged with sedition over his anti-war book *The Great Madness*, was barred from entering Britain because of his outspoken opposition to colonialism, and was expelled from the Communist Party in 1929 for refusing to change his views in his book on imperialism.

PART TWO:
ANALYSIS

ELITES AND SUPPRESSION

Brian Martin

To speak of "suppression of intellectual dissent" usually assumes the following context. First, there is a power structure of some kind, with some groups having vested interests in their power and privilege. Such groups are responsible for most suppression. Second, there is some set of ideas or practices from which intellectual dissent is possible. Third, there is some alternative source of power, or other potential threat to the powerful and privileged groups, to which the dissent may appeal.

For example, consider a scientist who speaks out about potential health hazards to workers on the job. In this case the powerful group comprises the corporation owners or management, who sometimes will have an interest in not taking action against the hazard, particularly if this is a threat to profits. The prevailing set of ideas from which dissent is possible might include responsibility of management for worker safety, or a public expectation of such responsibility. And an alternative source of power might be workers and trade unions who could take action to reduce the hazard. In speaking out, the scientist potentially threatens the interests of management, invokes, implicitly or explicitly, concepts of responsibility for the hazard, and potentially appeals to the power of workers and unions to take action against the hazard.

This simple framework can be used to analyse many cases of suppression. But to be useful in getting at the roots of suppression, a more detailed analysis and classification is required. That is my aim in this chapter. I look in turn at three sources of suppression: corporate elites, bureaucratic elites and professional elites. In each case there are characteristic types of suppression, types of dissent, and sources of support for the dissent.

To characterise suppression in the manner done here is to make a number of theoretical assumptions. Indeed, the terms "suppression" and "intellectual dissent" reflect a particular way of viewing the world in which the exercise of elite power often constitutes suppression and in which freedom of speech against elite frameworks becomes dissent.

Differing from this is the point of view of most elites who see their organisations or professions operating on the basis of standard principles or procedures such as profit, efficiency or service. They may perceive those who speak out or act against the interests of elites as malcontents, as naive or misguided idealists, as people lacking professional standards, or as malevolent opponents. Since elites seldom question the goals or procedures of their malevolent opponents. Since elites seldom question the goals or procedures of their organisations or professions, "suppression" for them typically is a nonexistent or seldom-used category.

The differing views of elites and dissidents reflect a more general point: the meaning of social reality does not present itself unambiguously or uniformly, but rather is socially constructed.[1] Social meanings are created and negotiated as part of ongoing social interaction.

To select and use a set of concepts — whether "suppression" and "dissent", or "bureaucratic efficiency" and "professional conduct" — is to use ideas as tools for political purposes.[2] This politicising of ideas is impossible to avoid. In analysing here the phenomenon of "suppression" in the context of the structural role of corporate, bureaucratic and professional elites, I have consciously adopted a framework which is selectively useful for those who would question business as usual in these dominant social institutions.

CORPORATE ELITES

Owners and top managers in corporations have a strong interest in profits, in market share and in corporate expansion. To ensure maintenance of profits and growth, most corporations proceed on the basis of standard operating procedures and generally understood assumptions about goals, methods and rationales. Many of those who dissent from accepted policies and practices and thereby threaten profits, corporate image, or commercial prospects, become potential targets for suppression.

In most corporations, suppression of dissent is so usual and expected as to be unremarked. Anyone who questions policy in a fundamental way — for example by refusing to carry out instructions — is likely to suffer quick dismissal, or perhaps reassignment or blocking of promotion. In corporations producing military components, for example, openly expressed opposition to military production, such as through distributing anti-war leaflets, is not likely to help one's career! Since most workers value their jobs and their career prospects, the likelihood of suppression is a strong disincentive to dissent.

In some companies — especially in smaller firms in the more competitive, "free enterprise" sectors of the economy — a certain degree of dissent is tolerated or encouraged. This is seen as "innovative thinking" which can provide a competitive edge. But even in this case tolerance of unconventional ideas has strict bounds: questioning which threatens profits is not allowed. In larger firms, action which exposes failings of management can lead to suppression irrespective of the benefits of dissent for profits.

Dissidents in corporations seldom have an independent power base, and often see their options as either remaining in the corporation and remaining quiet, or speaking up and getting out. For example, when the three nuclear engineers Dale Bridenbaugh, Gregory Minor and Richard Hubbard, who worked for General Electric in the United States, decided that they wished to speak out about reactor safety hazards, they did this at the same time as they resigned from the company in 1976.

Only a tiny fraction of corporate employees actually think seriously of openly dissenting from standard policy and practices. In most corporations the reigning orthodoxy of the corporate view is largely unquestioned. In the rubber industry, the social uses of rubber are assumed to be acceptable. In the housing industry, standard house designs and construction methods are mostly unchallenged. There are several reasons for this, besides overt suppression. First, people who decide to enter a particular occupation usually are sympathetic to its function and aims. Vegetarians seldom become meatworks employees.

Second, once working for a corporation or in an occupational field, a selection process operates to encourage those most committed to the activities of the enterprise and to filter out those with reservations. Those who are highly committed tend to work harder, to get on better with bosses and to have ambitions to rise in the occupation. To get ahead, it greatly helps to really believe in what one is doing, whether selling insurance or manufacturing cigarettes.

Third, inside most corporations there exists a standard view of reality, a basic perspective which pervades all discussions and activities. Within the automobile industry, for example, it goes without saying that cars enhance mobility, that the solution to excess traffic is not fewer cars but more roads, and that advertising on the basis of cars' power and glamour is acceptable. The standard view is usually so deep-seated that it is not even recognised as a set of assumptions. As a result, the very idea of dissent in any fundamental way from the goals of the corporate enterprise is almost unimaginable for most workers.

And this is also why those who do dissent are seen as such dangerous threats: dissenters could potentially puncture the corporation-serving hegemony over discussion.

While the corporate view of reality may seldom come under threat from employees, disagreement from the outside is more common. This may come from people in government, in universities, or from independent groups. How can corporations prevent or restrain such dissent? The most effective way is to ensure a widespread acceptance of the corporate view of reality. One way to do this is by providing benefits to those who support the corporate view: jobs, funding, contracts, etc. Government bodies meant to regulate the industry can be turned into faithful partners and academics can be brought on side by providing contracts, potential jobs and access for research.[3] The media can be provided with advertisements and stories. As a result, many industries have gone for long periods without facing any fundamental criticism, such as the automobile industry, the pharmaceutical industry and the insurance industry.

Forestry in Australia is an example of an area in which industry perspectives are dominant throughout most of the relevant government and university bodies.[4] The forest industries — timber, pulp, woodchip and other industries based on forest products — maintain strong links with government forest services and research organisations, and with university forestry departments. Avenues for maintaining the links include professional and commercial organisations, clubs, joint conferences, informal networks of communication and consultation concerning appointments.

One example of the link between personnel in the forest industries and forestry researchers is the international organisation called the Concatenated Order of the Hoo-Hoo. Members of this social and "service" organisation in Australia are "limited to male persons of the full age of 21 years, of good moral character and engaged in forestry, sawmilling, the manufacture of timber products, wood pulp and insulation materials derived from forest products, officials of the forestry service, forest commissions and boards, officers of timber organisations and makers of the allied industries". Despite its peculiar name and associated rituals, the Hoo-Hoo plays an important role not only in generally promoting the forest industries but in helping attune forest regulatory agencies and certain forest researchers to the interests of the forest industries.

The availability of jobs is a strong influence in maintaining commitment to the industry perspective. For example, quite a few leading figures in the government forest services have, on retirement, taken positions with forest industries. An interchange of personnel between industry, government and university is common in many fields besides forestry, such as nuclear power, armaments and agriculture.

Also important is the closed-shop nature of most recruiting into government forest services. Recruits are preferred to be from special forestry schools and graduates to be from one of the two university forestry departments (Australian National University and Melbourne University). These are the places where the influence of the forest services and industries is greatest.

Illustrating this influence, the electoral committee which was formed in 1974 for the filling of the post of Professor and Head of the Department of Forestry at ANU included a representative from the Australian Institute of Forestry and another from the heads of the forest services. In addition, the committee's terms of reference included seeking the views of the Commonwealth Forestry and Timber Bureau, the Australian Institute of Foresters and the heads of the state forest services — but not, for example, any conservation groups.

In many Australian states, the link between the forest industries and the government forest services operates through the structure of the state and federal government bureaucracies. The state cabinets appoint senior officials in the bureaucracy, including the departmental head responsible for forestry. Due to the political influence of industry in lobbying, creating jobs locally and supplying election funds, most departmental heads are chosen to be acceptable to industry.

As a result of the influence of the forest industries, the basic orientation of the government forest services and many forestry academics is to promote the exploitation of forest resources for the purposes of production and profit. This orientation carries over into government and university forest research, in which the criteria for valid and useful knowledge, and how it may be obtained, are influenced by the interests of the forest industries. In other words, the paradigm for many forest researchers is, to put it quite baldly, based around ensuring that forests exist primarily for the forest industries.

Corporations thus attempt to ensure that outsiders accept the corporate perspective. But sometimes dissent crops up. Corporate elites may try to suppress such dissent, but it is not as simple as suppressing dissent from employees. Somehow pressure must be brought to bear on the outside critics.

When the outsider works for a government, university or other body which subscribes to the industry view of the world, then the task of suppression is straightforward: apply pressure on the dissident's boss to have the activity stopped. Sometimes it is not even necessary for any pressure to be applied; the boss may subscribe to the industry perspective and take action quite independently.

How often overt pressure is applied is hard to say, since it is seldom publicised, and often the contact is by word of mouth rather than in writing or other permanent form. Two documented examples are the actions taken by Bayer and by Velsicol Australia after John Coulter had spoken out in a way that was critical of their corporate interests.[5]

Because of the powerful influence of corporations, open dissent in many areas comes from those on the periphery, outside the direct influence of the industry. In the forestry area, I have been informed of a considerable number of cases of suppression of people who had voiced dissent on the inside, but most of those suppressed are hesitant to have their cases publicised. The possible result of gaining a high profile critical of prevailing forestry practices or ideology would be a virtual blacklisting from many jobs in forestry. As a result, many of those who have openly challenged forestry interests are not directly employed in the forestry area: critics Richard Routley and Val Plumwood are professional philosophers, Peter Rawlinson is a zoologist and Philip Keane is a botanist.

The greatest threat to industry arising from dissent usually comes when a social movement develops which is in some way critical of industry activities. The environmental movement has posed such a threat to many industries engaged in environmentally damaging practices or producing environmentally damaging products. The peace movement is a threat to military industry. And the consumer movement poses a threat to many corporate activities.

When Ralph Nader in the middle 1960s exposed shortcomings of automobile design and production, General Motors tried to discredit Nader, and arranged for him to be spied upon to find ways to do this. Significantly, Nader was not employed by an automobile-related industry, and so the immediate avenues for suppression were not available. Once an entire consumer movement was more firmly established, not only did many people on the outside question corporate views, but this questioning led more corporate employees to speak up. With a potential power base outside the corporation — the independent consumer movement, plus allies in government, universities and the media — insiders have more leverage with their criticisms.

To summarise: Suppression of dissent within corporations is routine. And in most cases dissent does not arise in the first place, because of employee self-selection, peer pressure and the internal hegemony of the industry ideology. Dissent by outsiders often is inhibited also, by industry influence via jobs, funding and perspectives in government, universities and the media. When dissent by outsiders does occur, pressure on the dissident's boss — if the boss does not autonomously take action — may suppress it. But this sort of suppression is less successful once a social movement develops which can sustain critical perspectives and encourage dissent on the inside as well.

BUREAUCRATIC ELITES

pression by corporate elites to protect profits and market shares fits reasonably well with a traditional Marxist analysis of capitalist society, in which the power of the ruling capitalist class depends on its control over the means of production. But there are other sorts of suppression which do not fit so nicely within this framework. Suppression by bureaucratic elites is one such type.

Bureaucracy is a way of organising social interactions. It is characterised by hierarchy, a specialised division of labour, rules describing the duties and rights of members, standard operating procedures and impersonal relations between staff. In a bureaucracy, individuals become interchangeable parts possessing uniform, circumscribed functions.

Bureaucracy is typically seen as a way of organising people for the purposes of administration. But this perspective hides much of the dynamics of bureaucracy. It is much more fruitful to look upon bureaucracy as a political system.[6] People at the top — bureaucratic elites — have the greatest power over the organisation's policy, initiatives, internal decision-making and design of the organisational structure itself. People at the bottom — the rank and file — essentially do as they are told. Opportunities for popular participation in decision-making in bureaucracies are very limited. About the most that can be hoped for is that the bureaucratic elites may listen to or solicit opinions from the rank and file. But the elites do not have to act on the basis of opinions from below. In a bureaucracy, information flows up the hierarchy and instructions flow downwards.

Since a bureaucracy is a power structure, it can be expected that power struggles will occur. Sometimes these may be between competing elites, but of more interest here are challenges from the bottom, which can be called bureaucratic oppositions. Any person or group within a bureaucracy which challenges from below the actions, privileges, rights or status of bureaucratic elites constitutes a bureaucratic opposition. One response to such challenges is suppression.

Intellectual dissent is almost always a threat to bureaucratic elites. A bureaucracy is analogous to an authoritarian state in its hierarchy, its imposed uniformity of perspective, and in its intolerance of dissent. Authoritarian states can use, if necessary, violent repression to squash dissent. Most bureaucracies are different in that only nonviolent means for containing dissent are permissible or available. That means suppression: dismissal, blacklisting, legal action, and blocking of appointments, promotions, funds or initiatives.

It is useful to distinguish two sorts of dissent from within bureaucracies: dissent which threatens the organisation as a whole, and dissent which only threatens the position of bureaucratic elites. For example, a member of an intelligence agency who covertly provides information to foreign governments is usually considered a threat to the state as a whole, and branded a spy and a traitor. By contrast, a member of an intelligence agency who exposes misuse by the agency's director of power or funds — on an issue which is of no particular interest to foreign governments — provides a threat only to the director and associated cronies. The dissident in this case threatens the bureaucratic power structure of the agency. This sort of dissident may also be called a spy and a traitor, but only as a means for helping to suppress the challenge to the bureaucratic power structure.

Suppression to protect bureaucratic elites is common in as many areas as bureaucracy is common: government departments, trade unions, political parties, corporations, and many voluntary groups. Suppression by corporate elites can be seen as one special case of suppression by bureaucratic elites, since most corporations are organised bureaucratically.

One example of a bureaucracy in which top-level control is rigorously enforced and dissent not tolerated is the Leninist political party. Under so-called "democratic centralism", all decisions made at the top of the party are binding on everyone in the party. Dissidents are expelled. When such parties have gained national power, as in the Soviet Union, the ruling Communist Party penetrates all other power structures, such as the state bureaucracies, in order to enforce adherence to the party line and acquiescence to the party elites.

Another example of a rigid bureaucracy is the military. Indeed, the military is a model bureaucracy, and in many Third World countries bureaucratisation of the economic and political system is carried out by ruling military elites. Within military forces, dissent is harshly repressed, and obedience is encouraged by training and by rewards for loyalty.[7]

The idea of the "captured bureaucracy" should be mentioned here. Corporations, through their economic, political and ideological influence, are often able to influence state bureaucracies to serve corporate interests. One example is the Australian state forest services. Essentially, the "captured bureaucracy" becomes the pliant tool of the relevant industry, a corporate ally within the state sector.

Not all cases fit the captured bureaucracy model. Nuclear power, for example, has been almost entirely a creature of states rather than corporations. In most countries it has been developed, promoted and controlled entirely by state bureaucracies. Even in the United States in which state control of industry is ideologically an anathema, considerable state pressure was necessary before corporations would enter the nuclear industry in a big way, namely legal protection against claims from major nuclear accidents, subsidies from the military sector and other financial incentives. Admittedly, once General Electric, Westinghouse and other large corporations became deeply involved in the industry, they have been strong proponents of it and have opposed dissent. But the primary driving force behind nuclear power remains the state. And it has been within state bureaucracies where much suppression of dissent has taken place, for example the harassment and attempted discrediting of John Gofman and Arthur Tamplin of the former Atomic Energy Commission whose figures on likely deaths from given radiation exposures were too high to please AEC elites. Most funds for nuclear research have come from the government, and funds are simply not available for nuclear critics, and may be withdrawn from those who become even mild critics, such as Gofman and Tamplin were originally.[8]

Corporations are only one part of the overall power structure. In some areas corporations are the dominant influence, and spread their control via captured bureaucracies. In other areas state bureaucracies are dominant, and may spread their control through "captured corporations", as in the case of many firms producing military goods. And often the relationship between different dominant bureaucracies, especially when it comes to challenges made from below, is a symbiotic one. Indeed, one good way to analyse the locus of vested interests is to look at cases of dissent and suppression and to see what groups are willing to support the dissent and oppose the suppression.

Only in special cases is dissent within a corporation defended by government bureaucracies, or vice versa. The most common base for support of dissent is the general public, often via the media. The phenomenon of "whistle-blowing" — revealing to the public abuses within large organisations — occurs precisely because the media and its audience is a power base independent of bureaucratic elites. The challenge is a potent one. Bureaucracies operate on a close control of information, lack of open discussion, and internal determination of priorities. Whistle-blowing is an immediate and direct challenge to bureaucratic control over information and decision-making.

All the methods used by corporate elites to prevent and restrain dissent are also used by non-corporate bureaucratic elites: selective recruitment and advancement, uniformity of ideas, and suppression of dissidents. Also, as in the case of corporate dissent, opposition to bureaucratic activities is greatly encouraged by the existence of a social movement. For example, the 1980s peace movement has not only stimulated widespread public questioning of government policies and military activities, it has also encouraged dissent from inside the military among soldiers, even generals.

PROFESSIONAL ELITES

Bureaucratic elites owe their power to their position within a formal hierarchy. A somewhat different but often overlapping basis for power resides in expert knowledge used within a framework collectively controlled by professionals. Those who wield such power I call professional elites. Before describing their role further it is worth looking at ideas about a "New Class".

According to a classical Marxist analysis of class in modern capitalist society, the two key classes are the capitalist or ruling class and the working class or proletariat. (Other groups, such as small independent farmers, who are similar in role to peasants, and shopkeepers, fall outside this categorisation and are part of the so-called petite bourgeoisie.) In recent years quite a few socialist scholars have looked at this framework and decided that it is inadequate to take into account the role of those people and groups which owe their position and collective power to their knowledge and intellectual skills: managers in corporations, government bureaucrats, doctors, lawyers, teachers and so forth. Those in these areas seldom own much capital: they do not owe their power to ownership of the means of production. But neither are they simply characterised as workers who sell their labour power. Managers, administrators and professionals may be employees, but they are also bosses or in other ways are in a powerful position in relation to subordinates or clients. Their collective economic and political interests are different from those of the capitalists and also from those of the traditional working class.

This class of intellectually skilled workers has been called the "intellectual class", the "New Class" and the "professional-managerial class".[9] Normally the distinguishing trait for this class is taken to be involvement in intellectual work rather than manual work. But in my view whether one does intellectual or manual work is not a ready indication of one's power vis-a-vis others. Many intellectual workers, such as bottom-level bureaucrats, have as little independence and power over others as do assembly-line workers. Indeed, bottom-level clerks are essentially the process workers of "factories" that deal in papers and files. For this reason, I think the distinguishing characteristic of what I term the "administrative class" is having the power to influence the conditions of life of others. Those reasonably high up in bureaucracies set the agenda for lower-level employees, and also may set or execute policy which affects clients. Doctors, lawyers and other professionals collectively set the framework and individually make the decisions in which medical treatment and other activities take place. The boundary of the administrative class is necessarily fuzzy, but the criterion of power over the lives of others by setting the frameworks and individual requirements for action can still be a useful one.

Within the administrative class, I distinguish bureaucratic elites and professional elites. Bureaucratic elites owe their power primarily to position in a formal hierarchy. Their role in suppression has already been discussed. Professional elites owe their power to special knowledge and skills, both individually and collectively. Doctors, for example, are individually trained, and the medical profession as a whole maintains a near monopoly on formal treatment of ill health. Nonprofessional care, however effective in practice, is usually ignored, downgraded and uncertified. Medical practitioners collectively control many aspects of their own work situation: entry requirements, salaries, advancement to higher posts (such as hospital superintendents), protocols for patients, hours, etc. Medical decisions within the profession — about methods of treatment for example — are decided to a great degree on the basis of knowledge, skills and intellectual argumentation. The role of numbers or violence is minimal. In these ways doctors, like others among the professional elites, have considerable power which is not available to manual workers or to low-level bureaucrats or indeed low-level professionals. Cleaners, clerical workers and nurses have little power compared to hospital administrators and most doctors.[10]

Professional elites use their specialist knowledge in several ways to gain power. The monopolisation of a body of expertise serves to exclude both laypeople and other expert groups.[11] It also serves to legitimate a hierarchy within the profession, in which professional elites have the most power and privilege. Junior professionals and apprentices, in aspiring to elite positions, are thereby encouraged to conform to the prevailing professional standards and practices.

Professional elites also use their knowledge to gain power within wider institutions, for example to influence government policy. Indeed, such influence is essential in establishing and maintaining professions via educational certification and state regulation. In their interaction with corporations and the state, both the professionals and their knowledge are inevitably politicised. To gain access and influence, professionals develop political skills, and mould their knowledge to political ends. At the same time, the advice of experts is used by corporate and bureaucratic elites to justify pre-decided courses of action. The esoteric knowledge of the professional legitimises the exclusion of outsiders from the decision-making process.[12]

The development of nuclear weapons policy provides an excellent example of the role of professional elites in high-level policy in the United States. Nuclear scientists claimed a policy role by virtue of their special knowledge. Groups within the state bureaucracy — such as the military and the federal executive — mobilised experts to support their own views and interests. All combined to exclude public involvement in the nuclear issue.[13]

What is the role of professional elites in dissent and its suppression? It is a complex one. On the one hand, professional elites favour freedom for professionals to determine their own conditions, and as a result oppose suppression from corporate and bureaucratic elites. On the other hand, professional elites tend to oppose dissent which threatens their own vested interests.

Professionals justify their own autonomy by invoking professional freedom, or more generally freedom of speech. Professionals often have opposed constraints on free speech imposed by corporate and bureaucratic elites, and asserted the right to "professional freedom". The political power basis for "professional freedom" is the establishment of a monopoly on a body of esoteric knowledge which is alleged to be necessary before activity defined as professional can take place. For example, "scientific freedom" is supposedly required so that the full fruits of scientific endeavour can be realised; in other words, since only scientists know what they are doing, they must be given freedom over their own conditions in order to maximise social benefits. One may be cynical in many cases about the necessity for professional freedom, but the struggle for such freedom has had positive spinoffs. Claims for social privilege are most effective when they are based on a universalistic appeal, and "freedom of speech" is such an appeal. Professionals often have supported the general principle of free speech in the course of expanding and protecting their own professional freedoms, especially when the threat to such freedom comes from outside the class of professionals.

In 1977, both Peter Rawlinson of the Zoology Department and Philip Keane of the Botany Department at La Trobe University spoke out about the dangers of cinnamon fungus in Victorian forests. This was an open challenge to the interests of the forest industries and the government forest bureaucracies. As a result of their statements, the Chairman of the Forests Commission of Victoria wrote and had hand-delivered at least 10 letters to top officials of La Trobe University complaining about the statements by Rawlinson and Keane. But this pressure to take action against them was strongly resisted by the La Trobe University officials concerned. The Chairman of the Forests Commission was informed that all Australian University Statutes are framed to allow staff to speak publicly on controversial issues, thereby preserving academic freedom.[14] This is an example of how at times professional elites may act as strong defenders of dissent and open opponents of suppression.

The rhetoric and reality of professional freedom do not always match. During the cold-war period, university officials at Harvard and Yale collaborated with the FBI in vetting applicants for positions. But the officials, perhaps aware of the discrepancy between this complicity and the professional norms publicly espoused by the university, opposed revealing this connection both at the time and indeed ever since.[15] Similarly, the use of security checks to screen applicants for university positions in Australia during the 1950s has never been publicised by the universities.[16]

The role of professional elites in opposing suppression is limited by their incorporation into wider power structures. Many professionals work for corporations and state bureaucracies, and while many still identify with goals of professional autonomy, others collaborate with corporate and bureaucratic elites. Just as there are captured bureaucracies, so there are captured professionals and captured professional groups. Most nuclear scientists and engineers are solid allies of the nuclear industry. Those who are most likely to support free speech are those most independent of the industry, in particular university theoretical nuclear scientists. For example, Richard Temple and F. P. Robotham, two leading opponents of nuclear power and uranium mining in Australia, fall generally into this category. The usual path taken by professional elites is to cooperate with corporate and bureaucratic elites, maintaining on overall power structure in which each set of elites has its own independent interests which only mildly conflict with the interests of other elites.

Sometimes serious conflicts do arise between elite groups. A situation of special importance arises when aristocratic, bureaucratic or corporate elites refuse to make room in the economic and political system for all the aspiring professionals. Some of the intellectuals who are thereby "marginalised" — not given an opportunity to rise above lowly bureaucratic or teaching posts, for example — may throw in their lot with revolutionary bodies. Such marginalised intellectuals have been the elites of many revolutionary parties. If a crisis occurs which paralyses the existing state apparatus, and which stimulates peasant and working class revolts, a revolutionary party led by marginalised intellectuals may be able to shape the creation of a new state.[17] This has happened for example in the French, Russian, Chinese, Mexican and Vietnamese revolutions. The result of such social revolutions is the creation of a much larger, more centralised and more powerful state apparatus. Under state socialism, corporate elites are destroyed, and the power of bureaucratic elites is greatly expanded.

To return to the role of professional elites in capitalist society: on the one hand they support rather generally professional freedom, but on the other they oppose challenges to their own professional control. For example, even though corporate elites at times complained to the Institute of Medical and Veterinary Science about statements by John Coulter, no serious action against him was immediately taken by IMVS elites. The precipitating factor in John Coulter's dismissal arose when he provided results of tests for mutagenicity of environmental chemicals directly to workers. This was a serious threat to professional elites in the IMVS, since it undercut their control over expert knowledge and its distribution. Cedric Pugh's basic sin was to question the governance of the South Australian Institute of Technology, and thus to challenge the power of professional-bureaucratic elites at SAIT. Similarly, Sidney Orr questioned the governance of the University of Tasmania and challenged the power of professional-bureaucratic elites there. The challenge by Michael Spautz to the competence of Alan Williams, a professor, was a challenge to control over assessments of academic competence by academic elites.[18] In each of these cases, professional elites opposed rather than supported dissent, because the dissent was a challenge from below to their own power and privilege rather than an exercise of freedom mainly threatening to other elites outside the profession.

Within professions, power is often maintained on the basis of empires of specialised knowledge, whether this is specialist medical treatment or knowledge of a certain country's history. Fundamental challenges to a speciality from within are few, since those who have invested time and effort to enter the area seldom wish to tear it down. (Small challenges within a speciality, to gain prestige and position, are much more common, though currying one's way to advancement remains the standard approach.) Attacks from outside the speciality, which may be mounted to expand other empires, are also resisted. For example, within universities interdisciplinary studies are often opposed, since most academics rise to positions of power via successful research and publication within a narrow specialisation. The Human Sciences Program at ANU has been opposed by both scientists and social scientists on the grounds that it is not rigorous enough. But the problem is not rigour but the threat to disciplinary empires which the interdisciplinary program poses.[19]

THE POPULIST CHALLENGE

Common to the perspective of all elites is an opposition to activities which potentially expand the avenues for participation by non-elites in decision-making or judgement. Such activity provides a common theme for many cases of suppression. Making criticisms on the inside is often accepted or tolerated. But "going public" is usually going too far. This is what antagonises elites more than anything. And since many workers in corporations, state bureaucracies and professions identify their own interests with those of the elites, dissidents who go public often have little support on the inside. But it is precisely because there is so much potential support on the outside — among the "public", those who do not have formal positions or special knowledge — that going public is so frowned upon. It is not surprising that subjects such as workers' control are seldom studied even by academics, that genuine popularisation (that goes beyond public relations) is often denigrated, that deprofessionalisation is never discussed, and that all insiders look down upon "amateurs".

To illustrate the differing interests of elites and the public, I will briefly discuss a quite diverse set of examples: thalidomide, Velikovsky, wind power and fluoridation.

Thalidomide[20]

Those with immediate vested interests in promoting the tranquilliser thalidomide were the corporate elites of Chemie Grünenthal, the West German company which developed and marketed the drug, and of companies in other countries licensed to market it. When evidence began surfacing about the harmful side-effects of thalidomide — initially, the deadening of nerve sensations in fingers and toes, sometimes irreversible — attempts were made by company elites to suppress criticism. Attempts were made to discredit critics, to block publications critical of the drug, to falsify unfavourable research findings and to pay for sympathetic studies to counteract criticisms. Most importantly, the company continued to advertise thalidomide as being completely safe, discounting the mounting evidence of risks.

Corporate elites from drug companies not marketing thalidomide had no particular interest in supporting a competitor's drug, but on the other hand they had no particular interest in opposing it. Any clampdown on drug marketing, or a scare about the hazards of drugs, would not have been in their immediate interests. Corporate elites by and large were not active in the thalidomide issue.

The relevant bureaucratic elites are found in government regulatory bodies. Many of these are classic "captured bureaucracies": servants of the pharmaceutical industry. In most countries, bureaucratic elites did little to restrain the marketing of thalidomide, until forced into action after the arousal of public concern. One exception was the United States, in which only limited trials occurred. Full-scale marketing of thalidomide was blocked there partly because one government scientist, Frances Kelsey, refused to bow to strong pressure, by the company marketing the drug, on her and on her Federal Drug Administration superiors to give the drug the go-ahead.

Professionals played several different roles in the thalidomide case. Several of the key figures in Grünenthal who promoted the drug were chemical researchers: professionals who were attuned to corporate goals. Most doctors and medical associations took no special interest in the drug, which was only another addition to the great number already in use. Many doctors readily prescribed thalidomide without much suspicion about the amazing claims made for it. No study has been done to determine what fraction of doctors took notice of side-effects of thalidomide, but it is known that some who noticed this became quite concerned and tried to publicise the danger. The attempts at suppression instigated by Grünenthal were aimed at such doctors. In any case, it was mostly doctors who were not especially prestigious who did the most to sound the alarm. Like the corporate elites and bureaucratic elites, most professional elites were slow to act on the issue.

What finally broke open the case was publicity. Media coverage, especially of thalidomide babies, stimulated public pressure that governments could not ignore. The thalidomide case illustrates well the important role of popular opinion and popular challenges in opposing the interests of elites. Dissidents — in this case mainly medical professionals and researchers — played a vital role in puncturing the top-level silence about the hazards of thalidomide and providing the basis for public awareness and concern. The long rearguard action by the companies to limit payouts to thalidomide victims was sustained partly because ongoing court action prevented full public discussion.

Velikovsky[21]

In 1950 the book *Worlds in Collision* by Immanuel Velikovsky was published. In this and later books, Velikovsky challenged orthodox views on the history of the earth and the solar system, suggesting that planetary near-collisions occurred within the past several thousand years. Velikovsky's ideas were vehemently opposed by portions of the scientific community, especially certain of its elites. Vicious reviews of *Worlds in Collision* were published by scientists who admitted that they had not read the book. Scientists mounted a campaign to boycott the book's publisher. A few supporters of Velikovsky lost their jobs. For many years any sympathetic mention of Velikovsky's ideas in the scientific literature was strictly taboo. Periodically, attacks on Velikovsky by various scientists were made; replies were not published.

The attack on Velikovsky's ideas certainly was not instigated by corporate elites, who had no particular interest in the reigning ideas in the history of ancient civilisations or of the solar system. Indeed, a few industrial scientists have provided some of the rare sympathetic discussions of Velikovsky's ideas by working scientists. Similarly to corporate elites, bureaucratic elites have had no particular involvement in the opposition to Velikovsky's ideas. This has come almost entirely from scientific elites.

Velikovsky's ideas are a challenge to scientific orthodoxy. Ideas which challenge the established framework of ideas and set of practices — the current scientific "paradigm" — are almost always resisted by working scientists.[22] Velikovsky's ideas are particularly threatening because they are interdisciplinary to an extraordinary degree, involving historical analysis with implications for astronomy, geology and anthropology as well as historical disciplines. Such interdisciplinary ideas challenge the exclusive judgement rights claimed by specialists over the development of academic disciplines. What natural scientists would want to allow historical analysis to be included as an essential part of their discipline? Eminent astronomers and astrophysicists such as Harlow Shapley and Donald H. Menzel were prominent in the early opposition to Velikovsky's ideas. They apparently considered any research work offering potential support to Velikovsky's ideas to be off limits. For example, in 1960 a Sydney University professor of physics, V. A. Bailey, then totally unaware of Velikovsky, published research on the existence of net electric charges on planetary bodies. Menzel asked Bailey to revoke his theory since it was hindering efforts by Menzel and others to discredit Velikovsky.

It is difficult to explain the response to Velikovsky solely as a consequence of the behavioural norms of the scientific community or of collective commitments to scientific knowledge frameworks. Part of the explanation seems to be the popularity of Velikovsky's ideas, and the fact that Velikovsky was not a professional scientist. Challenges to scientific orthodoxy from within the scientific community often can be ignored. At most they pose a threat to the internal power structure of science. But challenges to scientific orthodoxy from outsiders, from "amateurs", are another matter. Most are simply dismissed as being the work of "cranks", and are ignored. But when publicity is obtained, the power and prestige of scientists vis-a-vis the public is threatened. *Worlds in Collision* in 1950 was a best-seller, and the basic ideas were presented in *Reader's Digest*. Such popularity was a serious threat to the professional control over the ability and methods for proposing and publicising theories. Popular involvement of any sort in the assessment of scientific theories is not in the interests of scientific elites.

Some of the most vocal and consistent opponents of Velikovsky have been well-known popularisers of science, including Martin Gardner, Isaac Asimov and Carl Sagan. These same people, interestingly enough, have themselves been involved in highly speculative scientific theories or science fiction. It may well be that popularisers of science have a vested interest in the ultimate sacredness of professional science and its monopoly on acceptable ideas about nature. The popularisers can then act as interpreters for the professionals, communicating the sacred word to the awestruck masses. Outsiders like Velikovsky whose ideas are directly accessible to the public are as a result often reviled by popularisers.

Wind power

By use of a windmill or aerogenerator, the power of the wind can be used to pump water or generate electricity, for example. Wind power is a renewable energy source. It can be used for small, medium and large-scale power production, but even a large-scale aerogenerator produces only one thousandth the average power of a large coal or nuclear electricity generating unit. Wind power, like other small-scale renewable energy sources, is not especially attractive to large corporations or government bodies involved in producing electricity and electricity-generating equipment. Corporate and bureaucratic elites prefer energy sources which can be monopolised for profit or bureaucratic expansion. And professional elites prefer energy sources which require the attention of experts. Nuclear power requires nuclear scientists and engineers, massive corporate investment, and heavy government involvement. Wind power potentially could be controlled by these or similar elites, but it also has the potential for being used by individuals and small communities.

In Australia, dominant corporate interests have shown little interest in wind power. Small companies which might be involved in constructing components for aerogenerators are more likely to be enthusiastic. But such small businesses have little pull with bureaucratic elites who hold the greatest control over electricity supply. In Tasmania, the Hydro-Electric Commission prefers nothing but hydro-electric schemes, and is a political empire of its own within that state. In other states, electricity authorities mainly use coal for electricity production, supplemented by oil and gas. Most have not been very responsive to the idea of wind power, and have been reluctant to allow independent producers of wind power to gain a reasonable price for electricity provided to the grid.

Opposition to wind power is also found among most scientific and technological elites, such as the CSIRO Executive and Institute Directors and the members of the National Energy Advisory Committee. Elite scientists mostly prefer the centralised methods of electricity production which are favoured by corporate and bureaucratic elites. CSIRO elites since 1982 have gradually shut down all wind power research under their control.[23] Funds provided by the National Energy Research Development and Demonstration Council for wind power research and development have been small compared with traditional technologies.

Support for wind power has come partly from scientists and engineers in middle-ranking positions — such as Mark Diesendorf and Hugh Outhred — and also from a wide-ranging collection of supporters including many farmers, amateur technologists and people searching for an alternative lifestyle. For example, in 1983 there were over 500 subscribers to *South Wind*, the journal of the Australasian Wind Energy Association. The underlying support for campaigns by the most active promoters of wind power is provided by general community sympathy for renewable energy sources.

Fluoridation[24]

Some corporations have an interest in fluoridation. Aluminium companies are able to improve the image of their worst environmental pollutant, and manufacturers of sweets support fluoridation since it shifts attention away from the role of sugary foods in tooth decay. But the key forces behind implemented fluoridation programs have been the dental and medical professions, especially professionals in academia and in state bureaucracies. Fluoridation is a prime example of the medical approach of a "magic bullet" — a wonder drug or other professionally controlled intervention into the body — as a solution to health problems. Approaches involving redesign of the environment (better working conditions, different systems of transport), nutritional programs designed to prevent disease, the advocacy of home births, the promotion of exercise and restraints on the production and distribution of chemicals, are not favoured by the medical profession as a whole, since these and other similar approaches remove the necessity for a great deal of professional medical activity and undercut the monopolies on knowledge and treatment which benefit medical elites.

Only in some countries have dental and medical elites supported fluoridation. Europe is largely unfluoridated, while Australia and the US are two of the most highly fluoridated countries. In the 1940s and 1950s when fluoridation was first proposed and introduced experimentally, a few individual dentists and other figures promoted fluoridation and tried to mobilise professional and state support for their position. The professions as a whole have generally fallen in line with whatever stance the professional elites have adopted, and this usually reflects the prevalence of actual fluoridation in a particular country.

To push fluoridation in the face of potential or actual popular resistance, the medical-dental strategy has been to claim that the benefits of fluoridation, and the lack of risks, have been scientifically proven beyond dispute. If this is the case, then opposition can only come from "irrational" individuals and groups, and in heavily fluoridated countries this is how opponents of fluoridation are painted.

One problem with this strategy is that disagreement with fluoridation on scientific grounds is quite possible: the scale of benefits can be disputed, and risks shown to exist for some people. But in fluoridated countries this disagreement has been almost completely suppressed from the standard medical-dental literature. A picture of scientific unanimity is presented to the public and to state elites. In addition a fair bit of unabashed promotion of fluoridation goes on.

As a result, most of the overt opposition to fluoridation has come from citizen groups who, due to the lack of scientific opposition, latch on to various arguments. Some of these lack any basis, such as the claim made by some United States opponents that fluoridation is a communist plot. More substantial arguments include the medical-ethical argument that people should not be exposed without their consent to uncontrolled dosages of a medication, in this case fluoride, and the nutritional argument that it would be healthier and safer to promote better general diet to prevent tooth decay rather than to use a magic bullet to do this. And, underlying much of the opposition to fluoridation, there seems to be an opposition to the uncontrolled impositions of the medical-dental elites themselves.

Conclusion

The cases of thalidomide, Velikovsky, wind power and fluoridation show that opposition to dissenting views can come primarily from either corporate, bureaucratic or professional elites, or from a complex mixture of them. In all these cases, the ultimate source of opposition to elite interests lies in some portion of the community, among the non-elites. The mobilisation of this reservoir of potential opposition is often aided by action by concerned insiders, such as doctors, scientists or academics. Usually these insiders occupy low or middle-level positions, or exist on the fringe of the area in question. Suppression is usually aimed at restraining the activities of these crucial people who work within corporations, state bureaucracies or professions, and yet are willing to speak up against the interests of elites in these areas. Suppression thus is a telling symptom of the distribution of power in society.

Acknowledgements

Useful comments on a draft of this chapter were provided by Ann Baker, Mark Diesendorf, Clyde Manwell, Cedric Pugh and Ian Watson.

References

1. This is a standard idea in the sociology of knowledge. See for example Peter L. Berger and Thomas Luckmann, *The Social Construction of Reality* (Garden City, New York: Doubleday, 1966).

2. On ideas as tools see Barry Barnes, *Interests and the Growth of Knowledge* (London: Routledge and Kegan Paul, 1977).

3. Many examples of the connections between science advisers and industry are given in Joel Primack and Frank von Hippel, *Advice and Dissent: Scientists in the Political Arena* (New York: Basic Books, 1974), and Phillip M. Boffey, *The Brain Bank of America: An Inquiry into the Politics of Science* (New York: McGraw-Hill, 1975).

4. Documentation for the examples from forestry here are provided in Brian Martin, "The scientific straightjacket: the power structure of science and the suppression of environmental scholarship", *Ecologist*, vol. 11, no. 1, January–February 1981, pp. 33–43, from which portions of the text here are directly taken.

5. See the chapter "Mutagens and Managers", on the Coulter case.

6. Deena Weinstein, *Bureaucratic Opposition: Challenging Abuses at the Workplace* (New York: Pergamon, 1979). The next several paragraphs draw on Weinstein's analysis.

7. Lawrence B. Radine, *The Taming of the Troops: Social Control in the United States Army* (Westport, Connecticut: Greenwood Press, 1977).

8. Leslie J. Freeman, *Nuclear Witnesses: Insiders Speak Out* (New York: Norton, 1981).

9. Barbara and John Ehrenreich, "The professional-managerial class", in: Pat Walker (ed.), *Between Labour and Capital* (Brighton: Harvester, 1979), pp. 5–45; Alvin W. Gouldner, *The Future of Intellectuals and the Rise of the New Class* (London: Macmillan, 1979); George Konrád and Ivan Szelényi, *The Intellectuals on the Road to Class Power* (Brighton: Harvester, 1979).

10. Eliot Freidson, *Professional Dominance: The Social Structure of Medical Care* (New York: Atherton, 1970); Eliot Freidson, *Doctoring Together: A Study of Professional Social Control* (New York: Elsevier, 1975).

11. On the political use of expertise to establish professional prerogatives, see for example Magali Sarfatti Larson, *The Rise of Professionalism: A Sociological Analysis* (Berkeley: University of California Press, 1977) and Norbert Elias, Herminio Martins and Richard Whitley (eds), *Scientific Establishments and Hierarchies* (Dordrecht: D. Reidel, 1982). Unfortunately most such analyses are written in a form which is accessible mainly to academic social scientists.

12. Hans J. Morgenthau, *Science: Servant or Master?* (New York: New American Library, 1972).

13. See for example Robert Gilpin, *American Scientists and Nuclear Weapons Policy* (Princeton: Princeton University Press, 1962); Eugene B. Skolnikoff, *Science, Technology, and American Foreign Policy* (Cambridge, Massachusetts: MIT Press, 1967).

14. See note 4 above.

15. Sigmund Diamond, "The arrangement: the FBI and Harvard University in the McCarthy period", in Athan G. Theoharis (ed.), *Beyond the Hiss Case: The FBI, Congress, and the Cold War* (Philadelphia: Temple University Press, 1982), pp. 341–71.

16. R. M. Hartwell, letter, *Vestes*, vol. 3, no. 4, December 1960, p. 51.

17. Theda Skocpol, *States and Social Revolutions* (Cambridge: Cambridge University Press, 1979).

18. See the chapters in this volume on the Coulter, Pugh and Orr cases, and reference to the Spautz case in the chapter "Archives of Suppression".

19. See reference to the Human Sciences Program in the chapter "Archives of Suppression".

20. Henning Sjöström and Robert Nilsson, *Thalidomide and the Power of the Drug Companies* (Harmondsworth: Penguin, 1972); The Insight Team of *The Sunday Times* (Phillip Knightley, Harold Evans, Elaine Potter and Marjorie Wallace), *Suffer the Children: The Story of Thalidomide* (London: André Deutsch, 1979).

21. Alfred de Grazia (ed.), *The Velikovsky Affair* (London: Sidgwick and Jackson, 1966); the journals *Pensée* and *Kronos*; Robert McAulay, "Velikovsky and the infrastructure of science: the metaphysics of a close encounter", *Theory and Society*, vol. 6, 1978, pp. 313–42; C. Leroy Ellenberger, "Heretics, dogmatists and science's reception of new ideas", *Kronos*, vol. 4, summer 1979, pp. 60–74; Brian Martin, "The determinants of scientific behaviour", *Society for Interdisciplinary Studies Review*, vol. 2, no. 4, 1978, pp. 112–18.

22. The classic work here is Thomas Kuhn, *The Structure of Scientific Revolutions* (Chicago: University of Chicago Press, 1970).

23. Neville Jones, Hugh Outhred and Alan Langworthy, letter, *Search*, vol. 14, nos 11–12, December 1983/January 1984, pp. 303–4

24. On the scientific criticism of fluoridation, see P. R. N. Sutton, *Fluoridation: Errors and Omissions in Experimental Trials* (Melbourne: Melbourne University Press, 1960); George L. Waldbott (with Albert W. Burgstahler and H. Lewis McKinney), *Fluoridation: The Great Dilemma* (Lawrence, Kansas: Coronado Press, 1978); Mark Diesendorf, "Is there a scientific basis for fluoridation?", *Community Health Studies*, vol. 4, no. 3, 1980, pp. 224–30. On suppression of evidence and individuals critical of fluoridation, see for example Geoffrey E. Smith, "Fluoride: the frightening facts", *Simply Living*, vol. 2, no. 1, 1983, pp. 29–36, and vol. 2, no. 2, 1984, pp. 112–15. On the politics of fluoridation, see Wendy Varney, *Fluoridation: A Case to Answer* (Sydney: Hale and Iremonger, to be published).

WHO LISTENS WHEN WOMEN SPEAK? THE STRUGGLE FOR FEMINIST CRITIQUE IN UNIVERSITIES

Cheryl Hannah

Suppression of intellectual dissent sometimes occurs in obvious and dramatic ways, such as a blocking of critical publications or sacking dissidents. These cases are important, but they may divert attention from even more important aspects of suppression: the systematic downgrading or denial of whole areas of thought and action. If the systematic suppression is highly effective, then overt suppression will seldom be required. One of the areas which has been suppressed in this way is feminist critique.

Feminism is a wide, diverse body of thought and political action. I define feminism here as the theoretical critique of patriarchy and the action being taken by women to remove male domination from their work and personal lives.[1] Feminism is not a new phenomenon, rather a new formulation of an old problem: how to prevent the power and integrity of women being denied or dismissed by men.[2]

Feminist critique, at the intellectual level, encompasses a number of challenges to established ideas, including insights into the nature of power and hierarchy, analysis of the importance of the gender[3] division of labour, the division between public and private, and a re-valuing of women's experience. Feminist critique is linked to feminist political practice, which includes struggles for equal opportunity, struggles against male domination over reproduction and women's sexuality, and struggles for a more just society.

Within universities, feminism has presented a challenge both to established ideas and to the structures of power, including staff control over curriculum and students and administrative control over job opportunities. It is not surprising then that feminist theory and action has been greeted with opposition, opposition both to the feminist critique of dominant intellectual frameworks in academia, and opposition to the advancement of feminist scholars within academia.

My aim here is to describe the structural nature of the suppression of feminist thought in universities, with some examples of strategies used to overcome it. It is important to note that I am concerned primarily with suppression of *feminist thought*, not with discrimination against and suppression of women because they are women. This latter phenomenon, though highly important, is peripheral to my concern here.

Also, I do not intend to catalogue individual struggles for feminist studies in particular universities, but only to mention a few such cases in passing. My primary focus will be the silence which has surrounded the work and ideas of feminists.

As well as including analysis and documentation of suppression of feminist critique, this account also includes many comments based on my personal experiences and perspectives because this is the only authentic voice in which I can speak. I am part of the process I am attempting to understand, not an independent anthropologist from another galaxy.

ORIGINS OF THE CONTEMPORARY FEMINIST CHALLENGE

It was not until my first few weeks of women's studies, lectures and tutorials at the Australian National University in 1981 that I realised the full impact of Simone de Beauvoir's observation[4] that men describe the world from their own point of view, which they confuse with absolute truth. I was outraged when I thought about my earlier studies at the same university. Apart from the few famous queens, wives, saints and whores, women had rarely been mentioned in the history and political science courses I had been taught a decade before. No serious attention had been paid to the concerns of *half* the humanity talked about in the humanities.

On reflection, even more disturbing than the absence of women's concerns and contributions was my uncritical acceptance of such scholarship as adequate. During my two years of Women's Studies I often pondered the paradox that the questions generated by a feminist critique were needed to discover that the central concerns of feminism were being ignored in the first place. It became clear to me that most of the analytic tools I had taken for granted in the social sciences were very inadequate since they did not incorporate a feminist critique.

When I, and many other women students like me, entered university in the early 1970s we were mainly aware that we were privileged to be there. Any unease we felt as women in an overwhelmingly male environment was repressed or dismissed, and attributed to our personal inadequacy rather than the environment. The absence of women's writing or anything which could be definitely identified as a women's perspective reinforced the ambient androcentric concerns of the university. Without any guidance or encouragement to explore women's work it was hard to sustain more than a fleeting glimpse of what was missing.

Universities in Australia expanded in both size and number during the post-war period. The legacy of the English tertiary system with its classical traditions and conservative outlook shaped the form of Australian academic life. Until the 1960s, the institutions remained the province of the wealthy and the few exceptionally gifted students who received government bursaries. The values enshrined by the institutions were those of the establishment they supported. The almost total absence of women both as teachers and students reflected the absence of women in significant numbers from any public sphere of life. It was taken to be the natural order of things and appeared to need no comment.[5]

Despite their rapid expansion through the 1960s, Australian universities seemed to manage to contain any challenges to established authority. The uprisings of student radicalism on Australian campuses were mild when compared with their American or French contemporaries. A wider cross-section of Australian youth was in attendance at university than ever before but the students did not, in general, bring much awareness of class politics into their classrooms. This is significant when trying to understand why women had so little awareness of the lack of feminist critique in their studies: even the more established radical critiques such as Marxism were ignored.

Towards the end of the 1960s, articulate, energetic women outside Australia were rediscovering their ability to join forces to claim better working conditions and personal rights for themselves as women. Some of their writings and accounts of their political action began to filter into the newspapers, magazines, bookshelves and discussion groups of Australian women. The early days of Australian Women's Liberation had begun.

Gradually universities found themselves confronted by feminists within and without who were demanding that women's views should be listened to and accommodated. Many women realised that they were no longer prepared to accept the privilege of a tertiary education at the price of silence about themselves. They began to speak out.

FEMINIST CRITIQUE

The second wave of feminist theorising began with the publication of *The Feminine Mystique* by Betty Friedan in 1963, and the further development of some of the same ideas in the 1970s by Kate Millet and Shulamith Firestone.[6] They, together with other women writers, articulated the unease of women in western societies about the gulf between what they had been taught from birth that they were supposed to feel and what they actually knew to be their experience.

Friedan and others argued that males and females were artificially differentiated from birth onwards by a series of pressures from family, school, church, workplace and other agencies of socialisation. These theories of gender socialisation suggested that while boys were being taught to be rational, logical and objective and to repress their feelings, the girls were learning to cultivate their emotions: to be directed towards the care of others and to ignore their facility to reason. Boys were being prepared for life-long occupations in the public domain — girls for immersion in the unpaid labour of domestic service, where child-bearing and child-rearing would constitute their only true vocation.

The new feminist theorists were drawing on the analysis of other women before them, women like Mary Wollstonecraft and Simone de Beauvoir[7], in trying to account for the position of women as "other". They sought to name the process by which women are made object, becoming a subject only by reflection on the face of the male mirror. They sought to explain why women were so vilified when they dared to reject their image on the face of patriarchy.[8] What followed the publication of their ideas was an explosion in thinking, writing and talking and publishing[9] on the cultural, social, historical, psychological, philosophical and anthropological condition of women.

The formulation and development of feminist perspectives has led to insights and challenges involving many areas of life, including personal self-image, the division of labour, child-rearing and macro-political practice. Here I am mainly concerned with the feminist critique of areas of scholarship and ideas.

The feminist demands were not new[10] but they were based on claims which had been so successfully suppressed in the past that it seemed to the women making them that they were new. They challenged the way in which the course content of the traditional disciplines was determined. Feminist scholars began to name the previously unnamed gaps in the orthodox descriptions of the world.[11] Some of these areas included:

rediscovery and re-examination of the role of women in history;

the role of women's labour, both domestic and public, in economic production;

the importance of gender socialisation;

the importance of gender in interpersonal power relations;

the gender division of labour;

the link between gender, violence and war;

the masculine formation of the deep structure of language;

the connection between masculinity and the notion of scientific objectivity;

the role of social hierarchies and patterns of domination in the creation and maintenance of ideologies;

the misogynist bias in medical research and practice;

the role of gender stereotypes in media and the arts;

the role of social institutions such as marriage in the maintenance of male domination;

the importance of concepts such as the "family wage" in the economic oppression of women;

the use of rape and sexual harassment in social power relations between men and women.[12]

From this list it should be clear that feminism has enormous potential implications for academic disciplines, ranging from philosophy and psychology to medicine and law. Furthermore, feminist analysis by its nature is trans-disciplinary because the established methods of inquiry do not fit with women's experience of the world. Thus feminist analysis threatens to break down barriers between many of the intellectual empires of academia. This is profoundly shocking to some of the traditional owners of knowledge.

When, for example, feminist anthropologists began questioning male views of their subject cultures, began re-interpreting geographical, historical and linguistic material on the basis of their perceptions as women, whole areas of anthropological study were severely shaken.[13] The boundaries between disciplines were no longer preserved as sacrosanct limits between separate "states" of knowledge to be defended, but rather as frontiers on a whole new landscape waiting to be traversed.[14]

Feminism thus provides a threat not only to established ideas and the prestige and self-image of their promoters and adherents, but also to the academic power structure which is built on hierarchy and the intellectual division of labour.

Is it any wonder that the academic response to feminist critique has largely been one of silence? This is the essence of the suppression of feminist critique.

Appropriately, feminism provides its own explanation of this suppression, in the theory of patriarchy.

PATRIARCHY AND THE RESISTANCE TO FEMINIST CRITIQUE

Heidi Hartmann defines patriarchy as

a set of social relations between men, which have a material base, and which, though hierarchical, establish or create interdependence and solidarity among men that enable them to dominate women. Though patriarchy is hierarchical and men of different classes, races, or ethnic groups have different places in the patriarchy, they are also united in their shared relationship of dominance over their women; they are dependent on each other to maintain that domination... in the hierarchy of patriarchy, all men, whatever their rank in the patriarchy, are bought off by being able to control at least some women.[15]

The university exhibits several features which are characteristic of patriarchy. First, most of the key decision-making positions are controlled by men, who have a vested interest in preventing collective challenges to their positions. Women overwhelmingly occupy subordinate positions, as tutors, research assistants, secretaries, typists and cleaners. Second, the university is built around the narrow-track, full-time career, which strongly favours men. Those who take breaks in their career for childbirth and child-rearing, or who start their career late or prefer to work part-time, have little chance of receiving academic preferment. Many men receive valuable career support from their wives, whose subordination in this is integral to the success of their husbands.[16] Third, the ethos of academic life is built around career competition, intellectual aggressiveness and emotional aloofness, which is typically masculine behaviour, rather than the feminine characteristics of cooperation and emotional support. Finally, female staff and students are sexually exploited by many academic men.

Contrary to these patriarchal features, the male self-image of academia is one of fair assessment of scholarly contributions and value-free intellectual endeavour. But the use of the terms "value-free" and "objective" obscures the hidden agenda of the institution. If, as I have suggested, the structure of the university itself is a snapshot of patriarchy, then it is extremely difficult to see how those with a vested interest in maintaining the structure can claim to know how to evaluate knowledge objectively. It is more than just an absence of women in the institution, it is a fundamental perception by men of differences between themselves and women. Simone de Beauvoir described it as being reduced to the status of the second sex. She says,

> just as for the ancients there was an absolute vertical with reference to which the oblique was defined, so there is an absolute human-type, the masculine...Thus humanity is male and man defines woman not as herself but as relative to him; she is not regarded as an autonomous being...she is defined and differentiated with reference to man and not he with reference to her; she is incidental, the inessential as opposed to the essential. He is the subject, he is the Absolute — she is the other.[17]

The belief, however, that universities are places of sophisticated, objective evaluation of knowledge is fundamental to the careers and self-esteem of the majority of the inmates. To find themselves confronted by a group of women proclaiming their right to focus on previously submerged areas was unpleasant, even frightening. In the words of Dale Spender,

> Patriarchy requires that any conceptualization of the world in which men and their power are a central problem should become invisible and unreal. How could patriarchy afford to accept that men were a serious social problem, to gather together what women have said on the subject and make it the substance of the educational curriculum, to treat women's versions of men with respect, and to discuss at length with impartiality the origins of male power and the means by which it is maintained?...Groups in power validate themselves by reference to those out of power — which they dismiss as *wrong* — and justify their own power in the process...[18]

The oppression of women and the suppression of feminist critique are different faces of the same beast. As Spender identifies, for women to really be listened to requires men to admit that their world view is inadequate in some fundamental aspects. Theory which addresses the inadequacy, if it is tolerated or encouraged, must eventually challenge the oppression also. Such a challenge would be uncomfortable and ultimately dangerous to the power monopoly of the dominant gender. Rather than engage in a systematic, rigorous debate leading to fundamental change in intellectual and political frameworks, the serious attempts to promote feminist critique were opposed. The implications of the deeply embedded misogyny of patriarchy need to be understood if any sense is to be made of the fear often associated with the idea of a "feminist".

It is this understanding which is necessary when women are called upon to endure the litany of sexist jokes which inevitably accompany any attempt to initiate a thoughtful discussion of the need for feminist critique amongst androcentric academics. Women who refuse to join in the laughter usually evoke the hostile charge of being "humourless feminists", adding insult to injury.

Not all women within universities were pleased about the feminist challenge. Having been trained for years to see the world through "masculine" eyes they were as disturbed as their male colleagues at the prospect of unworthy women receiving attention or recognition. Many of those who had been successful in achieving the male standard for themselves were even more reluctant to admit the validity of feminist perspectives.[19] Any challenge to the male hierarchy was a challenge to the system they had done well in, and after all, if they had done well then surely other women could if they chose to. While such a view ignores the benefit bestowed upon some women by virtue of their birth or special opportunity, it does not begin to explain the enormous disparity between the numbers of successful males and females at every level in the hierarchy.[20]

One of the ways used to justify exclusion of feminist critique was on the basis of its alleged emotionality and lack of objectivity:

Those who try to put forward an alternative to patriarchy and male values, when the male values are the basis of the society and men's opinions the very standard of reasonableness and veracity, are being *extremist* and acting as *politicos*. They too can be dismissed as subversive, or stupid, or sick.[21]

This charge essentially reflects the adherence to the notion of "objectivity" which in practice has meant unquestioning acceptance of the political and intellectual status quo. Admittedly, much feminist writing has been angry and polemical. Many people have found it very threatening. Some male academics have been indignant that such "ratbaggery" should try to pass itself off as serious theory-making. But to dismiss its importance as theory because it first appeared couched in highly emotional terms is to misunderstand the significance of theory which is created in active struggle.

Early feminist writing in England, America and Australia informed the groups of women who gathered together spontaneously in what became known as the Women's Liberation Movement (WLM). The Movement actively encouraged women to discuss and debate the issues which affected their lives and to raise their consciousness.[22] The early searching discussion of WLM groups played an important role in fostering personal skills and political determination. The interplay of theoretical ideas and group activity strengthened the belief of the participants in themselves and in the justness of their complaints.

Many of the women active in WLM consciousness-raising groups were studying or teaching in universities. Their determination to have feminism treated seriously carried over into their academic lives.[23]

The clamour of their demands was in part a response to the profound silence about women which was characteristic of the traditional disciplines. Women who agitated to change the content of courses quickly realised that changes in academic approach were needed as well. To add a few lectures about women to the existing courses, or even a few courses within a whole faculty, would mean taking the "add women and stir" approach. It might have livened up the existing mixture but feminists understood that the inclusion of women in course content should be more than a token gesture or for mere entertainment value. A feminist critique would need to address the structure and process of scholarship as much, or more, than content. It would demand a thoroughgoing re-examination of the whole enterprise.

How could feminist perspectives be introduced into existing disciplines? Because most university administrators were reluctant to listen to feminist demands and even more unwilling to do anything substantial about them, the task has fallen to feminist academics — mostly women, and a very few men, sympathetic to the claims of feminism.

Those secure or brave enough to risk publicising their feminist re-interpretations from within their disciplines provide a valuable opportunity for their students to explore a feminist critique. What might be described as an "osmosis effect" may operate: feminist ideas may be pulled from one course to another because students transfer the strength of the critique away from its original location.

However powerful such internal critique might be, it remains vulnerable because of the nature of the hierarchy mentioned earlier. Women who are admitted to the hierarchy are generally clustered at the lower, less secure levels as a matter of course.[24] Job insecurity may silence or modify the scholarship of women within the institutions even though they are aware that their academic integrity is compromised by such silence.

A woman anthropologist[25] of my acquaintance at another university, who dared to inject gender as a variable to radicalise her analysis of cultural development, encouraged (empowered) a number of her students to challenge what they were being taught in political science and sociology courses at the same institution because it failed to take account of the differences that the inclusion of gender would make to the analysis. Needless to say the anthropologist the students kept citing as their authority for the critique did not earn herself any favour with her male colleagues in other departments who regarded her "militancy" with abhorrence. They were extremely hostile to the presence of one feminist theoretician in their ranks who encouraged her students to awaken to patriarchy.

As there is much more discussion of feminism and women's history on the campuses around Australia in classrooms, student newspapers, collectives of women activists and on graffiti-sprayed walls, it is much harder for the hierarchy to completely contain or suppress the ideas generated by such discussion.

WOMEN'S STUDIES

Very few university course administrators were prepared to allow feminist critique to be included in the teaching of the traditional disciplines. Such a transformation would require teachers of the traditional disciplines to confront their own sexism and to adopt an open mind on the challenges to their accepted beliefs which feminist theory would be bound to throw up. If feminism were to be taken seriously, the very carefully conserved boundaries between the traditional disciplines would be called into question. Such challenges would threaten both the intellectual self-image and the disciplinary power base of traditional academics.

But in the face of feminist demands, opposition to any teaching at all of feminist critique was an unacceptably overt form of suppression. Those in universities who opposed the feminist demands laid themselves open to the charge of being intolerant, illiberal and unscholarly because they were unwilling to allow an area of ideas to be debated. Rather than be seen to be opposed to the discussion of important ideas, many members of the university hierarchies sought a compromise. They would allow the ideas to be explored as long as they were kept within certain limits. Thus, in many cases, feminist demands were accommodated by the establishment of small programs or area studies dedicated to women's studies[26], within a particular department of an existing discipline, as at ANU and Flinders.

Although certainly far better than nothing, such programs do have disadvantages. First, they may serve to reinforce the common perception of feminism as a marginal concern if their establishment excuses the wider academic curriculum from addressing the questions of feminism. It was sobering to hear women who attended the "Feminism and Academics" workshop at the third Women and Labour Conference in Adelaide in 1982 say that it was probably the perception of feminism as a peculiar, unorthodox ideological phenomenon which would prove to be of transient appeal to students that contributed to the willingness of university boards and departments to accept women's studies programs in the first place.

Second, women's studies programs are more readily suppressed than the incorporation of a feminist perspective in a range of established disciplines if that teaching in the disciplines is done seriously and in good faith. As long as the teaching of feminism remains dependent upon the existence of small, often understaffed, isolated programs then it remains vulnerable to being silenced with minimal disruption to the administration of the wider academic community. Students and teachers involved in women's studies programs have found that they need to be continually alert. Experience at both ANU and Flinders has proved that those engaged in analysing patriarchy are foolish to trust patriarchal institutions to deal generously with them.

To protect themselves from arbitrary closure, women's studies programs need to forge solid links with other courses in other departments. Developing a network of interdependencies with courses in related areas is difficult to achieve because of limited staffing and the innate resistance of most university teachers to interdisciplinary courses. But where it has been tried it has become a source of great strength to the women's studies programs.

Although women's studies programs have the disadvantages of potential marginality and vulnerability, these are outweighed by the advantage of actually having a part of academic discourse actively using and developing a feminist critique. Women's studies courses offer a place of support and self-validation for their women students which has proved to be crucially important in combating the wider academic silence about women. The women involved in one of the most successful of the early women's studies programs, the Bristol Women's Studies Group[27], noted that as the women became confident in thinking through concepts related to their own experience as women, they also became much more confident in speaking out and participating in other areas of their academic studies. Their battles to have a feminist analysis of traditional approaches considered legitimate were strengthened by their knowledge that at least one area of the academic discourse accepted such inquiry.

My own experience in the program at ANU bears out these observations. I have found that the women who grasped the feminist critique of psychology or learned to ask new questions about the position of women in a sociological framework inside the course work of women's studies were much more confident and better equipped to tackle the traditional content back in the psychology or sociology departments. They could not so easily be dismissed as eccentric individuals by the traditional disciplines because they could point to the legitimacy of their questions from women's studies. Even students not actually involved in the program themselves felt more confident in challenging the orthodoxies of their departments because they knew the challenge could be supported from at least one other area of inquiry in the university.

From overseas experience in women's studies courses it appears that the longer they run the stronger they become in terms of student participation, enthusiasm and commitment. However, they also encounter increased hostility from some established areas because of the discomforting nature of their endeavours.

One example of such resistance has concerned the credentialling of women who have sought to lecture and tutor in women's studies programs. Often the agitation to establish a program has come from one or two women who were able to draw on outside support and student demand. Their attempts to set up a functioning course using feminist critique may be interpreted by some women as attempts to get permanent jobs ahead of others "better" qualified in traditional terms.

The difficulty here is that many of those who have credentials acceptable to the establishment may be too well trained in orthodox modes of analysis to be able to meet the requirements of transdisciplinary thinking and innovative teaching to do the new studies justice, while those who are sufficiently radical are unlikely to have achieved the credentials normally required to teach at university level. Women's studies programs as a result may be caught between conflicting expectations by established women scholars and feminist activists.

Out of those few[28] women who have succeeded in the eyes of their own discipline, many seem oblivious to the structural suppression of feminist demands. These women may express the most hostile opposition towards those they perceive as "unqualified" entering their ranks.

Just as it is difficult for some women within the system to accept that less qualified women are capable or suitable to analyse patriarchy, it is difficult for many women who have worked hard for women's liberation outside of universities to accept that there is any real benefit to be gained from setting up women's studies courses within such institutions. They regard the energy invested in establishing a women's studies program as better spent improving the situation of women in the wider society. This may underestimate the particular advantage of locating feminist struggle in a university. Kathy Ferguson summed up the advantage quite succinctly when she noted:

> Sometimes (certainly not always) women's studies programs can maintain a commitment to radical, rather than liberal, feminism. Because the members provide a support structure for one another and because as a group they are providing a valuable resource to the university . . . they can disguise their radicalism externally and maintain it internally . . .[29]

The anxiety of some concerned feminists outside the university about the possibility of feminist critique being diluted or sold out in universities is valid. Those charged with the responsibility of teaching and administering women's studies programs need to be constantly vigilant about the degree of compromise they make with the keepers of the hierarchy. As Ferguson goes on to note

> . . . the requirements of organizational survival are likely to penetrate into the program itself and endanger the alternative values and processes that insurgents seek to maintain.[30]

Feminists inside the university system cannot afford to allow the evolution of feminist critique and theory-making to become too remote from the political action of other feminists.

Like other unorthodox critiques — Marxism[31], political economy, radical ecology — feminist theory draws strength from the activities of its committed practitioners outside the universities. The political action taken by women on issues that concern them and their children has taught feminists the importance of continually reviewing the processes of their actions while striving for their goals. Feminists know that the *personal is political* and are therefore reluctant to make artificial divisions between feminist theory and practice. Inevitably, tensions have arisen at times between the women committed to the frontline of feminist action and those who are more distanced from the action but actively thinking about it.

The women who seek to support women who have been raped, those who work for the provision of shelter for women who are the victims of domestic violence, and those who endeavour to provide alternative, woman-centred health care as cheaply as possible have important things to say about the way that feminist theory interacts with the everyday lives of women from diverse class and ethnic backgrounds.

In the efforts to establish viable women's studies programs it has been important for the women involved not to regard the lives of the women they seek to record, research and explain as something divorced from themselves as inquirers after knowledge. For example, a better understanding of the power relations which underlie rape and domestic violence is an important subject for feminist study. Such study would probably include observing the lives of women who are already vulnerable. The study would need to be conducted very sensitively in order not to contribute to accusations of academic exploitation and possibly even voyeurism, thereby risking alienating women from the very understanding it sought to promote. The charge of "voyeurism" springs from the common perceptions of academics as watchers of other people, not doers. Both the elitism and the intellectual orientation of university feminism is offensive to many activists of the women's movement.

While feminist activists may criticise women's studies programs for their lack of contribution to the feminist struggle, traditional academics may perceive the programs as radical and threatening. Even the existence of a separate program, once it is established, can be seen as a threat to other areas. The approach of the program at Flinders to assessment and to power sharing between teachers and students was deemed too radical by many of the other courses. Flinders' women's studies program emphasised the need for students to examine their personal lives and happiness as a part of understanding how they learned and how they decided what they wanted to learn.[32] Much of the later hostility towards the program, which undermined its credibility, probably reflected the unease about the challenges the program presented not just to traditional content but also to traditional methods within the university.

At ANU, the demands for a separate course focusing on the concerns and contributions of women was a part of more general demands for better teacher accountability and more appropriate forms of assessment across the whole of ANU. During the "Education Campaigns" of 1974–5 the needs of students were brought to the attention of the university hierarchy in a more forceful way than ever before.

One response to threatening programs within the university is suppression. This can take the form of limiting resources, denying flexibility in staffing and curriculum, and denigration of the intellectual content of the subject matter. The difficulties of the programs may even then, in typical scapegoating fashion, be blamed on internal tensions within the programs. The situation at Flinders, where staffing and funding difficulties led to the program being dismembered, serves as an excellent example of this process. The program at ANU has fared much better but there were some very shaky moments in 1983 when it appeared that the staff of two would be reduced by 50 per cent.

CONCLUSION

The feminist critique of patriarchy and of orthodox disciplinary knowledge provides women with a source of strength. But, unless the critique is available to draw on and *to transmit to the next generation of women* then it is in danger of lapsing once more into a deafening silence. In male-dominated society where men are still largely able to control knowledge, they are always in a position to deprive women of this source of strength. If they are able to assert that it is masculine experience which is to be valued, and to insist that it has always been this way[33], then any gains made by individual feminists or women's studies courses in this generation may be lost to the next. This is partly how patriarchy has sustained itself, and those who would seek to overthrow patriarchy forget this at their peril.

Certainly, significant gains have been made over the past two decades. The suppression of feminist theory has neither been complete nor automatic. The concerns of feminists have not been so readily ruled out-of-order or placed at the periphery of academic affairs. Neither have they remained isolated from the claims for justice proposed by other minority consciousness groups. However, the acceptance of the claims central to a feminist critique are still a long way from being realised in universities.

Consider the following scenario: a group of women are working collectively and non-hierarchically on a piece of research which reflects their perceptions of themselves as women. They are using language which in its very structure affirms them as equal with men. The content of their research is not considered exceptional or trivial if it is drawn from the domestic sphere. When it is finished their contribution to scholarship is treated with complete seriousness by other male academics who then cite it in their own publications without hesitation. If such a description sounds far-fetched it is a measure of how hard the feminist critique still has to battle to move from the margins of academic discourse to an accepted place in the methodologies of the disciplines within the universities.

The contributors to the critique itself have come a long way since the early days of WLM writings. All around the world there is now a formidable and rapidly expanding collection of books being published under the general heading "women's studies". The theories, descriptions and explorations undertaken by the pioneering works of second-wave feminism have been subjected to vigorous, creative analysis by later feminist writers.[34] There now exists a substantial body of core literature relating feminist critique to sociology, history, anthropology, geography, psychology, medicine, economics, political science, philosophy and linguistics.

It is less and less excusable for the universities to ignore or trivialise this large and growing body of thought, which is the basis of feminist critique. An increasing number of academic decision-makers have accepted that there is a profound gap in the evaluation of knowledge so long as no specific attention is paid to women's concerns. They have begun programs to address the issues.

The public interest outside the universities has slowly begun to recognise the structural inequality of women and this has provided the stimulus behind official moves towards remedying some of the inequality.[35] University hierarchies are subject to some of the same pressures as state bureaucracies and so general interest in equal employment opportunities has stimulated a climate of debate over the place of women in university, which fosters the increased demand for the inclusion of feminist critique to explain the mechanisms which underlie the inequalities.

In the universities, where at least lip service is paid to the belief in the freedom to pursue knowledge fearlessly, there is a chance for women to have their concerns and contributions taken seriously. The suppression of their demands can never be far away, however, while the majority of the most powerful members of the hierarchy continue to view women as *other* and regard current feminist analysis as dispensable.

The fear of what true equality for women might mean goes to the heart of patriarchy so it is not surprising that it has been so long lived. Feminist critique and all it implies for the liberation of women will go on being covertly or overtly suppressed in the spirit of this fear unless women refuse to be silent.

Part of that refusal is the quest for a secure place for feminist analysis and theory-making and for the acceptance of feminist critique across all fields of knowledge. There can be no true freedom to think, to write, to teach while women remain an unspoken, unrecognised component of those ideas: while women's reality is denied. It is one thing to unconsciously participate in an accepted practice of the dominant group and another thing entirely to choose to perpetuate an unjust practice after being confronted with its real nature. Those who would champion the freedom of academic inquiry should pay close attention to *whom* they would include in that freedom, and why.

Acknowledgements

Many valuable comments on drafts of this chapter were received from Ann Baker, Dorothy Broom, Heather Dornoch, Clyde Manwell, Brian Martin, Elizabeth O'Brien, Val Plumwood, Jennifer Rainforth and Julia Ryan. My thanks to each of them.

References

1. This is a working definition. It is similar to Linda Gordon's useful definition of feminism as "an analysis of women's subordination for the purpose of figuring out how to change it", in "The Struggle for Reproductive Freedom: Three Stages of Feminism", *Capitalist Patriarchy and the Case for Socialist Feminism*, (ed.) Zillah R. Eisenstein, (New York: Monthly Review Press, 1979), p. 107.

2. Merlin Stone cites archaeological evidence of the resistance of women against the systematic repression of their religious rites throughout the Middle East over a period of 1000 to 3000 years, probably beginning with the first invasions by the northern tribes around 2400 B. C. Merlin Stone, *The Paradise Papers: The Suppression of Women's Rites* (London: Virago, 1976), p. 79.

3. I use the word "sex" to refer to biological differences between men and women and "gender" to refer to feminine and masculine social roles into which women and men are socialised from the moment of birth.

4. Simone de Beauvoir, *The Second Sex*, transl. H. M. Parshley (New York: Alfred A. Knopf, 1953), p. 102.

5. See the chapters by Bettina Cass in *Why So Few? Women Academics in Australian Universities*, Bettina Cass et al. (Sydney: Sydney University Press, 1983).

6. Betty Friedan, *The Feminine Mystique* (New York: Dell Publishing, 1963); Kate Millet, *Sexual Politics* (London: Davis, 1971); Shulamith Firestone, *The Dialectic of Sex. The Case for a Feminist Revolution* (London: Jonathan Cape, 1971).

7. Mary Wollstonecraft, *A Vindication of the Rights of Woman* (Baltimore: Penguin, 1975, first published 1792), and de Beauvoir, op. cit. (first published in French, 1949).

8. For an exploration of this idea see Juliet Mitchell, *Psychoanalysis and Feminism* (Harmondsworth: Penguin, 1974).

9. It has been no coincidence that a number of all-women publishers have been established in the same period. Women are no longer prepared to suffer the restrictions and bias of the male-controlled publishing houses. The women have organised to do it for themselves. See, Lyn Spender, *Intruders on the Rights of Men, Women's Unpublished Heritage* (London: Pandora Press, 1983).

10. Dale Spender, *There Has Always Been a Women's Movement This Century* (London: Pandora Press, 1983).

11. Betty Friedan's analysis in *The Feminine Mystique*, op. cit., gave the lead for the important task of naming the previously unarticulated concerns of women, as women.

12. For an indication of the scope of feminist theory and analysis, see: Hester Eisenstein, *Contemporary Feminist Thought* (Sydney: Unwin Paperbacks, 1984); Gloria Bowles and Renate Duelli Klein (eds), *Theories of Women's Studies* (London: Routledge and Kegan Paul, 1983); and The Bristol Women's Studies Group (eds), *Half the Sky* (London: Virago, 1979).

13. See, for example: Diane Bell, *Daughters of the Dreaming* (Sydney: Allen and Unwin, 1984).

14. I am indebted to Fay Gale for this description in geographical terms. See her paper: "Seeing Women in the Landscape: alternative views of the world around us", presented at "Women and the Social Sciences, New Modes of Thought", Symposium of the Academy of the Social Sciences in Australia, Australian National University, 1983.

15. Heidi Hartmann, "The Unhappy Marriage of Marxism and Feminism: Towards a more Progressive Union", *Women and Revolution*, Lydia Sargent (ed.) (Boston: South End Press, 1981), pp. 14, 15.

16. Hanna Papanek, "Men, Women and Work: Reflections on the Two-Person Career", *American Journal of Sociology*, vol. 78, 1973, pp. 852–72.

17. de Beauvoir, op. cit., p. 316.

18. Dale Spender, *Women of Ideas and What Men Have Done to Them, From Aphra Benn to Adrienne Rich* (London: Routledge and Kegan Paul, 1982), pp. 7–8.

19. This is as difficult for many women as it is for men because of the androcentric conditioning both have received. See: Andrea Dworkin, *Right-Wing Women, The Politics of Domesticated Females* (London: The Women's Press, 1983).

20. Cass, op. cit.

21. Spender, *Women of Ideas*, op. cit.

22. For some interesting insights into the functions of consciousness raising (C. R.) groups, see: Betty Friedan, *It Changed My Life. Writings on the Women's Movement* (London: Gollancz, 1977).

23. Rita Helling, *The Politics of Women's Studies* (Adelaide: University Relations Unit, Flinders University of South Australia, 1981), pp. 167ff.

24. Cass, op. cit.; also, Marian Sawer, *Towards Equal Opportunity: Women and Employment at the Australian National University* (Canberra, March 1984).

25. She wishes to remain unidentifiable because of political difficulties over her reappointment which is due to coincide with the publication of this book.

26. For an attempt to describe the term "women's studies", see: Susan Magarey, "Women's Studies Programme", *ANU Reporter*, 28 November 1980. She suggests that women's studies is "a subject area, a field — but not a form — of intellectual inquiry".

27. The Bristol Women's Studies Group, op. cit.

28. Cass, op. cit.

29. Kathy E. Ferguson, "Feminism and bureaucratic discourse", *New Political Science*, no. 11, Spring 1983, p. 68.

30. ibid.

31. I have included Marxism because although it has almost become an orthodox critique, it still has the intellectual force to disrupt academic complacency, especially when combined with feminism and used to re-evaluate institutions such as the family. See for example: Zillah R. Eisenstein, op. cit.

32. Helling, op. cit., pp. 166–8.

33. Spender, *Women of Ideas*, op. cit., p. 13.

34. Eisenstein, op. cit.

35. Sawer, op. cit. (refer to the list of government initiated equal opportunity inquiries).

AUTHORITARIANISM IN STATE BUREAUCRACIES: THE PSYCHOLOGY OF BUREAUCRATIC CONFORMITY

Stuart Rees

INTRODUCTION

Nurses in hospitals, scientists in industry, lecturers, tutors and technicians in universities, secretarial staff in the world of commerce, administrators, telephonists, social workers, social planners, teachers and others employed by government departments frequently have grievances about the conditions of their employment. They feel dissatisfied because they feel unduly controlled. Yet they know that any improvement in their working conditions, even their very jobs, will be at risk if they openly express their resentment.

The employees listed above spend a large part of their lives in bureaucracies which have been defined as hierarchies "designed to coordinate the work of many individuals in the pursuit of large scale administrative tasks".[1] Such "coordination" can become a form of control aimed not only at achieving the official objectives of the organisation but also at perpetuating the power and status of key people.

Such controls are made possible by and contribute to the acquiescence of most employees, but why should acquiescence be so widespread? The means of control do not reach the dramatic, nightmarish means of an Orwellian Big Brother, and the consequences of such machinery may not always be similar to the fearful *1984* obedience of the mass of the people.[2] Yet, in the interpretation of bureaucracies' official regulations there exists an enormous potential for the abuse of authority. For example, the codes of conduct issued by public service boards in Australian states may not always appear military in their content and objectives, yet they retain a preoccupation with the means of control: justifying hierarchies, reinforcing the respect due to senior officials, outlining the consequences of disobedience.[3]

AUTHORITARIANISM DEFINED

Some uses of authority which I have examined by interviewing public service employees and by reading their records were described by those employees as "authoritarian". This is a notion which has already received exhaustive analysis in an examination of the traits which contribute to social discrimination in general and to the particular prejudice of anti-semitism.[4] My concern is not so much with individual traits but rather with those abuses of authority which have included practices such as a secret keeping of records, punishment of dissidents and the concealing of information.

213

These practices represent authoritarianism. Although such a definition facilitates the task of identifying authoritarian behaviour, other methodological safeguards have to be taken. For example, one should avoid the trap of merely recording as authoritarian that conduct which an interviewer or respondents did not like, or where this adjective was used uncritically in other ways. Authoritarian behaviour should not be equated with the exercise of authority; it represents an abuse of authority and is not necessarily a consequence of, nor synonymous with, bureaucratisation.

However, employees in large bureaucracies do object strongly to the *style* in which authority is exercised, as when a senior bureaucrat consistently fails to consult or when a politician goes out of his way to victimise his critics. Others might argue that such examples represent bullying, excessive forms of control or just irresponsibility. The question remains whether bullying, some kinds of irresponsibility and excessive control represent forms of suppression to be labelled authoritarian. This chapter analyses the conditions which contribute to such suppression.

THE MAIN ISSUES

In the following discussion, examples will be taken from the experiences of employees in several large organisations, including government departments in New South Wales. More important than the specific examples will be the identification of the conditions which would contribute to the abusive use of authority in any large organisation, including scientific establishments and institutions of tertiary education which are the subject of analysis in other chapters in this book.

A major question for analysis concerns the interrelationship of personality and organisational structure. In the examples which follow, are we seeing authoritarian individuals who happen to work in a particular organisation, or are we seeing unpleasant but obligatory administrative tasks which merely happen to have been made the responsibility of certain staff? To begin to answer these questions it is necessary to unmask an ideology of bureaucracy, that powerful set of ideas which enables large numbers of employees to explain, to make sense of, and seldom to question, their life at work.

AN IDEOLOGY OF BUREAUCRACY

Assumptions about correct behaviour in organisations are held by employees at different levels of a hierarchy and amount to an ideology of bureaucracy which sustains such employees' belief in their work, and their employing organisation. References to strong leadership and efficient administration are central notions in this ideology.

Strong leadership is illustrated by popular images of politicians and executives as being single-minded, willing to take unpopular decisions, and who allegedly do not vacillate under pressure. Efficient administration has been revered in a decade which has seen a preoccupation with cutting costs and which has sponsored the careers of management consultants who are paid to prescribe remedies for inefficiency. Yet, efficiency has hardly ever been operationalised in bureaucracies in terms of assessing and increasing staff motivation, morale and output. It remains a general praise word used to describe and justify what is actually done.

It hardly matters that these terms are problematical, unlikely to survive close examination. They are of particular use in dressing up the organisation in acceptable terms, in concealing the real goals of the organisation, such as survival, the maintenance of internal power structures, and expansion.

The notion of "strength" through strong leadership is instrumental in this ideology in underlining the force of personality, or at least certain kinds or personality. The notion of "efficiency" is often used to describe an allegedly ideal system of organisation. The fact that these nouns could be used to refer to either individual behaviour or organisational system, or both, brings us back to the problem of analysis, the intersection of psychological and social forces in their historical context.

HISTORICAL CONTEXT: STRENGTH THROUGH EFFICIENCY

Any current concerns to convey an impression of strength through efficiency have a long political momentum behind them. For example, the autobiographical accounts of those who joined the National Socialists and helped Hitler to power are filled with references to the importance of discipline as a means of achieving a "new social order".[5]

In Britain, during the general election of 1983, young voters interviewed by BBC reporters said that they regarded Prime Minister Thatcher as strong because she would "stand up and not back down to the unions". Thatcher's alleged triumph in winning the Falklands War, and the televised response, in 1983, of some Americans to President Reagan's invasion of Grenada, that "at last there's a real 'man' in the White House", serve to reconvince politicians and a majority of their electorates of the importance nationally of being unashamed in the use of power.

In the state of New South Wales, the importance of getting the media to convey images of strong government and a strong leader do not appear to have been dented even by inquiries into alleged government corruption. Authoritarian controls, such as secrecy and the dismissal of employees who tried to release information about malpractice, have so far been effective in preventing the exposure of corruption.[6, 7] Electoral techniques are used to present a macho image of the state's leader as in the caption "Wran's the Man", a claim substantiated by the argument that a powerful but usually invisible Secretary to the Premier's Department was the clever manager, the man behind the man.[8] Such images of strength through efficiency have provided cues for the administrators of government bureaucracies, those senior civil servants who are accountable ultimately to the men at the top.

The authoritarian practices which are the subject of analysis here are not occurring under fascist or other totalitarian political regimes. They have occurred in countries which pride themselves in their democracy and openness in government and which appear at first sight to oppose the strong centralising forces at work in contemporary capitalism, whether specifically in institutions of higher education[9], or more generally, in all public service departments.[10] In New South Wales a series of reports on proposals for reform in the public service have included an emphasis on a flexible management structure in which middle and junior personnel could develop their skills and would not be stifled by an excessively hierarchical organisation. Such reports also emphasised the value of sharing information among employees and with the public.[11]

The desire of some governments to appear strong by taking unpopular decisions has been evident in the 1980s in severe cutbacks in the funds for tertiary education. Such cutbacks were accompanied by concerted efforts, in Britain indirectly by the University Grants Commission, and in the province of British Columbia in Canada directly by the Social Credit government to tighten central control over universities.[12] These developments underlined the importance of the warning made a decade earlier that at least in one kind of public bureaucracy the staff should determine the structure of the institution that they worked in. Professor John Griffith wrote that, following the values of independence and self-direction applicable to social activities generally, the nature of working in universities should be "essentially anti-authoritarian, anti-oligarchic and anti-hierarchical".[13]

SYSTEMS OF CONTROL

In the New South Wales government reports referred to earlier, the author expressed the hope that bureaucratic practices of centralised control, failure to share information and promotion through seniority would become relics of a bygone age. Yet these "relics" have remained as inherent features of bureaucratic organisation and facilitate some individuals' concern to control other staff members' behaviour.

Sometimes the form of control is open, sometimes it is secret. Always it has included some forms of aggressive behaviour by men and women and a quick or eventual submissiveness by staff who were the subject of that aggression, or who carried out instructions. As in Milgram's famous experiments on obedience to authority, the cooperation of willing or even reluctant subordinates perpetuates tyrannical conduct as much as the destructive attitudes and initiatives of superiors.[14] Such a process is perhaps not too surprising. For example, in his analysis of the theories of Weber and Chester Barnard, Hopkins wrote "the giving of orders or the sending of communications are themselves forms of compliance because the orders a participant gives are assumed to derive directly from those he receives".[15]

The examples which follow come from interviews and correspondence with employees who had complained of various excessive uses of authority over them and their colleagues. The first set of examples refer to various official controls which were perceived by the recipients as overly aggressive but which were successful in ensuring the submission of these "recipients". The second set of examples illustrates intolerance of questions and debate.

(a) *Aggression and submission*

In a series of personal interviews, several social workers employed in a state welfare organisation described how their professional training had led them to expect that the work of their agency would be characterised by idealism. They were disappointed and all felt a sense of disquiet and discomfort. One of them observed, "the lives of hundreds and hundreds of people have been made miserable by working here". His observation was confirmed by groups of colleagues in different offices who spoke of their own low morale and who concluded that the way to survive was either to leave or to stay and be obedient.[16, 17]

The difference between a reasonable attempt to be efficient and unreasonable use of authority is a matter of interpretation, but employees usually resent secret attempts to check on and so influence their work. For example, in the State Electricity Commission, allegations have been made of excessive secrecy and rule by fear, as manifest in the filling out of pre-printed forms by supervisors on all the staff below them — forms which asked questions about an "employee's ability, initiative, time-keeping and so on".[18]

Under systems of secrecy, staff and public are maintained in states of relative ignorance and authoritarianism knows few limits. For example, the low state of morale among employees of the Department of Youth and Community Services was attributed to "an humiliating tradition of secrecy which has produced a well grounded fear that even small grievances cannot be discussed openly".[19] In the same organisation, some forms of control resented by staff included decisions to transfer some officers to different offices without consulting them.[20, 21] The employees in question were dismayed by such practices but felt powerless to challenge their superiors.

In a Public Service Board investigation of the Department of Agriculture, an Acting Assistant Director made notes, "quoted from memory, as close to verbatim as possible", of the alleged critical attitude of an officer and of his "intransigence". The Acting Assistant Director reported these comments to the management division of the Board and a senior member of the Board made a written note "The general conduct of the officer of the Department will be taken up at the completion of the appraisal, unless circumstances force the issue earlier". "Taken up" meant a further investigation to see whether "disciplinary charges" could be made against the intransigent staff member.

Language such as "charge", "disciplinary action", usually reflects military means of controlling subordinates or adversary systems governing the administration of justice. Accusations or imputations of guilt associated with the notion "charge" may be appropriate means of sustaining due processes of criminal law yet they have also been retained without question in public service bureaucracies. An alternative view, namely that conflicts in employee relationships could be dealt with by practices of careful consultation and negotiation, as between peers, finds no place. Notions of openness, debate, mutual problem solving and support for colleagues could replace that disciplinary language which has already had a long life, but such notions would challenge structures that are taken for granted, would challenge the convenient ideology of bureaucracy which gives employees a sense of order and security.

However, aggressive, hostile investigations and submissiveness as a response to such forms of control are usually neither sensational nor obvious. The suppression which lowers morale and demands redress is not so much the abrupt moments of humiliation as month after month of disregarding employees. Such disregard may be shown in valuing only the staff who give no trouble, or by providing no support for those who may be working under difficult conditions, as in community welfare offices where staff are expected to meet increased public demand with fewer resources.

Disregard establishes domination almost as effectively as more obvious forms of coercion. By making disparaging observations about other workers, or by seldom expressing interest in or feelings about their colleagues' work, people in power are able to grind down the sense of self-worth of lower status employees. "This, rather than open abuse, is how he [the employer] bends them to his will. When shame is silent, implicit, it becomes a patent tool of bringing people to heel."[22]

(b) *Intolerance of debate*

It is difficult to initiate open debate about the consequences of not consulting staff on matters which directly affect them because such non-consultation is often sustained on the grounds that correct administrative behaviour requires little obligation to take notice of subordinates. In the same tradition, outsiders' requests for information can be treated with indifference, criticism is ostensibly "not heard" and an image of business as usual is maintained.

The habit of not answering correspondence is a well-developed means of blunting opposition, of trying to make critics give up. In response to such refusal to reply, the writer can always use the option of going public, by distributing papers, by writing "letters to the editor". Such actions prompted a senior public servant to complain to this author: "You have no right to do this, why are you being so discourteous? If you want us to cooperate with you professionally, you cannot engage in such practices. If you have useful ideas, why don't you write a private letter to myself or the Minister?"

In his attempt to head off opposition, the civil servant makes a strong appeal to certain moral principles — to "being courteous", to "having no right", to "being professional". His appeal for obedience derives from an attitude which is often evoked in response to a variety of authority figures: parents, leaders, supernatural powers and so forth. All such appeals, says Adorno, have to do with the moral aspects of life, with standards, with offenders against them who deserve to be punished.[23] Some elaboration of this psychology of conformity will be pursued later in this analysis in a discussion of the functions, in organisational terms, of individuals' anti-intellectualism and their defence of certain moral principles. At this point it is more pertinent to describe further those circumstances which contribute to authoritarian behaviour.

In the field of welfare, the survival of voluntary agencies depends largely on state financial patronage which can vary according to assessments of the proper behaviour — duly respectful, morally worthy, and therefore deserving — of the representatives of voluntary organisations. Such agencies want to be successful in their annual submissions. The pun is deliberate. Not only must the financial request be presented in the appropriate manner, but respect for the father and mother figures must be considered genuine and consistent. For example, in a newsletter article, the representative of a NSW Voluntary Child Care Agency had criticised state government arrangements for funding substitute care. In response to this article, the Minister concerned was said to have blocked the agency's funds and said to the writer of the critical article: "If I had my way I'd throw your typewriter in the river". The leader of the voluntary agency explained, "Only when I pleaded on bended knee to have the funding renewed was I successful".

The practice of cutting off funds, or threatening to cut off funds as a means of reprisal persists in the context of dependency relationships, as between a Public Service Board's attempts to monitor and control the budgets of other departments of government and in the relationship between the State Welfare Department and the voluntary sector. In respect of this latter relationship, a leading member of a voluntary organisation was told that if she continued to even meet with a particular group which analysed state welfare policies, her agency would lose its funds. That person has explained that her management committee felt intimidated by the government civil servant's attitude and asked her to "back off putting pressure on the government, otherwise we will always have funding problems".

These examples, of appealing for courtesy, of refusal to answer correspondence, and of repeated threats to cut off financial help, derive from some individuals' apparent fascination with exercising power through handling money and their unwillingness to tolerate criticism.

Although there is an emphasis here on the behaviour of key individuals and although a certain structure has facilitated the promotion of such people to positions of prominence, it is at least plausible to argue that the economic climate also influences the defensive, often frightened, way in which they assert themselves. At a time of recession when jobs are scarce, the holders of such positions may be even more concerned than usual not to allow challenge to themselves or the organisation which sustains their self-image and self-interests.

Nevertheless, it is their intolerance of ideas, of imaginative policies, let alone debate, which remains the conservative motif of those who run organisations. They follow the notion of rational authority based on the belief and legality of rules and the right of those who occupy posts by virtue of these rules to issue commands. They have seen disruptions as removing the quality of omnipotence from themselves and from other figures of authority in the chain of command. The highest valued traits — loyalty and obedience — in these organisations are parts of that ideology of managerial fraternalism reminiscent of the "boss is father metaphor" which characterised the company town philosophies of the nineteenth century.[24] In reality, then, as now, the bosses were anything but supportive, protective, loving leaders of their employees.

In another context, the reluctant acceptance by working-class men of an annoying sense of personal inferiority has been described by Sennett and Cobb as the "hidden injuries of class".[25] To paraphrase these authors' conclusions, the hidden injuries of welfare employees are that they must think of themselves as unimportant, except inasmuch as they are industrious, compliant, unquestioning cogs in a machine. They are to be the "locals", whose preoccupation should be with the rules and routines of their employing agency as opposed to the "cosmopolitans" who place their loyalty to abstract ideals, to their profession, and to other social networks, above that of their employing agency.[26] The survival and promotion of those whose orientation is local produces an atmosphere in which in Merton's terms, rules, originally conceived as a means become transferred into an end in itself, "an instrumental value becomes a terminal value".[27] At this point it is pertinent to return to the question about the relationship between individual traits and organisational structure by unravelling those major ideological themes of strength and efficiency.

STRENGTH AND EFFICIENCY

The enduring psychological disposition of those politicians and civil servants whose behaviour I have just described is to keep good order, to be correct, to ensure that other people do not stray outside their roles. This concern with orderly conduct is part of that set of assumptions which breathes new life into an always potentially authoritarian ideology. As argued earlier, and as shown in other periods of history when severe economic difficulties have facilitated politicians' arguments about the need to impose discipline and defend old values, these assumptions have poignancy at a time of recession when ministerial concern is with knowing where the dollar is, with giving the public value for money, and with eliminating signs of inefficiency. Such ideas have produced this decade's pejorative political epithets, as in the distinctions between the wets and the drys — the wets, in Thatcher's terms, being those who are weak, who have not had the strength to stand up to adverse economic and political conditions, and the drys being those who are supposed to be strong because they are willing to face unpopularity by refusing to intervene to defend supposedly weak individuals.

In my observations of the grievances of employees such as social workers, secretaries, teachers and social planners, it appeared that two techniques, a defence of certain moral values and anti-intellectualism, were used by senior staff to express sentiments both about themselves and their particular ideology of bureaucracy.

(a) *Defending moral principles*

In their concern to bind the lines and bonds of authority, the proponents of images of strength also covered their own and their organisation's weaknesses, a technique which could be perceived in defensive behaviour in which a major concern was with moral scruples. Demonstrating strength could also be identified in forms of attack in which the work of imagination in politics, and in the day to day management of bureaucracies was to be distrusted.

Defence of current practices can be just as aggressive and humiliating as open forms of attack. For example, the senior civil servant who suspects sexual goings on among his junior staff and who reprimands them on the basis of his suspicions, is defending some notion of correct conduct. At this point one can only speculate on the religious or other beliefs of such senior staff and their assumptions about the correct behaviour of adult men and women. The point is that these beliefs have become part of an organisational agenda, they are examples of the fusion of the personal and the political, the process whereby personal habit becomes embedded in the objectives and machinery of an organisation.

Control, as a defensive response to any pressure to effect change, appears to be the mechanism used by career-oriented, loyal bureaucrats who cope with their jobs by adherence to rules. In defending the organisation, they defend themselves. In asserting their reverence for seniority, or for obedience to department heads, they try to conceal their own sense of threat, or their organisation's difficulties. An aura of infallibility must be maintained. Accountability is to the organisation, not to the client, to the powerful, not to the powerless.

As in a corral surrounded by hostile forces, threatened people can defend themselves by calling in outside helpers. In an age of monetarist beliefs, when cost-effectiveness becomes the objective, the outside helpers are often management consultants, but they are seldom asked to consider whether the corral is worth defending, whether departmental policies have much bearing on public needs. Instead, their tasks are to simplify management procedures, to examine structures, to produce diagrams about flows of communication and lines of responsibility. The net result is to mystify further the importance of hierarchies and so contribute to the belief that such forms of dominance and subordination are the only way to organise work if it is to get done.

The appointment of management consultants "to examine the management of the New South Wales Department of Youth and Community Services" was regarded on the one hand as a demonstration that the organisation was doing something[28] and on the other as another example of staff interests being ignored.[29] The need to be seen to be doing things has been documented as characterising manipulative type behaviour in which certain individuals divided the world into empty, schematic, administrative fields and treated everything and everyone as an object to be handled, but with indifference to the content of what was going to be done.[30] Doing something is politically more attractive than appearing to do nothing or even, says van Krieken, questioning some of those basic assumptions of the organisation by increasing staff participation in producing their own solutions.[31]

The tendency to call in outside management consultants illustrates a habit of thought which is superficially attractive because it seems to provide a short cut to understanding and can anaesthetise politicians, civil servants and others into thinking that there are simple remedies for complex problems. An image of being objective, above politics, above human foibles, appeals to those whose concern is with the correctness of things and who see management of people as non-ideological. Such a perspective is held not only by staff at the top of a hierarchy. The compliance of junior staff because they think it is in their best interests also facilitates the smooth running of organisations. Tutors and technicians in universities, nurses in hospitals, public servants in government departments can and do muzzle their sense of grievance. At least they do so in sufficient numbers to convey to their seniors that they need change neither their attitudes nor the structure of the organisation. In consequence the concern with administrative tidiness remains as part of that ideology, which says, implicitly or explicitly, that human interests should be subordinated to economic ones. It is a way of thinking which makes a spurious separation between economic and social affairs, between the concern of the accountant and the objectives of maximising the welfare of employees as well as of clients.

Management consultants have become the witch doctors in a decade of pragmatism when efficiency is the hallmark of strength, when a sense of vision generated through fascination with ideas finds no place in those political lobbies concerned with a kind of bureaucratic selfishness, protecting the organisation and those in power. This is an exact reversal of Titmuss' old adage that social policy is about the triumph of altruism over egoism.[32] Indeed, such a statement might now be regarded as wet, as weak, as something to be scoffed at by "strong people".

(b) *Anti-intellectualism*

Defence is usually concerned with protecting order. For example, protests against new ideas have appeared in the form of a defence by powerful conservative groups, such as public service unions in New South Wales, of existing conditions and their own interests.[33] By contrast, those who are regarded as symbolising disorder because they present new ideas are frequently attacked as "intellectuals", or as people who associate with intellectuals.

Writing about the paternalism of company towns in nineteenth and early twentieth century America, Jane Addams, the social worker, described the anti-intellectualism of company leaders who felt that they were being paternal and loving in their attitudes to their employees. They thought they were loving fathers of their children, and they expected to be perceived as such. They appealed for loyalty and felt betrayed by questions, let alone rebellion.[34]

Politicians and senior civil servants may be unable or unwilling to confront the inherent contradictions in their wish to demonstrate care *and* control. Other contradictions in state bureaucracies include the need for these organisations to employ both conforming bureaucrats and autonomous professions. In this respect, contradictions also exist between the values placed on developing policies and ideas at all levels of the bureaucracy *and* insisting on protocol and attention to detail as part of competent staff performance. Instead of debating these contradictions and welcoming the development of ideas as a criterion for taking seriously the proposals for reform in government administration, letters go unanswered, questions in the state Parliament are answered in monosyllables (usually "no"), and alternatives to existing administrative practices are described as arrant nonsense, or are answered by the well-developed habit of merely abusing the Opposition.[35] It is almost as though one of the hallmarks of a "democracy" that wants to sustain an image of strength is not to tolerate any challenge which might dent this image. Protecting that image leaves little room for toleration of ideas or the people who raise them.

If powerful administrators take for granted the value of the set of assumptions about maintaining good order, then any sense of unhappiness and tension in their departments can easily be attributed to the activities of those insiders who are seen as disloyal or disobedient, or outsiders who are "trouble-makers". That discipline which can be applied within organisations and which Merton has shown produces over-conformity and "induces timidity, conservatism and technicism"[36], may also be directed at an organisation's outside critics. For example, in the controversies in the agencies referred to above, outside critics were lumped together as "trouble-makers" or "intellectuals" or they earned that other monolithic label, "just Marxists". As an alternative, "anarchist" is apparently an even more disparaging and dismissive label since it can be applied to almost anyone who asks critical questions, who does not cooperate. As an extra dimension to the ideology of bureaucracy, staff who are known to associate with the "anarchists" are assumed to have been contaminated by them and should not be trusted.

CONCLUSIONS AND IMPLICATIONS

Are we any nearer to answering the question whether authoritarianism derives from the habits and values of individuals, or whether it is the product of some organisational tradition whose force is difficult to deflect?

The distinction in this question represents a false dichotomy. It is impossible to separate the individuals who behave so insensitively to their colleagues from the immediate contexts in which they operate. The interrelationship of potentially authoritarian individuals and that set of assumptions that good order and efficient administration are fulfilled through control, produces a self-fulfilling prophecy. If competence within the organisation is measured in terms of key staff being "solid, conservative and non-controversial"[37], promotion by other sets of criteria will take a long time to produce a different set of assumptions, a different atmosphere, different leaders and a reduction in existing forms of central control. Until that time is reached, those controlling individuals who like to appear strong will continue to be able to shape their own needs according to those bureaucratic conditions which they have helped to create.

Authoritarianism in organisations has been manifest in repeated forms of intolerance, as in an intense dislike, almost a fear, of questions and debate. It has been evident in aggressive assertion of power by superiors over their subordinates and in the submission to authority by people at different levels in hierarchies because they have wished to preserve their own influence or that of the system which had given them their status. This submission to authority is the binding principle, of both those who assert their power over fellow employees and of those who feel constrained by the system but who were socialised long ago into believing that obedience, loyalty and compliance were virtues which the organisation valued and which would usually result in rewards. By contrast, those who did not comply would be dealt with by at best having no reward, at worst by being punished.

Incidents of authoritarianism are evidence of a long, unfinished agenda for producing greater participation among employees and the development of experiments in a democratic tradition. A bureaucracy in which deference and obedience are not equated with competence would mean less rather than greater need to conform to superiors. The process whereby the allegedly efficient manager takes over in government as well as in business results in a decline in political debate and conflict. This negation, as in reluctance to openly share information and ideas about different forms of management, different ways to exercise authority, requires challenge. "Democracy requires institutions which support conflict and disagreement as well as those which sustain legitimacy and consensus."[38]

In concentrating on authoritarian practices between staff and the political conditions that facilitate such behaviour, no claim has been made about the possible connection between employees' negative reactions to their own treatment and their responses to relatively powerless clients. However, the literature on organisational theory is replete with examples of the relationships between internal and external relations in a bureaucracy. The regulation of the poor is an almost inevitable corollary of the internalised discipline of the bureaucrats.[39]

The powerlessness of patients is partly the product of the preoccupation of the medical profession with maintaining and enlarging medical dominance.[40]

At the tail end of a chapter it is inappropriate to embark on this new subject: the effect on the "beneficiaries" of organisations — clients, students, patients — of abuses of authority as exercised over employees. It is germane to ask questions about the effects of suppression on people's lives at work. On the one hand it is apparent that some employees are happy to conform. Others are miserable because they had perceived their jobs as potentially stimulating and productive: stimulating if they and their ideas could be taken seriously, productive if they could be encouraged to develop their potential and not feel constrained by excessive controls.

That psychology of conformity that has been derived from an ideology of bureaucracy has been evident in particular in welfare organisations. Although the processes described here almost certainly apply to all large bureaucracies, some sceptics may feel that there is a risk in drawing conclusions on the basis of a few controversial events. The alternative to taking the risk is to raise no questions, to place no obstacles in the way of practices which affront people's sense of fairness, which stifle talent and which are not in the spirit of democracy.

References

1. L. A. Coser and B. Rosenberg, "Bureaucracy", in Coser and Rosenberg (eds), *Sociological Theory* (New York: Macmillan, 1968), p. 463.

2. G. Orwell, *1984* (London: Penguin Books, 1954).

3. Examples which specifically illustrate these rules include, Tafe Gazette No. 22 of 1982, "Policy — public relations — addresses" and Public Service notices, administration, "Code of conduct and ethics for the N.S.W. Public Service", Sydney, 24 November, 1982.

4. T. Adorno, E. Frenkel Brunswick, D. J. Levinson and R. Nevitt Sanford, *The Authoritarian Personality* (New York: Harper and Row, 1950).

5. T. Abel, *Why Hitler Came into Power* (New York: Prentice-Hall, 1938).

6. B. Sweeney, "Arantz and De Groot — A Connection?", *Legal Service Bulletin*, vol. 8, no. 6, December 1983, pp. 264–6.

7. G. Boehringer, "Something rotten in the State of N.S.W?", *Legal Service Bulletin*, vol. 8, no. 6, December 1983, pp. 266–7.

8. M. Cockburn, "Profiles in power, the man behind the man", *Sydney Morning Herald*, 13 July 1982.

9. A. Arblaster, *Academic Freedom* (London: Penguin, 1974).

10. P. Wilenski, *Directions for Change* (Sydney: NSW Government Printing Service, 1977).

11. ibid.

12. FAUSA News, "Update on British Columbia", September 1983.

13. J. Griffith, *New Statesman*, 17 November 1972, and quoted in Arblaster, op. cit.

14. S. Milgram, *Obedience and Authority* (London: Tavistock, 1974).

15. T. K. Hopkins, "Bureaucratic authority: the convergence of Weber and Barnard", in A. Etzioni (ed.), *Complex Organizations* (New York: Holt, Rinehart and Winston, 1962).

16. S. Rees, "Crisis of confidence in Youth and Community Services", unpublished paper, University of Sydney, April 1982.

17. A. Gorman, "State welfare faces a crisis of confidence", *Sydney Morning Herald*, 23 April 1982.

18. G. Williams, "Power system's woes horrendous", *Sydney Morning Herald*, 10 July 1982.

19. S. Rees, "Social welfare: an opportunity for reform", *Sydney Morning Herald*, 29 June 1982.

20. Rees, "Crisis of confidence", op. cit.

21. Gorman, op. cit.

22. R. Sennett, *Authority* (New York: Vintage Books, 1982).

23. Adorno et al., op. cit., Ch. XIX.

24. Sennett, op. cit.

25. R. Sennett, and J. Cobb, *The Hidden Injuries of Class* (New York: Vintage Books, 1978).

26. Gouldner, A. "Cosmopolitans and locals: toward an analysis of latent social roles", *Administrative Science Quarterly*, vol. 2, 1957–8, pp. 281–306 and 444–80.

27. R. K. Merton, "Bureaucratic structure and personality", pp. 151–60, in Merton, *Social Theory and Social Structure* (Glencoe, Illinois: Free Press, 1949).

28. G. Pratt, "Administrative chronicle: New South Wales", *Australian Journal of Public Administration*, vol. XLI, no. 3, September, 1982, pp. 254–69.

29. S. Rees, "A bad time to question authority", *Australian Society*, vol. 2, no. 1, 1983.

30. Adorno et al., op. cit., p. 767.

31. R. van Krieken, "Participation in welfare: democracy or self-regulation?", *The Australian Quarterly*, Autumn 1981.

32. R. Titmuss, *The Gift Relationship: from Human Blood to Social Policy* (London: Allen and Unwin, 1970).

33. M. Cockburn, "From Machiavelli to Wilenski: reform is slow, frustrating", *Sydney Morning Herald*, 13 July 1982.

34. Sennett, op. cit.

35. Hansard, NSW L.A. 19 of 21 October 1982 and L.A. 15 of 9 November 1982.

36. Merton, op. cit., p. 153.

37. Cockburn, "Profiles in power", op. cit.

38. S. Lipset, *Political Man, the Social Bases of Politics* (New York: Anchor Books, 1963).

39. F. Piven, and R. Cloward, *Regulating the Poor, the Functions of Public Welfare* (New York: Vintage Books, 1976).

40. E. Freidson, *Professional Dominance: the Social Structure of Medical Care* (New York: Atherton Press, 1970).

In the Twilight Zone: Academia and Human Rights

Cedric Pugh

Introduction

In a general sense rights are claims which are enforceable in legal or other legitimate processes. Stated in this way, we can see that rights necessarily involve discussions about the nature of claims. Claims then become ultimately matters for justification and legitimation in terms of moral and political principles. For example, if we lay claim to a right to our private property, we believe that we can exclude others from our property and, when necessary, we could get this enforced in a court of law. The justification for this right lies deeply embedded in the history and ideology of the liberal democracies. This private property right is justified by arguments from social and economic theory which run along the lines that such a right improves the economic wellbeing and the functioning of society. Opponents will want to argue that claims to private property should be limited, by virtue of inequalities or some other social principle. In effect, they argue that property law should be rewritten, thus offering alternative justifications for claims, enforceability, and rights. Similarly in human rights, people will argue alternative justifications, depending upon the extent to which they want fundamental freedoms and other things recognised and ensured.

Human rights revolve around claims for basic freedoms in *expression* (as well as freedom in association and freedom from arbitrary arrest and imprisonment). They also have a historical connection to the development of liberal societies, and in some cases they are stated specifically in constitutions and charters. For example, the United States has a Bill of Rights attached to its constitution, and the United Nations has a human rights charter. In other places, such as Britain, freedoms and rights have evolved within a general political and legal development. But, as we know, countries which are less democratic fail to guarantee freedoms and fail to provide the "rule of law" in arrest, detention, and access to fair and open trials.

Academic institutions in liberal democracies are expected to observe basic freedoms and to provide fair procedures in determining tenure, promotion, dismissal, and so on. However, as will be evident in the other chapters in this book, academic institutions in the modern democracies do not unequivocally hold basic human rights as secure and protected in their statutes, which are supposed to establish rule of law principles and fair procedures. An academic's claims for human rights are not always enforceable in her or his institution, and sometimes they are not clear-cut in the wider society, with its legal systems, and other provisions. One of these other provisions which is worth special reference is the role of ombudspersons or "parliamentary commissioners". As public bureaucracies (including state-financed academic institutions) have become increasingly powerful, citizen concern about the misuse of power, the infringement of human rights, and crass administration has become more and more resented. One means of accountability and review is the use of ombudspersons generally and in academic institutions, with some further development of examples in the United States where some universities come within the scope of ombudspersons.

As a matter of basic enforceability of claims and rights, we need to discern what distinguishes enforceability in such things as property law from human rights law. The figure below shows a continuum in the means of dealing with claims.

CLAIMS AND OUTCOMES

Gratuitous benefit at	Twilight	Legally secured
the discretion of the grantor	Zone	interest

At the left side of the continuum we have the operation of an *administrative* principle, where the criteria are vague, they are unwritten, and they are not open to public view. Decisions on claims for such things as academic tenure, promotions, dismissals, and so on, are made by administrators. We have no prospect of appeal, and the conduct of administrators is scarcely subject to general rules. At the right side of the continuum we have the operation of an *adjudicatory* principle. Administrators have to make their decisions through definite rules and standards. Criteria for making decisions are specific, they are written, and they are open to public view. The decisions are accountable within law, where they have to be elaborated, consequently checking the use of arbitrariness and improper criteria in decision making. Between these two polar positions we get twilight zones with more or less observance of the adjudicatory principle in operation on such things as fair procedural standards, proper systems of appeal, and accountability on criteria and decisions.

This framework can be used to interpret the variability in practising the acceptance of human rights among academic institutions, enabling us to evaluate the performance of institutions in respect to basic freedoms and adequate justice. We expect the elite universities to abide by academic principles and to be concerned with human rights. Although there have been some examples of where elite universities have deviated from those principles, they have nevertheless tended to conform more closely to the ideals than most ordinary universities and tertiary institutions. The reasons for this are partly historical and partly because their students and academic staff are more proximate to the external establishment, consequently giving them more equality in the distribution of power. Sometimes academic institutions will have elaborated statutes with fair procedural standards, principles of natural justice, and proper rights of appeal. The key characteristics of natural justice are the rights to be heard and the clear association to decisional impartiality. By comparison, other academic institutions follow policies of administrative discretion, with scope for administrators to fudge the interpretation of criteria, to preclude appeals, and to arrange their formal adjudicatory apparatus with only the appearance of fair standards, but not its substantive reality in operation.

The extent to which academic institutions are accountable in the external legal system, in state ombudspersons provisions and so on, will influence the way they, in fact, operate and design their procedures in academic claims on matters of dismissal, termination, promotion, tenure, and others. Parliaments which insist on institutions writing proper statutes in these spheres, and connecting them to administrative law can drag reluctant institutions closer to full adjudicatory principles. However, the present reality in countries like Australia is that whereas things like property rights are within full adjudicatory principles with legally secured rights, human rights in academia are only variably secured, and for the most part they lie in the twilight zone of the continuum.

Once we recognise that human rights in academia are mostly in the twilight zone, then it becomes important to give socially based explanations of why there are so many threats to those human rights. When we have such explanations, we can more clearly discern remedies. Of course, we are mainly concerned with those many academic institutions which operate in the twilight zone, and thereby become somewhat vulnerable to demoralising human rights cases in the course of their history. This book indicates the nature and the prevalence of such cases. As an advocate, a critic, and a social scientist writing on this topic, I should set out my approach to my methodology underlying this study.

My method of study has been one that is based upon a wide reading of human rights literature, a continuous interest in administrative and policy changes in higher education, and having some insights from participant observation. This approach leads towards setting up a *pattern* model of administrative and policy matters in some academic institutions. A pattern model can be built up from the following sorts of experiences. First, the participant observer stands close to the system of administration in higher education. Second, he or she can observe the main themes and internal characteristics to derive a picture of the system as a whole. Third, the experience can be widened by discussions with academics in other institutions in Australia, Europe, North America, South East Asia, and so on. Fourth, we then obtain a number of linked ideas and tentative hypotheses about what makes modern academia tick; that is, we understand its "clockwork". Our purpose is to develop understanding rather than to make logically predictable statements. Finally, we remind ourselves that we are developing what is only a *partial* pattern model; some academic institutions are reasonably clean on human rights problems.

In our partial pattern model, we begin from the interpretative position that academic suppression occurs with a combination of external and internal circumstances. Elsewhere in this book, other authors have pointed to the relevance of key modern *external* forces — the narrow interests of large business and public bureaucracies, the ambivalence of the government to intellectual free expression, and the cutbacks in funds by cost-conscious governments. Internally, academic institutions have grown rapidly and have become more tied-in with the general political, social and economic developments of the wider society. Their administration has become more bureaucratic, with the enunciation of regulations, procedures and formalities. Power has enlarged and become more centralised, and consequently some of the genuinely "academic" qualities have been superseded by bureaucratic administration. Those who hold central bureaucratic power are necessarily selective in what they want to represent as their institutional image. They select and publicise things which add to public institutional image, including some items of academic research importance. The selection process is biased by the external circumstances, referred to above. It is seldom detached, egalitarian, or much concerned with real academic freedom. Rather, on occasion, the selection goes towards suppression and using administrative power to contend against good scholars within a context where human rights are not always legally secured.

Our course for developing our understanding in human rights issues goes in the following directions. First, we look at the state of international human rights law and evidence for problems in academic institutions. Second, where decisions are closer to administrators giving gratuitous benefits rather than operating within rule of law principles, we might expect some disputation on personal, ethical and ideological issues. We discuss those issues as part of human rights cases, with their consequent dimensions of personality conflicts. Third, we recognise that group dynamics and the high stakes of prestige involved in some human rights cases interact to influence the course of their history. We shed some light on those processes. Fourth, we extend our introductory theme that some prevailing characteristics of political-economic power have strong impacts upon academic institutions and their attitudes to human rights issues. Finally, we examine some wider changes in society, with particular relevance to human rights cases.

HUMAN RIGHTS AND INTELLECTUALS

In full development, human rights would be written into charters, given official recognition by governments, have enforcement provisions attached to them, and for academic institutions they would be elaborated in statutes with fair procedures to hear and determine cases. As we have noted, full development is rare, with most academic situations in a twilight zone. However, as we shall presently see, since the 1960s there has been both a growth of international human rights law and some movement towards enforcement provisions. In this section I describe and comment upon these developments, and I underline relevance by reviewing the human rights records of academic institutions in Australia and overseas. We should be concerned about the infringement of human rights. In a democratic country, human rights could be codified and have status as a standard of reference or a "touchstone". However, it seems that in the twilight zone an individual can only be free to make some sorts of public criticism if she or he can defend her position by the force of power, by guile, or by purchasing certain economic and legal services. It is a sober reflection on academia that suppression is more likely to be stopped by countervailing power, by guile in opening up administratively controlled information conduits to circulate evidence of suppression, or by involving legal and extramural leverage, than by arguing reasonably on grounds of human rights. Nevertheless, human rights considerations have some relevance and use, especially where they can be linked to power.

Human rights law revolves around the basic freedoms — expression, association, and freedom from arbitrary detention and arrest. Such rights have been connected to the United Nations in its charter and in subsequent international agreements. We might have circumspect reservations about the extent to which international human rights law is observed in a world which has totalitarian and authoritarian regimes. Also, as academics we know that even in the liberal democracies, academic institutions sometimes infringe principles of academic freedom. However, we should also recognise that there have been improvements in international human rights law, and this will have significance in the liberal democracies and in their institutions, including universities and colleges.

Since the late 1960s, international agreements on human rights have proliferated, with some key agreements specifically relating to intellectual and research activities. For example, in 1974, UNESCO's *Recommendations on the Status of Scientific Researchers* was agreed, with rights set out on the basic freedoms, and with recommended standards for contracts with employers, general conditions of employment, and career development. Alongside the growth and specialisation of human rights law, occasionally steps have been taken to set up courts and tribunals to strengthen enforcement provisions. Most progress has been made among western European countries, but in a range of United Nations activities, member countries have agreed, in ratifying the international laws, to go further and pledge the introduction of such things as human rights commissions. Much still depends, of course, on the commitment and the legislation of governments in their own countries, and away from the more pious atmosphere of UNESCO headquarters.

In overseas countries, academics have sometimes responded to the growth and development of international human rights law in positive and encouraging ways. For example, the very prestigious British Council for Science and Society collaborated with the British Institute of Human Rights to produce a booklet, *Scholarly Freedom and Human Rights*.[1] The booklet records the progress in human rights law, explains the social and academic reasons for new developments, and it gives practical recommendations on how academic freedom can be secured in universities and colleges. One recommendation is that directors of academic institutions sign public pledges to uphold academic freedom and fair procedures.

The Council for Science and Society and the British Institute of Human Rights outlined the reasons for the existence of suppression of academics. They pointed to the ambivalence of governments towards research and free expression. On the one hand, the political success of governments depends upon the impacts of research on technological change and economic development. On the other hand, intellectual expression on key issues, for example nuclear technology and environmental detriment, can challenge public policies. Scientific and academic institutions then become sensitive to this ambivalence, and external pressures along with internal bureaucratic power may combine to suppress free expression. The suppression takes a variety of forms — censorship, harassment, restrictions on research funds, blocking promotion, and expediently deciding to discontinue employment for those on short-term contracts.

The eminent authors of *Scholarly Freedom and Human Rights* perceive that intellectuals are especially endangered by administrators who opt for expedient suppression.[2] Although it is an intellectual's duty to express critical views, the modern academic is in a somewhat dependent situation, bound up with expectations in the professions and in some academic institutions. In asserting a full right to freedom and integrity, he or she can be vulnerable in tenure, promotion, access to research funds, and so on. Effective operation as an independent critic often depends upon association to a profession and to a university or college. This vulnerability is reduced when academic institutions practise academic freedom and guarantee fair procedures. The authors of *Scholarly Freedom and Human Rights* advocate the principles along the following lines:

> In defence of scholarly freedom, moreover, it must be recognised that a scientist's personal reputation is often his most precious asset. This right thus applies with some force in the circumstances envisaged in RSSR, (*UNESCO'S Recommendations on the Status of Scientific Researchers*, 1974), Article 28: "...decisions as to access by scientific researchers...to positions of greater responsibilities and correspondingly higher rewards should be formulated essentially on the basis of fair and realistic appraisal of the capacities of the persons concerned, as evidenced by their current or recent performances, as well as on the basis of formal or academic evidence of knowledge acquired or skills demonstrated by them."[3]

The principles and the rationales are clear enough. From our discussion in the introduction we can also see how human rights can be better protected in countries like Australia. Generally, we need to bring human rights closer to legal enforcement. We may not always be able to achieve easy legal enforcement because administrative law tends to restrict remedies, largely because if access were made wide open, there could be a large influx of litigation, putting pressure on the capacity of the legal system. However, tougher laws could be useful as a deterrent against unfair administrators. Meanwhile we do not have to accept that matters can be left entirely to the discretion of administrators in academic institutions. In Australia, each state has Discrimination in Employment committees which have power to conciliate, and, if necessary, to publicise academic wrongdoings under parliamentary privilege. The powers of ombudspersons can be tightened up and extended. Australia now has a human rights commission. Its jurisdiction in academic affairs is not clear, but perhaps it can be persuaded to play a role. Finally, the Council for Academic Freedom and Democracy in Australia can have roles in review, publicity and lobbying. As will be shown below, the Council has had some effectiveness in bringing some academic institutions into closer conformity with proper principle in tenure, promotions and other things.

Why is it necessary to press for more enforcement and persuasion in human rights issues? We begin to see cause and reason by examining the precise problems that have been reviewed and publicised by academics who examined human rights cases in Britain and Australia. First, let us look at the findings of the reputable British Council for Academic

Freedom and Democracy (CAFD). CAFD's findings from its public and careful case studies were:

Improper use of executive authority

The manipulation of appointments and promotions committees to block candidates who hold critical views on educational policy and administration. Using the appointments and promotions systems as means for suppressing dissent, or as a "gift" system of senior academics. Effecting dismissals with no apparent academic reason, and in the context of interpersonal difficulties among academics and executives.

Confused and improper roles of governing bodies

These range through a variety of problems:

1. Inertia on human-scholarship rights, leading to a failure to discharge duties, and raising doubts about the fitness of members to occupy positions assigned under statutory powers.
2. Failure to hear grievances properly where a governing body ought to be an honest and unprejudiced court of appeal.
3. Mistakenly regarding institutional autonomy as private property, and ignoring wider accountability to the general community of scholars, to the professions, and to the wider society.
4. Ignoring constitutional powers to set down statutes for: (a) appeal against arbitrary executive actions, and (b) establishing codes of fair practice in appointments, promotions, and the rights of staff in relation to senior executives and heads of departments.

Looseness in criteria, procedures, and justifications in promotions

1. Academia failing to set up conditions so that not only is justice done, but seen to be done.
2. Using nonacademic considerations — political views, personal styles, and misconceived notions of "obstructiveness", political behaviour, and so on.
3. Committees without relevant competence making decisions to reject candidatures where their composition is inadequate in the specific professional spheres under assessment, and not taking steps to get relevant advice.
4. Committees failing to take in external referees' reports and full curricula vitae, and neglecting to invite candidates for interview.
5. Committees failing to explain and justify their decisions publicly on the basis of accepted criteria.

CAFD's suggested ways of dealing with these problems, and achieving fair resolution of the cases if reviewed were:

1. By a governing body setting up a judical enquiry.
2. By getting a senior executive who may have misused authority to explain his/her actions before a special independent committee of enquiry.
3. Offering restitution to an academic whose rights had been violated.
4. Reforming the procedures to bring them into line with the precepts of British justice.

In Australia, its Council for Academic Freedom and Democracy (P.O. Box 217, Broadway NSW 2007) has begun to find similar problems, since its founding in 1980. The Council has publicised cases showing human rights violations in dismissals, nonrenewal of contracts, promotions, sexual discrimination, blocked access to research materials, and an institution expressly forbidding freedom of speech on matters of public interest. Some seven Australian universities and colleges have been blacklisted for their record in human rights issues. In some instances, the effect of the Council's correspondence and publicity has led to institutions reversing decisions on blocked promotions and other issues.

It is clear that arbitrary criteria and unfair procedures have operated in some academic institutions. This, of course, reflects that human rights tend to lie in the twilight zone between outright gratuitous administrative discretion and full legal enforcement. Academic freedom and intellectual human rights are more substantial than being merely rhetorical, and academic institutions will seldom overtly and explicitly disclaim proper principles. It is just that they act in more or less sophisticated ways in their bureaucratic interests rather than for human rights. In effect they use their inherent power in their roles as employers to follow expedient executive wants, sometimes without reference to justice and relative merits. Ultimately, intellectual human rights are about the distribution of power, as well as being declarations of principle with implications for institutional means of enforcement and public persuasion.

Whilst human rights issues get disputed in the twilight zones, the inherent contentions of power and principle will tend to spill over into personality conflicts involving moral, psychological, political and ideological issues. We now turn our attention to these aspects of human rights cases.

CONTENTION, DISSIDENCE, AND THE MORAL DIMENSION

As we have seen, human rights involve statements of claims which ultimately depend upon social and ethical-political arguments. It is therefore not surprising that human rights conflicts in academic institutions will get entangled in questions of personality, politics, ideology, and moral differences among administrators and the subjects of academic suppression. We are generally familiar with bureaucrats, officials, and those with power who assume or posture upon their moral superiority and use the information under their control in their institutions to suppress and isolate anybody who cares to contend a human rights case. When there are no proper rule of law procedures, no impartial institutions, and no proper enforcement of human rights, we would then expect extended grounds of conflict. We need to get a circumspect view of these things, and beyond that to indicate the bases upon which we take a reasonable position on the moral-ideological aspects of extended personality conflicts.

We should not expect to settle much simply by taking sides where a victim of a human rights case alleges bias among decision-makers, or where an administrator takes steps to display his or her moral superiority. Such steps can include propaganda objectives within the confined sources of information in an institution, more or less vague smear campaigns, the propagation of an academic "blacklist" (see the subsequent discussion on Veblen's ideas), and extractions of "confessions", and so on. Although we could not get very far in pursuing any detail here in what is a general thematic discussion, it is possible to take up some matters which lay a foundation for circumspect viewing in human rights cases. In the first place we recognise that general principles can apply to a situation where bias is alleged by one side or the other in a human rights dispute. Second, we can discuss moral principles and their relevance to academic institutions. We now address these two issues.

Our general and detailed knowledge of human rights cases in academic institutions shows that personal, political and ideological matters do get disputed in some blocking of promotions, dismissals, and other key conditions in employment. For example, in social science departments and faculties we can find cases where radicals (or conservatives) cannot make progress in their careers because those holding the decisional power have opposing ideological views towards conservatism (or radical reform). In other situations where there are interlocking committees in determining outcomes on dismissals, promotions, and so on, people associated with arbitrary decisions may also be represented on higher level committees with further decisional power in the same cases. Or, more generally, the oligarchs in academic power structures can make appointments to committees with a view to getting the outcomes they want. Biased decision-making can be played out in a variety of ways, especially when there is slender external accountability and where legal-style enforcement procedures are not readily available.

In the liberal democracies, administrative law generally recognises the *nemo judex in causa sua* principle. This is a part of natural justice where procedures and the composition of adjudicatory bodies should be free of the likelihood of bias. Sometimes in academic decision-making, which may be several degrees removed from the enforcement of administrative law, the victim in a human rights case quite properly objects to decisions and committees which have a strong likelihood of association with arbitrary criteria and bias. However, such objection can raise further problems. The decision-makers and the oligarchs in the academic bureaucracy, or in its governing body, may feel that merely by raising the *question* of bias, their motives, integrities and competences have been impugned. The important point then becomes not just whether bias has occurred or is likely to occur. Rather, what has to be shown is that bias has led to, or might lead to, decisions which on grounds of fact, logic, and reasonable interpretations could have been, or may become, invalid and arbitrary. The radical (or conservative) academics who in a human rights case have better records in publication, research, teaching and community service compared with conservative (or radical) academics, who are protected from termination or who are promoted, have every right to object on grounds of *nemo judex in causa sua*. Biases of more or less intensity and significance are an everyday routine reality of academic administration. They are often significant and consequential in intellectual human rights cases.

Bias gets connected to the internal politics and power in academic institutions. As we have suggested, sometimes disputes will become entangled in questions of which disputant has moral superiority. This takes us into the territory where issues are essentially connected to evaluative and subjective aspects of arguments and claims. How should we respond to a suppression and a contention where an institution claims that its moral view of the world is sufficient to justify termination, dismissal, blocking of promotion, and so on?

This takes us to the subject of philosophical justification of moral principles. It is a subject that is well handled by Professor P. A. Griffiths who proposes that justification can be pursued by relating it to discussion and to three principles[4]:

1. impartiality,
2. rational benevolence,
3. liberty.

The principle of impartiality is that any decision/action by authority is one which could be reached by anybody. It is associated with consistency: similar cases should receive similar treatment to avoid discrimination. The principle of rational benevolence is connected to the public interest. What is right or wrong should be determinable by other rational beings. This ensures that the outcome depends on reason, not upon who has the will or the power or the initiative in a course of action. Then the outcome is determined by what is true, rather than upon who has won. Liberty is necessary so that all rational and interested participants can enter the discourse.

These principles outline ways of resolving moral principles in contention. They would still need some procedural method and a mechanism to make reason hold in the decisional process. Where there is no procedural method within an institution's autonomy, that provides a good reason for wider public involvement. Some academic institutions may have internal ombudsperson powers, which should be sufficient to bring reason and to disengage the contentions of ethics, ideology and personality. Institutions need some procedural recognition of these matters, because it is well established in the theory of bureaucracy that the bureaucracy will believe it has superior information, purpose, and propriety. But, on the contrary, for reasons which we shall clarify below, a bureaucracy can be wrong in many ways, including the moral dimension.

It is probably inappropriate for an educational institution in the university-level context to have a published moral code. What is really needed is an understanding that bureaucratic and popular moralising will not resolve problems originating in dissidence, and in other academic controversies. Bertrand Russell[5] presents some useful reflections. He dismisses the notion that useful moralising can come from popular sources or from the generality of Protestant/Catholic prescriptions on ways to behave. Instead he proposes a secular and social perspective, identifying a good person as one who cares for the happiness of friends and for all humanity; cares for art and science; pursues personal excellence privately as well as does duties for fellow beings, and can show performance in creative personal excellence and respond positively when creativity is achieved. Russell adds that "society ought to allow me freedom to follow my convictions except where there are very powerful reasons for restraining me". These values are more consistent with academic objectives, and they can scarcely be used by suppressors to "legitimise" their use of authority in academic disputation. However, academic administrators can become enmeshed in a dispute situation which has its own logic of group dynamics and institutional prestige beyond a rational view of academic freedom. Our discussion now turns to these considerations.

DISCRIMINATION AND "GROUPTHINK"

We can think of discrimination cases broadly falling into two categories, though some cases interdependently cross into both categories. First, we can perceive the results of suppression following from the ordinary course of academic activity and from the hierarchically organised internal politics of the academic business. Others have shown in this book how academic oligarchs use their power to ensure the dominance of their theories, their research, and their social values. Like businesses, many powerful academics do not want too much competition or a fair ordering of the academic universe. They prefer power and personalised prestige. We shall not deal with this sort of thing further, because other contributors have shown precisely what is involved. Instead, we shall focus upon the second category, where an autonomous and insular academic bureaucracy organises itself (unconsciously) to provide bad decisions in human rights cases.

Often a case history will begin with a relatively minor indiscretion in administration, and when challenged, it is defended. As time passes further problems and errors occur, and the case collects more participants in a context where prestige, authority and reputation are at stake. Nobody wills the growing complications, but in the absence of independent review procedures it is difficult to obtain useful resolution. Resolution can come with a dying away of energies on the one side or the other, by changes in personnel in administration, or by the force of external power to take away things which are precious to the institution — reputation, autonomy and resources.

Janis[6] shows what happens when an in-group closes ranks. His example was the 1961 fiasco of the US-backed invasion of Cuba at the Bay of Pigs. *Groupthink* is the psychological drive for apparent consensus at any cost; it suppresses dissent and appraisal of alternatives within cohesive decision-making. It is about forced consensus seeking behaviour to get solidarity and the "we feeling". Beyond consensus seeking, groupthink results in deterioration of mental efficiency and disastrous decision-making.

How does it occur?

- By genuinely considering only a few alternatives;
- by failing to evaluate risks and drawbacks;
- by excluding courses of action, originally rejected as unsatisfactory, but becoming appropriate in changing circumstances;

- when excluding expert evidence;
- by bringing in outside information to the group only under selective bias;
- by having no contingency plans for when things go wrong;
- by making amiability and *esprit de corps* the end, rather than attending to general functions and basic principles.

Who succumbs and why?

- Vulnerability is greater when a chief executive depends upon just an inner circle of chosen advisers, and where the group norms favour unanimity or compliance.
- Group efforts heavily discount warnings, and there is a failure to properly reassess decisions.
- The group holds an unquestioned belief in its own morality and purpose, ignoring the moral consequences of its own decisions.
- The "enemy" is stereotyped as too evil to warrant negotiation, or too stupid or weak to take counter action.
- Pressures are put on deviates in the group to remain loyal.
- Doubts are minimised by a continuous process of self-censorship.
- Illusion arises because the in-group consensus is aimed at legitimising the action, and members of the group assume that external silence means consent.
- The group uses self-appointed mindguards to protect it from adverse information which would shatter its complacency in the effectiveness and morality of its decisions.

Academic institutions are as prone to these sorts of problems as other organisations. Awareness of *groupthink* could lead to more circumspection, but external criticism and power will be the main way to break down *groupthink*. The self-realisation of bureaucratic error will occur only when the organisation is constrained to the uncomfortable position of altering its decision. At that point we can expect it to seek scapegoats for earlier errors and to attempt to rewrite and to re-interpret history.

THE CARDINAL AND THE ICONOCLAST

Cardinal John Henry Newman took up his pen in the 1870s and wrote eloquently about the idea of a university.[7] Universities should have liberty; they must become a concourse of ideas with varied intellectual discourse, and they should pursue excellence. These were to be places of vibrancy, curiosity and respect for creativity in developing scholarship and teaching. The Cardinal's piece has been significant. For example, in the institution where I work, the enacting legislation from the South Australian Parliament refers to such objectives as nondiscrimination and pursuing a liberally conceived education. Writing some fifty years after the Cardinal (in the 1920s), Thorstein Veblen[8] the iconoclast took up his pen to write witty and clever stuff about realities in American academia. His historical context was the invasion from the style and thinking of businessmen into colleges. Course offerings were becoming more vocational; boards of governors included more captains of industry, and colleges competed to attract students. In the eyes of the iconoclast this led to inferior standards in scholarship and teaching, and the basic ethos in those colleges constricted initiative and liberty.

The iconoclast's explanation goes something like this:

The Problems Funding has to be won from fickle sponsors. Governing bodies have a habitual parochialism and delegate power to their academic executive. The academic executive has a duty to use publicity for enhancing college prestige.

Power What is virtually an autocratic power lies with the academic executive. The formal power of departmental heads and academic boards is of little significance. It is more significant that the executive will attract "a conveniently small number of advisers who are in sympathy with his own ambitions". Power will lie with this "cabinet" or "junta" which is likely to include administrators, "campus politicians" and a few putative scholars.

Measures of Effectiveness These are for publicity and to satisfy sponsors, not for learning, scholarship and social purposes. The key measures are: number of students enrolled, number of courses offered and number of graduations/awards. It is undergraduate courses/student numbers which make up the edifice of power.

Courses As stated above, the undergraduate fare will build up power. Courses will be standardised into unit equivalents to which measures of (political/publicity) effectiveness can be attached. Teaching will be mainly perfunctory, with recourse to a prescribed textbook occupying a standardised unit of time.

Frills These are there to attract students and to promote public image. They will include recreational facilities, architectural monuments, and glossy pamphlets which overstate the college facilities and its measure of success. Some of the accessories to college life are there for decorative rather than for substantial purposes. Professional titling becomes part of the decoration: in American colleges sports coaches became professors.

The Academic Staff In Veblen's words: "under this rule the academic staff becomes a body of graded subalterns, who share the confidence of the chief in varying degrees, but who have no decisive voice in the policy or the conduct of affairs of the concern in whose pay they are held. The faculty is conceived as a body of employees, hired to render certain services and turn out certain scheduled vendible results".

Scholarship Managerialism, not scholarship, is the primary quality sought for central and departmental executive control. Quasi-scholarship is useful for publicity. It will be necessary to get some well-ranked scholars, and these will be tolerated as long as their scholastic inclinations do not go against executive purposes. The whole show can be kept going by buying cheap and selling dear.

Liberty and Initiative These are constrained by the system of power. This power is led towards conventionality in the social "establishment" and the duties of publicity. Opposition can be "corrected" by appointment, perferment and the "academic blacklist". The academic blacklist ensures that "no one will openly say a good word for colleagues who have fallen under the displeasure of an aspiring or incumbent executive". Initiative and innovation yield to statistical magnitudes (for the sponsors) and conciliatory publicity. In social sciences "the executive is actuated by a sharper solicitude to keep the academic establishment blameless of anything like innovation or iconoclasm". The duties of publicity lead to the propagation of appearances and the surveillance of academic staff.

Veblen sums it all up in these words: "with the progressive substitution of men imbued with the tastes and habits of practical affairs, in place of scholarly ideals, the movement toward a perfunctory routine of mediocrity should logically be expected to go forward at a progressively accelerated rate".

How can we relate Veblen's evaluations with the current situation in Australian academia? We would need more research information on particular histories to see to what extent the "animus of businessmen" was prevalent, and a threat to scholarship. However, some modern conditions run parallel to Veblen's context of American colleges in the years 1900–20. Australian academic institutions are dependent upon fickle sponsors for finance, many governing bodies delegate power to the executive, and institutions compete for student numbers, courses, research funds and general finance. Perhaps the main modern difference compared with Veblen's time is the necessary growth and use of research in modern social and economic processes.

ACADEMIC INSTITUTIONS AND THE EXTERNAL WORLD

The Veblen analysis of cause and reason for problems in academia can be taken some steps further. First, it is appropriate to state qualifications and exceptions in respect to the roles and policies of central administrators. For example, the *National Times* (13–19 September 1981, p. 50) reported the appointment of Professor J. M. Ward as the new Vice-Chancellor of Sydney University, and showed how he would combine administration with the continuity of his eminent scholarship. Veblen's argument is that in many cases the scholarship is separate from the main activities and roles of central administrators. We view the academic institution as a large resource system, allocating finance, personnel and support to courses, administration, libraries, research, and so on. A substantial amount of power is centralised, information is controlled, and bureaucratic norms are often in conflict with academic objectives. This can be detrimental to education. Central administration will be concerned with student numbers, the amount of courses, and access to external finance. These priorities and roles for central administration can push to the periphery, at some distance from the administrator's roles, the substantial things in creative innovation and the relationships (the good intangible things in the processes) between teaching, research and student learning. The central administration's relationship with the external world revolves around finance, institutional reputation (often a conservative expectation in the community), political grantsmanship, and the confined social and professional networks connected with these things. In this context any discrimination or suppression case which breaks into publicity can be quite embarrassing. The choices are to prevent it before it happens, or to repress and quieten it down as soon as it is publicised.

For academic scholars and students, the external world has a different significance. The outside world has specialist libraries, a widening scope of non-university research, a knowledge from professional and administrative experience (not the sort of knowledge in most books), and an opportunity to pursue relevance in intellectual and social problems. A good scholar will have an "invisible college" of contacts in the outside world. It is powerful, useful, and can be used in teaching programs. But this is a different outside world from that known to central administrators.

When a suppression case does become public, central administration can be taken by surprise by the amount of support the dissident will have in the wider community. Apart from the "justice" and "scholarship" aspects of a case, the external support has another dimension. In the modern world most professionals, academics, and people generally, have experienced the touch of bureaucratic obstruction. They will side with the dissident, against evasive and ambiguous bureaucracy. Many of them will know exactly how to counter bureaucratic power. That is an outside world beyond the control of central administrators in democratic societies. It is an indictment of modern institutions that this "outside world" has to be used, because these institutions do not have the procedural mechanisms and the attitudes to resolve some crucial problems within their own jurisdiction.

CONCLUSION

My theme has been that most academic institutions operate in a twilight zone in respect to human rights. Academic institutions in democracies owe their historical inheritance to the Age of the Enlightenment, and it is something of an irony that they are largely in the twilight on principles of central significance. Clearly they can remain where they are in twilight, or with the right circumstances they can be moved towards light, or they can drift into real darkness. What the future holds depends entirely upon relevant circumstances. I discuss those circumstances, drawing upon contrasting moods of circumspection, and optimism, and pessimism. Beyond this I give some statements on personal experience and general testimony, having been at the centre of a human rights controversy and having acted as adviser to human rights organisations in academic–bureaucrat contentions.

It is always easier to stay put than to move deliberately away into a different environment. In the twilight zone we expect that in human rights large gaps will continue to exist between the prescribed values of dissident free expression and the realities of suppression. Without full legal enforceability of human rights, cases will be contended by using countervailing power (usually external to the academic institution concerned), guile in opening up bureaucratically controlled information systems in academia, and occasionally by purchasing legal and other services. Justice will be contingent upon the particular circumstances and the dynamics of individual cases. Many academic institutions would find comfort in the twilight zone. Administrators retain their power, unless a countervailing bloc is ranged in opposition. Many mediocre academics and ordinary people who like a quiet life will find the twilight zone to be a safe haven. Injustices will remain unattended, with some being profound and significant and others being passing and less important. Some of the best academics will face dismissal, termination, and restricted opportunities in research, promotion, and the development of society. The familiar consequences are well discussed in other chapters in this book.

If we were optimistic, we would draw attention to some of the following circumstances. Being cautious, our optimism would be qualified in various ways, keeping us within the bounds of reality. First, since 1980 in Australia the media have been more interested in problems in academia. In the recent past it was extremely difficult to run a counter information system to the bureaucratically controlled system of the suppressors. However, the media are not always responsive, and they are often connected to conservative owners and editors. Second, the Council of Academic Freedom and Democracy in Australia, itself reflective of the scope and extent of modern academic problems, has been a useful new activist. Interestingly, central administrators sometimes view these sorts of advocates for civil liberty as ''the lunatic fringe'' and ''not having status in Australian academic life''. In fact, these advocates and activists have had success in some cases, and occasionally suppression has been checked.

Third, in the wider community Australian professionals will join cause, and write critical correspondence to administrators. But the critical correspondents will be from outside the institution where suppression occurs and the case will have to be very convincing. Few academics within an institution will be prepared to oppose their central administrators. Fourth, all political parties have some civil libertarians. It is the Australian Democrats, as a minority party, and being less connected to entrenched power blocs, that have a greater proportion of parliamentarians who will work for individuals. But the scope of parliamentarians goes wider. Some younger men and women in the Labor Party were involved in anti-Vietnam War campaigning and/or in feminist movements. They know what it is like to be at odds with authority and social opposition, and some know how to break through bureaucratic inertia in academia and elsewhere. However, the power of parliamentarians is limited. Those in the party in government will be cautious in making public statements on an issue which could be interpreted as running counter to present educational policy. The ordinary backbencher can write letters to administrators and sometimes raise questions or make comments in Parliament, but that is often as far as he or she can go. Some politicians are strong and persistent, and others are weak; they are usually very busy and are themselves dependent upon colleagues for support and advice.

Finally, for optimism, if the external trends in publicity and general political life are towards favour to human rights in academia, then academic institutions will become ready to create better mechanisms and fairer procedural standards for dealing with academic controversies, dissidence, and other problems. This may be linked to external legal enforceability. Once that is done, the suppressors will be at risk, rather than the dissidents.

By contrast, it is now the turn of pessimism. If academic institutions move from the twilight to darkness, it will be because they will drift there on the tide of external circumstances. Suppression will be rewarded with administrators simply following their expedient wants. That is easy when they are not opposed in publicity, in the public opinion and politics in the wider community, and in being brought to account in terms of basic human rights. Modern society has some general processes which run to the advantage of powerful executives in academia.

First, consider the general student dissent and activism of the late 1960s and the early 1970s in Australian academic institutions. Although it left a legacy of some student representation on some committees and a vague acceptance that in some sense students count in decision-making, in substance, not much has changed. The teaching–learning process has scarcely been changed, and in many courses academic success is interpreted as reproducing ideas from a set textbook and a set of narrowly confined lectures. This hardly leads to critical thought or to broad understanding of what is possible in educational and social relationships. Without these values and understandings, academic institutions are more readily run by systems men. (There are few women in key positions in academia.) Also, many good scholars are not closely in touch with suppression. A good scholar will prefer to spend time and energy in teaching and in research and writing than in administration. Consequently, academic administration ends up in the hands of those more attracted to power than to scholarship. Or, the good scholars who have administrative responsibilities are in a dilemma as to whether to pursue loyalty to their subjects and their professions or to write some mundane memoranda to central administrators and administrative peers. Australian academia is not always well organised to get both good scholarship and good administration. Bad administration, in itself, can lead to human rights contentions.

Since 1974 many modern democracies, including Australia, have experienced stagflation. Under monetarist economic policies, higher education has experienced slow growth or, sometimes, financial cutbacks. Although the consequences in academia have not been fully documented and written up in good evaluative studies, perceptive observers can see what has happened in many instances. In some academic institutions, there has been internal faction fighting, with coalitions forming to curtail courses or groups which are vulnerable. It has been opportunistic, with little real recourse to fair procedures, independent and impartial reviewing, and with scarcely any reference to broader social, economic, or educational needs in the wider community.

In large measure, national policy-making in education has contributed to the arbitrary and clumsy processes within academic institutions. On the one hand, politicians do not really understand the nature of academic administration and the way financial cuts are actually operated. On the other, they want better science and technology, and a smoother fitting of graduates to the changing occupational structure. But academic institutions speak rhetorically about "academic autonomy", seeking to keep politicians away from any proximity to academic administration. At the same time, the academic institutions have scarcely been effective at publicising the real problems brought about by cutbacks in finance. The end result is that there is a large gap between the requirements for reform in academic administration on the one hand, and bringing power authority in relation to those requirements on the other. In short, there is more noise than reason. Dissidents and potentially good reformers are extremely vulnerable in these circumstances. Terms like "academic autonomy" and "academic freedom" become the slogans for expediency. It is sometimes quite a nasty business.

My closing lines are very much dependent upon my participant observation and action in varied human rights cases. That participation and action includes access to primary documentation and numerous discussions over a period of some ten years or so. I have seen three cases of attempted dismissals, several of discrimination in blocking promotion, a situation where administrators arbitrarily usurped power from a departmental head who was one of the leading scholars in his institution, and instances of summary and arbitrary withdrawals of benefits in the ordinary terms and conditions of service. At first hand, and in these contexts, I have had discussions and meetings with international authors on human rights, with heads of departments, with council members elected by academic staff, with politicians from the major political parties, and with directors and retired directors of academic institutions. Some cases I have seen were unresolved for years, others quickly settled, and yet others accommodated by negotiation after the balance of power was shifted in favour of the object (they are usually treated as objects, not subjects) of the suppression or discrimination. From all of this, the obvious question to ask is what essential conclusions and interpretations follow. Seen from another angle, we might ask what a subject of discrimination can expect to experience in his or her situation. What happens when a competent Asian academic has his promotion blocked whilst less qualified white Australians in his department advance their careers? Or, where a young woman with a good record in teaching, research and publications sees less experienced men awarded higher positions, what can she expect as events unfold in her challenge to the university's vice-chancellor?

The people who become involved and informed in the cases will, with some notable exceptions, take their positions according to their situational context. The situational context is broadly divided into those who are in the same institution as the subject of discrimination — the insiders — and outsiders. The insiders who have full information and have duties in relation to the case will be few in number. They will tend to acquiesce in the decisions of the chief executive. Even elected representatives of academic staff will acquiesce, largely because they are caught up in a conflict of interest situation and do not see their role as truly "representative" of subordinate staff. Their responses will range from silence to the occasional justification of their position in terms of the generally irrelevant arguments favoured by the chief executive. They prefer silence and secrecy. Chief executives will resist concession, sometimes going further by placing the onus of responsibility on the subject of discrimination of suppression. Within the institution, things will be organised to act in cohesive "groupthink" against the dissident or claimant. Exceptions can occur. Occasionally staff or students may petition and change things. Also, sometimes an individual may support a dissident against central administration, but without any real power to change things.

It is outsiders who see things differently and can act to change an unsatisfactory state of affairs. Given access to facts and logic, some academics from other institutions, some politicians, and some people in public affairs, may act positively in human rights cases. If such opposition can be concentrated and publicised, there is a chance that suppression will be checked. The insiders will continue to claim that they have superior information, much as the conventional theory of bureaucracy predicts. But exposure and wider discussion bring more varied and more relevant perspectives. I can recall an example where a politician reacted so strongly to correspondence which an academic institution sent to a dissident that he was ready to establish it in the parliamentary record and to make fulsome criticism of the institution under parliamentary privilege. Reasonable and activist outsiders will recognise dissidence and suppression when they see the evidence.

All of this can be interpreted in terms of power — an important aspect of human rights. Tawney[9] presents a useful perspective on power. Power is at once both awesome and tenuous. It is often limited, and the powerful, like the spider, can be dominant only in the scope of their webs and hopeful that more powerful forces do not destroy their webs. To be a dissident is sometimes to perceive that power is tenuous, because the dissident is not dependent upon or attracted to the rewards and things within the disposition of the powerful. Others who are within the employee status of an academic institution will often be more conscious of their dependence and their conflict of interest dilemmas. That will include members of governing bodies elected by academic staff and some leaders of staff associations. By contrast, outside academics, politicians and commentators are simply not totally within the power of the chief executives in institutions which are prone to suppress. Clearly, as things stand, the existing contours of power, without enforceable human rights, are a comfort to some and a threat to dissidents. This is bad for society, because as Clyde Manwell and Ann Baker show in the chapter, "Evaluation of Performance in Academic and Scientific Institutions", the dissidents will frequently include some of the more capable teachers and researchers.

This is not all. Tawney has some more significant views of power. It should serve public, not sectional interest. It should rest upon consent and the rule of law. Public institutions, of which academic institutions are a part, should have statements of specific duties and definitions of rights to ensure reasonable freedoms. It is then clear that the general solution is to legislate so that reasonable claims on human rights are enforceable. The real point about power is not who has it, but rather how it is used and how it is limited. For democratic societies, suppression of the kind I have seen amounts to a misuse of power. Power needs to be limited and conditioned so that academics do have rights to free expression.

I have shown here what is involved in human–scholarship rights, in moralising against dissidents, Veblen's analysis of modern academia, and in the social/political context of modern Australian society. These are all, at base, political questions, with relevance to values in society and to relationships between the rulers and the ruled. The remedies lie in creating various administrative and legislative reforms so that external review is available, and by strengthening fair procedural standards in academic institutions. In short, human rights matters move from twilight areas of gratuitous administrative discretion towards procedural enforcement and wider publicity.

Acknowledgements

I am grateful for helpful comment on an earlier version of this chapter from Brian Martin, Ann Baker and Clyde Manwell. The responsibility, of course, remains with me. The secretarial support at the National University of Singapore has been excellent.

References

1. *Scholarly Freedom and Human Rights* (London: Barry Rose, 1977).
2. ibid.
3. ibid, p. 37.
4. P. A. Griffiths, "Ultimate moral principles; their justification", in Paul Edwards (ed.), *Encyclopaedia of Philosophy* (London: Macmillan, 1967).
5. In R. E. Egner and L. E. Dennon (eds), *The Basic Writings of Bertrand Russell, 1903–1959*, (London: George Allen and Unwin, 1961).
6. I. L. Janis, *Victims of Groupthink* (Boston: Houghton Mifflin, 1972).
7. J. H. Newman, *The Idea of a University* (New York: Image Books, 1959).
8. Thorstein Veblen, *Higher Learning in America* (Stanford, California: Academic Reprints, 1954).
9. R. H. Tawney, *Equality* (London: George Allen and Unwin, 1964).

PART THREE:
RESPONSES

OPTIONS FOR DISSIDENTS

Brian Martin, C. M. Ann Baker, Clyde Manwell and Cedric Pugh

What can individuals do to deter and oppose suppression? The previous chapters have given some idea of what suppression looks like in practice and what causes it. In this chapter we give an overview of the available avenues for action against suppression, with comments on their advantages and disadvantages. Because suppression takes many forms, and because the best course of action against it depends on the particular circumstances of each case, we do not wish to suggest a single solution, but rather to outline the options so that individuals and groups are better able to choose a successful defence.

PREVENTION

Once action has been taken to block a person's appointment, to prevent teaching of courses, or to institute dismissal, the struggle against suppression is much harder than if such actions had been prevented. As in the case of war, deterrence is better than battle, and removal of the causes is best of all. The most effective time to overcome suppression is before it begins. There are several avenues for helping deter suppression.

Legislative reform

Liaison with politicians who are interested in amending the Acts under which institutions operate can open up possibilities for developing statutes that ensure good procedures and appeals, and achieving access to administrative review by ombudspersons or other independent reviewers.

Better procedures

Grievance committees, appeal procedures, ombudspersons and similar channels, if they provide a known and effective way of addressing cases of discrimination, exploitation and suppression, also provide a deterrent to their occurrence. Therefore it is important to press for better procedures. Often this is only done after particularly blatant cases of suppression expose their inadequacies.

The existence of formal procedures is not always an advantage for dissidents. For example, an institution's representatives may claim "qualified privilege" or even "absolute privilege" on the grounds of the existence of formal procedures within the institution. What are needed are properly codified rules which really guarantee fair treatment. Providing the rules are good, their too flagrant abuse can result in bad publicity for the institution.

Better legal channels

Legal avenues for redress are a special case of formal procedures, often used as a last resort.

Legal channels are usually ill-suited for addressing cases of suppression, because of the lack of suitable laws and because of the large expense involved.

Informal response methods

Formal channels often do not deter suppression because the person or group suppressed does not wish to make a major issue of the case. Deterrence would be aided by the existence of well-known *informal* methods for resolving disputes. For example, individuals or groups might be prepared to act as mediators to attempt to propose solutions and to informally point out proper and improper courses of action to potential suppressors. The availability of such mediators might serve to restrain suppression, especially in cases where people in powerful positions do not realise the ethical implications of their actions.

Channels for publicity

If standard avenues for obtaining publicity for cases of alleged suppression were available, this would serve to deter its occurrence. At the moment obtaining publicity is an uncertain business: newspapers, journals and organisation newsletters may or may not take an interest. If for example a journal or other outlet were available to publish accounts of alleged suppression, this would help deter as well as oppose suppression.

Support networks

For individuals or groups who speak out or take action on controversial topics, having a support network is a good way to help deter suppression. A support network is essentially a collection of people or groups who are aware of and sympathetic with the general concerns or goals of the individual or group in question. The network may be held together by personal contact, newsletters or occasional publicity. For example, John Coulter's support network consisted of both friends and environmentalists who knew of his work. A support network can be mobilised into action when suppression occurs. The known existence of a support network can help deter suppression. For this reason it is important for dissidents to maintain contact with sympathetic people. Sometimes a low profile may serve to help avoid suppression, but once a person or group becomes known as a dissident, publicity may serve to deter suppression, by bolstering and expanding a support network more than it aggravates potential suppressors.

Social reform

If suppression arises from entrenched interest groups, such as chemical companies which try to stop publication of critical comment about their products, suppression may be prevented by reforming the social and political environment. For example, standard procedures may be brought in by governments for testing chemicals and documenting their hazards, or independent institutes set up for evaluating chemicals. Reform here refers to political change which makes it unnecessary for people to become dissidents and risk suppression to expose particular information.

Reforms within intellectual organisations are important. Some possible general long-term reforms which would reduce the power of elites responsible for suppression are as follows:

1. Remove rank and either remove or reduce salary differentials, to reduce power-striving within scientific and academic organisations.

2. Reduce work loads and hire more staff. This should be coupled with a general reduction in both hours worked and total years worked, to provide opportunities for intellectual work by all interested people.

3. Strengthen "freedom of information" at all levels.

4. Reduce asymmetries in decision-making power. For example, positions on committees for job selection, research coordination or administration might be filled by rotation.

Social transformation

Instead of simply testing and publicising the hazards of a chemical, an alternative is to remove the necessity for its use. Often such a change requires changes in social, political and economic structures. To replace much of the unnecessary routine spraying of herbicides might require tight government regulation or alternatively local community control over agricultural practices. To accomplish this would also require reducing the powerful organisational interests behind agricultural chemicals within chemical companies and government agricultural departments. Another example is the removal of the need for nuclear power by promoting energy efficiency, renewable energy sources and redesign of communities to reduce energy requirements. The social transformation to accomplish this would also remove the sources of suppression within the nuclear industry and state bureaucracies.

RESPONSES

Suppression cannot always be prevented. Sometimes, in spite of the availability of procedural channels and support networks, individuals or groups find themselves harassed, blocked and attacked. There are quite a few options. Here we outline them, mentioning some advantages and disadvantages.

Acquiesce quietly

Probably in the majority of suppression cases the suppressed individual makes no attempt to challenge the actions taken. Perhaps most commonly this is because the person is not aware of any suitable response, or is afraid of the possible repercussions. Other occasions when suppression is not challenged are when there is not enough overt evidence to mount a formal challenge, when the person does not want to become a focus of attention, and when the person wrongly accepts some of the blame. In some cases silence or a quiet exit may allow an individual's career to continue otherwise uninterrupted. But nonresistance may also allow or even encourage further suppression, such as blacklisting, as in some cases known to us.

The wider consequences of habitual nonresistance to suppression are a reinforcement of acquiescence to the status quo and the discouragement of critical scholarship. Furthermore, the power structures which generated suppression are allowed to continue intact. When indication was given to John Hookey — who among other things had introduced the first Australian course on environmental and resources law — that he would be denied tenure at the Australian National University, he took another job without making a full challenge to the decision. Several years later, attempts were made to deny tenure to Jeremy Evans, who had helped set up the environmental Human Sciences Program, in very similar circumstances.[1]

Use formal procedures

If resistance to suppression is contemplated, the first and most obvious channel is the formal procedures provided, typically by the organisation in which one is employed. For example, various procedures may exist to appeal against a blocked promotion.

Sometimes these so-called "proper channels" may be all that is required to rectify the situation. But this requires that a person have a strong case in a formal sense and that the system rules be respected by all parties. When suppression is initiated from top levels within an employing organisation, formal procedures may provide only a travesty of justice, as in the Orr case.[2] More importantly, in many cases formal procedures do not apply to the circumstances, or do not exist at all, or sufficient documentation may not exist to provide a reasonable case in pursuing them. For example, often there are no channels available to appeal against rejection of a job application. Even if there are appeal channels, there may be no way of showing that the rejection was caused by some form of unjust discrimination.

Nevertheless, even when formal channels are largely irrelevant to the case, it may be wise to pursue them just the same. This is not so much to realise the small chance of success, as to provide a justification for the use of other methods. When taking one's case to staff associations, courts or the media, it is often quite important to be able to say that one has tried the "proper channels" first.

On the other hand, formal channels often serve to defuse issues and obscure the justice of a case. When the formal channels are known to be slow and ineffective, then it may be wise to pursue other channels simultaneously or even exclusively.

One positive wider consequence of using formal procedures — or indeed any open resistance to suppression — is encouragement to others to resist when appropriate. In addition, some improvement in formal procedures may result if they are shown by a challenge to be inadequate. Australian National University tenure review procedures were changed after both the Hookey and Evans cases, though the reasons for the changes can only be inferred. On the negative side, formal channels provide no challenge to the institutional forces behind suppression, such as bureaucratic or corporate elites. In addition, by using them the formal channels, however inadequate, may be legitimised.

When using any methods of overtly opposing suppression, whether this is through formal channels or other methods, *it is vitally important to document one's case*. When possible, written records should be obtained and kept concerning all aspects of the case; sometimes it is useful to obtain written statements about occurrences from people who have observed what is happening. This is especially important when rumours abound or subtle forms of harassment occur. Without documentation, formal channels are usually entirely useless. And documentation is also vital when obtaining publicity and support from outsiders. (For suggestions on documenting a suppression case, see below under "Write-in campaigns".)

Dissidents under suppression should also keep a diary or "attendance notes" of any interviews, discussions and telephone calls with those holding authority or with those associated with "official" positions. That is important for documentation and for any possible future legal procedures.

A dissident being considered for discipline, or an individual claiming discrimination, may opt or may be required to undergo a quasi-legal hearing administered within the institution. A word of warning is appropriate. Some of the most blatant abuses in universities have involved such quasi-legal hearings. Furthermore, the very existence of such formalised hearings may prejudice access to remedy through the courts.

Thus, if at all possible, insist upon *proper* formalised procedures. The complaint should be *particularised*. The exact allegations should be in writing. There should be a written transcript of *all* testimony and copies of that transcript should be freely available to the dissident. All witnesses should be examined and cross-examined. Whether you are represented by an advocate, perhaps legal counsel, is a difficult problem. The *right* to be represented should certainly be there.

If an administrator suggests an "informal" hearing, it would be wise to have an exchange of correspondence stating clearly the precise nature of that hearing, its object, its possible consequences and its procedures. If the administrator wishes to have jurors or their equivalent, insist that their selection be done fairly. The right to challenge for cause, to be able to eliminate proposed jurors with conflicts of interest, should be honoured and used when necessary.

Staff associations

As well as formal procedures set up by the employing organisation, another set of formal procedures is often available through trade unions or staff associations. The existence of case histories such as the sample provided in this book shows that there are some weaknesses in many professional organisations, including staff associations and professional unions, in responding to suppression. But in some cases unions and staff associations do take a strong role against suppression. Taking a case to these groups can stimulate them to look at a wider range of problems. Also, even if staff organisations are not willing or able to take formal action, individuals within them may be willing to make deputations, organise publicity or otherwise act on one's behalf.

Many union activists and officials are unsympathetic to non-members who suddenly come to them requesting considerable support and action. If one is an actual or potential dissident, and union support is a potential option, then it is wise to belong and, if one is so inclined, to be active in the union.

In summary, unions and staff associations can provide valuable support in opposing suppression, and this possibility should be carefully considered. But all too often unions and staff associations may be unwilling or unable to take action. Expectations of solutions from this source should not be raised too high.

The law

The legal system is often the final resort in formal challenges to suppression, and use of this system epitomises the positive and negative features of using formal procedures. If one has a strong legal case, just the threat of legal action may serve to induce a favourable settlement. Those who go to court should try to choose their preferred issues, the timing and the point of initiative, rather than letting the institution have primacy in these things. The courts often provide a partially independent locus of power to corporations, governments and universities, and *sometimes* this power can be used to restrain suppression.

On the other hand, court procedures are usually heavily weighted against the victim of suppression. Unless legal aid can be obtained, legal costs can be financially crippling. Even when this is not a problem, the time and energy required to fight a court case can be exhausting physically and emotionally. By comparison, one's legal opponent, usually an organisation such as a government or corporation, has virtually unlimited financial support for the court case, and individual suppressors risk little.

In addition, the court is seldom a forum for getting at the truth. The court may be only able to rule on whether an alleged dismissal is harsh, unjust or unreasonable, as in the Coulter case[3], and issues of corporate pressures, harassment, and rumour-mongering are out of bounds. Getting a case into court often diverts or obscures the real issues, and even a successful court case may not provide emotional satisfaction. And like other formal procedures, there is little opportunity for changing the structures which lead to suppression.

Informal procedures

Sometimes suppression results from misunderstanding, lack of communication, cultural clashes or subtle differences in values. One way of overcoming the problem is to try to sort it out informally. The most obvious way is for the suppressed person to talk with the suppressors and help them understand why their actions were wrong or inappropriate. Often, this should be the first thing done. What is apparently a blocked publication may be only an oversight. Sometimes the suppressors may genuinely be surprised and embarrassed on realising what they have done.

Rather than a direct approach by the suppressed person, another possibility is the involvement of a third party who looks at all sides of the issue and talks with everyone concerned. The third party should be someone not obviously identified with the other parties, and someone who is discreet and sensitive to the issues involved. Sometimes formal procedures will require, suggest or allow involvment by such a third party. It is often a good way to overcome problems bound up with personality clashes or with cultural misunderstandings. Anybody taking up informal discussions should first acquire a working knowledge of conciliation and arbitration principles and, as suggested above, should keep "attendance notes".

Informal approaches have the great advantage of avoiding polarisation which often occurs in disputes after formal procedures are taken up or publicity is obtained. But informal approaches have clear limitations. For instance the suppressed person or, more often, the suppressor may refuse to be involved. Sometimes the suppressor is unknown, as when complaints are made to a person's boss without informing the individual complained against. And informal approaches seldom do anything to help remove the source of suppression.

Write-in campaigns

Apart from formal and informal procedures, the other major way to oppose suppression is by mobilising support and applying pressure on decision-makers. There are several ways to do this, and perhaps the most circumspect is the write-in campaign. The basic idea is for supporters or concerned people to write letters to an appropriate body requesting information or expressing concern. In the case of a dismissal, the appropriate body is usually the employer.

Writing letters may seem an innocuous activity, but it is the same method used by Amnesty International in opposing torture around the world, and it is a method used with considerable success. Essentially letters show that certain people are aware of the situation and are concerned about it. The more people that do this, and the more influential or prestigious they are, the more this demonstrates that the prestige of the institution being written to is in jeopardy. Furthermore, letter-writing campaigns are often a prelude to wider forms of publicity.

To initiate a letter-writing campaign, it is necessary to inform the potential letter-writers. At this stage it is important to prepare one's arguments carefully. Mustering evidence and argument for a letter-writing campaign or any form of public pressure is somewhat different from doing it for formal procedures. Emphasis should not so much be on technical violations of statutes and so forth, which are most relevant for formal channels, but on presenting a sound and reasonable argument. The following features are important:

- Include a summary in a few short sentences, including what happened to the dissident and the situation which appears to have precipitated it. A mention of any singularly awful procedural violation might also be added.
- In the more detailed description of the case, a chronological order usually is best; important interconnections can be indicated by cross-referencing.
- Stick to areas of principle and justice, and don't get bogged down in technicalities or digressions. Try to avoid "who-said-what-to-whom" accounts. Sometimes these are crucial, but then give supporting evidence.
- Present only information that can be verified if challenged. Remember that those whose actions are being questioned will scrutinise statements, looking for the slightest inaccuracy or weakness. Whenever possible, use documentary material. This is a courtesy to all sides.
- Avoid personal attacks. Perhaps rightly, you may feel that certain individuals are dishonest, unfair, malicious or ignorant. Do not say it. Just give the facts as clearly and concisely as possible. Launching into personal attacks can lead to alienation of supporters.
- Be succinct. The gory details of the case are seldom interesting to outsiders. Pick out what is important or most representative, and save the rest for other occasions.
- Obtain advice on presentation of arguments. Sympathisers and outsiders may be able to offer suggestions on improving clarity, accuracy, and conciseness. Especially where one is emotionally involved, it is easy to make errors and to miss important facts.
- Even if the case does not look as if formal legal proceedings will be necessary, it may be useful to obtain the advice of a good lawyer in summarising your case. The problem is finding a good lawyer. Personal connections may be your best bet, but an alternative is to seek out legal firms with experience in employee rights, industrial law, or a good record on civil rights. There is also the difficulty that a lawyer may prefer a legalistic description instead of a document to convince others.

Also bear in mind that most lawyers are on at least the fringe of the local establishment, if not part of it. Although their primary allegiances are supposed to be to their clients, that has not been true in several situations known to us. Bear in mind that members of the judiciary are often prominent on university councils and that, in both their legal and academic capacities, they can bestow many favours on local lawyers.

- Often it is desirable for affected parties — those involved against the dissident — to have the opportunity to comment on the case history. Comment should be confined to correcting any errors or possible misunderstandings but not censoring the facts. Whether to solicit such comment depends on the case. Where one is dealing with a demonstrably repressive administration, the courtesy of allowing the opposition to comment may not be a viable option.

- Be persistent, be prepared for a protracted struggle (if necessary), and go for saturation and variety. The institution will find it difficult to be both credible and consistent in designing its "line" and its answers to varied, diverse, and well-organised enquiries. It may have to resort to a generalised letter of reply which is done by way of a word processor and which says virtually nothing relevant.

- If possible, allow the main activities to be carried out by supporters rather than oneself. For example, a third party, perhaps a friend or a concerned person, may be willing to prepare or send out an information sheet documenting the events of the case and requesting letters to be written.

- Spell out one or more possible solutions to the situation, including one that you would be happy with. Without some cues, it may be that those who would like to resolve the case will not know what to do, or that they will take an inappropriate action.

Publicity

Letter-writing campaigns constitute a form of limited publicity. The next stage up from this is publicity in newsletters, journals, newspapers, radio and television. There is a considerable difference between different media outlets, for example between a staid presentation in an academic journal and an up-beat story in a tabloid newspaper. Coverage should be sought according to how one wishes the campaign to proceed. If one is still pursuing formal channels with some hope of success, sedate treatments in professional journals may be appropriate. If the aim is to apply pressure to entrenched elites, it might be best to pursue mass media treatments. One use of media treatments is to photocopy newspaper clippings and pin them on noticeboards, and to use them to persuade correspondents in write-in campaigns.

In their analysis of responses by journals to submissions about the Coulter case[4], Brian Martin and Clyde Manwell reach the conclusion that the mass media are often more willing to provide coverage of suppression cases than professional journals. Because mass media coverage often can be obtained without too much difficulty, it is important to only seek this when it is really wanted and needed. As in the case of letter-writing campaigns, it is important to have prepared a documented, clear and concise presentation of the vital features of the case.

Reporters are people too! They need stories; it is part of their job to get them. Some of them may be concerned about suppression and interested in your case. After all, they have probably been suppressed, or seen suppression in action, more times than they can count. You can make life easier for them by providing a clear and considered written or verbal account of your case, and being as courteous to them as you would to anyone else. Remember that unless you have specified that your discussion is "off the record", anything you say to a reporter may appear in print, or on air if you are being recorded. It pays to be honest, open, cautious and completely accurate.

Pressure group action

Another extension of the letter-writing campaign by individuals is action by sympathetic groups. In the Coulter case, trade unions and environmental groups took action to oppose the dismissal. There are many avenues for action. Groups (and individuals too) can write letters to employers, write letters to newspapers, lobby politicians, get questions asked in Parliament, make public statements, hold public meetings, hold demonstrations and organise occupations.

Elite bureaucrats detest public campaigns. Often they have no idea how to handle the situation. Sometimes they are prone to make logistical and decisional errors, which can accumulate to turn the process to the favour of the suppressed as errors are compounded upon errors. The initial response of bureaucrats usually is to ignore publicity and pressure. If this is not effective, then everything will be done to squash the campaign or divert it into formal channels.

Public campaigns have several positive wider consequences: they delegitimise inadequate formal procedures and organisations; they encourage similar action by others, especially by making many people aware that suppression has institutional roots; they can sometimes induce organisational change, or result in imposition of controls from the outside; and they promote solidarity between dissidents and their supporters. On the negative side, public campaigns may result in greater cohesion among vested interests against challenges, depending on how the campaign is run.

Public campaigns often are quite powerful because the majority of the public is in sympathy with the dissident's activities. When a government employee exposes waste or corruption, it is usually only those who think that the actions of those in high places should not be questioned who want this hushed up. Most people will want the waste, corruption or injustice rectified. Public channels tap the basic sympathy for good action and the basic antagonism to abuse of power and privilege. It is often the dissident's strongest base. On the other hand, public sympathy cannot be guaranteed. Sometimes racism, sexism, rumour or systematic counter-publicity may swing sympathy to the suppressor. These possibilities should not be discounted.

As well as the previous suggestions about the preparation of arguments and coordinating campaigns, the involvement of pressure groups raises some delicate issues. Most importantly, dissidents should on no account manipulate, or be seen to manipulate, individuals or groups in order to gain support. For example, it may be that a threatened academic program has potential support from other staff and from students. But if the organiser is, for example, a member of a staff association and a teacher of the students in the program, these positions of formal or de facto power should not be used to induce support. In our opinion, it is quite all right to discuss the situation with individuals or groups, and to suggest courses of action. But often it would be politically unwise to propose a staff association motion to take action to protect one's job, or to convene a meeting of students and outline plans for a student strike. Campaigns are best run by other staff or students, and the threatened individual plays the role of adviser. Not only is this better for the sake of appearances, but more importantly it ensures that the goodwill of supporters is not jeopardised by misuse of their concern, even if the misuse is unwitting.

Manipulation is usually only a problem when dissidents are in formal positions of power in relation to potential supporters. The avoidance of manipulation should not be taken to imply that support cannot be solicited. It can, and should be. People will not take action unless they know about the case and have some ideas of what to do about it. Furthermore, although it is useful to have one's case taken up by a third party, often this is not possible. Do not be hesitant in actively promoting your own case if necessary, by writing letters, putting out press releases and making public speeches.

Unfortunately, many reforms only occur after considerable bad publicity. In several of the cases we have examined, it was only mass student protest that motivated university administrations to reconsider their actions. If the situation at an institution has reached the point where mass protest is required, then it is important that those involved behave with restraint and decency. There is nothing to prevent an unscrupulous administration using the agent provocateur technique to induce violence which is counterproductive for the protesters. When there is a convincing case of injustice, the presence of a large number of nonviolent, firm and courageous protesters can work miracles in restoring, if only temporarily, a sense of fair play into the administrators of intellectual organisations.

Personal resources

At times you may stand alone. You'll need the psychological resources to handle that, and the skills to win support. Don't expect too much initial support from colleagues in the pay of your institution. Once a power bloc begins to get at a dissident, many others may join in against the dissident for a variety of reasons. It is because of the isolation resulting from such unified opposition that many dissidents simply drop out, refuse publicity, resign (even though the charges are false), or even commit suicide. To counteract such isolation, support networks are vital. Support networks thus serve a double role: they provide both moral support and some source of countervailing power.

If you retain your composure and consistency, you may be fortunate enough for the arguments and the balance of power to move eventually in your favour, providing you with more confidence. If things start to go in your favour, the suppressors may begin to disagree among themselves, looking for scapegoats or a "rationalised" rewriting of the case history to make things look better for themselves.

DECIDING ON A STRATEGY

There are many possible methods and courses of action in opposing suppression. How can one decide what to do? One can carefully consider the options, consult friends, and get advice from others with similar experiences. In a major case, it may be useful to use some of the methods of nonviolent action training in designing a strategy meeting.[5] Here is a possible sequence of events.

- Carefully examine your own motives, and assess why you are acting to oppose suppression. Is it mainly for your own interests, or because of wider principles? What do you hope to achieve personally? Is there a grudge element in pursuing the case?

- Call a meeting of supporters (or participate in a meeting called by a supporter). Allow plenty of time away from distractions and deadlines. Invite supporters, especially those who will be taking action or who will be affected personally by the campaign. It may be useful to have a sympathetic person who is not actively involved in the campaign to facilitate the meeting.

- Evaluate the current situation. Assess who are current and potential supporters and opponents. Assess the degree of support and opposition likely from different groups.

- Decide the goals of the campaign. Is for example reinstatement sufficient or is public vindication sought? Or are changes in procedures desired, or penalising of suppressors sought, or social reforms aimed at? It is vitally important to be clear about aims, so that one is not enticed by minor concessions or carried away by side issues.

- In the light of the present situation and the future goals, evaluate the strengths and weaknesses of the different options. Assess these options not only according to their immediate relevance to the goal, but also according to their effectiveness in sustaining motivation and outside support. For example, a petition may not have much effect on the authorities it is addressed to, but it can be an effective way of exposing more people to the issues and publicising the case through press releases.

- Assign specific tasks to specific people. If there are not enough people ready to do what is planned, the program is probably too ambitious. After any planning meeting, it is important for all involved to know what they are supposed to be doing and how it all fits together. Often it is useful to prepare a "time-line", a week-by-week or day-by-day schedule of when different avenues of action will be undertaken. For example, if a submission is to be made to a union meeting, time must be allowed for writing, verifying and reproducing it. If a time-coordinated set of activities is developed, it can be possible to generate a crescendo of pressure focused on a particular crucial event, such as a faculty meeting to decide funding priorities.

• Don't be totally tied to a fixed course of action. Periodic reviews of options are useful, especially when events open up new possibilities. It is also effective not to be too predictable. If the suppressors can take your actions for granted, this can help them plan their own campaigns against you. Be original.

• Be persistent and prepare for a long struggle if necessary.

References

A few points in this chapter are taken from Brian Martin, "Suppression of dissident experts", *Crime and Social Justice*, no. 19, Summer 1983, pp. 91–9.

1. Brian Martin, "The scientific straightjacket: the power structure of science and the suppression of environmental scholarship", *Ecologist*, vol. 11, no. 1, January–February 1981, pp. 33–43.

2. See the chapter by Clyde Manwell and C. M. Ann Baker, "Not Merely Malice".

3. See the chapter: "Mutagens and Managers", on the Coulter case.

4. See the chapter by Brian Martin and Clyde Manwell, "Publicising Suppression".

5. Virginia Coover, Ellen Deacon, Charles Esser and Christopher Moore, *Resource Manual for a Living Revolution* (Philadelphia: New Society Publishers, 1981).

Publicising Suppression

Brian Martin and Clyde Manwell

Publicity is one of the most powerful avenues for opposing suppression of intellectual dissent. Suppression usually takes the form of blocking publications or free speech, or of victimising those who hold the dissenting views, such as by harassment, smear campaigns and sackings. Publicity is an immediate challenge to suppression in two ways. First, it exposes or threatens to expose the suppressed views themselves. Second, it threatens to mobilise opposition to the practices, policies or power of the groups instituting the suppression.

There are some specific examples which suggest that publicity does help. Soviet dissidents have reported that when foreign publicity exposes their mistreatment, conditions usually improve. In the case of Zhores Medvedev the pressure of outside publicity assisted in effecting his release from a mental institution.[1] Andrei Sakharov has written of the helpfulness of publicity in countering secret repression within the USSR — although he has also warned that inaccuracies in the publicity, as in the overly zealous anti-communist propaganda published in *Nature*, "almost cancelled its usefulness".[2]

Amnesty International has used the method of writing letters to the authorities in countries where political prisoners are held. This seemingly innocuous approach has achieved the release of thousands of prisoners, among other successes. Amnesty also recommends attempting to communicate with gaoled dissidents to let them know that there is someone on the outside who cares.

In this chapter we address a specific question about obtaining publicity for dissidents. Where is coverage of suppression of intellectual dissent more likely to be obtained: in scholarly journals or in the mass media? We obtained an answer to this question from an unplanned experiment in trying to publicise a case of suppression treated earlier in this book, the dismissal of Dr John Coulter from the Institute of Medical and Veterinary Science.

When news of Dr Coulter's impending dismissal became known in April 1980, many people rallied to his defence. It seemed apparent that Dr Coulter was being victimised for his environmental activities: a case of suppression of a dissident scientist. The official justifications for the dismissal did not stand up at the time, as correspondence in the Adelaide *Advertiser* showed, nor later during the court hearings. Dr Coulter was supported by scientists, environmentalists, trade unionists and others who wrote letters to newspapers and parliamentarians, passed resolutions and published information about the case.

We were two of those who tried to publicise the Coulter case. Since each of us had been concerned about suppression of scientists for some time, we also tried to place the Coulter case in the context of suppression generally and in the context of the system of power relationships within science and the wider society.

In the course of writing and submitting letters and articles about the Coulter case and about suppression in science, we carried out an unplanned experiment in determining the receptiveness of different types of journals to information about suppression. A summary of the responses to our efforts is presented in the table below. Details, qualifications and further comments are given elsewhere.[3]

TABLE

Fate of submissions by Brian Martin or by Clyde Manwell about the Coulter case or about suppression generally, to various journals.

Technical, scientific and medical journals

British Medical Journal: letter submitted July 1980, rejected July 1980.

Medical Journal of Australia: letter submitted July 1981, rejected September 1981.

Nature: letter submitted July 1980, revised version of letter not published.

New Scientist: article submitted September 1980, rejected October 1980.

Science: article submitted April 1980, returned May 1980; letter submitted May 1980, published September 1980.

Search: article submitted March 1981, rejected April 1981; letter submitted May 1981, published April/May 1982.

Journals treating social issues

Arena: article submitted May 1981, rejected November 1981.

ANU Reporter: article submitted May 1980, revised version published August 1980.

Bogong: solicited article submitted September 1980, published September/October 1980.

Crime and Social Justice: solicited article submitted September 1982, published mid-1983.

Current Affairs Bulletin: article submitted February 1982, declined March 1982.

Ecologist: letter submitted July 1980, accepted July 1980 but not published; article submitted October 1980, published January/February 1981; letter submitted August 1982, not published.

Higher Education Research and Development Society of Australasia: article submitted May 1980, revised version published December 1980.

Metal Worker: article submitted February 1981, published March 1981.

New Doctor: letter submitted September 1981, not published.

New Society: article submitted February 1981, rejected March 1981.

Probe: article provided August 1981, published October 1981.

Progressive: article submitted November 1980, story published February 1981.

Science for the People: information submitted February 1981, nothing published.

Social Studies of Science: article submitted May 1980, declined July 1980.

Waikato Environment: solicited article submitted March 1981, rejected April 1981.

Newspapers and television and radio stations

Adelaide *Advertiser*: article submitted April 1980, not published.

Melbourne *Age*: unsolicited interview July 1980, article published July 1980.

Australian: information requested September 1980, article published September 1980.

Australian Broadcasting Corporation, radio and television: several interviews in 1980, broadcast in the following weeks.

Canberra Times: letter submitted May 1980, published June 1980; talk given September 1980, article on talk published September 1980.

Capital 7 Television: unsolicited interview September 1980, broadcast September 1980.

National Times: information provided October 1980, nothing published.

We have grouped the journals into three categories. First are technical, scientific and medical journals. By and large these journals were uninterested in or hostile towards publishing material on the Coulter case and suppression. Partial exceptions were *Science* and *Search*, where letters were published after considerable delay and some persistence on our part, and *New Scientist*, which solicited (but did not receive or publish) an article after rejecting a submission from one of us.

The second category includes a diverse collection of journals which can be said to treat social issues. The response from these journals to our submissions was quite mixed, seeming to depend considerably on the particular editors involved. Of left-leaning journals, *Arena, New Society* and *Science for the People* were not interested in our material, but *Crime and Social Justice* and the *Progressive* were quite receptive. Of environmental journals, *Bogong* and *Probe* quickly published articles, the *Ecologist* was interested but did not publish all our submissions, and *Waikato Environment* was not interested. The two journals closest to the professional orientation of journals in the first category, namely *New Doctor* and *Social Studies of Science*, were similarly hesitant to publish our submissions.

The third category includes newspapers and television and radio stations: the so-called mass media. By and large these outlets were quite interested in the Coulter case and in suppression generally, more even than the table suggests. Although the Adelaide *Advertiser* did not publish an article written by one of us, it did publish many letters and an article about the Coulter case. Likewise, while the *National Times* did not use the material provided by one of us about a variety of cases of suppression, earlier it did publish one of the most substantial articles on the Coulter case. Many reporters requested information or interviews with us; we have not listed in the table the many radio stations which requested and recorded interviews about suppression.

The contrast between the first and third categories is considerable. On the one hand, editors and referees for prestigious scientific and medical journals tended to be sceptical of the existence of suppression and wary of making comment. On the other hand, reporters for newspapers and the electronic media were ready and sometimes eager to publicise stories on suppression. Journals intermediate in scientific status were also on average intermediate in receptiveness to material on suppression.

How can the differences in receptiveness to material on suppression be explained? One possible explanation is that scholarly journals have higher standards of verification. This does not stand up to examination. When we submitted material to scientific journals, we also sent supporting evidence, including newspaper accounts and internal memos. Rejections of our accounts were not claimed to be based on lack of evidence. Sometimes no reasons were offered, sometimes the editors were not convinced of our explanations, but in only two cases did they request further information. Furthermore, in every case we personally were taking responsibility for accuracy by offering letters or signed articles.

Inaccuracy in scientific journals is more common than is usually recognised. It is telling that the exposure of fraud in science, as in the case of Sir Cyril Burt, often has taken place in the mass media rather than in the scientific journals that published the fakes in the first place.

While examples of inaccuracies in the mass media abound, the mass media must be very careful in reporting cases dealing with individuals. The laws on defamation — which are quite severe in Australia — provide a source of feedback on accuracy in reporting cases such as the Coulter case. Not only would it be much easier to sue a local newspaper or television station than an overseas scientific journal, it would be more lucrative.

In summary, scientific journals are not as concerned about high standards of verification of suppression as might be expected, whereas the mass media are forced by defamation law to be very careful in these cases.

Nor can differences in responses to information about suppression readily be explained by differences in types of articles published in journals. Most of the scientific and medical journals to which we sent letters and articles normally include some articles or editorials on ethical issues. Several of these journals routinely publish material about suppression of scientists in communist countries. The few reasons offered to us for not publicising the Coulter case — that it was only of local interest, or that it might be solely a personality clash — do not sit well with the willingness to expose victimisation of dissident scientists in communist countries.

In our opinion, the differences in response to information about suppression are largely due to the role of many scientists, especially influential editors and referees, in sanctioning or not protesting against suppression close to home, compared to the important if occasional role of the mass media in exposing various abuses in society. Many scientists have submerged their own dissent or qualms — or even tolerated or used the suppression of others — in order to obtain degrees, jobs and research grants. In these circumstances the way to avoid guilt and cognitive dissonance is to deny that suppression occurs at all.

More importantly, exposure of suppression is a threat to the power and prestige of scientific elites. For example, Dr Coulter in his public statements cast doubt on the safety of certain environmental chemicals. This provided a direct threat to the profits of companies and an indirect threat to the funding and status of scientists and scientific institutions patronised by the chemical corporations. Is it any wonder that chemical corporations forwarded complaints to the IMVS, and that influential figures in the IMVS were upset by Dr Coulter's activities?

Historically, the press became a business in itself in the mid-1800s by selling itself via catastrophes, scandals, crime and war: bad news in moral terms became good news in commercial terms. Once news became a commodity rather than just information, the press was able to become partially detached from the political and economic bases of capitalism and parliamentary democracy. As a semi-autonomous force in society, the press on occasion is able to publicise or even support movements or activities, such as the labour movement, which are antagonistic to dominant groups. Journalists, editors and proprietors do not have a great stake in protecting the image of science and academia. Some pressures in this direction exist, but contrary pressures exist to publish anything that makes a good story — and suppression fits this bill well.

Would better national and overseas publicity have made a difference in the outcome of the Coulter case? It is impossible to know for sure, but we strongly suspect that extra publicity — especially in scientific journals — might well have encouraged a better and quicker settlement in Dr Coulter's favour.

We conclude that "scholarly standards" are not always sufficient to produce the truth. At least as important is freedom of the press, and more than this the willingness to speak out on controversial issues.

Acknowledgements

We thank Ann Baker, Barry Hailstone and Cedric Pugh for valuable comments.

References

1. Zhores A. Medvedev and Roy A. Medvedev, *A Question of Madness* (New York: Norton, 1979).
2. Andrei Sakharov, letter, *Nature*, vol. 288, 13 November 1980, p. 112.
3. Brian Martin and Clyde Manwell, "The fate of suppression submissions" (available from the authors).

SUPPRESSION AND SOCIAL ACTION

Brian Martin

Suppression of intellectual dissent can be seen as one part of a general historical struggle between on the one hand powerful and privileged interests in society and on the other grassroots initiatives for a more equal and just society. Here I will first describe this context for understanding suppression in general terms. Then I will discuss the ambiguous relation between intellectual dissidents and social action groups.

It is common historically for the mass of people in complex societies to be dominated economically, politically and ideologically by particular elite groups.[1] In the history of European peoples, the earlier primary elite group of the feudal aristocracy and church hierarchy was supplanted several hundred years ago by capitalist owners and managers. More recently power has been shifting to political and bureaucratic state elites, most notably under state socialism but also in capitalist societies. These shifts in the locus of power have resulted from economic, political and social development, and the ensuing struggles between interest groups.

The other essential component in this process has been the struggles of the mass of the people, the non-elites. These struggles have waxed and waned, but have been marked by progress in some areas, such as the ending of slavery, development of mass literacy, spreading of the franchise, redistribution of some economic benefits to workers, and ending of colonialism. These struggles have become increasingly self-aware and organised. But new struggles are required as new forms of exploitation and oppression arise or expand, such as neo-colonialism, technology designed to control workers, and weapons of mass destruction.

What is the role in this historical process of intellectuals and institutions for cultivating intellectual skills? For centuries one primary function has been the ideological legitimation of current social arrangements. This legitimation has at various times included religious certification of the god-givenness of the social order, the alleged social and biological necessity of capitalist competition (social Darwinism), and the alleged necessity to have experts to manage all aspects of society (technocracy). This sort of legitimation has been important because ruling groups have usually been in the minority and have depended for their power and privilege on the support or acquiescence of the bulk of the population. Besides legitimation, in the past century or so schools and universities have played an increasing role in training more people in intellectual skills useful for the maintenance and expansion of industrial society.

Intellectual skills are indeed used widely for justifying power structures and for ensuring the normal functioning of industrial society, but they also contain the seeds of liberation, for supporting struggles for democratisation. It is this potential for ideological unmasking of the present order that makes universities periodically become hotbeds of dissent, and leads to attempts by elite groups to throttle these movements. The institutions of learning are

257

protected in two ways: first by their own service in the maintenance of society, and second by the intellectual tradition of liberal education and freedom of opinion. This tradition — which represents the intellectual self-justification of higher learning and which often masks the reality of intellectual service to vested interests — can also be used to defend the existence of dissent.

Within academia and other intellectual institutions, suppression is one mechanism to ensure that the main beneficiaries of paid intellectual activities are the dominant groups in society, in particular corporate, bureaucratic and professional elites. The main forces forging this orientation are the hierarchy, division of labour, privilege and status of paid intellectuals.[2] Suppression is essentially a back-up mechanism, to keep those in line who are not induced or seduced by privilege and status to support the powers that be by keeping to their narrow activities and staying out of political struggles on behalf of oppressed groups. Suppression is important precisely because dissidence is so infrequent. When the consensus of expert intellectual opinion is virtually unanimous, a single dissenting voice can make a big difference in helping to legitimise contrary views.

The driving force behind challenges to dominant institutions in society comes not from intellectual dissidents themselves but rather arises from the potential for mass action at the grassroots such as by the labour movement. But dissidents can expose the nature and abuses of the ruling elites, puncture the standard legitimations and thus help to weaken support for the elites and to catalyse mass action. Dissidents in many cases are essentially subversives within the more privileged levels of the power structure. They break the bureaucratic and professional monopolies on knowledge and thus provide avenues for challenge from below. For example, John Coulter's public statements about the hazards of particular environmental chemicals in themselves did not threaten the profits of corporations. But by providing information about these hazards to public audiences — for example via the media — community group protest and possibly government action concerning the chemicals might be mobilised or focused, thus threatening profits. Similarly, by providing information about work hazards directly to workers and unions, John Coulter broke the ranks of professional control over such knowledge and provided leverage for workers and unions to take action.

Before Ann Baker and Clyde Manwell wrote their letter to the Adelaide *Advertiser* about fruit fly spraying, several other individuals had written similar letters. Clyde Manwell was singled out for attack because he was the first person to write from a prestigious position: his co-authorship of the letter was seen as breaking the monopoly on "expert" opinion on the fruit fly spraying issue, and thus greatly weakening the establishment view on the subject.

There is an interactive process between intellectual dissidents and mass movements, and this process is sometimes a complicated one. In many cases, the rise of mass movements encourages or allows dissent within intellectual institutions. For example, the rise of the environmental movement has encouraged and enabled many scientists and academics to undertake research and make public stands on environmental issues. On the other hand, a few courageous intellectuals are often found promoting an issue before it becomes the basis for a mass movement. Rachel Carson and some other scientists played this role in relation to environmental issues in the 1950s and early 1960s. In the case of nuclear power, various individual scientists — such as, in the United States, Henry Kendall, John Gofman and Arthur Tamplin — took critical stands in the early 1970s, before popular concern about this technology had reached major proportions. These scientists played an important role in legitimising anti-nuclear concerns, and laying the intellectual basis for mass action years later. And once the mass anti-nuclear movement developed, other scientists and intellectuals took stands, such as the three General Electric nuclear engineers who resigned in 1976.

Those intellectuals who take stands contrary to elite interests before mass concern develops are often suppressed, as were Carson, Gofman and Tamplin.[3] But once mass concern is aroused, it may become acceptable to do research or teaching in the once ignored or taboo area. For example, programs in peace studies, environmental studies and women's studies are in numerous cases set up in response to general public concern on these issues, and sometimes due to direct public pressure. In the United States, not a single holistic study program in the area of energy and environment was established at a university before 1971, by which time widespread public interest and the definition of the main problems had already been developed.[4] A similar situation applies in Australia in this area. Intellectual institutions are but rarely in the forefront in developing new areas of study relevant to social problems. They are much more likely to move into areas after popular concern has well and truly developed. In this they are similar to other basically conservative institutions, such as the law, major political parties and the churches.

From this perspective, the role of dissidents within intellectual institutions, and the role of small social action groups, is much greater than first appearances might suggest. Although their immediate impact may seem small, they can provide the stimulus for development of mass concern and mass action on social issues, and thus do more to induce institutional change than the more immediate method of working through "proper channels".

I will now look at the problem of social change from the point of view of those in social action groups. What should be their orientation with respect to intellectual institutions, and towards dissidents?

SUPPORT FOR DISSIDENT PROFESSIONALS

The most immediate thing social activists can do is directly support dissidents in their battles against suppression. Social activists often are experienced in political campaigning and are much better equipped to organise defences of dissidents than are professional intellectuals. Support for dissidents by outside social activists sometimes happens, but not as often as might be expected. The reason is the distance maintained by most senior professional intellectuals — including many dissidents — from social action groups. Personally, I think this distance should be bridged through efforts on both sides. Social activists can help in this by supporting dissidents.

Another problem in supporting dissidents is different perceptions of the motivations and value of the dissident activity. Some dissidents may be seen by outsiders to be taking a stand only in order to gain personally. A university program under threat may contain some committed, hard-working, socially conscious and outspoken scholars and others who are more interested in a job or in expanding their power. Or the program leaders may oppose internal staff democracy or oppose more participation by students. Social activists can legitimately feel ambivalent about supporting such programs and the individuals in them. Should an imperfect but generally desirable program be supported unconditionally, or should criticisms of the program by social activists be made privately or publicly?

Compounding these problems are differences of opinion and splits within social movements about the role of professional intellectual activity in social activism. For example, many people in the Australian peace movement have spent much time and effort promoting the establishment of a peace research institute. Others would not oppose such an institute, but do not see it as a high priority. Still others see efforts for setting up an institute as a diversion from more important tasks of building up mass involvement in the peace movement and developing grassroots strategies. These and other perspectives will influence the willingness and approach of anti-war activists in supporting professional intellectuals who speak out on issues of war and peace. Divergences in perspective can be quite major, and are important in, for example, the feminist, political economy and environmental movements.

SUPPRESSION WITHIN SOCIAL MOVEMENTS

Social movements can be organised in various ways, but they almost always contain some individuals with greater formal or informal power than others, such as officials, paid workers, key spokespeople, and editors of movement journals. This power can be used to suppress individuals from a different clique or with unorthodox opinions. Suppression within social movements can take forms such as:

- withdrawing union membership, blacklisting, beating and even killing of rank-and-file trade union activists[5];
- expulsion of dissenting members from political parties;
- sacking of politically minded environmental workers from environment centres;
- social ostracism, character assassination and sacking of feminists with "incorrect views" from community service organisations dominated by particular types of feminists;
- blocking of dissenting views from ostensibly pluralistic social movement journals.

Suppression within social movements typically involves many of the methods found in suppression elsewhere, including personal attacks such as threatening phone calls, spreading of slanderous stories, ostracism, criticising work, failing to provide information about meetings and social functions, and public confrontation. Especially revealing of power inequalities is the use by social movements of formal mechanisms against dissidents such as defamation suits and legal challenges concerning elections or administrative action. For the dissidents, suppression is especially difficult to handle psychologically when the social movement espouses values such as emotional honesty and participatory democracy, since expectations of fair treatment are much greater than in mainstream institutions.

Sometimes suppression within social movements is justified by conventional criteria: shortage of funds, incompetence of the suppressed, or personality clashes. At other times the exercise of power by a particular faction or clique is justified by alleging that the dissident is insufficiently committed to the movement.[6]

Suppression of intellectual dissent is most rigorous in those left-wing parties which maintain a strict "line", but also can occur in more broadly based movements. Most movements base their activities on a set of more or less unquestioned assumptions, and challenging these assumptions may not be well received.

Like suppression in general, suppression within social movements is an area in which documentation is scarce, and so my comments here are based largely on personal observations and discussions. Social activists sometimes argue that public discussion of internal dissent and its suppression is undesirable because it will be seized upon by critics to attack the social movement. This argument is often used to make activists feel guilty about protesting against abuses within their own groups. But silence and nonaction, besides being ethically unacceptable, are often even more harmful to the movement than speaking out. Tolerance or support for internal suppression can cause entrenchment of factions or cliques, alienation of supporters, neglect or loss of new ideas and constituencies, and corruption of principled behaviour. In making compromises to attain power or influence, the movement may come to resemble the institutions it aims to transform or displace.

If social activists are to be consistent and effective in opposing suppression of intellectual dissent, then they need to make sure their own house is in order. In my opinion, tolerance of a diversity of opinions is essential in developing a program and practice for beneficial social change. Social activists could well take to heart the principles of academic freedom which are so seldom used by academics.

INSTITUTIONALISATION

Besides defending dissidents, another thing social activists can try to do is to promote institutionalisation of their concerns within intellectual institutions. This is a difficult task. A frequent result of the development of mass concern on an issue is the establishment of government departments or academic programs which treat the issues but without the critical force behind the original concern. Government departments of industrial relations may serve to integrate workers and unions into the capitalist system. Environmental studies departments may study environmental problems and develop policy within the context of existing practices and assumptions of industrialisation and the existing distribution of political and economic power.[7] Even after a "radical" program is set up, an ongoing struggle may be required to prevent expropriation of the original social concern into service to elite interests, such as building "environmentally sound" car parks for yacht clubs.

To have some chance that programs on social issues will maintain some critical concern, social activists need to be involved directly in designing the form and content of the programs. One important model is the science shop, well developed at several Dutch universities.[8] Groups such as trade unions or community welfare, peace or environmental groups can contact the science shop for advice about questions involving expertise in science and technology. The workers at the science shop try to connect the requesting groups with scientists willing to work on the problem. Another example is the Centre for Alternative Industrial and Technological Systems, a research unit set up at North East London Polytechnic to study problems relevant to the alternative corporate plan developed by Lucas Aerospace workers.[9]

What about the structure of the university? The basic problem is the power structure of the university, especially the power of academic elites and administrations.[10] The most fundamental challenge to this power is flattening the academic hierarchy. This would do more to allow genuine academic freedom than marginal fiddling with tenure, procedures, or staff and student representation on committees. If all high salaries were reduced — for example to the average wage — then staff members could be greatly increased and everyone given tenure or extended contracts. This would free numerous people from publication rat-races, bureaucratic infighting and bootlicking, and permit a great deal of innovative teaching and research.

The typical strategy by radicals in academia has been to try to get more radicals into positions within the present academic structures, whether this is via promotion of talented radicals to high positions or by increasing staff and student representation on decision-making bodies. The more fundamental strategy of flattening the hierarchy has seldom been adopted. The challenge — as yet largely unmet — is to develop persuasive campaigns with this more fundamental change as a goal.

INTELLECTUAL SELF-MANAGEMENT

A third avenue for action by social action groups is in this final direction: developing models and campaigns to challenge power structures in society, including those within intellectual institutions. If the structures of unequal power and privilege can be transformed, then the use of suppression will be reduced. For example, in the labour movement the normal goals are improved wages and conditions within the existing structures of state-regulated capitalism. A more radical goal is that of workers' control, which looks towards a more egalitarian work environment in which workers themselves decide the organisation of work and the products produced, in conjunction with community interests.[11] In the women's movement the liberal goal is equality for women within the existing career and family structures. A more radical feminist goal is transforming the power hierarchies and establishing equality between the sexes within a more egalitarian society.

If this perspective is applied to intellectual activity, the goal becomes not experts for social movements but a spreading of expertise. One standard approach within social movements is to develop or cultivate "counter-experts": experts in a field who use their knowledge to criticise the activities or ideology of dominant interests. For example, scientists who were public opponents of nuclear power helped the anti-nuclear power movement by puncturing the mystifications of the pro-nuclear experts. Those within intellectual institutions who subscribe to this approach generally think in terms of the "social responsibility" of experts to make use of their knowledge to oppose social wrongs.

The approach of using counter-experts and promoting social responsibility of intellectuals is good as far as it goes, but it does not question the nature and role of expertise itself. Knowledge produced and used by professional intellectuals is for the most part esoteric, jargon-ridden, separated from its ideological context, and hence irrelevant to social issues. Because intellectual institutions are geared to the interests of corporate, bureaucratic and professional elites, the knowledge they produce is likewise biased in form and content. Counter-experts can rectify this situation to some extent — especially as regards the content of knowledge — but may at the same time reinforce the dependence on certified expertise itself, to the detriment of social movements.

Underlying most social issues are questions of values, not of facts. Rather than use counter-experts to challenge the facts put forward by the supporters of elite interests, a more radical approach is to focus on the values underlying the differing sides to the debate. For example, instead of only spelling out the hazards of plutonium, the instances of reactor malfunctions and the limitations of proliferation treaties, emphasis can be put on the political and economic implications of centralised, high-cost and expert-dependent nuclear power technology, along with the implications of an energy future based on energy efficiency and small-scale decentralised use of renewable energy technologies and accompanying social changes.

To avoid dependence on the counter-experts, social action groups can promote the spreading of intellectual and practical skills: research, writing, speaking. This is encouraged in action groups which try to be non-hierarchical, participatory and self-managing, such as sections of the feminist, environmental, anarchist and non-violent action movements. These groups provide a base outside the intellectual institutions where intellectual activity and social action can be linked together in an ongoing process of building campaigns, undertaking cooperative research and learning, and communicating via journals and newsletters.[12]

Grassroots social activism linked with self-critical evaluation and study provides an alternative to relying on professional intellectuals and at the same time strengthens the positions of those intellectuals who do engage in or promote genuinely critical research or teaching. If a participative social movement with a sound set of principles and strategies for social change can be built, then intellectual institutions may eventually join the bandwagon.

In some ways, egalitarian social action groups are a greater long-term threat to the privileged professional intellectuals than are corporate or bureaucratic elites or powerful working-class organisations. The irony is that many of those who join and become most active in such groups are products of the academic system. While the academics pursue autonomy, academic freedom and control over work conditions for their own self-interest, these action groups are attempting to apply these same ideals to a much broader constituency.

Acknowledgements

Useful comments on a draft of this chapter were received from Ann Baker, Marilyn Chalkley, Clyde Manwell, Cedric Pugh and Wendy Varney.

References

1. The following several paragraphs are taken from Brian Martin, "Suppression of dissident experts: ideological struggle in Australia", *Crime and Social Justice*, no. 19, Summer 1983, pp. 91–9.

2. This point is developed at some length in: Brian Martin, "Academics and social action", *Higher Education Review*, vol. 16, no. 2, Spring 1984, pp. 17–33. A few paragraphs from this article are used in this chapter.

3. Frank Graham, Jr., *Since Silent Spring* (Boston: Houghton Mifflin, 1970); Leslie J. Freeman, *Nuclear Witnesses: Insiders Speak Out* (New York: Norton, 1981).

4. David J. Rose, "New laboratories for old", in: Gerald Holton and William A. Blanpied (eds), *Science and its Publics: The Changing Relationship* (Dordrecht: D. Reidel, 1976), pp. 143–55.

5. Suppression and repression within trade unions are especially serious in the United States. See for example: Burton Hall (ed.), *Autocracy and Insurgency in Organized Labor* (New Brunswick, NJ: Transaction Books, 1972).

6. Katherine Newman, "Incipient bureaucracy: the development of hierarchy in egalitarian organizations", in Gerald M. Britan and Ronald Cohen (eds), *Hierarchy and Society* (Philadelphia: Institute for the Study of Human Issues, 1980), pp. 143–64, see especially pp. 157–8.

7. Brian Martin, "Academics and the environment: a critique of the Australian National University's Centre for Resource and Environmental Studies", *Ecologist*, vol. 7, no. 6, July 1977, pp. 224–32.

8. Ad Meertens and Onno Nieman, "The Amsterdam science shop: doing science for the people", *Science for the People*, vol. 11, no. 5, September–October 1979, pp. 15–17, 36–7.

9. Hilary Wainwright and Dave Elliott, *The Lucas Plan: A New Trade Unionism in the Making?* (London: Allison and Busby, 1982).

10. The increasing power of academic administrations is noted in: Lionel S. Lewis, *Scaling the Ivory Tower: Merit and its Limits in Academic Careers* (Baltimore: Johns Hopkins University Press, 1975), Ch. 6; Anthony Arblaster, *Academic Freedom* (Harmondsworth: Penguin, 1974).

11. Ken Coates and Tony Topham, *The New Unionism: The Case for Workers' Control* (London: Peter Owen, 1972); Gerry Hunnius, G. David Garson and John Case (eds), *Workers' Control: A Reader on Labor and Social Change* (New York: Vintage, 1973).

12. See for example: Virginia Coover, Ellen Deacon, Charles Esser and Christopher Moore, *Resource Manual for a Living Revolution* (Philadelphia: New Society Publishers, 1981); The Training/Action Affinity Group of Movement for a New Society, *Building Social Change Communities* (Philadelphia: Movement for a New Society, 1979).

EVALUATION OF PERFORMANCE IN ACADEMIC AND SCIENTIFIC INSTITUTIONS

Clyde Manwell and C. M. Ann Baker

Covert discrimination cannot exist without falsehood...Often the blame is placed on the victim...

You will cause the least trouble to the university if you can be persuaded to doubt your own worth and to believe that your opponents are being objective. The university may also rely on your fear of what will happen to you if you resist its authority. If, however, you do struggle, the university will put forth a powerful effort to get you to fight the case on its own grounds (usually the quality of your scholarship, occasionally the quality of your teaching).

Those who have the power to practice discrimination understand its mechanisms far better than do their victims. Many of us are burdened with a sense of inferiority; though we know better, we are nevertheless likely to believe authorities who assure us in a seemingly rational and objective or even benevolent tone that our work is mediocre. People who possess the critical vocabulary, who know the lingo, can always find the words and means to support a predetermined negative judgment; all that is needed is the will to make that judgment.

There are stock methods of creating such a negative assessment: discovering "inconsistencies" between parts of your work; distorting the argument; suggesting that the development lacks complexity; asserting that your work failed to include some other aspect of the subject.

When discrimination is being practiced, the publication of an article, even in a prestigious journal, is no longer a sufficient guarantee of the article's quality...

Marcia R. Lieberman[1]

INTRODUCTORY REMARKS: OBJECTIVES AND SUMMARY OF THE TOPICS SURVEYED

The primary purpose of this chapter is to help individuals defend themselves against inadequate or inaccurate allegations. Many fail to fight good cases because they do not know the Marquess of Queensberry's Rules — and how some administrators hit below the belt and get away with it. As the above quotation from Marcia Lieberman points out, the academic system can force the innocent victim to believe in his or her own guilt. The system, with its potential for bias in peer review at a number of levels (thesis examination, refereeing of manuscripts and research grant proposals, hiring or firing, promotion and other awards), destroys much individual creativity.[2] This destruction is done in an inefficient and hypocritical way: discrimination for irrelevant reasons is practised in the name of academic excellence. The dissident is sacrificed on the altar of administrative convenience.

This chapter needs to be longer than previous ones for three reasons: first, there is a wide range of honest opinions about what constitutes good performance in research or teaching. However, complications arise in interpreting the words used to justify some guilty verdicts.

Second, when the suppressors strike, the victim may not have the time or the resources to sift through the literature on evaluation of performance in order to prepare an adequate defence. As Professor R. D. Wright described so well in the preface to Eddy's book on the Orr case, the victim will find himself deserted by his fairweather academic friends.[3] The victim, even if a dues-paying member of his staff association, may find that staff association officials regard him as a threat to their own negotiations for improved pay or working conditions, negotiations carried out in a cosy manner with the administration. While there are a variety of options open in countering suppression generally, the options are narrowed when the suppressors attempt to effect dismissal. Especially where the administration seeks publicity so that sacking becomes a means to discredit the dissident, the victim may be presented with no viable alternative but to fight his case — and fight it on the administration's terms. We choose the words "viable alternative" deliberately, for we know of two cases where unfairly victimised academics committed suicide. It is impossible in our review to anticipate all possible allegations, or procedural tricks. Our case histories reveal a sample. Our aim here is to provide enough background material, and a varied enough range of topics, to allow those who are unfairly discriminated against to prepare their best case.

Third, several of the scholars who have attempted to improve the accuracy and fairness of the evaluation of performance have themselves been subjected to harassment. These case histories are included in this chapter. They provide additional evidence for the ubiquity of suppression in the self-styled "free world" of Western science and academe.

The organisation of this chapter, together with certain important conclusions, is summarised in five stages: first, there are five short sections providing background: why complaints centre on work performance rather than the dissident act itself; how the private ideology of academic power-brokers charges certain words and phrases with new and subtle meanings (words and phrases that often appear in letters of recommendation, dismissal complaints etc.); how "commitment" to research or to teaching, often an important criterion in hiring or firing, is situationally variable; how "personality", also a stock word in evaluating candidates, seems to be associated with teaching, research, dissidence and excellence — and how *radical chic* behaviour complements administrative *repressive tolerance*.

Second, we consider the *inputs*: the time and resources available to the individual whose performance is being evaluated. It is unfair to consider only large publication lists as a criterion for excellence without also considering such matters as the money available to buy equipment and to hire technicians — or, as covered in the chapter "Academic Exploitation", without also considering how some academics appropriate the efforts of students, staff and wives.

Third, we consider the *outputs*. These are often estimated by the opinions (frequently secret opinions) of other scholars. How reliable is *peer review*, especially with the absolute power enjoyed in secret peer review? This has many consequences, not least of which is the necessity to insist upon proper legal procedures in formal disciplinary actions. There must be examination and cross-examination of all witnesses before the defendant, who must receive a verbatim copy of all that is said or written.

Fourth, we consider the *outputs* as measured by the more quantitative methods of bibliometrics. This is much more than just counting publications. In recent years *Science Citation Index* has been used (and abused) in evaluating the performance of individuals. Properly used, the citation indices can be a protection against erroneous allegations, as in the example provided in the chapter "IMVS versus John Coulter: Charges and Cross-examination", charge number three. While there are many caveats, the citation indices are some protection from certain types of erroneous charges; in particular, they allow a comparison to be made of individuals who are, and who are not, up for administrative action. The antagonistic attitudes expressed by certain establishment figures suggest that they regard these bibliometric tools as a threat to their own "wheeling and dealing" in the reward system of science and academe.

Last, but by no means least, we survey means for the evaluation of teaching, probably the most controversial of all aspects of staff performance.

WHY COMPLAINTS ABOUT DISSIDENTS ARE PHRASED IN TERMS OF UNSATISFACTORY PERFORMANCE — AND NOT THE DISSIDENT ACT ITSELF

...the President of the University was a man for whom I conceived, I think justly, a profound aversion. If a lecturer said anything that was too liberal, it was discovered that the lecturer in question did his work badly, and he was dismissed.

Bertrand Russell[4]

As mentioned in the Introduction to this book, the belief system which has become enshrined as "academic freedom" means that suppression is not usually considered openly justifiable by university administrations. The situation described in the chapter "The Fruit Fly Papers", where the first official letter of complaint about the performance of a senior staff member is solely an unparticularised charge that the senior staff member (and his wife) had made some public criticisms about a local pesticide-spraying program (which had affected them at their residence), would probably be considered too direct an infringement on academic freedom, if not freedom of speech, at most universities.

In general, complaints about the actions of dissidents in universities are phrased in terms of a failure to perform satisfactorily, usually in regard to their responsibilities for research or teaching.

Even in government research institutions, which make no pretence at "academic freedom", this rule is sometimes followed. Although in government laboratories sanctions against certain types of public comment are formalised (for example Official Secrets Acts, or their equivalent), the tendency is to phrase the complaint against the dissident more directly in terms of work performance. For example, there is the recent dismissal of Dr Ross Hesketh from the research laboratory of the Central Electricity Generating Board (UK), allegedly for failing to heed "proper management instructions".[5] It appears that Hesketh's real offence was to co-author a letter to the editor of *The Guardian* (with Professor Martin Ryle of Cambridge University), which suggested that British civilian nuclear reactors were generating weapons grade plutonium which was exported to the United States and used for nuclear weapons.

WHY COMPLAINTS ARE IMPRECISE — PUBLIC VERSUS PRIVATE IDEOLOGIES

In attempting to understand how criteria are chosen for describing performance in teaching and research, one must bear in mind the distinction between attitudes and behaviour. What academics say should be done, and what academics actually do, need not necessarily be the same. One example, epitomised in the slogan "publish or perish", is discussed later.

Attitudes may be expressed differently for different audiences. Superficially, we recognise two levels. Each set of attitudes expresses an ideology — but there is one for public display and another for consenting academics in private. The *private ideology* shows itself in many of the expressions used to describe performance. Marcia Lieberman's quotation[6] referred to "stock methods of creating . . . a negative assessment". Caplow and McGee's[7] classic study of the academic profession provides many examples in their quotations from interviews. Commonly used phrases are: "X lacks commitment", "Y has an unsuitable personality", and "Z may be bright but is he *sound*?"

These phrases are a kind of code, the expression of a private belief system. Like all ideologies it is promulgated by a power bloc for the purpose of preserving its privileges.

"Commitment" is to the hierarchical system itself, or to narrow academic specialisation. An academic who is said to lack "commitment" may have, in fact, shown too much commitment to unpopular ideas or social causes. Such an individual is regarded as a threat to academics who find it profitable to serve the state or business. The allegation of a lack of "commitment" is sometimes used when it would be better to make a straightforward allegation of inadequate research or publication.

"Unsuitable personality" can be translated as "likely to rock the boat". Allegations of "unsuitable personality" have two marked advantages over other types of allegations. First, it is so clearly a matter of opinion that it is virtually impossible to disprove. Second, it is an allegation that is likely to get a sympathetic hearing from many academics, who, in turn, have suffered from the actions of superiors whose personalities were "difficult", to use another word commonly found in letters of recommendation.

"Sound" as a description of research often means the routine application of accepted paradigms.

There are also stock words and phrases for where a power figure is pushing a protégé for a job or a promotion. For example, when confronted with a lack of publications, one can always write "he shows promise".

It can be difficult to penetrate this private ideology, with its subtle changes in the meanings of words and phrases. These subtle changes colour the way complaints about performance are expressed. These changes allow discrimination on irrelevant or marginal criteria to sound impressive.

The *public ideology* of academics is epitomised by the rhetoric at graduation ceremonies, as well as at other official occasions. Speakers use a combination of the time-honoured phrases of pompous elegance and the current trendy buzz-words: "dedication to truth", "without fear or favour", "producing the well-rounded man", and "the pursuit of excellence". The existence of case histories of the kind that fill this book is evidence enough that the public ideology is now little more than public relations window-dressing. It is regrettable that the disparity between expressed attitudes and actual behaviour has created so much cynicism. The true goals of educational institutions are being eroded and devalued.

The differences between public and private ideologies show in the way complaints are phrased. The public ideology allows appeal for a general concern about teaching, or "gross moral turpitude" (which, revealingly, is almost always used for cases of sexual misbehaviour rather than academic dishonesty, although the term could as well apply to plagiarism or to bringing false charges). A head of a school refers to the stock phrases in certain letters of recommendation[8]: "I do not trust this man with girls" — or the more damning "I do not trust this man with boys".

In summary of this section, in studying dismissal complaints, letters of recommendation and other forms of peer review, we note that allegations are often imprecise. The existence of conflicting public and private ideologies accounts for some of this vagueness. There is also the "Vicar of Bray" syndrome shown by many intellectuals: a desire not to commit oneself too far and, above all, to be on the winning side. It often becomes necessary to devote considerable effort to get complaints about performance properly particularised. Although not without its own difficulties in terms of professional bias and a complex vocabulary, legal advice can be useful in cutting through the woolliness in complaints about performance, and, in particular, getting to the kernel of specific, testable allegations.

TEACHING VERSUS RESEARCH?

There are strongly held views about whether the relationships between teaching and research are antagonistic, neutral, or mutually supportive. These views often influence the choice of candidates for jobs or for promotions. On occasion, these views are used to mask discrimination against dissidents.

Some universities and private colleges in the United States, and certain Oxbridge colleges in the United Kingdom, discriminate against researchers in their hiring policies. This is justified publicly on the grounds that research-motivated individuals are "too narrow" or "likely to neglect their students". One wonders if this policy, while often sincerely believed, has not arisen from a fundamental fear of dissidence. Good research sometimes poses a difficult challenge to authority. The kinds of higher educational institutions which profess this preference for teaching over research often either train the offspring of the rich or have a strong religious base.

Certain elite universities, notably Harvard in the US and Cambridge in the UK, have placed emphasis on research quality as well as teaching. Especially in the era after the Soviets launched Sputnik I, in 1957, the emphasis at a number of American universities shifted dramatically towards excellence in research. The quality of research was sometimes measured by quite crude criteria, as in the following advertisement for a vacant position: "Cellular immunologist wanted for position of associate professor level...Candidates must have documented proof of scientific quality, for example at least $100,000 per year in grant funds".[9] The sudden influx of large amounts of research money was accommodated by a corresponding ideological shift in the relative merits of teaching versus research. A belief developed that good researchers were automatically good teachers.

Despite the dogma and the money, there are few useful data to answer the question about whether teaching and research help or hinder each other. The situation also brings us back to that elusive word, so frequently used (or abused) by academics: personality.

In studying the staff of Canadian universities who were involved in the teaching of psychology, J. P. Rushton and colleagues[10] found some differences in the *average* for certain dimensions of personality when comparing good teachers with good researchers — but there was great individual variation in each category. The personality traits of the good teacher are largely neither congruent with, nor opposite to, those of the good researcher. Largely, the personality characteristics of good researchers and good teachers are orthogonal. However, certain characteristics are common both to good teachers and to good researchers, for example high intelligence and ability in leadership. The better researchers tended to be ambitious, aggressive, authoritarian, persistent, and non-supportive. The better teachers tended to be liberal, sociable, non-anxious, supportive, non-authoritarian, and aesthetically sensitive. But, what is especially important is the wide variance in each category. This means that the superficial assessment of personality by appointment committees is unlikely to be effective in the accurate assessment of the effectiveness of individuals.

Furthermore, even the thorough study by Rushton and his colleagues is limited to but a single subject discipline and to a homogeneous type of academic setting. It may well be that quite different personality traits will make for the best research, or best teaching, in other subjects, or in smaller, more democratically organised institutions. A few scientists have written perceptively of the personality traits required for research in different fields, for example the botanist Edgar Anderson[11], the physiologist Hans Seyle[12], and the molecular biologist Atuhiro Sibatani.[13] Their impressions have been confirmed in the results on psychological testing of scholars from different fields, although considerable variability occurs.[14]

Thus, it would be unwise to use casual estimates of personality traits to make decisions on hiring or firing in the absence of information on actual performance in teaching or research. Generalisations about the personality traits that preadapt individuals for teaching or for research in particular subjects must recognise the nature of the academic reward system, the vague vocabulary arising from public and private ideologies, the absence of precise data on psychological testing of the individuals being considered, and the rather random application of what criteria for good teaching, or good research, actually exist. When an administration places all the rewards on research, rather than a balance between research and teaching, it is hardly surprising that teaching and research become antagonistic. And, it can require a strong personality to get something done in spite of the system.

SCHOLARSHIP, DISSIDENCE AND RADICALISM

The personality of teachers and researchers can be examined in the perspective of conservative versus liberal attitudes. Good scholarship requires intellectual independence. There must be a constant willingness to challenge the status quo, including one's own preconceptions. This must be balanced by certain social restraints: a willingness to consider views differing from one's own; politeness to opponents; and, a refusal to let rank, rather than content, settle an argument.

In our case histories the dissidents usually had at least an average level of performance (when compared with their appropriate peers, matched for age, rank etc.). Yet, administrators had alleged that the performance of these dissidents was so bad as to warrant the rarely used, ultimate sanction: sacking. Information from the literature suggests that, although there are exceptions, dissidence (both social and intellectual) and performance are positively associated.

In the extensive survey of the social characteristics of university staff in the UK, A. H. Halsey and M. A. Trow[15] collected data for self-assessed general political and social characterisation, i.e., "far-left", "left", "centre", or "right". These characterisations were compared with the quality of their degrees, with the following results:

Self-reported assessment	Number of Staff with particular classes of degrees		Academic "quality ratio": $(I + IIa)$ divided by
	$(I + IIa)$	$(III + IV + pass)$	$(III + IV + pass)$
"far left"	8	2	4.0
"left"	105	83	1.26
"centre"	54	50	1.08
"right"	33	66	0.50

Treated as a 2×4 contingency table: $\chi^2 = 17.33$, three degrees of freedom; $p = 0.0006$

These results suggest that there is some positive association between self-reported radicalism and the quality of the degree which they obtained (in many cases a number of years before the interview). One might like more direct measures of dissidence versus performance. However, the quality of an academic's first degree is positively correlated with later performance.

It can also be argued that more objective criteria of the inclination towards dissent are needed than just self-reported assessment of "far left", "left", "centre" or "right". However, the tendency for brighter students and staff to be more radical has been observed in several American studies.[16] Radicalism in one direction can be offset by conservatism in other directions, quite apart from the inevitable arguments about what constitutes radicalism or conservatism. Clark Kerr has written: "Few institutions are so conservative as the universities about their own affairs while their members are so liberal about the affairs of others".[17]

Despite the reservations, there is sufficient tacit agreement among academics that dissidence and intellectual achievement are positively correlated that there has been the evolution of a phenomenon sometimes called *radical chic*: a small number of academics cultivate radical or eccentric behaviour. Unfortunately, their concept of radicalism is sufficiently distorted as to suggest that this includes rudeness, anti-intellectualism, unkemptness, and extremes of sexual behaviour — depicted so well in the British Broadcasting

Corporation's televised version of Malcolm Bradbury's *The History Man*.

This radical chic behaviour is usually tolerated by administrators. Sometimes it is rewarded (as in *The History Man* example, with the "hero" ultimately shown in his true reactionary colours). Such tolerance is a form of *repressive tolerance*: "Within the solid framework of preestablished inequality and power, tolerance is practiced indeed. Even outrageous opinions are expressed, outrageous incidents are televised."[18] Radical chic behaviour is welcomed because it allows administrators to prove they defend academic freedom. It does not threaten the existing power structure. It is not to be confused with dissidence.

While we would not wish to claim that all dissidents are excellent scholars, the data available suggest an association between, on one hand, academic and social dissidence, and, on the other hand, certain measures of ability in performance in the academic milieu. Thus, by penalising dissidents, the university selects against the very excellence that, in commencement day rhetoric, it claims to defend.

SUPPRESSION OF ATTEMPTS TO IMPROVE THE EVALUATION OF RESEARCH PERFORMANCE: "CONVERGING PARTIAL INDICATORS"

There is a fascinating contradiction in the behaviour of some establishment scientists. On one hand, they show a willingness to rank order the accomplishments and abilities of other scientists. On the other hand, these same establishment scientists show an unwillingness to have their own accomplishments evaluated by relatively objective means.

This contradiction came to the surface recently when part of the English astronomy elite overreacted to a study on the scientific productivity of the Isaac Newton telescope and of Jodrell Bank. One reads: "legal proceedings, initiated by members of the Advisory Board for the Research Councils"[19] and "[Sir Bernard] Lovell threatened to take legal action against the journal *Research Policy* if it published..."[20]

The two researchers who precipitated this reaction, John Irvine and Benjamin Martin, of the Science Policy Research Unit of the University of Sussex, have provided a detailed study of methods for evaluating research performance. They have devised a method of "converging partial indicators", using several distinct criteria of performance, ranging from opinions from a large sample of relevant scientists, to the actual citation impact of publications.[21]

Irvine and Martin are hesitant to apply such methods in comparing individuals — even though some of the techniques are widely (if often inadequately) used by scientific administrators, for example taking opinions on what one scientist thinks about another scientist's research or teaching. Irvine and Martin prefer to apply their "converging partial indicators" to comparisons of different laboratories, departments or institutes, that is, to *groups* of individuals. This allows statistical comparisons to be made with much more discriminatory power. Nevertheless, on occasion it is necessary to evaluate the performance of individuals; in such instances the work of Irvine and Martin provides much good cautionary advice.

INPUTS AND OUTPUTS: MEASURES OF OPPORTUNITY AND QUALITY?

It is a curious reflection on administrative values that the measurement of performance is so frequently incomplete. Despite the current emphasis on input/output economics, administrators often fail to consider all the input and output variables when assessing staff performance.

Too often, output is measured only in terms of *publications*, such as papers, reviews and books. However, less formal means of publication are occasionally of value, for example computer programs, bibliographic lists, printed notes, and laboratory direction sheets. All of these items, often circulated within "invisible colleges", can be important contributions to the research of others. Patents are a form of publication, emphasised more in technological institutions.

The object is often to estimate the *quality* of output. Few administrators we have encountered have read enough about the history of science (or other subjects) to realise just how difficult it is to judge quality. One indirect method is by *recognition*, the way the scholarly community expresses its collective judgement about the value of the contributions of an individual scholar. Of course, there are many examples of where proper recognition came only posthumously. Recognition can be measured by counting citations, a technique discussed later. Other measures of recognition include invitations to speak at meetings, to write reviews, or to assess manuscripts or research grant proposals. Recognition is also manifested by requests for advice from other scholars, or requests for assistance in building apparatus, and requests for help in locating source materials. Translation of articles from foreign languages is a valuable service, sometimes ignored in assessing scholarly performance. Recognition is often measured in terms of prizes or election to prestigious societies, but the reward systems of scholarship are not always accurate measures.[22]

There are two other types of output which may count positively or negatively, depending on the situation: participation in community organisations and communication in the mass media. In both situations, which sometimes overlap, an academic can play an important role, both in expanding knowledge and in disseminating it. However, whether or not such activities are counted for or against an academic can on some occasions depend upon whether or not administrators approve of the organisations or the nature of the communication.

Participation in the "wrong" community organisations can result in peer disapproval, or even administrative action. Participation in the affairs of business or government is usually regarded as laudatory, although sometimes it can result in neglect of students and research, or in serious conflict-of-interest problems.

Attitudes about communication in the mass media present some contradictions. On one hand, academics have often looked down on popularisation. However, there is in the hiring process a desire to appoint individuals whose names are recognised, not only by other scholars but by influential members of the wider community.[23] Thus, visible scholars are sometimes sought after.

The sheer size of the scholarly community, plus the marked increase recently in the number of unemployed and underemployed intellectuals, all competing for very limited job opportunities, has resulted in some academics using communication in the mass media. Furthermore, this is sometimes encouraged by administrators who are attempting to influence politicians in order to reverse the trend to budget cutting. Many universities have employed media relations officers in order to feed information to local newspapers and television. An increasing number of academics realise that they must sell their product to the tax-paying public. But at the same time, this has meant that university administrations are becoming more sensitive about the occasional academic who criticises publicly some vested interest, especially if it can be tapped for money.

There still is, even if in an eroded form now, a general academic ethos of avoiding publicity. This ethos serves business and government, for it gives access to important information for entrepreneurs and bureaucrats but denies it to the less powerful.[24]

We would argue that, given the definition of a university as a centre for the discovery and dissemination of knowledge, the less formal means of scholarly communication should not be ignored in evaluating performance. At least the standards should be clearly spelled out. There should not be one rule for corporate interests and another rule for community interests.

Inputs, especially time

An inconsistency in the evaluation of performance is a failure to take into account differential access to *inputs*. The question should be asked in comparing staff members: what opportunities have the individuals been given — or denied?

Allowance must be made for *professional age*, the number of years spent in research or teaching. It is accepted that time spent in the armed services, especially in time of war, is exempted. There were opinions voiced at the recent Australian tenure hearings, conducted by Senator Teague's committee[25], that allowance should be made for women to take time off for child-bearing. It was even suggested that this activity should be counted towards professional advancement. We would suggest that this is a purely personal matter — and we note that no mention was made of the problems of many single or married women who spend considerable time caring for parents or other relatives.

Allowance must be made for how duties are distributed in the organisation. Since not all staff in a university are equally capable or motivated in teaching and research, it is reasonable that duties be distributed with some allowance for this. However, it is unacceptable that an individual, assigned years of heavy teaching loads, should be expected to have the same count of publications as colleagues who have had light teaching loads. In a university teaching and research are interdependent activities. There should not be a wide variance in the time that different staff members have for these twin responsibilities.

Administration

A disturbing trend, visible in some Australian universities, is to elevate administration to the status of a duty comparable with research or teaching. Indeed, Sir Mark Oliphant complained about the tendency of Australian universities to reward administration more than either teaching or research.[26] Since Sir Mark made his complaint, the situation has worsened. In the last five years of relatively declining budgets the University of Adelaide lost over 60 teaching staff members. Almost none have been replaced — but a nearly identical number of administrative positions have been filled. We find it disturbing that universities can maintain constant numbers of administrative staff, or even increase numbers, while the number of teaching staff declines — and the number of new doctorates, who are unable to find a job in academe or research, continues to rise.

Why do administrators put more emphasis on outputs than inputs in evaluating staff?

In many cases examined by us we have noted that administrators put much more emphasis on outputs rather than inputs. The fact that a staff member may have been denied fair shares of research funds, or given an extra heavy teaching load, is ignored when publications are counted. We suggest that the answer to this question is simple: administrators have much more *control* over inputs.

This is not to deny the possibilities that an establishment can influence access to publication outlets — for example the massive amount of financial support for publication which the CIA administers clandestinely to willing academic recipients.[27] However, local elites do have more control over staff members' access to time for research and to research funds, whereas local elites usually cannot influence decisions concerning the rejection or acceptance of manuscripts submitted for publication in international journals.

Many research granting agencies require, or at least allow, a secret statement on the applicant and his intended research to be made, often by a department head. This occurs in spite of the fact that in many cases the administrator is clearly outside the area of his professional competence to pass on the merits of the researcher or his proposal. Abuse of this administrative prerogative was admitted by a former Chairman of the Australian Research Grants Committee:

In the early years of its operation, the [Australian Research Grants] Committee asked as a matter of routine for a detailed comment and recommendation by Heads of Department. It has ceased to ask in this way for these reports, leaving it to the discretion of the Head of Department to make a comment where he considers it is needed. The simple situation was that most Heads of Department appeared to have only swans on their staff. Where Y, a Head of Department, reported "X is a goose", the Committee was inclined to wonder what X and Y had been fighting about.[28]

It is with such opportunities to keep dissidents from getting a fair share of inputs that an administrator can, almost effortlessly, make the allegation of inadequate performance a self-fulfilling prophecy.

In some cases administrators, or other staff members, intent on harassing a dissident, have interfered in research by removing equipment (that did not belong to them) or by taking away technical staff. This happened to Dr Struan Sutherland at the Commonwealth Serum Laboratories in what has been called "the bureaucratic civil war of ludicrous pettiness".[29] We had similar experiences at the University of Adelaide. Furthermore, Clyde Manwell was assigned additional teaching duties while preparing his defence against the dismissal charges. The fact that these duties were the same as what the complainant felt were unsatisfactory suggests that the administration either didn't care about the duties or didn't really believe the complaint.

Thus, as administrations have so much power in controlling access to inputs, it is not too surprising that, in comparing the performance of staff members, they pretend that everyone has had an equal chance. Hence, more emphasis is placed on comparing outputs, rather than inputs.[30]

OPINIONS OF OTHER SCHOLARS: PEER REVIEW IN HIRING, FIRING, PUBLICATION AND RESEARCH GRANTS

We took him on the basis of the enthusiastic support of an outstanding professor at Harvard. That's very important. If Princeton pushes a man, I know it means I'll have to look somewhere else. I don't trust Columbia either, or Chicago. With one or two exceptions in each department, those bastards are shysters; they'll say anything about anyone to get a man placed.

> From one of the interviews conducted by
> Theodore Caplow and Reece J. McGee[31]

In the attempt to measure *quality* of output, *peer review* forms the basis for the commonest method. It is also commonly abused. In several dismissal cases the administration justified its action largely or solely on the basis of one or two adverse opinions, solicited from individuals who had a clear conflict of interest or a known personal dislike for the individual being assessed.

A distinguished expert in computer science and artifical intelligence has commented as follows on the peer review sampling procedures that are occasionally used:

A fairly senior official of a [research granting] agency, whose nationality I shall not disclose, once told me that if for any reason he felt justified in short-circuiting the system in order to get a given result, he would make a judicious selection of referees — either the scientist's particular friends or his particular enemies, according to which result he wanted. He needn't have told me. I knew it already. In his heart of hearts so does any scientist who has been in the game any length of time.[32]

There are examples that suggest that errors and bias in peer review result in the frequent rejection of good manuscripts. One editor rejected at least three manuscripts which, when ultimately published elsewhere, helped to win their authors Nobel Prizes. Hans Krebs' first description of the citric acid cycle, Urey's work on heavy hydrogen, and Fermi's research on beta decay were all rejected by *Nature*.[33] Other examples of inconsistencies and differences in opinion have been observed in studies on peer review.[34] Among the most conspicuous failures of peer review are the examples of the publication of faked or plagiarised research.[35] Another type of failure of peer review is where conspicuous errors are published; scholars in many fields have their favourite examples.

Errors in the use of statistics are common — although there are strong differences in opinion about the most appropriate statistical tests or the possible inferences in certain cases.[36] Three statisticians who examined a highly prestigious medical publication concluded:

> Sixty-two reports that appeared as Papers and Originals... in 13 consecutive issues of the *British Medical Journal* included statistical analysis. Thirty-two had statistical errors of one kind or another; in 18 fairly serious faults were discovered. The summaries of five reports made some claim that was unsupportable on re-examination of the data.[37]

IMPORTANCE OF OPEN COURT PROCEDURES IN EXAMINING OPINIONS

An episode related to a case history is useful here. It is chosen because it illustrates several problems dissidents have encountered. The example shows the importance of the careful evaluation of opinions, in particular the use of the methods evolved by the legal profession for examination and cross-examination of witnesses in open court.

A dismissal complaint included an allegation of "a number of flagrant mistakes" in the use of the Chi-squared statistic in a book (which was not about statistics but had used some statistical procedures in one chapter). The complainant wrote that these mistakes "will undoubtedly have upset the general conclusions of the book but how profoundly I do not know". The complainant then made a request that the Professor of Genetics be asked to comment.

In correspondence to the Vice-Chancellor the dissident admitted one statistical error (in the number of degrees of freedom in a Chi-squared test) and pointed out that another "error" was simply a typesetting mistake which had no other implications. It was, however, maintained that two other alleged errors were themselves incorrect. It was also maintained that, even if all the alleged errors were indeed errors, these were a very small part of the book and not important to its purpose or its conclusions.

This was apparently not acceptable to the administrative powers that be. In the ensuing correspondence the complainant reasserted his views and now stated that the Professor of Genetics was in agreement with him.

Later the contents of the letter of complaint were examined in open court. The Professor of Genetics was *not* listed to appear in court as a witness to support the claim (by the complainant) that he had agreed with the selection of four errors. Surely, had he been that certain of the importance of those errors, he would have been willing to appear.

In court the complainant, under cross-examination, admitted that the alleged errors were not important — and that some of the errors were not as erroneous as he had thought at the time. The upshot of all this was to leave a residue, which basically featured the one mistake admitted from the very beginning. Even that mistake did not alter the specific conclusion, let alone other aspects of the book.

In contrast, another professor, knowledgeable of statistical techniques (and Fellow of the Academy of Sciences) was willing to appear for the dissident as an expert witness, although the results of the cross-examination, combined with a settlement before judgement, made further examination unnecessary.

It can be argued strongly that such matters should not have to be settled in court. However, when a university administration acts as if such allegations are important (and accepts a dismissal complaint with such allegations when the Statutes allow the Vice-

Chancellor to refuse to accept the complaint), fairness demands that its contents be evaluated critically.

The episode shows that opinions in secret correspondence can differ significantly from opinions expressed in proper, formal, non-secret procedures. Complaints about such details in a dissident's work are common. This is not to excuse error but to maintain a sensible perspective in evaluation of an individual's work. Secret opinions are open to suspicion.

PROPER PROCEDURES FOR OBTAINING OPINIONS

"Honesty is the best policy." Any solicitation for a professional assessment should state clearly the reasons for the solicitation. The individual being assessed should receive copies of all correspondence. Secrecy is out.[38] If an individual's job is at stake, proper court procedures for the examination and cross-examination of witnesses should be followed. Care must be taken to ensure that the sample of opinions is made fairly and that the sample size is reasonable. One possibility is to allow each side to select an equal number of names as possible assessors. In this way biases for and against will tend to cancel out. Care should be taken to avoid soliciting opinions from individuals who have a conflict of interest. This is often easier said than done, given the nature of the academic profession. The person who is being assessed should be able to challenge opinions that come from individuals with a clear conflict of interests, including personal dislikes.

We would also insist on the *control experiment*: a similar solicitation of opinions about the peers of any individual who is being considered for sacking. After all, the question is whether or not an individual is doing such a bad job, in comparison with his colleagues who are not being considered for dismissal, as to warrant the ultimate sanction. Peers should be of two types: colleagues in his department, or related departments within the institution, of approximately similar professional age and rank; and his "invisible college" of colleagues at other institutions throughout the world who are doing research in the same subject.

Inside or outside the institution?

A point of some contention is the extent to which opinions should be obtained from individuals inside or outside the university or research institution where an individual's performance is being evaluated. On some matters only individuals in the same institution can make knowledgeable comment, but in reference to professional accomplishments the comments are best obtained from individuals located at other places. Outside opinion is not always as independent as one might wish. The outside assessor may be a direct competitor, or a friend of some important party involved in the complaint.

Probably the safest situation is where a large number of opinions are randomly sampled. One can argue endlessly about the fairness of certain procedures. It is the blatant disregard for natural justice that should be opposed. In one case the individual who authored a dismissal complaint was allowed to assist in choosing two academic jurors, whom he later acknowledged in writing were in agreement with him. Moreover, this information was kept from the individual being considered for sacking. We doubt if many individuals would wish to be tried under such a "kangaroo court" system.

Limitations of letters of recommendation

It is chastening to read the only detailed study we know of on letters of recommendation.[37] Scientists and non-scientists alike frequently placed more emphasis on trivial and irrelevant factors in letters of recommendation than information on research or teaching. Comments on female candidates are particularly prone to be focused on physical attractiveness, on qualities which are perceived by the writer as feminine or masculine, and on speculations about commitment to research or to child-bearing.

Clyde Manwell has seen several hundred letters of recommendation and finds no reason to disagree with Lionel S. Lewis's conclusions.[40] In truth, it is extremely difficult to predict how well an individual will perform. As the very nature of letters of recommendation will determine the candidate's chances, such letters are likely to be self-fulfilling prophecies.

The historical perspective on opinions

In evaluating opinions, administrators who wish to do a fair job, or dissidents who wish to protect themselves, should read the literature on peer review.[41, 42, 43] It is useful to examine historical cases from science or other forms of scholarship. Had Mendel been considered for dismissal from the Abbey in Brno, there would have been no difficulty in finding experts who considered his research to be worthless, or worse.[44] Mendel was so far ahead of his time that it took nearly forty years before biologists began to realise that Mendel had, almost singlehandedly, revolutionised the science of genetics, and thus much of the biology that depends upon it. Furthermore, R. A. Fisher's suggestion, that Mendel (or his assistant) "doctored" his experimental results, has been countered by several researchers.

SUPPRESSION OF ATTEMPTS TO STUDY PEER REVIEW

The most original approach to studying peer review is that performed by Douglas P. Peters and Stephen J. Ceci.[45] They took twelve papers which had been written by prominent psychologists and published in high status journals. The papers were typed out as new manuscripts. The texts were left essentially unchanged. However, Peters and Ceci replaced the prominent names, and also the prominent institutional affiliations, with imaginary names and institutional affiliations. In other words, the papers were left unaltered except that the authorship and institutional affiliation were changed from high status to low status. What then was the fate of these manuscripts which were, in fact, almost verbatim copies of papers already considered by peer review to be good enough to be published?

Of the 38 referees and editors involved, only three detected the resubmitted articles. Of the nine manuscripts that proceeded further into the peer review process, eight of the nine were rejected. In many instances the grounds for rejection were "serious methodological flaws"!

Behavioral and Brain Sciences published Peters and Ceci's paper, together with the comments of 55 scientists from a wide variety of disciplines, including many individuals with experience in refereeing papers and several individuals who were editors of journals. The comments, and the cited references, provide a wide range of opinion about peer review. Some, though not all, editors and other establishment figures objected to the Peters and Ceci study, largely on one or both of two grounds: the sampling procedure itself, in particular the small sample size, and the ethics of deception. We do not believe that these two grounds are valid criticisms of the Peters and Ceci study. Indeed, we do not believe that these two grounds, taken together, represent an entirely consistent point of view. If the experiment were unethical, would it not be compounding the unethicality by taking a larger sample, or by variations in the procedures which would amount to further deception of referees and editors? It is like telling a child: What you did was wrong — but you should have done more of it.

Being a referee or an editor is a sacred position of trust. Especially with so much peer review being done in secret, those who are in the extremely powerful position that secrecy automatically confers must be held accountable. Peters and Ceci executed a simple experiment which established a fact that many suspected but others denied. Their demonstration, that peer review is at best a chancy process, is of the greatest importance. Not only is the morale, indeed the livelihood, of many researchers dependent upon peer review in getting jobs, promotion, papers published, or receiving research grants, but peer review also serves society as a whole, for we are all dependent upon the flow of accurate information. Even results in scholarly publications become translated into action by politicians, by bureaucrats and by industrialists. Such individuals often practise "the principle of unnatural selection"[46], choosing from among the variety of opinions and contradictory "facts" those items which are perceived as most useful for the actions they wish to rationalise to a sceptical public. Peer review, in its broadest sense (which includes the publication of criticism of already published articles), reduces the opportunities for error and for antisocial action.

The research by Peters and Ceci represents dissidence at its best. Their demonstration of the imperfections in peer review, as currently practised by establishment figures, constitutes a healthy challenge to their power. It is instructive to read in Ceci and Peters' own words what happened to them:

> Upon collection of the data we entered a period lasting approximately two years during which we experienced an intense and negative reaction from many powerful individuals in our profession for having conducted our study. One editor in the study wrote a letter threatening a lawsuit for copyright violations. Actually, we had obtained permission from the original authors and copyright holders (publishers) to use their materials in our study.
>
> Quite unexpectedly, several editors who had not been directly involved with our study wrote scathing letters calling into question our professional ethics because of our use of deception (which, according to our national code of ethics, requires a careful cost-benefit analysis before employing). Actually we had given serious consideration to alternative, nondeceptive means of examining peer review but we ended up rejecting them. There simply was no experimentally sound way to study the issues we were interested in studying without using some form of deception. [We agree fully with Ceci and Peters.]
>
> The field of psychology has a long, somewhat tarnished, history of using deception in studies where the subjects are relatively powerless individuals, like children, college students, and unsuspecting citizens in the community. In our investigation the subjects were anything but powerless. We felt that if ever deception was justifiable, it was in the context of our study because the data were of great potential importance to the academic and research community and there were no sound, nondeceptive means of collecting them. Given the large role of peer review in determining people's lives (e.g., tenure, promotion, hiring, grant awards, professional status and recognition), it is urgent that we learn more about the practice and specifically more about factors influencing a reviewer's judgement before we assign [disproportionate] importance to that judgement in, say, a promotion decision.
>
> Recognizing the potential hazards, such as embarrassment to editors, we never divulged names of editors or journals...
>
> Other negative repercussions included several threats to professionally censure us, and threats to reject the work of our colleagues, supposedly because they had been part of a department that had approved such ethically bankrupt research.
>
> This charge is sadly ironic. Our department had no screening mechanism for nonfunded research, thus they were neither asked nor had they given, their approval, although two senior colleagues were consulted about the study's design. Later, when our chairman was personally contacted by an angry editor, he withdrew all of our departmental resources until we finished the study. We were sent a memorandum informing us that typists, photocopy, mail, etc. were "off limits" to us as long as we continued using the procedures we had adopted. When challenged on the grounds that this amounted to a violation of our academic freedom [the department chairman] offered to have the decision reviewed by the entire faculty. Because of the timing (right in the middle of a tenure review), we declined his offer and moved the project off campus. It was completed at our own expense.
>
> These personal attacks took their toll... Finally, after two unsuccessful attempts to publish our findings, replete with personally insulting, *ad hominem* reviews, we found a publisher and positive reviews. Soon press releases were telling a diverse audience of our findings. Letters of support (over a thousand) came pouring in. Every one was complimentary.[47]

PUBLICATION COUNTS: THE MYTHOLOGY OF "PUBLISH OR PERISH"

Given the uncertainties in personal opinions, some administrators have sought more quantifiable means for comparing candidates in regard to research productivity. It is common among academics to make jokes about administrators counting numbers and pages of publications, or even weighing them. It has all become part of the mythology of "publish or perish".

Yet, providing it is not the only criterion which is used, and providing it is done in a sensible way, such publication counts do have some value. Among other things they prove that the obsessive concern about "publish or perish" is unwarranted by evidence from the *realpolitik* of academic institutions.[48] Lionel S. Lewis, a sociologist of the academic profession, has concluded:

> . . . the idea that one must publish or perish is somewhat of a myth, perpetuated by the notoriety given a few cases. But it is no accident that [this myth] is widely accepted. First, it is a protection for those who wish to rid themselves of an unwanted colleague; it is a real explanation to conceal the true reasons for some dismissals. Second, it helps [to keep] those who are fearful of losing their positions busy doing research and writing (a good deal of which may be useless), diverting them from an active role . . . Third, it promotes the idea that an objective standard is used in arriving at decisions which are really made subjectively.
>
> Although academicians quarrel with the dictum of publish-or-perish, there appears to be little interest in investigating its credibility. Nor is there an attempt to abolish it; this might lead to an awareness that its importance has been exaggerated. It is too convenient a myth to abandon.[49]

The fact is that a researcher who is conscientiously performing his scholarly duties will be doing *some* publication. He may be prolific and write lots of little papers with minimal information content — "the least publishable unit".[50] He may be a perfectionist and write only a few papers in a lifetime. In the latter case, however, those papers are likely to represent either major breakthroughs or large reviews or presentations of new data, works of monographic size. Thus, counting the pages as well as the number of papers reduces the discrimination against the perfectionist. The use of citation index counts is also sometimes a protection for the perfectionist, for his smaller total output is likely to get proportionately greater recognition, that is, a higher citation count per paper per unit time; but care must be taken to allow for the large difference in citation counts between different subjects.

Another justification for counting pages as well as publication numbers is as follows. Although exceptions abound, on the whole editors guard journal space. Editors often insist that authors remove material from otherwise acceptable papers. Thus, the opportunities for padding are fairly limited. The variance may be great, but on average larger papers represent more work.

Some would argue too that allowance must be made for the format of different journals. A one-page paper in a journal like *Science* or *Nature*, with three columns of fine print per page, is likely to contain more information per page than a ten-page paper in a single-column format and with large print.

There are important differences in publication style, both between subjects and between individuals in a given subject. Our impression is that in certain sciences there is relatively little variation in the size and structure of papers, for example mathematics, physics and chemistry, but in biology and in many non-scientific disciplines there are great differences in publication styles. For example, biologists who specialise in the classification of animals and plants (taxonomists) have diverse publication styles. Many taxonomists write lots of short papers, describing one or a few species at a time, or reporting an extension of the range of a previously described species. Other taxonomists prefer the perfectionist approach; their lifetime output is a few big monographs, but each monograph deals with hundreds of species. The different styles each have advantages and disadvantages. Somewhat similar individual variation is common in the arts and humanities. Certain scholars prefer to publish a number of book-length studies, others favour many short articles.

On the whole there is some association between quantity and quality[51,52] but that association is not so strong that one should become obsessive about it. We all know of examples of where an individual leaves only a few papers, but where those publications are of seminal importance for many other researchers.

Access to publication differs markedly between subjects. A far greater proportion of manuscripts submitted to social science journals are rejected than those submitted to physical science journals.[53] Contrary to the situation for most other fields of study, medical journals receive lucrative subsidisation from advertisements placed by "ethical" drug companies. This has allowed the proliferation of journals publishing in biomedical fields. Has this resulted in any deterioration in the standards of published work in biomedicine? On the other hand, biologists often find it very difficult to find publication outlets for large studies, unless they happen to be lucky enough to be at a museum or university which has its own "house journal". This situation does not always select for high quality because such "house journals" often have lax peer review procedures, or no peer review at all.

This is not the place for a detailed discussion of publication counts but three complications need to be considered: abstracts, multiple authorship, and journal prestige or rank.

ABSTRACTS: THE QUANTUM OF PUBLICATION?

In some subjects a common form of publication is the *abstract*, a short summary of work in progress. Abstracts are often published as summaries of research presented at conferences. Certain scholars have perfected the art of padding their publication lists with abstracts and other non-definitive means of communication. First, there is the "paper read at conference"; this is followed by an "abstract", often with an impressive title nearly as long as the abstract itself; there may even be a separate "paper published in the proceedings of the conference" (and in some cases, to be fair, that may be a definitive paper); finally, hopefully, there is the definitive publication in one of the standard journals. With some care in the wording of titles and the arrangement of authors (in multiple-author works) there can be several "papers read at conference" and "abstracts" for each definitive paper that is finally published.

One way of detecting abstracts in publication lists is their shortness, usually a page or less in length. Occasionally job applicants evade this detection tactic by providing only the first page for *all* their publications.

Abuse of abstracts is probably greatest in biomedical research, which is highly competitive and has absorbed some of the ethics of the medical profession and the drug companies. However, we have seen also the use of abstracts to pad out publication lists in other subjects.

A large proportion of all the abstracts in biomedicine represent research which is never published in a definitive form.[54] There are many possible reasons for this, and some of the reasons are no fault of the authors. However, it is not unknown for the non-appearance of a definitive paper to be the consequence of the authors' inability to repeat the original experiment. This problem of the lack of reproducibility has resulted in a not inconsiderable amount of scientific humour, with jokes about journals with mythical names like "*The Journal of Unreproducible Results*" or "*Acta Retracta*".

Another problem of abstracts is *self-plagiarism*, where the same work is repeated in two or more different abstracts. This problem is not unknown in definitive publications, but is rarer there. Abstracts are rarely refereed before publication; this state of affairs may encourage more self-plagiarism.

This is not to criticise the use of abstracts in scientific communication. Abstracts play a role in establishing contact between different researchers. For those concerned about priority (and the reward system of science forces that concern on many scientists), abstracts have some significance. Abstracts form a convenient way to place small amounts of important information into the scientific literature in a way that is economical of journal space.

Our object here is to ensure that abstracts are not used to inflate publication counts and thereby not used to set unreasonably high expectations as to the number of published items. Certain conscientious and capable researchers only rarely use abstracts as a means of communication. Furthermore, the opportunity to publish (and to pad bibliographies with) "abstracts", "paper read at conference", and similar non-definitive publications, depends considerably on financial support, either from the institution or from research grants. Universities can be very capricious in providing funds and free time for staff to attend conferences and thus accrue an impressive list of abstracts and conference-related publications. We have a number of examples of where Australian universities have discriminated against dissidents in this way, not allowing them to attend, or refusing to contribute to expenses, even when the invitations came from such organisations as the Royal Society, the US National Academy of Sciences, the Israeli Academy of Science and the academy of sciences of various eastern European countries.

Multiple Authorship: Who Did the Work?

Probably the most vexatious question in evaluating research performance through publications is: who did the work? As science tackles the more complex problems, which often demand the use of a number of difficult and specialised techniques, more and more research involves groups of people in collaboration. In the period 1960 to 1980 the average number of authors on each paper increased from 1.67 to 2.58 (see note 50). In physics, especially high energy physics, occasional papers have 20 to 50 co-authors.

If allowance is not taken of multiple authorship in comparing peers, there is the likelihood of penalising the perfectionist, for most of his work is solitary, or done with one or two other researchers. Large teams of researchers can be expected to publish more papers per unit time.[55]

Whether or not a name is included in multiple authorship does not depend entirely on whether or not the individual made a substantial contribution to the research effect. Non-Ph.D. subordinates, and women generally, whatever their degree status, are frequently excluded from co-authorship, even though they have done much of the work.[56]

This problem is especially serious for students. Some staff feel that they have a kind of *droit de seigneur*, a right to appropriate the first research efforts of their students. In fairness, on some occasions the staff member has put a lot of time and effort into a rescue operation. Also, an occasional staff member will lean over backwards and include a student's name when it is not warranted — but more likely that type of action will be done when it is the name of a famous individual or a powerful academic administrator. Postdoctoral fellows usually get their contributions recognised by co-authorship, even if there are conflicts about name ordering. It is realised that success in recruiting more postdoctoral fellows into a large laboratory depends upon placing the former fellows into good jobs. To this end they must receive some share of co-authorship. However, even junior staff are not safe from having their efforts appropriated by senior "operators".

It is also difficult to assign relative credit on the basis of the position of names in multiple authorship. The usual rule is that the individual who did the largest share of the work is first author. Groups where two or more individuals had essentially equal roles often rotate the authorship positions in a series of papers.

Occasionally, alphabetical ordering of names is adopted, either by certain laboratories or (very rarely) as an official editorial policy. Harriet Zuckerman found differences in the etiquette of name-ordering, both between subjects and even between different workers in the same subjects. Her data for Nobel Prize winners are instructive and she concluded:

> On the assumption that authors' names are listed in order of the value of their contributions, [Nobel] laureates should be first-authors more often than other scientists; in fact, they are not. Instead, they exercise their *noblesse oblige* by giving credit to less eminent co-workers increasingly as their eminence grows. They do so more often after the prize . . .[57]

A further complication is that, with the increasing necessity to obtain grant funds for research, the successful "operator" who is adept at getting money insists upon co-authorship, even though he has played little if any role at the laboratory bench or in the analysis of the data. There is also a tendency for a group to wish to include the names of eminent individuals, or powerful scientific administrators, both to curry favour and to convey status on the group's efforts. William Broad quotes the Managing Editor of the *American Journal of Psychiatry*:

> ...it's sometimes a glory kind of thing, putting the chairman in (as coauthor) even though he was not directly involved, trying to bask in the light of a greater name.[58]

Broad also describes one attempt to solve the question of how much effort each co-author contributed. Each co-author was asked independently what percentage of a particular paper represented his contributions. One would hope that the sum of these estimates for all co-authors in a given publication would not be far from 100 per cent. In fact, the totals were as high as 300 per cent!

Given all the uncertainties over co-authorship, we believe that simple correction factors should be applied. One possibility is to divide by the number of co-authors. Another possibility is to give somewhat more weight to the first position, for example $2/(n+1)$, counting the other efforts all equally as $1/(n+1)$. For a useful discussion of various weighting systems see the review by West, Hore and Boon.[59]

JOURNAL PRESTIGE: *"IT'S NOT ONLY WHAT YOU PUBLISH BUT WHERE YOU PUBLISH"*

Quite commonly administrators guess the quality of individual papers from their general assessment about the quality of the journals in which they are published, although, as our opening quotation[60] suggests, this behaviour can be modified by the circumstances. There is a strong competitive drive for some scholars to publish in what they consider to be high prestige journals. There is also sometimes a kind of "halo effect", where an individual defines a journal as "high quality" if *he* publishes in it, or is on the editorial board.

Access to a high prestige journal sometimes depends upon being the protégé of a powerful patron. Providing you have a good friend in the Royal Society or the National Academy of Sciences, you can escape both the rigours and the biases of the usual peer review process. This is a delicate issue, seldom discussed openly. An exception is Stephen Fretwell's[61] description of how the now widely recognised ecologist Robert MacArthur had great difficulty in getting his earlier papers published. It was only because he found a distinguished patron, G. Evelyn Hutchinson, that he could bypass peer reviewing by other ecologists and get his papers into the *Proceedings of the National Academy of Sciences, U.S.A.* Fretwell concludes his discussion of this sensitive topic by asking: "Without the Proceedings of the NAS, I wonder how far MacArthur would have gotten?" Although no one can object to the publication of the seminal papers by MacArthur, there have been so many examples of abuse by the bypassing of peer reviewing that members of the US National Academy of Sciences have complained, in a few cases publicly[62], and some reforms have been recently instituted.

Thus, many good quality papers get published in low prestige journals and vice versa. Some of the most serious faking scandals in science, and also cases of plagiarism, have appeared in high-ranking journals.[63, 64] Nevertheless, *some* weight should be given to where a candidate has published, providing allowance is made for the complicating factors. There is a useful rank ordering of journals by citation impact.[65] It has certain limitations but is the only way to get away from the subjective judgements of individual administrators. It is imperative to bear in mind that acceptance or rejection of a manuscript is rather capricious. The system is noisy, with many biases, including bias against dissidence, both scholarly and social.

The words of the editors of the very prestigious *Physical Review Letters* bring us back to the peer review theme:

It is a plausible hypothesis that, in spite of the responsible and conscientiously prepared counsel that we receive from our referees and Divisional Associate Editors, our selection of papers is too often ruled by chance. Under ordinary circumstances, each newly received paper is sent to two referees at once. *The agreement between the referees is scarcely better than chance.* A simplistic model which states that one-sixth of the papers are so clearly superior that each referee approves and one-sixth are so clearly poor that each referee advises rejection, leaving the other two-thirds to be decided by the flip of a coin, fits the correlations that we observe. On this model, *if two-thirds of the papers that we accept were replaced by two-thirds of the papers that we reject, the quality of the journal would not be changed.*[66] [Emphasis added]

Also, the words of Lynn Margulis, given below, turn our attention back to peer review when we consider judging individual contributions solely on the basis of where they are published. Margulis is a fine example of the dissident researcher. She originally championed the theory of the origin of subcellular organelles from separate microorganisms (the endosymbiont theory) against a unified disbelieving establishment. Now, as a result of research by her, and by many others, this theory is widely accepted, at least for chloroplasts and mitochondria. Margulis writes of her own experiences with peer review:

Every one of our papers containing new ideas was rejected at least once; this was especially true of a prize-winning paper that generated 1,100 reprint requests...

My experience on the question of a possible endosymbiotic origin for the microtubule system is a case in point. Six years ago I was told by an NSF [National Science Foundation] grants officer... that ''important'' scientists did not like the theory presented in a book I had written and that they would never fund my work. I was actually told that I should never apply again to the cell biology group at NSF, since my work ''only appealed to the small minds in biology... the naturalists''.[67]

CITATION INDICES: CATCHING "THE EEL OF SCIENCE"

How Index-learning turns no student pale,
Yet holds the Eel of science by the Tail.[68]

That refrain from Alexander Pope's *Dunciad* is part of his testimonial for a candidate for the Chair of Dullness. The lines, published in the eighteenth century, seem strangely appropriate in summarising the utilisation in the 1960s and 1970s of citation indices.

In publications scholars cite the work of other scholars, as well as of themselves. These citations can be used to construct a measure of information flow. The study of citation patterns has been used to work out the linkages in different fields of study.[69]

Highly cited papers or books are important landmarks in a subject. Citation indices, thus, can also be used to measure the impact of publishing scholars, although there are many caveats discussed below. Between the original *Science Citation Index*, starting in 1961, and the later *Social Science Citation Index* and *Arts and Humanities Citation Index*, essentially all forms of academic scholarship are now covered.

The basic procedure is to look up the individual's name in the appropriate citation index. One counts the number of times the publications by that individual are cited. One can also look up the items which do the citing in order to find out what type of use is made of the particular scholar's work.

At this point one runs into a problem. By 1978, *Science Citation Index* sampled over 2500 journals, including nearly 495,000 authored source items, which, in turn, had cited slightly over 7,475,000 items. *Science Citation Index* in 1978 refers to 920,039 ''unique cited authors''

— but, in fact, these authors are not "unique" in the sense of being individually identified. Individuals with the same surname and the same initials, for example all A. Smiths, are lumped together. These "homographs" can be a source of confusion. (Why bibliometricians do not call these homonyms, the more usual word for identical names, instead of homographs, we do not know.) When in doubt, each cited item must be checked. Obviously, homographs are most likely to occur for common surname and initial combinations, but there are examples even for very unusual names.

PROBLEMS IN THE INTERPRETATION OF CITATION INDEX COUNTS

Given the potentialities of citation counts for both use and abuse, it is desirable to have a brief discussion of some of the complications:

1. Professional age

The longer an individual has been publishing, the greater the opportunity to be cited. Nevertheless, although there is some controversy about the matter, with the possibility of different patterns in subjects differing in coherence and in the rate of growth, the professional age of the author of a cited item does not have much effect on the number of citations it receives, at least in sociology.[70]

2. Differences between and within fields of study

Citation practices vary greatly between disciplines, journals and authors. For science as a whole the average publishing author who is cited at all receives close to eight citations per year, though the actual figure is probably closer to seven because of the "homograph" confusion mentioned earlier. In the social sciences the average number of citations is about four. On the whole, chemists cite twice as many items per paper as do zoologists; thus, a chemist should get roughly twice as many citations as a zoologist of comparable age, quality etc.

3. The time factor: differences in persistence

Related to items 1 and 2 above is the time factor, which is partially dependent upon the differences in the rates of growth in different fields. In a faster growing field, relatively more papers become obsolete quickly. For science as a whole, the average cited paper has a "half-life" of only five years. Furthermore, in various fields between one-third and one-half of all papers are not cited again (or, to be more accurate, not cited again in the journals covered by the citation indices, a point to which we shall return). In biochemistry 62 per cent of all references were within the last five years of the date on the publication in which they were cited, whereas in sociology only 40 per cent were within the last five years.[71] Our impression is that researchers in unpopular areas, for example the classification of esoteric groups of animals or plants, get few citations in the short term; however, their work is likely to be relatively persistent, also picking up a few citations many years later.

4. Reasons for citing a paper

There are many reasons for citing a paper and useful short summaries of these reasons have been prepared by Lawani[72] and Gilbert.[73] Most of these reasons are, however, favourable to the use of citation counts as an approximate measure of impact. Nevertheless, the author's choice of citations is often consciously or unconsciously chosen so as to persuade the reader, and this results in subtle bias.

It is commonly argued that citation counts are meaningless because of the "fact" that many citations are made for the purpose of calling attention to errors. In fact, it is relatively rare for a paper to be cited only because of a trivial error in it. A paper may occasionally be cited because the citer disagrees with the cited, but that does not necessarily mean the citer is right and the cited is wrong. Even when it does, one must remember that science progresses in part by falsification (to use a Popperian oversimplification). Citing a work because the citer has, with the benefits of time and the further advances of science generally, a better technique or a wider perspective, is all part of scholarly progress. Needless to say, the best way to avoid being cited for errors is to publish nothing at all.

5. *"The Public Relations Web"*

This phrase has been used by Rodger Mitchell[74] and Leigh Van Valen[75] to denote the situation where the work of a particular ingroup is promulgated by confining citation and other forms of recognition to within the ingroup, failing to cite outsiders' publications, even when they have clear priority. We believe that this is probably the most important bias in using the citation indices, either to evaluate individuals or to trace out the origins of scientific developments.

Using an example provided by Daryl Chubin and a colleague, Timothy Lenoir[76] points out that the individual who had most clearly postulated the existence of "reverse transcriptase" (the enzyme that transfers information from RNA to DNA, an RNA-dependent DNA polymerase) had the importance of his work "severely underrepresented by citation counts". Lenoir concludes that " ... biomedical researchers at large laboratories tend to project similar citation profiles due to intra-laboratory co-authorship and self-citation. The effect is to inflate the importance of work done at these large laboratories".

In the prolonged and intense rivalry between Andrew Schally and Roger Guillemin, in pursuit of the chemical structure of the hypothalamic releasing factors which control the output of hormones from the pituitary gland, Nicholas Wade refers to the allegations of " ... the practice of citing as little as possible of each other's work".[77]

The noted historian of science, Derek J. de Solla Price, who had much to do with demonstrating the utility of quantitative methods, including citation counts, warned of " ... the evident malpractice of some authors in preferentially citing their own papers, those of their special friends, or those of important scientists that confer status on their work".[78]

Comments about the failure to cite the relevant research of others are often heard in gossip among scientists. No doubt some of these comments are exaggerated. It is easy to assume the elitist mode and dismiss such comments as "the squeals of second-raters", as one scientist said to us. It is, therefore, salutary to read the words of Sir Gustav Nossal, an eminent immunologist and Director of what many consider to be the top medical research institute in Australia:

> The process of citation, which used accurately ... guide[s] readers to the sources that inspired a particular piece of research, is now frequently nothing more than a kind of game, and a rather dirty one at that. In its most extreme form, the game seeks to hide the foundations for the work amidst a mass of trivial or irrelevant references, and seeks to establish the author's own laboratory as the sole source of wisdom ... In a complex competitive world, these problems will not disappear. Rather, they will intensify ...[79]

6. *Citation as ritual*

In certain subjects very important work may not be cited, as the source is regarded as common knowledge. On the other hand, a few older references become *de rigueur* as citation landmarks, for example Darwin's *Origin of Species*. Here too, however, the "public relations web" has left its imprint. It is generally accepted that Alfred Russel Wallace independently discovered the theory of evolution by natural selection and published the outline in the same year as Darwin. Furthermore, it is known that there were important predecessors who had formulated the essential elements of the theory.[80] In contrast to Alfred Russel Wallace, Darwin came from a wealthy and intellectually prominent family. Perhaps it is no surprising, then, that he received most of the immediate recognition, with the result that his name provided the convenient mark of recognition for subsequent citation. True, Darwin provided in *The Origin of Species* the most exhaustive documentation for the theory of evolution by natural selection (though in spite of the title Darwin devoted very little of that book to the central problem of evolution, the origin of species). On the other hand, Wallace's contributions in scholarly analysis were by no means unsubstantial. The present organisation of zoogeography owes much to Wallace — and to another neglected pioneer, Alfred Wegener, whose ideas on "wandering continents" were considered lunacy or heresy by the geological establishment for half a century.

It is also common for early important work to be missed. Although Mendel received a few citations prior to his "rediscovery"[81], it was only after the beginning of the twentieth century that citations revealed his true impact. Thus, there are time-dependent fashions in science, with Kuhn's[82] periods of paradigm change, or "revolutionary science", alternating with periods of gradual growth, or stasis. The periods of paradigm change will be marked by changes in ritual citation.

There is an aspect of ritual citation which is in need of study. We had noticed, in tracing out the literature on animal domestication, that a number of authors cited Hahn's *Die Haustiere und ihre Beziehungen zur Wirtschaft des Menschen*, usually for the first suggestion of religious and aesthetic factors as motives for animal domestication. Yet, we have been unable to locate a copy of this book in either the United Kingdom or Australia, even with the aid of interlibrary loan services. If the book is that difficult to obtain, one wonders how many of those who have cited this work have actually read it.

Somewhat similar is the pattern of ritual citation observed by Erwin Chargaff:

> ...bibliographies usually are wafted in their entirety from one paper to the next, except for the insertion of the respective authors' own contributions which, if luck has it, may then accompany, plasmidlike, the standard package in its subsequent passages.[83]

BIASES IN THE CITATION INDEX STRUCTURE ITSELF — AND THE POSSIBILITY OF SCHOLARS CHANGING THEIR CITATION AND PUBLICATION BEHAVIOUR

The citation indices only tabulate citations to the *first* author of a publication. A researcher whose name appears only in the second or subsequent positions in multi-authored papers will have a citation index score of zero. Will this intensify further the struggle for the first authorship position on papers?

An analysis of authors contributing articles to the *Journal of Physiology* is pertinent here. That journal has had the unusual practice of listing the co-authors in alphabetical order. The result is that, in comparison with other physiological journals, where the authors can be in any order, the *Journal of Physiology* has relatively more authors whose names begin with A–E and relatively fewer authors whose names begin with P–Z.[84] Thus, the publication behaviour (in this case, choice of journal for publication) can be influenced by authorship position.

Another serious bias in the citation index structure is that, until recently, *Science Citation Index* did not record the citations in the bibliographies of books, an extremely important nodal point in communication. The citation indices are still haphazard about picking up citations in books which are actually collections of papers or review articles. The problem is that the reference citations may be scattered through the text (usually as footnotes, though not invariably), at the ends of chapters, or collected together at the end of the book.

In general, the structure of the citation indices reflects the American dominance of many (but by no means all) areas of scholarship, dominance in terms of numbers, not necessarily quality. We have found that many important eastern European publications are missed. Although *Science Citation Index* has been used to compare the impact of scientists from different countries[85], we wonder how much these results will be biased by differences in the availability of publications, differences in the ease with which scientists can read different foreign languages, and the increasing use of the citation indices as bibliographic tools.

Biases in the Sources Sampled by Citation Indices and Current Contents — Information Capitalism versus Left-wing Journals?

The Institute for Scientific Information, which brings out the various citation indices, also brings out *Current Contents*, with different modules for different major research areas. *Current Contents* is essentially made up of copies of the table of contents of the most recent issue of a number of journals (often with an editorial by Eugene Garfield, the founder and director of the Institute of Scientific Information). The selection of journals for *Current Contents* is said to be on the basis of the frequency with which these journals are cited.

Jon Wiener[86] alleges that *Current Contents* is biased against left-leaning journals. For a time the appropriate modules of *Current Contents* did not include *Monthly Review*, a socialist American journal of considerable importance.

Not being listed in *Current Contents* probably has a serious effect on visibility. There are so many journals that scholars have great difficulty in keeping up, even in the narrowest specialties. Many researchers use *Current Contents* as a quick way to browse through the contents of the journals which are of most interest to them. *Current Contents* is extremely useful, for it allows researchers to know quickly about the existence of articles in journals not carried by their libraries, an important service in Australia where the combination of woefully inadequate journal subscriptions and the delay, from one to six months (as most journals are sent by sea mail to Australia), aggravates the already serious intellectual isolation.

The convenience of having the listing of titles and the authors' addresses in *Current Contents* means that many researchers (or their students or secretaries) flip through the listings and send off reprint request forms to the authors, or obtain a copy through their library. The decision to select certain source items for further inspection is reached largely on the basis of the title of the paper, although no doubt the reputation of the authors and the institutions from which the research was published also have some importance. A biochemist at Cambridge University, E. F. Hartree[87, 88], published a modification of a commonly used method for determining the amount of protein in samples. Because of a minor difference in the way Hartree's address was printed in the journal itself and in *Current Contents* he was able to score how many reprint requesters had seen the article in the journal in which it was published versus how many reprint requesters had learned of it from *Current Contents*. There were 375 who saw the actual article — compared with 2125 who used *Current Contents*.

This example warns us that *Current Contents* does play a dominant role in determining *access* to a researcher's publication. If the Institute for Scientific Information decides that a journal is not important enough to be included in *Current Contents*, many researchers (perhaps a majority, as in the above example) will miss relevant papers. While some of these may be picked up later by other literature retrieval methods, for example abstracting journals or the citation indices, the situation has all the elements of self-fulfilling prophecy. Many libraries now use *Current Contents*, or the citation index journal rankings, as criteria for deciding whether or not to purchase certain journal subscriptions.

Given that new journals will not have any citation score, and thus start at the bottom rank, they would automatically be excluded from *Current Contents*. The alternative is for the Institute for Scientific Information to favour some new journals which it *thinks* will be important.

All of this places an inordinate amount of power in the hands of one organisation — a privately owned organisation, not accountable to society, or its elected representatives, nor to the scientific community. While it can be said that, as a private corporation, the Institute for Scientific Information is accountable to the marketplace, it has no competitors and therefore completely controls the marketplace. The prices charged for many of its publications are so high that they are beyond the means of nearly all scientists and some libraries.

The Institute for Scientific Information is very profitable — and with its "fleet of chauffeur-driven cars [which] includes a Cadillac, a Lincoln, [and] a Jaguar"[89], it has clearly become indulgent in the luxuries of monopoly capital. Perhaps then, we can see a little better Jon Wiener's[90] concern about the absence of left-wing journals. George Orwell would have understood.

However, to be fair, the inventor of the citation abstracts, Eugene Garfield, who is also President and Chairman of the Board of the Institute for Scientific Information, and owns 65 per cent of its stock[91], has tempered his enthusiasm for his product with a warning to the scientific community:

> Like most other scientific discoveries, this tool can be used wisely or abused. It is now up to the scientific community to prevent abuse of the SCI [*Science Citation Index*] by devoting the necessary attention to its proper and judicious exploitation.[92]

We are now faced with an ominous situation; not only is there potential for error in the evaluation of individuals and groups of individuals, but there is also the potential for ultimately distorting the development of many fields of scholarship. The fault for allowing the Institute for Scientific Information to be a private organisation rests with the bureaucrats and scientific administrators in the US National Science Foundation, who failed to follow up Garfield's promising initial efforts in creating the citation index system and who refused to set up a publicly owned information agency.[93] There is really no excuse. The opportunity arose in that immediate post-Sputnik era, when funds were readily available and the Soviets had developed an impressive information service for their own scientists.

The result of that faulty decision within the US National Science Foundation is likely to have far-reaching consequences: first, as mentioned earlier, the high prices charged by the Institute for Scientific Information already limit the access to these useful bibliographic tools. Libraries must pay high charges for the ISI's subscriptions. This has come at an unfortunate time, for the economic recession has resulted in drastic cuts to the budgets of many university libraries, which have responded by purchasing fewer books and by cancelling journal subscriptions.

Second, leaving the situation in private hands may have inhibited further improvements. For example, probably only government financing and direction from the scholarly community could accomplish the necessary access to totally computerised citation indices that would so greatly speed the search for useful references, as well as assist in the analysis of the structure of science and other forms of scholarly activity. One vital project is to extend the citation indices back in time so as to be able to obtain a better historical perspective on the emergence of the structure of science.

Third, ways need to be found to prevent the system from being perverted by self-fulfilling prophecy. Especially with the citation indices being used uncritically for the evaluation of individual scholars, there are risks of intensification of overcompetitiveness and a widespread further demoralisation of much of the scholarly community. It will be necessary to institute some mechanisms for feedback, and that, at least in theory, is more likely to occur with an organisation funded directly by the taxpayer.

"Freedom of information" was a catchcry used by politicians and academics a few years ago. The concept was never rigorously explored. One form of implementation, the passage of Freedom of Information Acts or their equivalent, has had little effect except in the United States and Sweden. Despite the limited successes in penetrating unnecessary secrecy, the fact is that the control of many types of information is becoming increasingly concentrated into the hands of an oligopoly of information entrepreneurs and high-level bureaucrats. Nevertheless, the citation indices are a fascinating revelation in the flow of information. Like many inventions they can, at least temporarily, disturb existing power structures.

AMBIVALENCE OF ADMINISTRATORS TO BIBLIOMETRICS: THE CITATION INDICES GIVE SOME POWER TO THE ACADEMIC PROLETARIAT — AT LEAST TEMPORARILY

We are unable to find information about how frequently academic or scientific administrators use the citation indices in deciding the fates of staff. Nicholas Wade[94] claims that citation analysis is used at some American universities as "part of the evidence for deciding cases of promotion and tenure". Wade writes too that "the National Science Foundation (NSF) is using the technique to assess its funding of chemistry departments and as a safety net to catch chemists who write bad grant proposals but are heavily cited". However, Wade's latter claim drew a denial from an administrator in the chemistry section of the NSF.[95]

Wade[96] also mentions that citation counts were used in evidence in a court case to show that a female biochemist at an eastern American university was discriminated against in being denied tenure. Her citation count was better than that of a male staff member who had been granted tenure.

What is of significance is that in 1979, years after the introduction of citation indices and after much discussion of their uses in scholarly journals, we met two prominent British academic administrators, both involved in "life-or-death" decisions over staff being considered for redundancy. Yet, neither of these academic administrators knew about the citation indices — and didn't seem to want to know.

Many of the books and articles cited by us earlier in this section provide evidence for a *partial* association between various measures of quality and the citation counts. If due allowance is made for the biases discussed briefly by us earlier, the method can be used on individuals. This does *not* mean that one individual who gets 10 citations a year is better than another individual who gets eight. In fact, the 95 per cent confidence interval for comparing the citation impact of two different individual papers is very large. Just the sampling variation is so great that the 95 per cent confidence intervals are three versus 10, 10 versus 20, or 99 versus 124 (see note 97). When one adds the counts over the years, and for a number of publications, the techniques become more discriminatory — providing that the interpretation of the numerical data is tempered with the caveats discussed here.

Probably the most important source of error is the ingroup effect, or the "public relations web" mentioned earlier. This tends to give dissidents and other outsiders a low score. One possibility is to use the method employed by Dennis Dieks and Hans Chang.[97] They measured "strangeness", the percentage of citations arising from outside the country of the cited. Dieks and Chang showed that this measure was different for different groups of Dutch workers publishing on various aspects of magnetic resonance spectroscopy and suggest that "strangeness"..."can be useful to identify 'incrowds' in science". Presumably, researchers in another country will be less influenced by local favouritism or disfavouritism.

Such an example may seem a striking exception to R. K. Merton's basic norms of science, notably *universalism* and *disinterestedness*.[98] However, we know of a number of instances where researchers refused to cite a dissident's papers, even though these papers had clear priority or described techniques which they had copied. One of the individuals actually confessed to us that he was afraid to cite these papers lest he offend a powerful senior academic.

The overriding importance of *status* in influencing citation practices is evident from the research performed by Richard Whitley, which also gives a useful suggestion for reducing bias from the "public relations web". Whitley studied the citation impact and practices of two groups of physiologists: HIPP physiologists, who were "high in power and prestige", versus LOPP physiologists, who were "no power and low prestige".[99] Although LOPP physiologists received only six citations in physiological journals, versus 156 citations for HIPP physiologists, this overwhelming difference was greatly reduced when citations in non-physiological journals were measured. In journals outside the field of physiology the LOPP physiologists received 165 citations compared with 500 citations for HIPP physiologists. In other words, the no-power-and-low-prestige physiologists were making a relatively greater impact outside their field than inside. The HIPP physiologists still had a greater total impact but their dominance inside the physiology journals (156/6 = 26) was weakened outside the physiology journals (500/165 = approximately 3). What is especially important is Whitley's observation that HIPP physiologists *never* cited LOPP physiologists. Rank rules!

Now, with the review of various biases, we can return to the question of why many scientific administrators are reluctant to use the citation indices in obtaining an *approximate* measure of quality. We believe that, despite the many biases inherent in the use of citation indices, these methods do take some power away from the administrator. *It is easy to get the desired result by seeking a couple of anonymous opinions about a researcher. Despite the many biases in the citation indices, it is far less easy to "tilt" the counts in an open publication, accessible to administrator and to dissident alike.*

Furthermore, the tables can be turned: the dissident can always check up on the scholarly impact of the administrator, or upon the impact of a complainant or his supporters.

In the course of defending dissidents we have noticed a wide range of behaviour of staff association officials. Some are helpful and ready to protest injustice, but others are not. It gradually became apparent that the more vigorous defenders of dissent had, on the whole, better records of publication and citation. These results go along with the literature reviewed towards the beginning of this chapter, the partial positive association between social dissidence and scholarly accomplishment. However, such results have an important implication in the defence of academic freedom: the selection of mediocre individuals for staff association positions can be a threat to intellectual freedom and fairness. Some staff association officials are well motivated and have sufficient scholarly status to be able to stand up against academics or administrators participating in a witch-hunt. Unfortunately, a few individuals use their election to staff association positions as a conduit into the corridors of administrative power.

We conclude the discussion of citation indices by returning to the couplet from Alexander Pope, used at the beginning of this section: "Index-learning" does now "hold the Eel of science by the Tail". When allowance is made for the biases, the citation indices can also help to catch the eel-climbing academic who advances by means distinct from scholarly recognition.

"When All Else Fails, Try Reading . . ."

We have passed from the deviousness of personal opinions to the elegance of bibliometrics. At this point of desperation in the discussion of methods for the evaluation of performance we draw attention to a relatively neglected means for the evaluation of both research and academic staff. We suggest that administrators should try reading the publications of staff about whom they must make decisions of hiring, firing, or promotion.

Many specialist papers can only be fully comprehended by similar specialists. But a senior academic administrator should at least be able to judge certain general qualities of books, review articles or more popular presentations. Clarity of expression, logical development and enthusiasm for the subject should be evident to the capable administrator. It may also sometimes be possible to judge originality, if the field is not too far removed from the administrator's experience. Such qualities are desirable in both researchers and teachers.

We have no data on the extent to which academic administrators, or staff members generally, actually examine the publications of those on whom they pass judgement. We hope that the following confession revealed in the interviewing of an academic administrator by Caplow and McGee does not reflect the norm:

Q: Are the men's publications read?

A: Oh, yes!

Q: By whom?

A: By the tenure members, at least.

Q: All of them?

A: Yes.

Q: Did you read them?

A: Yes.

Q: Did you read those of the man you finally hired?

A: Yes.

Q: What was the one which you remember best about?

A: Well...I didn't read it, exactly. I looked it over. It was in a good journal. Nothing trashy gets in there.

Q: What do you mean by you "looked it over"?

A: Well, I looked at it, looked at his references, read his abstract.

Q: Is that the way the rest of the committee handles the publications, do you think?

A: I think so, yes, they look them over.[100]

EVALUATION OF TEACHING

Powerful evaluation procedures can yield results from which the administrator may have no place to hide. Weak methods yield results that can be interpreted to his advantage. To many administrators weak methods seem better...

[J. G. Stanley]

Of course, not only teachers are opposed to evaluation. Administrators, who are wise in the way of politics and organizational behaviour, realize that reverberations may take place on the campus; once evaluation of students is echoed by evaluation of teachers it may not be long before the evaluation of the administration is called for.

[G. L. Geis][101]

It is generally agreed that the evaluation of teaching is even more difficult than the evaluation of research. The topic of what makes a good teacher is one that is discussed frequently in books and papers, but with little agreement. A recent collection of review articles by the Canadian Association of University Teachers[102] provides a useful introduction to the literature on evaluation of teaching in higher education.

The lack of agreement about what constitutes good teaching is not surprising. Criticisms of teaching performance often do not allow for individual differences, both among teachers and among students. Certain styles of teaching suit some lecturers better than others. Conversely, some students prefer one type of teaching to another. A teacher who is considered dull and pedantic by one person might be considered well organised and carefully paced by another.

A further problem is that evaluation of teaching is coloured by one's own experiences, politics and value systems. One study of different teaching styles, assessed by different people, found that the same example could be judged "exemplary, trivial or unethical".[103]

Individual variation in learning ability cannot be ignored — especially in this time when more people are going on to higher education and when universities are encouraged (or forced) by politicians to reduce the ranks of the unemployed. Some students need "high arousal". They prefer exciting and enthusiastic speakers. When such "high arousal" students are inspired, they do excellent work. The slow-but-steady student, who may in the end reach a high standard of performance, usually does better with a more carefully paced and not-too-stimulating lecturer.

There is also now a pronounced generation gap between staff members in their opinions about what constitutes good (or bad) teaching. We believe that this divergence in opinion has probably arisen as a result of television and its influences on students. Thus, older and younger staff members often disagree about the means needed to encourage (or to coerce) students to study. For the last twenty years in Western countries, students entering university differ from their predecessors in their massive exposure to a novel means of communication. (They also differ from earlier students in being recruited from a broader social and ethnic base.)

The exposure to television, with viewing times of twenty to thirty hours per week, presents problems for teachers. Students have become conditioned, like Pavlov's dogs, to brief, pre-digested tidbits of knowledge, sugar-coated with a false lucidity. Concentration span has shrunk to the time for the average television commercial. It requires a determined personality on the part of the teacher to get students to break through the self-imposed barriers of mass mediocrity, indeed, just to get the students to read.

Television is also a one-way flow of information. If exposure to television makes students restless in ordinary lectures, it can also make them strangely passive recipients to knowledge. Some teachers, of course, prefer students who do not answer back. Other teachers deplore the intellectual deadness.

At the same time, television, for all its faults, has made the average student much more aware of what goes on in the world. Teachers who isolate their subject from the reality that students perceive run the risk of losing credibility, if not attention.

Whatever the differences in opinion about the value of television, few will deny that it hasn't changed attitudes about what constitutes good presentation. There are the rare examples of high quality lectures on television, combined with the visual presentation of examples from film or TV cameras in a way that would be beyond the funds available in any university.

Some qualities in a good teacher

In the course of interviewing candidates for academic jobs, it is common to ask them to give a seminar. This allows one to judge not only some of their research but, in particular, their ability to present material clearly. The results may not be representative of their day-to-day abilities at teaching a range of subjects, including, unavoidably, many for which the lecturer has not had first-hand research experience. Academic appointments more often go to specialists rather than generalists, but the specialist may have more difficulty in lecturing on the wide range of subjects necessary in teaching.

Other aspects of teaching performance need consideration besides lecturing. In the sciences a quite different approach is needed in organising effective laboratory practicals or field studies. Working with small groups, for example in tutorials, requires yet different talents.

Perhaps the most important quality in a teacher is being able to make effective contact with students, encouraging critical examination, both of their own efforts and the efforts of others. Some subtle factors are involved in balancing encouragement and discipline. A brilliant lecturer may be so personally arrogant that students are "turned off". We recall one lecturer who epitomised "radical chic" in his trendy dress and bizarre personal activities; but, he was the only staff member who could reach certain students and stimulate them to do excellent research. It takes all kinds to make an effective teaching world. By passing judgement too hastily, especially on nebulous concepts such as "personality", administrators reject many individuals who have that innate ability to make contact with certain students.

Some of the most effective teaching takes place in informal settings, often in casual conversation between staff member and student. Yet, in the evaluation of the performance of teachers, credit is rarely given to those who spend long hours helping, guiding, inspiring or just listening to students.

Thus, allowing for the wide range of opinions about what constitutes good teaching, the best procedure is to ask for a large number of independent assessments. Such evaluations should include some standard set of questions, such as: How well prepared is the lecturer? How well read is the lecturer? How effective is the lecturer in using visual aids? Does the lecturer show a willingness to answer students' questions? Does the lecturer respect the views óf students, especially when they differ from his own? Does the lecturer inform students ahead of time how they will be graded? In grading examinations, does the lecturer give students a good idea of what errors they made?

Our list is not intended to be complete and, obviously, must be adjusted to the requirements of different subjects, in particular the relative emphasis on lectures, tutorials and laboratory practicals. The standard set of questions should be used in the evaluation of *all* staff, not just the individual being considered for promotion (or sacking). The results should be freely available so that there is no suspicion of abuse in secrecy, although, at least for ordinary situations, the privacy of individuals will need to be preserved. In other words, for routine matters, each lecturer would be given only his or her own results, the results for others being presented as a general numerical distribution. However, when dismissal charges are being prosecuted — charges alleging unsatisfactory teaching — then the right of the individual to a fair trial transcends the rights of other staff members to their privacy.

Student evaluation of staff teaching performance

So far we have said nothing about student opinion in assessing academic performance. This is anathema to many academics. The very suggestion that students should be permitted to express an opinion, let alone that it be given some weight in evaluation, has on more than one occasion contributed to a dissident being given a one-way ticket out of the academic profession. It is thus welcome to find the example of a Vice-Chancellor[104] who points out the salutary role of student opinion, including even the candid comments which occasionally occur in student newspapers or counter-calendars.

Student opinion is no better and no worse than any other opinion. It is sometimes coloured by the prevailing subculture of anti-intellectualism ("ockerism" in Australia) and by a general hostility to what it perceives as parental authority. But, beyond the generation gap and mediocrity cult, there is sometimes an intolerance for unfairness and a youthful ability to detect — and to puncture — pomposity. Students have often sampled more of a lecturer's efforts than his professional colleagues have; also, students will have an immediate perception of how those efforts compare with the efforts of other staff.

The sensible way to use student opinion is the same as for any other kind of opinion. Ask a number of questions (rather along the lines of those listed in the previous section). The questions should not be "loaded" and should allow for the multiple facets of good teaching. A reasonably large random sample of students should be taken. One should allow for the fact that a staff member who expects students to work hard will always receive complaints that the lectures are too difficult to understand or that the reading assignments are too long. After all, one is supposed to be assessing performance in a university, not a kindergarten.

What we find odious in some attempts to dismiss staff is where the administration presents the opinion of only one or two selected students. The administration never reveals how many students were sampled to get a few who would give the opinion they wanted. This is a standard of unsatisfactory sampling that those same academic administrators would not tolerate in their own research (or at least we would hope that they would not tolerate it).

The claim is sometimes made that students' opinions are influenced by the grade they receive.[105] That may not be as bad as it sounds. Since a student who likes a particular teacher often works harder in the subject, it is not surprising that there is a positive partial correlation between grades and student opinion. We know of no evidence that students are more likely to be subject to faulty judgement arising out of conflicts of interest than are academics. The answer to such problems is, as mentioned before, to ensure that the sampling procedure is valid and that there are data available for opinions about other staff besides the one being considered for administrative action.

It is unsettling to note that in several cases where dissidents were alleged to have had poor performance in teaching, their non-dissident colleagues, whose performance was much worse, were not considered for dismissal. When a staff member frequently misses his lectures, fails to turn in his grades on time, arrives at lectures late or unprepared, fails to keep up in the subjects about which he is lecturing, treats the students unfairly, or even indulges in what is euphemistically called "sexual harassment", why are not the dismissal statutes invoked? Such behaviour would appear to qualify as "gross and persistent neglect of duties". Senator Baden Teague, the Chairman of the Senate Standing Committee on Education and the Arts, investigating the tenure of academics, complained: "... one could wax quite loudly about this almost national scandal of teaching inadequacies amongst tertiary staff".[106] That may be a bit extreme, but a problem exists and it is not helped by administrators spending so much time and effort in trying to sack dissidents on inadequate charges when consistently poor teaching, plagiarism, false charges, and sexual exploitation of students by other staff go unpunished.

In summary, the essence of fair evaluation is to have a thorough comparison of the individual being considered for some administrative action (appointment, promotion, tenure, or dismissal) with the performance of appropriate peers. The limitations of different methods of evaluation must be recognised. If the administration really has a good case, it need not rely on procedural ploys. Nor need the administration rely on inadequate sampling, either of an individual's work or actions. As Marcia Lieberman[107] wrote in the quotation given at the beginning of this chapter: "Covert discrimination cannot exist without falsehood... Often the blame is placed on the victim".

References

1. Marcia R. Lieberman, "The most important thing for you to know", in: Gloria DeSole and L. Hoffmann (eds), *Rocking the Boat: Academic Women and Academic Processes* (New York: Modern Language Association of America, 1981), pp. 3–7, quotation from p. 5, with a change in paragraphing.

2. The establishment view of creativity is exemplified by Jonathan R. Cole and Stephen Cole, "The Ortega Hypothesis", *Science*, vol. 178, pp. 368–75 (1972): only a very small percentage of scientists have the "sacred spark" to make really significant contributions.
   However, the evidence marshalled by the Coles is capable of an alternative explanation. Since the research by the mathematical biologist A. J. Lotka in the 1920s, it has been known that the number of scientists producing n papers is roughly proportional to n^{-2}: see, for example, Derek de Solla Price, *Little Science, Big Science* (New York: Columbia University Press, 1963). In other words, the majority of scientists who publish, publish only one or two papers in their lifetime. *This resembles the life-table data for a species with a high rate of random mortality where the mortality rate is especially high at the early stages*, e.g., Raymond Pearl's "Type III" mortality: see C. J. Krebs, *Ecology* (New York: Harper & Row, 1972), p. 158. This is contrary to what we would expect, given the requirement for some minimal intelligence, motivation and perseverance in order to do successful science (or other forms of scholarship). Truncating the normal distribution of human abilities should still yield a much flatter mortality curve for publication. This result, the n^{-2} distribution, automatically biases

the results on citation which the Coles use as their main evidence for elitism! There are other limitations to the use of citation data and some of these are discussed later in this chapter.

This alternative explanation of data which the Coles choose to interpret in an elitist manner illustrates a problem that also underlies much of the evaluation of performance. Intellectuals subconsciously (and sometimes consciously) "push" their hypotheses, experimental designs, and interpretation of results in a direction determined by preconceived ideas (or outright prejudices) or the source of research funding. The reader is well advised to study: Brian Martin, *The Bias of Science* (Canberra: Society for Social Responsibility in Science, 1979).

3. R. D. Wright, "Prologue", in: W. H. C. Eddy, *Orr* (Brisbane: Jacaranda, 1961), pp. xiii–xvi.

4. Bertrand Russell, *Autobiography* (Boston: Little, Brown, 1957), vol. 2, years 1914–44, p. 332. Because of his pacifism in World War I, Bertrand Russell was dismissed from his lectureship at Trinity College, Cambridge: see Ronald W. Clark, *The Life of Bertrand Russell* (New York: Knopf, 1976), pp. 289–92. Because of his alleged sexual permissiveness, Bertrand Russell was prevented from taking up a position at the City College of New York: see John Dewey and Horace M. Kallen (eds), *The Bertrand Russell Case* (New York: Viking Press, 1941, and 1972 reprinting); and, Paul Edwards, "Appendix", in: Bertrand Russell, *Why I Am Not a Christian* (London: Allen & Unwin, 1957), pp. 207–59.

5. D. Dickson, "Firing spotlights plutonium exports", *Science*, 221, p. 245 (1983); S. Bhatia, "Electricity Board critic is dismissed", *The Observer* (London), 12 June 1983, p. 3; see also the anonymous editorial, "Don't fire the messenger", *New Scientist*, 23 June 1983, p. 838. A useful exchange of letters is: Trevor Broom, "CEGB answers back", *New Scientist*, 7 July 1983, p. 50; and, R. V. Hesketh, "CEGB fired", *New Scientist*, 28 July 1983, p. 29. Confirmation of Hesketh (and Ryle) has come from Tony Benn, formerly the Secretary of State for Energy in the United Kingdom. Benn is quoted as saying: "Every British nuclear power station becomes a nuclear bomb factory for the US" (*New Scientist*, 8 December 1983, p. 724).

6. Lieberman, op. cit.

7. T. Caplow and R. J. McGee, *The Academic Marketplace* (New York: Basic Books, 1958).

8. R. T. Spooner, "Will you give me a reference?", *Education*, 27 August 1976 issue, pp. 173–4.

9. Advertisement in *Science* 195, p. 1370 (1977).

10. J. P. Rushton, H. G. Murray and S. V. Paunonen, "Personality, research creativity, and teaching effectiveness in university professors", *Scientometrics* 5, pp. 93–116 (1983).

11. E. Anderson, *Plants, Man and Life* (Berkeley: University of California Press, 1967 reprinting; originally published in 1952).

12. H. Seyle, *From Dream to Discovery* (New York: McGraw-Hill, 1964).

13. A. Sibatani, "You carry out eukaryote experiments on shellfish selfish DNA: an essay on the vulgarization of molecular biology" in: *Science and Scientists: Essays by Biochemists, Biologists and Chemists* (Tokyo: Japan Scientific Societies Press, 1981); and, A. Sibatani "Molecular biology: a paradox, illusion and myth", *Trends in Biochemical Sciences,* June 1981 issue, pp. vi–ix.

14. Anne Roe, "A psychological study of eminent biologists", *Psychological Monographs*, vol. 65, no. 14, pp. 1–68 (1951); B. T. Eiduson, *Scientists: Their Psychological World* (New York: Basic Books, 1962); Liam Hudson, *Contrary Imaginations* (London: Methuen, 1966).

15. A. H. Halsey and M. A. Trow, *The British Academics* (London: Faber & Faber, 1971).

16. See the review and new data in: S. M. Lipset and G. M. Schaflander, *Passion and Politics: Student Activism in America* (Boston: Little, Brown, 1971) and E. C. Ladd, Jr. and S. M. Lipset, *The Divided Academy: Professors and Politics* (New York: McGraw-Hill for the Carnegie Commission on Higher Education, 1975).

17. Clark Kerr, *The Uses of the University* (New York: Harper and Row, 1966), p. 99.

18. H. Marcuse, "Repressive tolerance", in: R. P. Wolff, B. Moore, Jr., and H. Marcuse, *A Critique of Pure Tolerance* (Boston: Beacon Press, second printing, 1969), p. 119.

19. Anonymous, "Angry astronomers gag their critics", *New Scientist*, 17 February 1983, p. 424.

20. David Dickson, "Study of big science group hits raw nerve", *Science* 220, pp. 482–3, quoting p. 483 (1983).

21. J. Irvine and B. R. Martin, "Assessing basic research: the case of the Isaac Newton Telescope", *Social Studies of Science*, vol. 13, pp. 49–60 (1983); B. R. Martin and J. Irvine, "Assessing basic research: some partial indicators of scientific progress in radioastronomy", *Research Policy*, vol. 12, pp. 61–90 (1983).

22. With regard to the "fickleness in the reward system" and the failure of multiple awards to represent *independent* estimates of quality, see A. Carl Leopold, "The act of creation: creative processes in science", *BioScience* 28, pp. 436–40 (1978). Even the Nobel Prize has in its history a number of examples of serious controversy and belatedly recognised error; see, for example: Deborah Shapley, "Nobelists: Piccioni lawsuit raises questions about the 1959 prize", *Science* 176, pp. 1405–6 (1972); Wallace Cloud, "Winners and sinners", *The Sciences (New York Academy of Science)*, December 1973, pp. 16–21; Anonymous, "A Nobel scandal?", *Time* Magazine, 7 April 1975, p. 55; H. Inhaber and K. Przednowek, "Quality of research and Nobel prizes", *Social Studies of Science* 6, pp. 33–50 (1976); M. Benarie, "Nobel Prize rules", *Nature* 288, p. 8 (1980); Danah Zohar, "The science prizes: they get those wrong, too", *The Sunday Times* (London), 23 November 1980, p. 35.

23. Caplow and McGee, op. cit.

24. Brian Martin, "The scientific straightjacket", *Ecologist*, vol. 11, Jan./Feb. issue, pp. 33–43 (1981); Brian Martin, "The naked experts", *Ecologist*, vol. 12, July/Aug. issue, pp. 149–57 (1982).

25. For example, see the Senate Standing Committee on Education and the Arts, *Tenure of Academics* (Canberra: AGPS, September 1982), p. 83 and the relevant Hansard transcripts and submissions, especially Senator P. J. Giles, pp. 1731–5.

26. M. Oliphant, "The quality of Australian universities", *Vestes*, vol. 3, issue 2, pp. 45–9 (1961).

27. Select Committee to Study Governmental Operations With Respect to Intelligence Activities, US Senate, Book I: *Foreign and Military Intelligence*, and Book II: *Intelligence Activities and the Rights of Americans* (Washington, DC: US Government Printing Office, Report 94–755, 1976). By 1967 the CIA had sponsored more than a thousand books. For the names of a number of eminent academics whose research or publication were financed by the CIA see: John Marks, *The Search for the Manchurian Candidate: the CIA and Mind Control* (Allen Lane, Penguin Books, 1979).

28. W. M. O'Neil, *Advice to A.R.G.C. Applicants* (Canberra: Australian Research Grants Committee, 1972, mimeographed document). Subsequent versions of the advice to applicants retain much of O'Neil's mimeographed document but this telling passage has been deleted.

29. Robert Drewe, "How bureaucratic venom threatens your life", *Bulletin* (Sydney), 12 January 1982, pp. 18–24. The case history is included in the "Archives of Suppression" chapter.

30. Our comments are not to be interpreted as pardoning the absence of *some* output. An academic with approximately half of his time free to do research ought to publish about one paper a year, or a book or a major review article at less frequent intervals. Even when denied research funds, there is much to be done in the way of theoretical and review work. It is revealing of the standards of administration that some staff members are allowed to spend years without showing any evidence for productive work. Tenure is no excuse, for dismissal statutes would allow the sacking of staff who neglect their scholarly duties for long periods.

31. Caplow and McGee, op. cit., p. 153.

32. Donald Michie, "Peer review and the bureaucracy", *Times Higher Education Supplement*, 4 August 1978, p. 11.

33. D. Fifield, "Nature", *New Scientist*, 30 October 1969, pp. 230–2.

34. C. Manwell, "Peer review: a case history from the Australian Research Grants Committee", *Search*, 10, 81–6 (1979); I. I. Mitroff and D. E. Chubin, "Peer review at the NSF: a dialectical policy analysis", *Social Studies of Science* 9, pp. 199–232 (1979); D. P. Peters and S. J. Ceci, "Peer-review practices of psychological journals: the fate of published articles, submitted again", *Behavioral and Brain Sciences* 5, pp. 187–95 (1982); see also the comments by others in the same issue, pp. 196–255. The Peters and Ceci paper, together with the comments, have been published separately: S. Harnad (ed.), *Peer Commentary on Peer Review. A Case Study in Scientific Quality Control* (Cambridge University Press, 1982). See also the chapter "Prejudice in Granting Research Grants".

35. C. Manwell and C. M. A. Baker, "Honesty in science", *Search* 12, pp. 151–60 (1981); William Broad and Nicholas Wade, *Betrayers of the Truth* (New York: Simon & Schuster, 1982); Nicholas Wade, "What science can learn from science fraud", *New Scientist*, 28 July 1983, pp. 273–5; C. Ian Jackson and John W. Prados, "Honor in science", *American Scientist* 71, pp. 462–4 (1983).

36. Useful discussions about the differences in opinion among statisticians can be found in: S. Siegel, *Non-parametric Statistics for the Behavioral Sciences* (New York: McGraw-Hill, 1956); L. Hogben, *Statistical Theory* (London: Allen and Unwin, 1957); and, R. R. Sokal and F. J. Rohlf, *Biometry* (San Francisco: W. H. Freeman, 1969).

37. S. M. Gore, I. G. Jones and E. C. Rytter, "Misuse of statistical methods: critical assessment of articles in BMJ from January to March 1976", *British Medical Journal*, 8 January 1977, pp. 85–7.

38. For an excellent discussion of the evils of secrecy see: Richard Davis, "Anonymity — the cancer of academia", *Education Research and Perspectives*, vol. 6, issue 2, pp. 3–11 (1979).

39. Lionel S. Lewis, *Scaling the Ivory Tower: Merit and Its Limits in Academic Careers* (Baltimore: Johns Hopkins Press, 1975). See also Caplow and McGee, op. cit. and Spooner, op. cit.

40. Lewis, op. cit.

41. See notes 34 and 35 above.

42. See note 39 above.

43. S. Cole, J. R. Cole and G. A. Simon, "Chance and consensus in peer review", *Science* 214, pp. 881–6 (1981). In their earlier work dealing with peer review the Coles took a strongly elitist position. Although they still maintain some of their earlier opinions, the data in this article argue strongly that peer review is characterised by a marked disagreement among assessors.

44. R. A. Fisher, "Has Mendel's work been rediscovered?", *Annals of Science* 1, pp. 115–37 (1936). R. A. Fisher's conclusions, that Mendel's data were deliberately trimmed (by Mendel or by his assistant), are disputed by several authorities: Sewall Wright, "Mendel's ratios" in: Curt Stern and E. R. Sherwood (eds), *The Origin of Genetics* (San Francisco: W. H. Freeman, 1966), pp. 173–5; Åke Gustafsson, "The life

of Johann Mendel — tragic or not?'', *Hereditas* 62, pp. 239–58 (1969); B. L. Van der Waekden, "Mendel's experiments", *Centaurus* 12, pp. 275–88 (1968); Robert Scott Root-Bernstein, "Mendel and methodology", *History of Science* 21, pp. 275–95 (1983). The last-mentioned reference has missed Sir Gavin de Beer's suggestion (although citing the paper) that one of Mendel's assistants had an "inclination towards bibulousness" and worked "subconsciously in the direction of obtaining the results that were expected, by discarding doubtful material or bad specimens, and by making honest mistakes": G. de Beer, "Mendel, Darwin and Fisher", *Notes and Records of the Royal Society (London)*, vol. 19, pp. 192–226, quoting from p. 201 (1964). Robert Scott Root-Bernstein's assertion that "Mendel counted all the peas he grew" is too strong; even if Mendel or his assistants attempted to count every last pea, the point is reached where damaged material, accidental loss, or removal by pests, intervenes. Thus, although Root-Bernstein provides an interesting suggestion, which proves Mendel's honesty, the explanations by some earlier authors are not so easily ruled out. Perhaps the best evidence for Mendel's honesty is his willingness to publish research which did *not* conform to his ratios, the work on hawkweeds: see L. C. Dunn, "Mendel, his work and his place in history", *Proceedings of the American Philosophical Society* 109, pp. 189–98 (1965).

45. See note 34 above.

46. C. Manwell, "Dissident scientists: hard versus soft science", *Physics Bulletin* 29, pp. 267–8 (1978).

47. S. J. Ceci and D. P. Peters, "Peer review: a study of reliability", *Change*, September 1982 issue, pp. 44–8, quotations taken from pp. 46, 47 and footnote no. 3 on p. 48.

48. Lionel S. Lewis, "Publish or perish: some comments on a hyperbole", *Journal of Higher Education* 38, pp. 85–9 (1967). See also, L. S. Lewis, "Getting tenure: change and continuity", *Academe*, November 1980 issue, pp. 373–81. See also Peter Blunt, "Publish or perish or neither: what is happening in academia", *Vestes*, vol. 14, issue 1, pp. 62–4 (June 1976).

49. Lewis, *Journal of Higher Education*, op. cit. pp. 88–9.

50. W. J. Broad, "The publishing game: getting more for less: meet the Least Publishable Unit, one way of squeezing more papers out of a research project", *Science* 211, pp. 1137–9 (1981).

51. J. R. Cole and S. Cole, *Social Stratification in Science* (University of Chicago Press, 1973). While they have overstated their case, we would agree with the general conclusion that there is a weak association between quantity and quality. Such studies need to be corrected for *visibility* (a person who publishes lots of papers is more likely to get his work seen in the random browsing of journals by readers) and for *opportunity* (the very fact that the reward system favours quantity means that prolific publishers will get more grants and more students to do more, and sometimes better, research). For a discussion of other biases in the work of the Coles see C. Manwell and C. M. A. Baker, "Reform peer review: the Peters and Ceci study in the context of other current studies of scientific evaluation", *Behavioral and Brain Sciences* 5, pp. 221–5 (1982); and, Stephen P. Turner and Daryl E. Chubin, "Chance and eminence in science: Ecclesiastes II", *Social Science Information* 18, pp. 437–49 (1979).

52. Eugene Garfield, *Citation Indexing: Its Theory and Application in Science, Technology and Humanities* (New York: Wiley, 1979).

53. Harriet Zuckerman and Robert K. Merton, "Patterns of evaluation in science: institutionalisation, structure and functions of the referee system", *Minerva* 9, pp. 66–100, see especially Table 1, p. 76 (1971).

54. A. R. Kraft, J. A. Collins, L. C. Carey and D. B. Skinner, "Art and logic in scientific communications: abstracts, presentations, and manuscripts", *Journal of Surgical Research* 26, pp. 591–604 (1979); L. Goldman and A. Loscalzo, "Fate of cardiology research

originally published in abstract form'', *New England Journal of Medicine* 303, pp. 255–9 (1980).

55. Garfield, op. cit.

56. A. G. Heffner, "Authorship recognition of subordinates in collaborative research", *Social Studies of Science* 9, pp. 377–84 (1979).

57. Harriet Zuckerman, "Patterns of name ordering among authors of scientific papers: a study of social symbolism and its ambiguity", *American Journal of Sociology* 74, pp. 276–91 (1968).

58. Broad, op. cit.

59. L. H. T. West, T. Hore and P. K. Boon, "Publication rates and research productivity", *Vestes*, vol. 23, issue 2, pp. 32–7 (1980).

60. Lieberman, op. cit.

61. Stephen Fretwell, "The impact of Robert MacArthur on ecology", *Annual Review of Ecology and Systematics* 6, pp. 1–13 (1975).

62. Phillip M. Boffey, *The Brain Bank of America: An Inquiry into the Politics of Science* (New York: McGraw-Hill, 1975); Claude E. Barfield, "Science Report/National Academy of Sciences tackles sensitive policy questions", *National Journal* 3, pp. 101–12 (1971). That protégé favouritism has resulted in some substandard papers getting into the Proceedings of the US National Academy of Sciences is only part of the problem. There is also the matter of poor quality reports, often biased in favour of big business or government; see, for example, Nicholas Wade, "Letter from Washington: credibility counts", *Trends in the Biochemical Sciences*, September 1980 issue, p. xiii. Some similar problems exist in the Australian Academy of Science; see the penetrating review by Ann Moyal, "The Australian Academy of Science: the anatomy of a scientific elite", parts I and II, *Search* 11, pp. 231–9 and 281–8 (1980). Ann Moyal reports (p. 283): "In interviews with the author, many Fellows sharply criticised Academy Reports..."

63. See note 35 above.

64. W. A. Hendrickson, R. E. Strandberg, A. A. Liljas, L. M. Amzel, and E. E. Lattman, "True identity of a diffraction pattern attributed to valyl t-RNA" (correspondence), *Nature* 303, p. 195 (1983); see also comments in the same issue, pp. 196–7.

65. Eugene Garfield, "SCI Journal Citation Reports: a bibliometric analysis of science journals in the ISI* data base", *Science Citation Index*, vol. 14 (1980).

66. Robert K. Adair and George L. Trigg, "Editorial: should the character of Physical Review Letters be changed?", *Physical Review Letters* 43, pp. 1969–74 (1979).

67. Lynn Margulis, "Peer review attacked" (letter), *The Sciences (New York Academy of Sciences)*, vol. 17, January/February issue, pp. 5, 31 (1977).

68. Alexander Pope, *Dunciad*, A, Book I, lines 233–4 (1729); version edited by James Sutherland (London: Methuen, 1943), p. 90.

69. Garfield, op. cit.

70. M. Oromaner, "Professional age and the reception of sociological publications: a test of the Zuckerman–Merton hypothesis", *Social Studies of Science* 7, pp. 381–8 (1977).

71. S. Cole, J. R. Cole and L. Dietrich, "Measuring the cognitive state of scientific disciplines", in: Y. Elkana, J. Lederberg, R. K. Merton, A. Thackray and H. Zuckerman (eds), *Towards a Metric of Science* (New York: Wiley, 1978), pp. 209–51, especially p. 223.

72. S. M. Lawani, "Citation analysis and the quality of scientific productivity", *BioScience* 27, pp. 26–31 (1977).

73. G. N. Gilbert, "Referencing as persuasion", *Social Studies of Science* 7, pp. 113–22 (1977).

74. Rodger Mitchell, "Scaling in ecology" (letter), *Science* 184, p. 1131 (1974).

75. Leigh Van Valen, "Note on the 'Public relations web'", *Evolutionary Theory*, vol. 1, issue 4, p. 106 (1975).

76. Timothy Lenoir, "Quantitative foundations for the sociology of science: on linking blockmodeling with co-citation analysis", *Social Studies of Science* 9, pp. 455–80 (1979), p. 478.

77. Nicholas Wade, "Guillemin and Schally: a race spurred by rivalry", *Science* 200, pp. 510–13 (1978), pp. 510–12; see also: N. Wade, *The Nobel Duel* (New York: Anchor/Doubleday, Garden City, 1981).

78. Derek J. de Solla Price, *Little Science, Big Science*, cited in reference 2, quoting from p. 78.

79. Gustav Nossal, "Information flow within scientific peer groups", in *59th Annual Review: Director's Report* (Victoria: Walter and Eliza Hall Institute of Medical Research, 1978), p. 8.

80. Loren Eisley, *Darwin's Century* (New York: Doubleday, 1958); and, L. Eisley, *Darwin and the Mysterious Mr. X* (New York: Dutton, 1979).

81. Eugene Garfield, "Citation indexing for studying science", *Nature* 227, pp. 669–71 (1970). See also the references cited in note 44 above.

82. T. S. Kuhn, *The Structure of Scientific Revolutions* (University of Chicago Press, 1970, second edition).

83. Erwin Chargaff, "Triviality in science: a brief meditation on fashions", *Perspectives in Biology and Medicine* 19, pp. 324–35 (1976), p. 324. Chargaff's writings provide entry into many controversial corners of science. See, for example: E. Chargaff, "Building the tower of babble", *Nature* 248, pp. 776–9 (1974); and, E. Chargaff, *Heraclitean Fire: Sketches from a Life before Nature* (New York: Rockefeller University Press, 1978).

84. R. Over and S. Smallman, "Citation idiosyncrasies", *Nature* 228, p. 1357 (1970).

85. J. D. Frame, F. Narin and M. P. Carpenter, "The distribution of world science", *Social Studies of Science* 7, pp. 501–16 (1977).

86. Jon Wiener, "Footnote — or perish", *Dissent* (New York), fall 1974 issue, pp. 588–92.

87. E. F. Hartree, "Reprint distribution", *Nature* 242, p. 485 (1973).

88. William J. Broad, "Librarian turned entrepreneur makes millions off mere footnotes", *Science* 202, p. 857 (1978).

89. ibid.

90. Wiener, op. cit.

91. Broad, op. cit.

92. Garfield, op. cit., p. 671.

93. Broad, op. cit.

94. Nicholas Wade, "Citation analysis: a new tool for science administrators", *Science* 188, pp. 429–32 (1975), p. 429.

95. O. W. Adams, "NSF and citation analysis", *Science* 189, p. 86 (1975).

96. Wade, op. cit.

97. D. Dieks and H. Chang, "Differences in impact of scientific publications: some indices derived from a citation analysis", *Social Studies of Science* 6, pp. 247–67 (1976), especially p. 257.

98. Robert K. Merton claimed that the behaviour of scientists followed four *norms: Universalism:* "The acceptance or rejection of claims entering the lists of science is not to depend on the personal or social attributes of their protagonist... The imperative of universalism is rooted deep in the impersonal character of science" (p. 607). *"Communism"* (sometimes called *communality*): the complete sharing of information (basically through publication in the open literature) — "Secrecy is the antithesis of this norm; full and open communication its enactment" (p. 611). *Disinterestedness:* self-interest is suppressed — the "virtual absence of fraud in the annals of science... There is competition in the realm of science... and under competitive conditions there may well be generated incentives for eclipsing rivals by illicit means. But such impulses can find scant opportunity for expression in the field of scientific research" (p. 613). *Organized*

Scepticism: "The suspension of judgment until 'the facts are at hand' and the detached scrutiny of beliefs in terms of empirical and logical criteria . . ." (p. 614). The quotations are from Robert K. Merton, *Social Theory and Social Structure* (New York: Free Press, 1968 enlarged edition). There appears to have been considerable confusion between public and private ideologies, between ideals, expressed attitudes, and actual behaviour. Merton, as a pillar of the American "eastern establishment" in the sociology of science, has had his norms accepted by many in this field; however, there have been some important challenges or modifications to Merton's norms. See, for example, S. B. Barnes and R. G. A. Dolby, "The scientific ethos: a deviant viewpoint", *Archiv europ. sociologie* 11, pp. 3–24 (1970); Robert A. Rothman, "A dissenting view of the scientific ethos", *British Journal of Sociology* 23, pp. 102–8 (1972); Ian I. Mitroff, "Norms and counter-norms in a select group of Apollo moon scientists: a case study of the ambivalence of scientists", *American Sociological Review* 39, pp. 579–95 (1974); and, Michael Mulkay, "Interpretation and the use of rules: the case of the norms of science", *Transactions of the New York Academy of Sciences*, series II, vol. 39, pp. 111–25 (1980). Basically, Merton's norms are largely ideals. In practice scientists do not always behave ideally. For example, demands on time and the limits to human information processing force many scientists to judge some research on the basis of *who* published it, i.e., ascription. This violates the norm of *universalism*. The "anthropological" style of research conducted by Latour and Woolgar, who observed the behaviour of scientists in a highly competitive laboratory, revealed that the initial reception of nearly all ideas and facts was determined by *who* originated them, a striking refutation of Merton's universalism; indeed, there appeared to be a pathological obsession about the personality characteristics and other attributes of individuals used in evaluating performance. See: Bruno Latour and Steve Woolgar, *Laboratory Life: the Social Construction of Scientific Facts* (Beverly Hills: Sage, 1979).

99. R. D. Whitley, "Communication nets in science: status and citation patterns in animal physiology", *Sociological Review* 17, pp. 219–33 (1969).

100. Caplow and McGee, op. cit., p. 127.

101. C. K. Knapper, G. L. Geis, C. E. Pascal and B. M. Shore (eds), *If Teaching Is Important: the Evaluation of Instruction in Higher Education* (Clarke, Irwin and Co. in association with the Canadian Association of University Teachers, 1977), p. 19.

102. ibid.

103. N. L. Smith, "Sources of values influencing education evaluation", *Studies in Educational Evaluation* 6, pp. 101–18 (1980), p. 101.

104. D. R. Stranks, testimony given before the Senate Standing Committee on Education and the Arts, Adelaide, 11 February 1982, p. 1727.

105. J. E. Dolin, testimony given before the Senate Standing Committee on Education and the Arts, Adelaide, 11 February 1982, p. 1791.

106. Baden Teague, comments recorded in the proofs for the Hansard record of the Senate Standing Committee meeting in Melbourne, 9 February 1982, p. 1389.

107. Lieberman, op. cit.

INDEX

Only individuals mentioned by name in the
text are included